THE GENERAL'S
GOOSE

FIJI'S TALE OF CONTEMPORARY MISADVENTURE

THE GENERAL'S
GOOSE

FIJI'S TALE OF CONTEMPORARY MISADVENTURE

ROBBIE ROBERTSON

Australian
National
University

PRESS

STATE, SOCIETY AND GOVERNANCE IN MELANESIA SERIES

Published by ANU Press
The Australian National University
Acton ACT 2601, Australia
Email: anupress@anu.edu.au
This title is also available online at press.anu.edu.au

National Library of Australia Cataloguing-in-Publication entry

Creator: Robertson, Robbie, author.

Title: The general's goose : Fiji's tale of contemporary misadventure /
            Robbie Robertson.

ISBN: 9781760461270 (paperback) 9781760461287 (ebook)

Series: State, society and governance in Melanesia

Subjects: Coups d'état--Fiji.
            Democracy--Fiji.
            Fiji--Politics and government.
            Fiji--History--20th century

Cover design and layout by ANU Press

For Fiji's people

Isa lei, na noqu rarawa,
Ni ko sana vodo e na mataka.
Bau nanuma, na nodatou lasa,
Mai Suva nanuma tiko ga.
Vanua rogo na nomuni vanua,
Kena ca ni levu tu na ua
Lomaqu voli me'u bau butuka
Tovolea ke balavu na bula.[*]

Contents

Preface

In 1979, a young New Zealand graduate, who had just completed a PhD thesis on government responses to the Great Depression in New Zealand, arrived in Suva to teach at the University of the South Pacific. Everything about Fiji and the university challenged that graduate's limited understanding of the world and offered a steep learning curve that ultimately transformed his academic and personal life. The result has been a fascinating educative journey, sometimes tumultuous but always rewarding. Now, at the end of that journey, it is time to take stock of what he has learned and to bring his story of Fiji up to date.

Histories are invariably partisan, which is one reason they are always rewritten. Their biases derive from the status of their authors (are they insiders or outsiders?), the sources used and the ideologies conveyed. None of these biases necessarily determine whether the result is good history or bad history; that derives almost solely from the quality of the work produced. But biases can also be time-bound. Early histories of Fiji were invariably captured by the prevailing colonial ethos and, later, by its postcolonial antithesis.[1] Across both perspectives strode the spectre of race, which came to dominate many interpretations of Fiji during and after the 1980s when military interventions added yet another dimension to Fiji's troubled history. Understanding these transformative dimensions is a central goal of the first two parts of this book. Fiji's contemporary history, however, slid into unchartered territory after its military crushed a populist revolt in 2000. On this occasion, neither colonial nor postcolonial explanations sufficed, nor crude references to racial divides. Instead attention shifted to the military and its radical transformation from indigenous Fijian protector to multiracial enforcer.

---

1   Two contrasting examples are RA Derrick's *A History of Fiji* (Suva: Government Press, 1950) and Jai Narayan's *The Political Economy of Fiji* (Suva: South Pacific Review Press, 1984).

The second two parts of this book tell the complex story of that uneasy and messy transformation and its impact on democracy within Fiji, with a conclusion examining post-2014 politics until 2017.

For many people, Fiji is simply a typical Third World basket case. For those who journey to Fiji from Australasia, North America and Asia for restful holidays, Fiji remains an uncomplicated small South Pacific island paradise. Of course it is neither. As one of the most developed Pacific states, Fiji strides the South Pacific islands as a colossus. It is a regional hub for travel and trade. It possesses outstanding infrastructure for tourism and education, and its economy is increasingly diversified. But, like any country, success depends ultimately on the quality of leadership. In this regard Fiji has suffered most. Partisan interests that are prepared to exploit populist and identity divisions for political and economic gain have often captured its leadership. Hence, the story of Fiji is a human one, rather than an exceptional one, but no less relevant as a consequence.

Too many people, especially colleagues and friends in Fiji and beyond, have assisted me over the years to mention them all here, but one who does stand out for helping me (the imperfect student) most to understand the intricacies of Fiji and for enduring my frequent absences (both real and virtual) is my wife, Jita. To her I owe an enduring debt of love and gratitude for a life well lived and shared.

Swinburne University of Technology
Melbourne
February 2017

iTaukei pronunciation

The iTaukei language contains consonants that are pronounced differently from their representation in English. These include:

b – pronounced *mb* as in *number*
c – pronounced *th* as in *they*
d – pronounced *nd* as in *candy*
j – pronounced *ch* as in *chest*
g – pronounced *ng* as in *singer*
q – pronounced *ngg* as in *finger*

Abbreviations

3FIR	Third Fiji Infantry Regiment
ABC	Australian Broadcasting Corporation
ACP	African, Caribbean and Pacific Group of States
ACS	Adi Cakobau School
ACTU	Australian Council of Trade Unions
ADB	Asian Development Bank
AFL	Airports Fiji Ltd
ALTA	*Agricultural Landlord and Tenant Act*
ANC	All Nationals Congress
ATHL	Amalgamated Telecom Holdings Ltd
BKV	Ba Kei Viti
CAMV	Conservative Alliance Matanitu Vanua
CCF	Citizens' Constitutional Forum
CEO	chief executive officer
CIAC	Constitution Inquiry and Advisory Committee
CO	commanding officer
Col	colonel
CRC	Constitutional Review Committee
CRW	Counter Revolutionary Warfare
CRWU	Counter Revolutionary Warfare Unit
CSR	Colonial Sugar Refinery Company
DPP	director of public prosecutions
ECREA	Ecumenical Centre for Research, Education and Advocacy

EIMCOL	Equity Investment and Management Company Limited
EPG	Eminent Persons Group
EU	European Union
FAB	Fijian Affairs Board
FAP	Fijian Association Party
FBC	Fiji Broadcasting Corporation
FCC	Fiji Constitution Commission
FDB	Fiji Development Bank
FEA	Fiji Electricity Authority
FFP	FijiFirst Party
FHL	Fijian Holdings Company Limited
FHRC	Fiji Human Rights Commission
FICAC	Fiji Independent Commission Against Corruption
FINTEL	Fiji International Telecommunications Ltd
FIRCA	Fiji Revenue and Customs Authority
FLP	Fiji Labour Party
FLS	Fiji Law Society
FMF	Fiji Military Forces
FNP	Fijian Nationalist Party
FNPF	Fiji National Provident Fund
FNU	Fiji National University
FPSA	Fiji Public Service Association
FRU	Force Reserve Unit
FSC	Fiji Sugar Corporation
FTUC	Fiji Trades Union Congress
FWCC	Fiji Women's Crisis Centre
FWRM	Fiji Women's Rights Movement
GARD	Group Against Racial Discrimination
GCC	Great Council of Chiefs (Bose Levu Vakaturaga)
GDP	gross domestic product
GVP	General Voters Party
HQ	headquarters

IBA	International Bar Association
ILO	International Labour Organization
IMF	International Monetary Fund
ISD	Internal Security Decree
ISI	import substitution industrialisation
LOPP	leaders of political parties
Lt	lieutenant
MIDA	Media Industry Development Authority
MP	member of parliament
MSG	Melanesian Spearhead Group
NAP	National Alliance Party
NBF	National Bank of Fiji
NCBBF	National Council for Building a Better Fiji
NFP	National Federation Party
NFU	National Farmers Union
NGO	non-government organisation
NIC	newly industrialised country
NLTB	Native Land Trust Board (later TLTB)
NVTLP	Nationalist Vanua Tako Lavo Party
NZ	New Zealand
OBE	Order of the British Empire
PACER	Pacific Agreement on Closer Economic Relations
PAFCO	Pacific Fisheries Company
PANU	Party of National Unity
PCPI	Pacific Centre for Public Integrity
PDP	People's Democratic Party
PER	public emergency regulations
PICTA	Pacific Island Countries Trade Agreement
PIDF	Pacific Island Development Forum
PIF	Pacific Islands Forum
PINA	Pacific Islands News Association
PNG	Papua New Guinea

PPDF	President's Political Dialogue Forum
QEB	Queen Elizabeth Barracks (Nabua, Suva)
QVS	Queen Victoria School
RBF	Reserve Bank of Fiji
RFMF	Royal (later Republic of) Fiji Military Forces
RKS	Ratu Kadavulevu School
RTU	Reconciliation, Tolerance and Unity (Bill)
SAS	Special Air Service
SBS	Special Broadcasting Service
SDL	Soqosoqo Duavata ni Lewenivanua
SODELPA	Social Democratic Liberal Party
SPARTECA	South Pacific Regional Trade and Economic Cooperation Agreement
STV	Soqosoqo ni Taukei ni Vanua
SVT	Soqosoqo ni Vakavulewa ni Taukei
TFF	tax-free factory
TFZ	tax-free zone
TLTB	iTaukei Land Trust Board
TNC	transnational corporation
UN	United Nations
UPP	United People's Party
US	United States (of America)
USP	University of the South Pacific
VAT	value added tax
VDCL	Vanua Development Corporation Ltd
VKB	Vola ni Kawa Bula
VLV	Veitokani ni Leweni Vanua Vakaristo Party
WUF	Western United Front

Maps

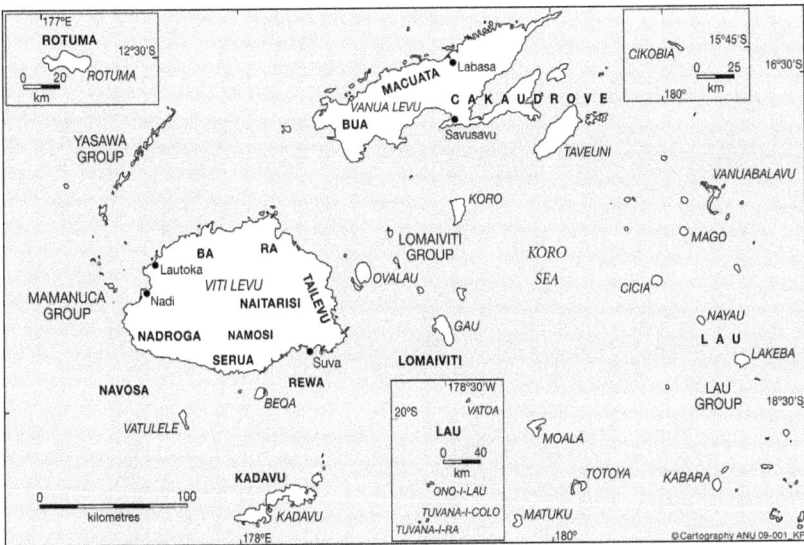

Map 1: The provinces of Fiji
Source: CartoGIS Services, College of Asia and the Pacific, Australian National University

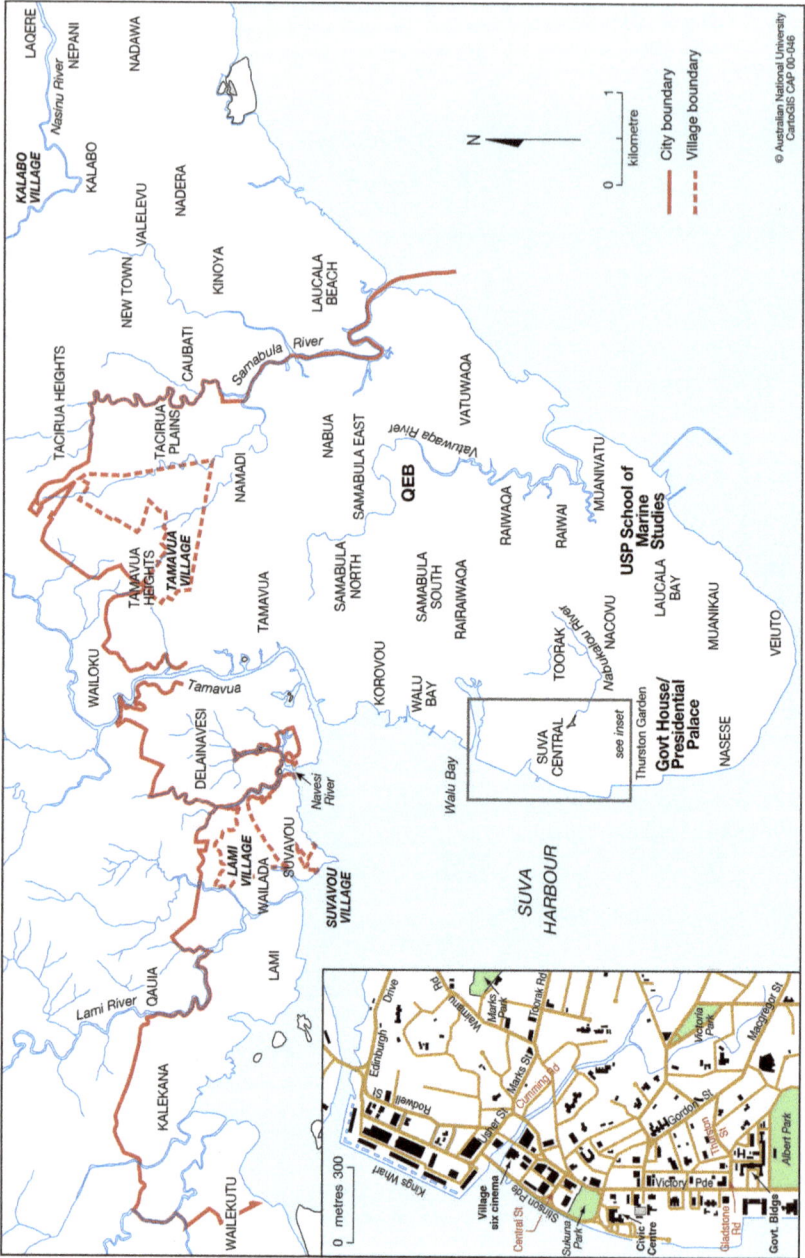

Map 2: Suva

Source: CartoGIS Services, College of Asia and the Pacific, Australian National University

Introduction

His admirers said he was a charismatic leader with a dazzling smile, a commoner following an ancient tradition of warrior service on behalf of an indigenous people who feared marginalisation at the hands of ungrateful immigrants. One tourist pleaded with him to stage a coup in her backyard; in private parties around the capital, Suva, infatuated women whispered 'coup me baby' in his presence. It was so easy to overlook the enormity of what he had done in planning and implementing Fiji's first military coup, to be seduced by celebrity, captivated by the excitement of the moment, and plead its inevitability as the final eruption of long-simmering indigenous discontent. A generation would pass before the consequences of the actions of Fiji's strong man of 1987, Sitiveni Rabuka, would be fully appreciated but, by then, the die had been well and truly cast. The Major General did not live happily ever after. No nirvana followed the assertion of indigenous rights. If anything, misadventure became his country's most enduring contemporary trait.

Rabuka understood from the very beginning that the path he took in overthrowing a new and democratically elected government on 14 May 1987 might ultimately prove his undoing, and not only for logistical reasons. Assertions of racial exclusivity or supremacy hung uneasily in a world that was still mired in post-fascist politics. Globalisation and its accessory, multiculturalism, had yet to be fully comprehended, let alone embraced globally, not that his followers paid much attention to how the world viewed their actions.

Rabuka declared himself the saviour of tradition in a country whose indigenous peoples still saw themselves as respectfully hierarchical. Democracy threatened that feature because it threatened the paramountcy of what they held to be indigenous interests;[1] it threatened Fijianness and the traditional relationships that Fijianness entailed. This was justification enough, and Fiji's first coup followed this script. Soon after, the country's traditional chiefs met and returned leadership to the Fijian elite who had ruled the country since independence in 1970. There the matter might have rested, perhaps uncomfortably for a time but, nonetheless, with inevitable finality. Unfortunately for its architects, political actions tend to promote unintended consequences that are less easily dismissed.

Rabuka came to power by overthrowing a democratically elected government that many Fijians viewed as illegitimate because the basis of its power lay predominantly with the votes of the descendants of Indian migrants. But he did so by first overthrowing his own military commander, a high-ranking Fijian chief. Within five months, he would also turn his overwhelmingly Fijian military machine against the same chiefs to whom he had initially entrusted power. He believed that they were about to cut a deal with the very politicians he had overthrown, leaving him out in the cold and possibly exposed to charges of treason. This unscripted intervention, however, brought its own difficulties.

Declaring Fiji a republic could not hide for long the fact that the military was not itself well positioned to seize control. Nonetheless, this second coup set the scene for a new and prolonged confrontation with the Fijian elite, even after Rabuka changed his mind three months into his second coup and restored the Fijian elite to power and delivered a new constitution heavily weighted in its favour. When solely communal elections were finally held in 1992, Rabuka emerged as the country's first elected, republican prime minister. For commoners like himself, democracy enabled a more meaningful future. But the experience took its toll. Within a short time

---

1   The 'indigenous' peoples of Fiji, the Taukei, have until recently called themselves Fijian, a description derived from assuming ownership of the country's name, itself reputedly derived from the Tongan pronunciation of Viti (Fisi). Until 2010, no other communities in the country (including the equally indigenous Rotumans) were permitted to use the national name to describe themselves; instead, they were identified solely by ethnicity, although, in the case of peoples deemed Indians, it is a national rather than ethnic description that is used. The decision to democratise Fiji's national name in 2010 addressed one longstanding grievance held mainly by non-indigenous citizens but overlooked the issue of indigeneity, the definition of which in Fiji never fully aligned with that accepted by the UN Working Group on Indigenous Populations, which describes peoples who not only have continuity with precolonial society and also belong to non-dominant sectors of society. In Fiji since independence, the Taukei have always been politically dominant. With that ambiguity in mind, I will use the standard naming conventions of the periods where possible, and refer to the Taukei (or iTaukei) as Fijians until 2010. Similarly, I will describe the migrant community as Indians until independence, thereafter as IndoFijians.

he would learn that democracy is best practiced by reaching consensus with all of a country's citizens. In other words, apartheid and aristocratic privilege could not form the basis for the economic growth and prosperity everyone craved, especially the Fijian people on whose behalf he claimed to act in 1987.

Reaching that point proved difficult, not least because accommodating his country's marginalised minorities and introducing a new democratic power-sharing constitution in 1997 meant challenging everything he had at one time stood for, including his popular support base. Rabuka would not be the first political leader to discover that hero status has a short shelf life. More importantly, he would learn that there were others less persuaded of the value of his transformation who would seek to emulate his past and, in time, earn his country the epithet 'Coup-Coup Land'.

The Rabuka legacy was not confined to military coups. It also ensured that democratisation assumed limited economic characteristics. In part this was both a colonial and postcolonial legacy but it was also a contemporary defensive mechanism. Rabuka could only avoid the personal consequences of his actions and maintain control over the levers of power by prioritising the growth of his military, buying elite support with access to state resources, paying off cronies and increasing the roles of traditional chiefs. Despite the politically important rhetoric of affirmative action for Fijians, these political priorities meant paying lip service to economic and social development for the mass of his people. For those of Indian descent, at best it meant neglect.

Coups are by their nature fixed firmly on control of the state as their primary prize. Hence they are unlikely to weaken the centrality of the state in economic and social life. Despite some attempts after 1987 to suggest a new and determinedly postcolonial economic trajectory, Fiji's early coups were far from revolutionary. If anything they were backward-looking, embracing a false memory of peaceful communal harmony and order but with one important difference: the colonial era was over, government had been restored to Fijian leadership. That was the central purpose of the coups and it would remain the raison d'être of post-coup administrations. There were limits, then, to what ordinary Fijians could expect from the restoration, as Rabuka told an Australian journalist in 1988:

> Fijian people will have the political say in their country and [a constitution to] safeguard their birthright, their land, their forests, the minerals and things; but not one that would make them so strong that they do not need a central government.[2]

In other words, authority would never be decentralised, civil society would always face constraints and development would continue to be bureaucratically led, as it had been ever since the country's high chiefs and colonial authorities had created the golden age of Fijian administration back in the 1940s. The legacy of its chief architect, Ratu Sir Lala Sukuna, was honoured from that time on, and Rabuka never had any intention of challenging it, even if sometimes when out of favour with the chiefs – and, in particular, Sukuna's protégé, Ratu Sir Kamisese Mara – he articulated the frustration it engendered in neglected commoners. Central government should never be challenged, he reminded a group of Fijian trade unionists in 1991. It was 'the goose that lays the golden egg'.[3] But for whom did the goose lay its golden egg? Clearly not ordinary Fijians; at least, not those who subsisted in rural villages and certainly not those who increasingly flocked to urban slums looking for work. There were limits to what they could expect if hierarchies of administration and power were to be respected.

This view, while not originating with Rabuka, had tremendous repercussions for the small state. Fiji might have the largest and most diversified economy among the independent island states of the south-west Pacific, but its economic performance over the next two decades served only to promote emigration and spiralling poverty. It added to the background dissatisfaction that Fijian rivals would employ to challenge Rabuka electorally in May 1999 and to mount their own 'civilian' coup one year later against the political coalition that they had inadvertently caused to succeed him. The coup could not succeed without military backing, but it did enable the formation of a new post-Rabuka political force that, over the next six years, would achieve the kind of Fijian political unity Rabuka had only been able to dream of, in part by reaching accommodation with supporters of the abortive 2000 coup. Yet, in terms of economic strategy, it was essentially Fijian Paramountcy 101, the post-1987 strategy reasserted and with a similarly narrow group of Fijian beneficiaries who were intent on capturing for themselves what wealth remained to be squeezed from the nation.

---

2   R Foley, 'Rabuka says interim government a "sideshow"'. *Canberra Times*, 11 August 1988.
3   *Fiji Times*, 6 May 1991.

In itself, this did not doom the government, which won fresh elections in 2006 and finally made significant overtures to its parliamentary opposition by forming a multi-party cabinet as the 1997 Constitution had intended. Multiracial accommodation now seemed possible. But the coup attempt in 2000 left another, less easily resolved legacy in exposing deep fractures within the military that, within months of the coup's resolution, exploded into a bloody mutiny designed to remove the military commander, Frank Bainimarama, and restart the coup. The mutiny collapsed but, from that moment in November 2000, the Commander became increasingly intolerant of the government he had put in place and especially of its efforts to accommodate those responsible for the 2000 coup, against which he publicly campaigned. An increasingly shaky multi-party cabinet and continued controversy over affirmative action programs provided his officers with additional ammunition to question the direction of the Fiji state and to launch its 'coup to end all coups' in December 2006.

Unfortunately, like all coups, the immediate impact of this fourth coup simply made long-term planning more difficult. Its economic consequences proved as disastrous for the beleaguered nation as those experienced nearly 20 years before. It further debilitated already weakened state institutions and it bitterly divided once-thriving civil organisations. Despite fluid promises to introduce transformative constitutional changes, the military consolidated its role as the nation's final political arbiter, leaving citizens to wonder at the state in which they would find Fiji by the time they emerged from the glare of elections in 2014 to survey their new democratic landscape.

This is a story of those tumultuous years, but of course it cannot be a story solely of Fiji. The events that occurred in Fiji did not take place within a vacuum. Instead they are part and parcel of the human story that is every bit as connected to the world as any other national story. This is not to deny the uniqueness of the Fiji experience, but to view it in terms of the broader stories of which it forms as essential an example as that from any other nation. Fijians exist because they derive from a wider set of Pacific migrations and interactions that began over 6,000 years ago far away in the South China Sea. During the 19th century, their diverse descendants were enveloped by the global reach of European economic, social and political activities, their peoples Christianised and their social structures transformed. For the first time they became Fijians, rather than Lauans or Kai Colo, although those late precolonial identities persisted, at least for political purposes, in the contemporary era.[4] Any form of identity, whether based on race, religion or nation, is a social invention. Becoming a British colony from 1874 further deepened change: new political structures and a colonial economy based on sugar and the labour of imported Indians, whose own country had been even more transformed as a result of British conquest. Fijian chiefs fought to retain some measure of control over their people and were accommodated in so far as the colonial system of indirect rule proved effective in maintaining order. But historically, accommodation was short lived; during the 1960s the global anti-colonial 'wind of change' swept also across the Pacific and, from late 1970, Fiji found itself an independent Third World nation, active on the world stage in pursuing postcolonial agreements on trade access and sugar, the law of the sea and peacekeeping duties for an increasingly pressed United Nations.

Fiji may be a small and relatively insignificant Pacific island compared with large Pacific rim countries, but it is nonetheless just as integrated into the globalised world of aid, education and training, health, labour, media, militaries, migration, mining, non-government organisations (NGOs), politics, religion, regions, tourism, trade, transport and unions; the list is endless. It might seem odd today that a country that is so successful in utilising global opportunities for the benefit of its people has been so undermined by insular introspection.[5] But, in the age of Donald Trump and Brexit, we should more easily recognise Fiji as an unexceptional example of humanity, one whose study offers insights just as useful for understanding our world as that of any society. Of course Fiji has not always been seen in this way. We often fail to look beyond superficial differences or at what appears unique. This is an examination of those perceptions and of the kind of society Fiji has become.

Central to an examination of both are notions of development and modernity. We sometimes patronisingly assume that development is a concern only for countries seeking to catch up with already 'developed' countries. Indeed, since the Second World War, modernising and

---

4   These older identities are increasingly undone by the fluid movement of Fijian (Taukei) people as they marry, raise children and work across the country (and beyond), outside old physical, ethnic and political boundaries. In that sense, Fijians have themselves again become more diverse.

5   The former judge and Fiji Vice President Ratu Joni Madraiwiwi once argued that 'Those who wish to turn back the clock or shake their fist at the outside world are an endangered species. There is no ... turning back'. The aspirations of the young 'can only be fulfilled pursuant to engagement with the world at large on its own terms' ('Ethnic tensions and the law', *Fiji Times*, 25 September 2004).

collectively improving society has become a central goal of almost all societies, and a vast array of multilateral and international civil organisations now exists to assist states to achieve economic growth or direct attention to human and social development. But, this focus should not seduce us into overlooking the reality that development concerns all societies, however they rank themselves globally. It is the shifting character of development debates, from basic infrastructure and social wellbeing to issues concerning ageing populations, changing technologies, economic competitiveness, inequalities and climate change that shapes perceptions in ways that often obscures commonality.

If we were able to return to the early 19th century, when a quickly evolving industrial revolution created the most dramatic changes human societies have ever faced, we might be less inclined to view development in binary terms. Many of the features of what was once called Third World development were then in evidence as people sought to reconstruct states and systems of governance to cope with the stresses of change and their consequences for regional balances of power. At that time, development came to be conceived of as progress, and its leaders took great pride in asserting that it denoted also national or racial superiority, using it to justify acts of aggression against neighbours or distant peoples. What we sometimes call the age of colonialism or imperialism, a time which not only saw the world carved up between a few leading industrial nations but also afflicted by devastating wars, was simply one manifestation of the desire to actively develop and change societies. And, for much of the 19th and 20th centuries, notions of fitness and human evolution were used to justify either the occupation and incorporation of whole societies or the rapid expansion of inequalities within societies. Development, always universal, carries with it tremendous baggage.

Part of that baggage is our tendency to dichotomise the world. How easily comparisons such as First World–Third World, developed–developing, north–south, East–West, tradition and modernity roll off our tongues, encapsulating generalisations and stereotypes that have long since lost their validity, if indeed they ever held any. In addition, nation-building responses to industrialisation over the past two centuries have also led us to regard nations as essentially natural homogenised units, to neglect or suppress evidence of internal diversity, and to reify culture and modernity. Consequently, we still tend to believe that homogeneity is an essential element for successful development, with the result that we fail to accommodate diversity within our models for growth.

Contemporary globalisation renders failure more dangerous. One only has to listen to debates on multiculturalism and migration to appreciate the continued strength of attachment to perceived national norms. Because many developing countries were created with attention to essentialised differences rather than national norms, their inability to successfully pursue the development examples purportedly set by the early industrialising countries, those we often misleadingly describe as the West, has been attributed – over the past half century or more – to their plurality or lack of cohesion. The argument becomes more convoluted still if we claim that the basis of Western development lies in free markets and democracy, something that most Western countries never enjoyed until recently. In other words, these features were products of development, not its prerequisites.

Democracy is an excellent case in point that is often held to be the result of a peculiarly Western cultural inheritance traced back to classical Greece or the English Magna Carta. This interpretation obscures the complex social and economic struggles that made different forms of democracy possible, a triumph of mass society and the growing middle-class nature of developing societies. This feature is evident also in Fiji. Democracy was never a historical feature of European societies or something that grew naturally from their past. Many only became democratic after 1945 and some have only experimented with democratic institutions since 1989. Even the United States only extended democratic rights to all its adult citizens in 1965, Australia in 1967.[6]

---

6   Kwame Anthony Appiah makes a similar case in relation to the notion of the West really only having assumed its modern meaning with the Cold War. People, Appiah argues, believe that an identity that survives must be propelled by some potent common essence. In the case of the West, that essence hung around a grand narrative about Greek democracy, the Magna Carta and the Copernican revolution, and a culture that became individualistic, democratic, liberal-minded and tolerant, progressive, rational and scientific. Of course, finding evidence for such a common culture across premodern Europe or even 20th-century Europe is impossible. It did not exist. Consequently, claims Appiah, we need to abandon the idea of an organic whole for a more cosmopolitan one. Every element of culture is separable, and open for adoption by anyone. Values are not a birthright; instead, they are choices that people need to make, 'not tracks laid down by … destiny'; 'Culture – like religion and nation and race – provides a source of identity for contemporary human beings. And, like all three, it can become a form of confinement, conceptual mistakes underwriting moral ones. Yet all of them can also give contours to our freedom.' Hence social identities can expand our horizons beyond our small-scale lives, even to the global human level. But our local lives still need to make sense ('There is no such thing as Western civilisation', *Guardian*, 9 November 2016).

Of course difference can always be used to rationalise pathways and institutions that are markedly dissimilar to the norms of many comparatively wealthy countries today. Invariably such arguments amount to little more than political point scoring. Development is not a Western project. The goals of development and the circumstances under which it occurs constantly change. At one time development was simply a state project. Today it is far more diverse, enveloping everything from the individual to regions.

It is important to understand the fluid nature of human relationships and development. Nothing is homogeneous or static. Everything interacts and is in constant flux. Under such circumstances, dichotomies do not describe reality, only perceptions of reality. We might look at subsistence farmers and regard them as traditional, but how traditional are they if they also produce for an urban market, make use of motorised transportation, and possess mobile phones to mobilise market data?

Globalisation introduces another dynamic that confounds narrow readings of the past and understandings of change. By fostering novel relationships, it has enabled new ways of seeing the world that prioritise human empowerment. It is this agenda that is often perceived as a threat to 'traditional' powerholders who fuel the modernity–tradition dichotomy for self-serving purposes. Thus globalisation, democracy and contemporary social movements have more in common than many people realise. Rather than assume a dichotomy between modernity and tradition, we might better argue that almost all societies are modern because they are all engaged – however unequally –with a globalised world. In this respect, Fiji serves as a useful example.

Modern Fiji in 1970 confronted development through the lens of race and privilege. When development failed to satisfy Fijian expectations and constitutional paramountcy tempered by multiracialism failed the privileged elite, Fiji's coup season began with Rabuka's 1987 attempts to mandate absolute Fijian dominance. When they too failed to deliver economic transformation, Fiji restored multiracialism in 1997, hoping that communal electoral reform alone might compensate for its development biases. That initiative was, however, doomed by two responses. First, a civilian coup in 2000, which swept aside a multiracial government and, through the military, reinstated the country's elite to power; and, second, a military coup in 2006 that rejected the communal basis for multiracialism and sought to address the biases inherent in Fiji's development strategies. That latter coup has, to date, endured; following elections in 2014, Bainimarama emerged as prime minister, leading a new multiracial party that overwhelmingly dominates the new parliament. But a weakened and confused iteration of the old party of the Fijian or Taukei elite survived. In an echo of the past, it would soon be led by the very man who had first sought to transform Fiji by military means – a resurrected and much older Rabuka, a man now haunted by his past.

This, then, is the story of Fiji's prolonged contemporary misadventure and its impact on the south-west Pacific's leading island state.

1

The challenge of inheritance

Sitiveni Ligamamada Rabuka derived from Nakobo, an isolated village in Natewa Bay, south-eastern Vanua Levu. Although a commoner, he was educated at Queen Victoria School (QVS), an elite colonial boarding school established in rural Tailevu for the sons of Fijian chiefs. Graduates of QVS have dominated the upper echelons of government in Fiji, sometimes bringing with them insular views of Fiji that neglected both its multicultural character and the diverse nature of the people they claimed to represent. This was unfortunate; Fiji's past has never been as insular or singular as they often asserted, and the political repercussions of such claims would be profound.

Indeed, 3,000 years of settlement has left legacies that we are only beginning to understand. The first migrants to the south-west Pacific islands of Fiji[1] were the coastal-based ancestors of today's Polynesians, who had travelled over 1,000 kilometres from the Bismarck Archipelago in present-day Papua New Guinea or from the eastern Solomon Islands. They were descendants of Austronesian migrants from Southern China and Taiwan over 6,000 years ago who had reached the Pacific via the

---

1   Fiji lies between 15 and 22 degrees south latitude and 175 degrees east and 177 degrees west longitude. It consists of two main islands, Viti Levu (10,386 square kilometres) and Vanua Levu (5,535 square kilometres) and some 330 smaller islands (2,151 square kilometres combined) predominantly within archipelagic thrusts west (the Yasawa group), south (Kadavu), and east (Taveuni and the Lau group). The small Polynesian island of Rotuma lies 400 kilometres to the north. From north to south, Fiji stretches some 1,000 kilometres and, from west to east, 500 kilometres.

Philippines and Indonesia.[2] They settled along Fiji's coasts, on its western grasslands and in its valleys, becoming increasingly pressured by climate change and the massive migration of Melanesians from the Solomons and Vanuatu after 1,000 CE. The latter migrants bestowed over 300 related languages on the Fiji group. But they also transformed Fiji in other ways, revolutionising agriculture and establishing the basis for the social and political structures that are today regarded as traditionally Fijian.[3] Population pressure at a time of climate change resulted in competition for resources that rapidly intensified warfare in Fiji. Fortified villages sprung up and, during the 19th century, they were augmented by increasingly large political confederacies (*matanitu*) and alliances for defensive and offensive purposes.[4] Huge wars were fought.

By then, Fiji had divided at least superficially into the Kai Colo of inland Viti Levu (nominally western Fiji) and the Kai Wai of Fiji's coastal regions and islands (again nominally eastern Fiji), with south-east Viti Levu (containing the fractious Bau, Rewa and Verata *matanitu*) the most densely populated region in the South Pacific.[5] The peoples of maritime Fiji were heavily influenced by trade and political alliances with Polynesian island groups, especially nearby resource-scarce Tonga, which colonised parts of eastern Fiji and lent troops to Fijian allies. Polynesian influence gave eastern Fiji a more hierarchical social and political character, which contrasted with the comparatively egalitarian nature of western Fiji. Whether the Kai Colo peoples of western Fiji are remnants of an early Melanesian wave that was pushed inland by successors is uncertain, but this late period of Fijian history undoubtedly left its people deeply scarred and disoriented. It also dislocated and scattered whole tribes across Fiji on a scale never before imaginable. In 2006, when working on the history of a Tailevu village that was seeking to recreate its ring ditches and fortifications for an ecotourism project, Canadian anthropologist Tara Mar and I learned of its people's movement from Ra and down eastern Viti Levu, possibly as a consequence of warfare. The Tai village's ancestors

2   B Su et al., 'Polynesian origins: Insights from the Y chromosome', *Proceedings of the National Academy of Science*, 97: 15, July 2000, pp. 8225–28.

3   C Walsh, 'Fiji's prehistory: Lapita', in C Walsh, *Fiji: An Encyclopaedic Atlas*. Suva: University of the South Pacific, 2006, pp. 394–95. Fijian social organisation began first with the family and then the extended family as the land holding unit, either the *i tokatoka* or the larger sub clan – the *mataqali*. The *yavusa* or clan is a grouping of *mataqali*, and related clans comprise a *vanua*.

4   In the east, the Tovata confederacy of *vanua* dominated the Lau group of islands and most of Vanua Levu. In eastern and northern Viti Levu, Bau held sway under the Kubuna confederacy while the Rewa confederacy of Burebasaga dominated southern Viti Levu.

5   Walsh, 'Fiji's prehistory: Ring-ditch fortifications', in Walsh, *Fiji*, 2006, pp. 396–97.

eventually found sanctuary as warriors for Verata, but the secrets of their past remain jealously guarded by family groupings (*mataqali*) and are not shared for fear of resurrecting ancient quarrels.[6]

At the University of the South Pacific during the 1990s and 2000s, a team of scholars led by Paddy Nunn revealed something of the many layers of that past and, in the process, challenged the general Fijian perception that they are derived from a single people, who arrived from the west with a great fleet led by the chiefly canoe, Kaunitoni, and then dispersed across Viti Levu. So powerful is the myth that, in 2005, the Fiji Museum and Radio Fiji sponsored its recreation. Fiji TV also broadcast a series devoted to exploring the myth, among others, although less for purposes of resolution than for reinforcement. That the myth bestows legitimacy on rivals (such as Verata) to dominant traditional powerholders of the country (Lau and Bau) is perhaps not insignificant. Nor the fact that the myth was cobbled together in the late 19th century by missionaries and ethnographers and later embellished with the notion that Fijians were a lost tribe of Israel that had arrived in Fiji via East Africa. Today, these stories remain enmeshed in the struggles of chiefs to reclaim heritage or status lost during the great remaking of Fiji under colonialism and in their desire to make Fijians a singular people.[7]

That remaking began before the arrival of Europeans, being most marked in south-eastern Viti Levu as the tiny island Bau gradually dominated over its hinterland and, in particular, Verata.[8] Europeans, however, provided fresh opportunities to exploit during these ongoing struggles. Bau's military chief or *vunivalu* quickly used access to European beachcombers to gain weapons to resolve its conflict with Verata more expeditiously. European plantation owners similarly created opportunities to silence opponents. A later *vunivalu*, Ratu Seru Cakobau, sold Ovalau's Lovoni

---

6   T Mar, 'A village based eco-tourism venture: A case study of Tai village', in R Robertson (ed.), *Livelihoods and Identity in Fiji*. Suva: University of the South Pacific, 2006, pp. 35–56.

7   Steven Ratuva claims that 'myths of common ancestry, origin, migration and history' are an important 'basis for constructing an ethnic ideology' to 'justify certain claims' ('Politics of ethno-national identity in a post-colonial communal democracy: The case of Fiji', *Identity & Belongingness in Fiji*, 18 June 2008, ecreanfriends.wordpress.com/2008/06/18/politics-of-ethno-national-identity-in-a-post-colonial-communal-democracy-the-case-of-Fiji).

8   See David Routledge, *Matanitu: The Struggle for Power in Early Fiji*. Suva: University of the South Pacific, 1985; and Peter France, *The Charter of the Land: Custom & Colonization in Fiji*. Melbourne: Oxford University Press, 1969.

people to planters in 1871 when they challenged his control over Lomaiviti. The same fate awaited *vanua* in Colo five years later after a series of unsuccessful attempts to establish Bauan dominance.

Christianity provided another tool for ambition. Cakobau converted to Christianity to ensure Tongan support for his next struggle on Viti Levu against Verata's neighbour, Rewa. The already Christianised Tonga was always something of a wild card in these struggles. Bau feared that it might try to usurp its authority. Indeed, Tonga sent a member of its ruling family to the Lau islands in eastern Fiji to consolidate Tongan influence there and, after a series of attempts, Ma'afu established the Tovata confederacy linking Lau with Cakaudrove, Macuata and Bua on Vanua Levu. Bau responded with its own Kubuna confederacy, but this soon found itself under pressure from the United States for a 20-year-old, dubiously inflated debt. The debt was paid, but by a commercial company in return for land. Settlers soon followed in 1871 and Cakobau sought to retain control by forming a Fijian kingdom with European advisors, hoping to gain recognition from foreign powers. It failed and, in desperation, Cakobau tried once more to cede Fiji to Britain, hoping again to maintain authority in the face of growing internal and external pressures.

Historian Alumita Durutalo argues that Christianity also helped chiefs to extend their power in other ways; certainly the translation of the Bible into the Bauan dialect extended Bauan authority and laid the foundation for a neotraditional order under colonialism.[9] Christianity destroyed the primacy of local gods; so too the power held by their priests or *bete*. The elaborate separation of gender and caste to stabilise population and maintain tribal hierarchies also disappeared from Fijian society. Missionaries demanded that husbands and wives live as nuclear families. Villages were transformed. Unexpectedly, in the midst of this revolution, came a great pestilence. In 1875, measles swept the land, wiping out nearly one quarter of the population.[10] Among the Tai warriors, a complex hierarchy of villages collapsed and the survivors huddled together for the first time within a single village. Thus weakened, Fijians made easier pickings for colonial land grabbers.

---

9   Alumita Durutalo, 'Of roots & offshoots: Fijian political thinking, dissent & the formation of political parties, 1960–1999'. PhD Thesis, The Australian National University. Canberra, 2005, p. 61.
10   The true demographic impact may never be known, but official estimates in 1879 place the death rate at 27 per cent of the 150,000 population (Andrew D Cliff & Peter Haggett, *The Spread of Measles in Fiji & the Pacific*. Canberra: The Australian National University, 1985, p. 35).

The colonial heritage

Historian Mike Davis once argued that underdevelopment – in his view the hallmark of most Third World countries on the eve of independence – had its origins in colonialism.[11] In Fiji, we can glimpse something of that origin in the way that the colonial desire for stability reduced the capacity of ordinary Fijians to engage with the modern economy, although reality was never as straightforward as Davis suggested. Colonial demands for raw materials, in particular sugar, also gave shape to an economy lacking the intersectoral linkages needed to capitalise on the creative potential of its people. An economy with such characteristics is not uniquely colonial but, under colonialism, development meant explicitly creating the conditions necessary to establish and maintain a viable export industry beneficial to the colonising power or its empire. Colonialism did not exist to benefit the colonised. Swiss sociologist Gilbert Rist argues that this approach to development cost colonialism any chance of success.[12] It was not inclusive. It could not win the hearts and minds of its subjects, no matter how much it pretended. Nonetheless, in the interim, it transformed societies like Fiji and created new dynamics that ultimately it could not control. By the early to mid-20th century, most colonies were under challenge internally, even before the Second World War and its aftermath swept away the international environment that had spawned it.

The modern era of colonialism began with the European arrival in the Americas in the late 15th century and the subsequent globalisation of trade routes. Colonies began to fulfil new economic functions, such as the production of tobacco, sugar and, later, coffee, tea and opium. Opium financed the British conquest of India and enabled it to control much of China's foreign trade by the late 19th century. Indian cotton fed British mills. The Pacific islands were incorporated for similar purposes. By the early 19th century, whalers plied the seas. Traders arrived for sandalwood and bêche de mer to sell to the Chinese. In the early 1860s, planters entered Fiji to capitalise on the American Civil War's impact on cotton supply. Cotton, already the world's most important crop, drove the mercantilist fortunes of the British East India Company and encouraged the use of slaves trafficked from Africa for American plantations. In Fiji,

11   M Davis, 'The origins of the Third World', in S Chari & S Corbridge (eds), *The Development Reader*. Oxon & New York: Routledge, 2008, pp. 14–30.
12   G Rist, *The History of Development: From Western Origins to Global Faith*. London & New York: Zed Books, 1997, p. 58.

blackbirded Pacific islanders provided the necessary plantation labour. But, most importantly, cotton drove Britain's industrialisation, earning it wealth and power of a magnitude never before imagined. The surpluses that Britain drew from India and China enabled it to sustain deficits with its self-governing dominions and new industrial rivals.[13] In addition, India became an important market for British products.

Industrialisation changed the nature of global dynamics and offered societies very different futures, but only if they appreciated the threat that industrialisation posed to their autonomy should they fail to respond. In the North Pacific, Japan appreciated that threat and, after 1868, began a development program to strengthen its already impressively commercial state through modernisation and industrialisation. This meant adapting what had been successful in existing industrialised countries, particularly Britain. And, if colonies were regarded as an important key to Britain's success, then countries that wished to emulate that success also sought colonies. This kind of thinking was all pervasive and long-lasting. When Hitler invaded the Soviet Union in 1940, he declared: 'What India is for England, the territories of Russia will be for us.'[14] In this way, colonies served the age-old zero-sum perceptions then held of development and change. Land and peoples were monopolised for the exclusive benefit of the coloniser. The exclusions and the inequalities they generated were justified as the reward for the coloniser's fitness and superiority. Progress possessed no universal application.

Societies unable, unwilling or unaware of the need to respond urgently to the industrial era became colonies, robbed of autonomy and incorporated into the economies of industrialising nations to supply raw materials and cheap labour. The experience was often brutal and harsh. Often, existing systems of governance were refashioned to disempower the very subjects that colonisers claimed they sought to civilise. The result was a process of dissolution and conservation that trapped future generations in legacies of disadvantage and bitterness.[15] It mattered little that these consequences contradicted the mission promoted by most colonising countries

---

13   Davis, 'The origins of the Third World', 2008, pp. 24–27.
14   A Bullock, *Hitler: A Study in Tyranny*. London: Penguin, 1962, p. 656.
15   C Bettelheim, 'Theoretical comments', in A Emmanuel, *Unequal Exchange: A Study of the Imperialism of Trade*. New York: Monthly Review Press, 1977, pp. 293–99. Bettelheim argued that, in conserving those parts of social formations deemed functional in practice, colonialism made them seem separate from its other institutions. This appearance of isolation gave rise to the notion of duality.

to justify their actions to their own people. In the end, empire sustained national pride and made nations appear great. Conquering lesser peoples fulfilled their historic destiny. Lesser peoples were not their equal. They did not possess the same rights; certainly not the right to develop similarly, create democratic institutions or engage with the wider, more globalised world on their own terms. Those possibilities could only occur after independence. Until then colonialism induced deep psychological barriers between colonised and coloniser that perpetuated distrust and violence. Such impacts often continued long after the colonial period had ended wherever local collaborators sought to inherit the colonial state. It gave birth to a form of neocolonialism in which the social divisions that promoted or sustained colonialism simply continued, invariably with destabilising consequences. Colonial experiences also generated deep suspicions of the motives of former colonial powers, affecting reactions to development advice after the 1950s and encouraging many former colonies to pursue disastrous separate development strategies.

Many of these features of colonialism were found in Fiji and made their way into the language of revolt that was demonstrated during times of upheaval long after colonialism had ended. So, too, the struggle for supremacy between Fiji's leading chiefs that had played such a vital role in the decision of Cakobau, the *vunivalu* of Bau, to cede Fiji to Britain in 1874. Cession provided a means to deal with the outside world now rapidly crowding in, while giving scope to preserve existing structures of power. The ageing *vunivalu* provocatively styled himself Tui Viti or King of Fiji and vainly hoped that the negotiated cession might consolidate his claims to paramountcy. It was not to be, but the title he claimed and his rivalry with the Tongan Ma'afu, who laid claim to eastern Fiji, continue to resonate through Fijian politics today, in part because the colonial settlement preserved the semblance of power held by high chiefs. At least some Fijians were far from passive recipients of colonialism; from the start they collaborated and benefited, finding in their state within a state a new means to exert authority and continue old rivalries.

From a security perspective, indirect rule made immediate sense. The first governor of Fiji, Sir Arthur Gordon, established what became known as the Native Administration or Matanitu iTaukei, a hierarchy of control that began at the remodelled village level (*koro*) and moved through to the district (*tikina*) and province (*yasana*). At its apex was an assembly of high chiefs, all from the victorious eastern sections of Fiji, known as the Bose Vaka Turaga or Council of Chiefs which advised the governor.[16] As historian Brij Lal aptly records, Gordon also 'imposed a uniform, inflexible set of land laws on a people whose traditional patterns of landownership showed kaleidoscopic variety and fluidity'.[17] They were laws derived largely from eastern Fiji.

This neotraditional orthodoxy became both a means of control and a focal point for dissent, in ways that Gordon never anticipated. He sought to maintain chiefly support and domestic peace, and avoid the costly war that colonialism had caused in New Zealand. And, in Fiji, colonialism did present risks. Not only were colonisers (around 2,600) vastly outnumbered by Fijians (possibly 140,000),[18] but cession brought revolt from Colo tribes in central and western Viti Levu. Bau joined with Britain to suppress Colo and gain advantage. This 'Little War of Viti Levu' (1875–76) left a legacy of dissent, in part borne from Colo's cultural distance from maritime Fiji and historical antipathy to Bau, but also from its continued neglect and relative poverty. It would find voice in anti-colonial and anti-Bauan movements such as the Tuka (led by Dugumoi or Navosavakadua), the Luveniwai in the 1880s and 1890s, and in Apolosi Ranawai's anti-colonial and anti-chiefly Viti Kabani movement of the early 20th century.[19] That all these movements adopted protective millennial or commercial forms should not detract from their intent. Not until independence would Fijians be permitted a political voice, but the dissent that was first demonstrated during the early decades of colonialism continued to echo in many of the small anti-establishment political parties formed in the late 20th century, in the victory of the Fiji Labour Party in 1987, and in the involvement of the Colo province Naitasiri in the 2000 coup, which also saw descendants of the Cakobau clan pitted against the Mara clan, the successors to Ma'afu and Tovata's 20th-century

---

16   This later became known as the Bose Levu Vaka Turaga or the Great Council of Chiefs.

17   B Lal, *Broken Waves: A History of the Fiji Islands in the Twentieth Century*. Honolulu: University of Hawaii Press, 1992, p. 15. Ratu Joni Madraiwiwi makes a similar point: 'Fijians were only united with the coming of the British colonisers' (Madraiwiwi, 'Ethnic tensions and the law', 2004).

18   The Fijian population declined from approximately 140,000 in 1881 to 86,000 in 1904. Europeans (half of whom derived from Australia, New Zealand or England) grew slowly in number from 2,671 in 1881 to 3,707 in 1911 (Peter Robinson, 'The Crown Colony Government & the regulation of relations between settlers & Fijians, 1880–1910'. Master of Letters Thesis, Oxford University, 1984, pp. 122, 137).

19   The best work on anticolonial resistance in Fiji is Robert Nicole's *Disturbing History: Resistance in Early Colonial Fiji* (Honolulu: University of Hawai'i Press, 2011). See also Timothy J McNaught, *The Fijian Colonial Experience: A Study of the Neo-Traditional Order under British Colonial Rule prior to World War II*. Canberra: The Australian National University, 1982.

resurgence under Ratu Sukuna. It would find echoes also in the marijuana plantations that, for much of the 2000s, provided the most viable cash crop for the isolated and impoverished but still defiant Colo region.

Gordon left another legacy that would prove equally long lasting in its impact. In order to make the new colony pay for itself, he imported Indian indentured labourers (61,000 between 1879 and 1916) to work on sugar cane fields that were eventually managed by the Australian Colonial Sugar Refinery Company (CSR). The use of CSR avoided the presence of British settlers who might demand rights similar to those enjoyed by settlers and their descendants in self-governing colonies like Australia and New Zealand.[20] The use of indentured Indians ensured the availability of cheap labour that would not disrupt the Fijian economy, as the withdrawal of Fijian labour would most certainly have done, and provoke anti-colonial agitation.

Fijians would later claim that the creation of the sugar industry excluded them from economic participation and marginalised them. The claim made use of notions of dualism, of a dichotomy between the tradition of the Fijian way of life and the modernity of the new economy, to assert postcolonial inequality and disadvantage, which are hallmarks of underdevelopment. This assertion became the central justification for Fijian paramountcy during the coups of 1987 and 2000. Many writers, including the political economist William Sutherland, have demonstrated that this is incorrect, or at best a gross simplification. Certainly Fijians had only marginal involvement in the sugar industry to start with, but they were never excluded from the colonial economy. Many Fijians worked as wage labourers; during the 1880s possibly one quarter of the Fijian workforce laboured in copra plantations. By the end of the 1930s many were also working in the Vatukoula goldmines. In addition, Fijians were forced to contribute indirectly to the new economy in other ways. Communal tax-in-kind made up 30 per cent of state revenue in

---

20   Nonetheless, settlers in Fiji still pressed for direct representation in government (their birthright), demanded Fiji's incorporation into a federated Australasia in the 1880s and with New Zealand in 1900, and pressed for access to more land, even though they never utilised more than a fraction of the land they already held. Fiji's colonial government briefly flirted with a political agitators ordinance to prevent colonists undermining Fijian support for the communal system, but eventually agreed to the representation of colonists (six) and Fijians (two) in a Legislative Council dominated by government appointees (10) (Robinson, 'The Crown Colony Government', 1984, pp. 16, 60–88, 95, 109–10). See also France, *The Charter of the Land*, 1969, pp. 149–75.

the 1870s[21] and the cost of Fijian labour set the national benchmark for wages. Fijians were not excluded from the colonial economy, but they were integrated differently from Europeans and Indians, and it was this difference that always ensured that labour possessed a racial dimension within Fiji.[22]

Rigid segmented labour markets were by no means unique to colonialism in Fiji. But, without doubt, its combination with other forms of separateness (social, political and educational) encouraged the divisions and stereotyping that would later haunt Fiji's political and economic development. Writers in the 1980s, like the sociologist Simione Durutalo, saw all this as grist to the mill for colonialism, but for those colonised it helped foster a victim mentality.

> During the greater part of British rule knowledge except that provided in carefully limited doses by the missionaries, was disdained. The people were discouraged from thinking for themselves; a thirst for knowledge was considered dangerous and subversive. Trained to obey and follow, and mindful of the misfortunes that befell the poor 'native' who, using his or her reason, questioned however timidly the decisions of someone in authority, the people later transformed this training and fear into a conviction that one should allow one's social and economic superiors to do the thinking for the community. One's betters eventually included, besides the British officials and white missionaries, those members of the local elite who were by then benefitting from colonial rule. This passivity was gradually transformed and glorified as tradition.[23]

In divesting its subjects of their humanity, colonialism created a sense of inferiority, and fostered a victim mentality. Above all it encouraged the idea that only colonisers were dynamic and capable of leadership and innovation. That idea – a form of cultural cringe – took some undoing.

---

21   If anything, the tax burden increased on Fijians because the amount in kind to be paid was never adjusted after 1881 to take into account the dramatic fall in the Fijian population (Robinson, 'The Crown Colony Government', 1984, p. 100).
22   W Sutherland, *Beyond the Politics of Race. An Alternative History of Fiji to 1992*. Canberra: The Australian National University, 1992, pp. 28–29.
23   S Durutalo, 'The liberation of the Pacific Island intellectual', *Review*, 4, September 1983, SSED, University of the South Pacific, p. 14.

Creating a plural society

The colonial approach to development and its failure to empower its subjects ultimately cost it any chance of success. It was challenged, not least because colonialism transformed societies and created dynamics that colonialists could not control.

The importation of Indian labour is a case in point. It gave labour a new racial dimension: Indian, Fijian, European, part European, Chinese, Pacific Islander and Rotuman. As Sutherland notes, however, such appearances can be deceptive.[24] Most indentured labourers (*girmitiya*) came initially from Hindi-speaking Uttar Pradesh in north India, but a large minority later came also from the Tamil- and Telugu-speaking south.[25] Southerners found fitting into a predominantly North Indian settler society difficult, partly because northerners were more established in Fiji at the time of their arrival, but partly also because of religious, linguistic and ethnic discrimination. Indians were never a singular community.

They arrived on five-year contacts to desperate conditions[26] in an industry dominated by a single company extracting even greater profits than its Australian operations were able to muster and paying wages seven times lower. According to economist Wadan Narsey, between 1883 and 1913, CSR profits in Fiji rose 600 per cent, despite a 53 per cent fall in sugar prices.[27] The colonial government saw no reason to interfere; indeed for many years the state's courts were employed to routinely discipline indentured labourers. Over time the position of Indians improved, especially once CSR ended plantation farming and leased land to free Indians as small farmers, who not unexpectedly now also carried most of the risks previously borne by the company. The indenture system ended by 1920 but, after a generation of harrowing experiences, post-indentured farmers became decidedly more assertive. Lal notes:

---

24   Sutherland, *Beyond the Politics of Race*, 1992, pp. 50–54.
25   See Brij V Lal, 'Girmitiyas: The Origins of the Fiji Indians'. Canberra: *Journal of Pacific History*, 1983.
26   V Naidu, *Violence of Indenture in Fiji*. Lautoka: Fiji Institute of Applied Studies, 2004. See also KL Gillion, *Fiji's Indian Migrants – A History to the End of Indenture in 1920*. Melbourne: Oxford University Press, 1963.
27   W Narsey, 'Monopoly, capital, white racism and superprofits in Fiji', *Journal of Pacific Studies*, 5, 1979, pp. 66–146.

Indenture had taught its lessons well. The Fiji-born were more on their own, more individually oriented, more conscious of and sensitive to the relative deprivation they experienced in the larger society. India did not loom large in their consciousness, as it had perhaps done in the lives of the *girmitiya*, including my grandfather, who even in old age still hoped to die in his *janmabhumi* 'motherland'. In contrast Fiji was the only home the new generation had, and they did not shy away from pursuing the rights and opportunities they thought were properly theirs.[28]

That assertiveness was most marked in a series of strikes in 1921, 1943 and 1960 over the cost of living and it was assisted also by a new but small class of Indian professionals and businessmen who migrated to Fiji, most notably after the First World War, especially from the Punjab and Gujarat. They added further to the linguistic and religious diversity of the Indian 'community' and also to the tensions within it over work, religion and political representation.

One recent migrant was a teacher from North India who had temporarily become a cane farmer in the early 1930s. Ayodhya Prasad formed the Kisan Sangh or Farmers Association in 1937 to negotiate on behalf of farmers with the CSR to reduce the huge impact of rising costs on their livelihoods. The CSR kept tight control over what farmers could do on its land, even restricting private gardens and animals, and its contracts with farmers often left them at the mercy of moneylenders and shopkeepers. The Kisan Sangh's goals were popular with farmers, and it eventually succeeded in influencing the terms of a new farmer's contract with the CSR. But its focus on debt reduction and farmer cooperatives, which released pressure on the CSR, potentially threatened the livelihoods of shopkeepers, many of whom were Gujaratis or Punjabis.

In 1941, Gujarati lawyer AD Patel formed a rival Maha Sangh devoted to the interests of the much discriminated South Indians, who were mostly employed directly by the CSR and less inclined to see the commonality of interests with the CSR that the Kisan Sangh projected. Increasingly they saw the Kisan Sangh as a North Indian association. Thus divided, cane farmers entered a period of great uncertainty. War increased inflation and hardship for farmers. A cane strike over conditions in 1943 saw the two associations assume diametrically opposed positions with disastrous consequences for farmers. Although the issues faced by the

---

28   Lal, *Broken Waves*, 1992, p. 75.

farmers would not be resolved until the dying days of colonialism, farmers had organised and stood up to the autocracy of both the CSR and the colonial government.[29]

Sutherland argues that, in Fiji's highly racialised atmosphere, it was all too easy for the class nature of farmers' struggles to be obscured by ethnicity, either that of North and South Indians or of Indians in general.[30] Sometimes it was in the interests of the state and farmer leaders to present issues in diversionary ethnic terms. Even during the political turmoil of 1987 and 2000, cane farmer issues and access to land were similarly presented. But, in the early 20th century, there were other struggles underway in Fiji – again the unintended consequences of colonialism – and they too were portrayed as racial. Among the most significant were those concerning chiefs.

Fijian chiefs, particularly those among the dominant eastern clans, had done well from the post-cession settlement but, with the Colo peoples under control, colonial authorities considered encouraging Fijian individualism by promoting the movement of Fijians from villages and relaxing communal obligations. To that end they sought to give Fijians more opportunity to break away from the confines of their villages and, during the 1920s, they downgraded the role of chiefs in native administration. But their efforts were always somewhat ambivalent; certainly following Ranawai's launch of the subversive western Fijian Viti Kabani in 1913, the state rediscovered the value of chiefs. Apolosi formed his Fijian Company as a cooperative to monopolise Fijian commerce and unite Fijians against colonial and chiefly control. For his pains he would spend much of his final 30 years in exile within and outside of Fiji. The colonial authorities should have welcomed him as a model enterprising commoner Fijian but his activities potentially threatened European traders. He also challenged the authority of the state and its Native Administration and raised the ire of chiefs, whom he blamed for the problems facing his people. Chiefs like the Tui Lau, Ratu Lala Sukuna, gradually convinced authorities of the importance of chiefly authority for maintaining law and order, particularly as more Fijians moved from their traditional places of residence. 'Whatever his real merits as a leader, or

---

29   B Lal, *A Vision for Change: AD Patel and the Politics of Fiji*. Canberra: National Centre for Development Studies, The Australian National University, 1997, pp. 64–80.
30   Sutherland, *Beyond the Politics of Race*, 1992, pp. 57–58.

failings as a demagogue,' one historian writes, 'Apolosi had become the Fijian bogeyman who served the authorities as the negative example to the good natives, chiefly and loyal civil servants like Ratu Sukuna.'[31]

The Great Council of Chiefs (GCC) took the lead, encouraging the formation of a Native Land Trust Board (NLTB) in 1940 to oversee the leasing of Fijian land, and mobilising many of its young men (in contrast to Indians) for war service. Loyalty eventually won Fijians a Fijian Administration in 1944, which re-established many of the old features of Fijian communal life that consolidated chiefly authority. Additionally, it assisted to paper over historic divisions and create the mythology of Fijians as one people, indivisible and united under their chiefs, with interests diametrically opposed to those of Indians. It survived until the eve of independence. Thereafter, many Fijians made its recreation an essential element in the assertion of Fijianness. Ironically it would also feature strongly in the Fijian military backlash in 2006, but for opposite reasons.

The increased assertiveness of Indians and apparent defensiveness of Fijians grew in part from demographic changes. Indians comprised 29 per cent of the population in 1911 (which totalled 140,000), 43 per cent in 1936 (160,000) and 50 per cent by 1946 (200,000). The change made electoral representation more difficult, minimal though it was in reality. By the late 1930s the advisory Legislative Council continued to be dominated by officials, with representation from subjects communalised and unproportional. Only half the European and Indian representatives were elected; Fijians were nominated by the GCC.[32] Efforts by Indians to achieve more democratic forms of governance were met by European claims that the Deed of Cession necessitated European dominance to protect Fijian interests. Exaggerated though they were, such

---

31   Some 17 per cent of Fijians had left their villages by 1946; see J Heartfield, 'You are not a white woman: Apolosi Nawai, the Fiji Produce Agency and the trial of Stella Spencer in Fiji, 1915', *Journal of Pacific History*, 38: 1, 2003, p. 82. See also Nicole, *Disturbing History*, 2011, pp. 70–97; and McNaught, *The Fijian Colonial Experience*, 1982.

32   Indians were permitted only one member nominated by the governor in 1916; Fijian chiefs, two; and Europeans, seven. The remaining 11 members were nominated officials. Agitation for change had little impact; in 1929 European representation fell to six, and Indians and Fijians were permitted three members each. Indian representatives called for a common roll rather than communal voting, but received little support either from chiefs opposed to democracy or from Europeans fearful of Indian demographic supremacy. In 1937, a revision produced a 31-member council of 16 officials, three elected and three nominated Indians, three elected and three nominated Europeans, and five Fijians nominated indirectly by the GCC. Local government representation produced similar distortions and arguments, with the state maintaining control through a preponderance of officials.

claims sent a powerful signal of support to the Fijian elite. Consequently, a new constitution prior to independence in 1970 rewarded Europeans with an equally exaggerated proportion of seats, effectively giving them the balance of power.

Colonial apartheid, represented by separate communal schools, separate suburbs, separate working environments and separate political representation marked the extremities of pluralism, a term increasingly used by social scientists after the 1930s to describe the mutually exclusive social, cultural and structural features of colonies or former colonies. Lacking any national binding, these predominantly tropical societies could only be held together by force, not consensus, or so they said.[33] Political scientists and historians echoed such views. They described two homogenous blocs confronting each other, with conflict the inevitable result. Guyanan academic Ralph Premdas believed that 'left to themselves these ethnic groups [in Fiji] would probably opt for separate states'.[34] 'The different social groupings are divided from each other in every respect,' claimed historian Deryck Scarr, 'the only common link is that they live in the same country.'[35]

Politicians and ethno-nationalists similarly echoed these views. Rebel George Speight argued in 2000 that differences between Fijians and Indians were immutable: 'They have their own religion; they don't dress the same; they don't speak the same language; they don't smell the same.'[36] Joji Banuve, an assistant Minister for Education, later suggested that racial characteristics could be inferred from how people combed their hair. Fijian women combed their hair outwards, demonstrating how Fijians reached out to people to help them. Indian women combed their hair inwards, signifying that they only cared for themselves, not others.[37] Similarly, Banuve's contemporary, Adi Asenaca Caucau – Minister for Women and Social Welfare – described Indians as 'weeds': 'pushy, inconsiderate and always demanding'.[38] Her Prime Minister, Laisenia Qarase, described

---

33   See JS Furnivall, *Netherlands India: A Study of Plural Economy*. Cambridge University Press, 1939; L Kuper & MG Smith (eds), *Pluralism in Africa*. Berkeley: University of California Press, 1969.
34   R Premdas, 'The foundations of political conflict in Fiji', Suva, mimeo, 1986.
35   D Scarr, *Fiji, Politics of Illusion: The Military Coups in Fiji*. Sydney: NSW University Press, 1988, p. 16.
36   *fijilive*, 23 May 2000.
37   *fijilive*, 14 April 2002. Banuve neglected to note that not all Fijian women wore the traditional *buiniga* hairstyle, and that those of Polynesian descent often had straight hair.
38   *Fiji Times*, 10 August 2002.

Fijians as 'the rarest breed of people in the world'.[39] 'The past is too much with us and cannot be wished away easily', Vice President Ratu Joni Madraiwiwi, noted at the time: 'While one may decry communalism, it is a difficult beast to subdue.'[40]

When anthropologist Alexander Mamak applied the plural analysis to Fiji's capital, Suva, during the 1970s, he wanted to know exactly how mutually exclusive communities had become and whether a tipping point existed after which a nation fell beyond redemption, its communities having achieved such separate autonomy that any process of de-pluralisation became impossible. Instead he found that internal divisions among Indians and Fijians created 'bases for cross-cutting alliances between sections previously unrelated'. Hence de-pluralisation was a real possibility because most Indians and Fijians shared low pay and low status employment.[41] Thus class could play a role in breaking down rigidities and providing space for the development of national goals and interests. Of course this did not explain why communities came to see their interests as so divergent in the first place. Could leaders gain in some way from promoting conflict pluralism? Could this explain the longevity of race as an organisational concept in countries like Fiji?

Political scientist Stephanie Lawson sees the overwhelming focus on race in Fiji as mistaking 'the social myth for reality and [giving] it both a force and a form that is not necessarily warranted'. Such focus distorts the nature of race relations and obscures other explanatory factors.[42] By using race, culture or religion as a way to define societies, we accept at face value the criteria by which groups define themselves. Harold Wolpe once argued with respect to South Africa that this kind of thinking reflected the internalisation of colonial attitudes. Internal colonialism, he argued, treats racial groups as distinct essentialised entities. It takes appearances for

---

39   *fijilive*, 12 March 2003.

40   To these opening remarks at the Fiji National Consultations on a Global Partnership for the Prevention of Armed Conflict, Pacific Theological College, Suva, Madraiwiwi added: 'In the heat of political confrontation, the electorate takes refuge in the familiar and eschews difference'. In such situations 'it is critical that one engages the political actors whatever their beliefs' ('Building the peace', *Fiji Times*, 17 March 2005).

41   A Mamak, *Colour, Culture & Conflict: A Study of Pluralism in Fiji*. Sydney: Pergamon Press, 1978, pp. 5–6, 178.

42   S Lawson, *The Failure of Democratic Politics in Fiji*. Oxford: Clarendon Press, 1991, p. 39. Steven Ratuva ('Politics of ethno-national identity', 2008) argues instead for a more 'complex inter-relationship of opposition and accommodation taking place between political and cultural discourses'.

granted. It glosses over internal differences within groups. It accepts the notion of separateness and that race drives social and political processes.[43] Wolpe argued for critical analysis instead.

Of course conflict pluralists also contrasted the diversity of developing societies with the presumed homogeneity of developed countries, where common norms and values enabled consensus not conflict. Such convenient simplifications flowed easily in the postwar period. Economist Walt Rostow maintained that modernisation produced homogeneity and the kind of society that the United States had become. Political scientist Samuel Huntington added a caveat: where homogeneity existed only within conflicting ethnic blocs, national consensus for stability and growth would be frustrated.[44] Neither acknowledged that the perceived homogeneity of developed countries emanated from long processes of social and economic change that gradually made states fiscally accountable and democratic. In other words, the transcendence of ethnic or other identities derived from political processes; it did not derive from a fixed inherited or natural condition. No similar process occurred with Third World countries. Colonialism never developed similar institutions of accountability or public goods like education and communications. Rather, it frustrated changes that might have created a sense of nationhood.[45] Hence only exceptional political leadership and prosperity could overcome the lack of cohesion and consensus and many newly independent states experienced neither.

---

43   H Wolpe, 'The theory of internal colonisation: The South African case', in I Oxaal, T Barnett & D Booth (eds), *Beyond the Sociology of Development*. London: Routledge & Kegan Paul, 1975, p. 283. More recently Paul Collier notes the near convergence of pluralism with the long-held views of late 19th-century urban middle-class romantic nationalists who retrospectively imagined 'the sense of a common ethnic origin blended to the national soil' (*Wars, Guns & Votes: Democracy in Dangerous Places*. London: The Bodley Head, 2009, p. 169).

44   WW Rostow, *The Stages of Economic Growth: A Non-Communist Manifesto*. Cambridge University Press, 1960; S Huntington, *Political Order in Changing Societies*. New Haven: Yale University Press, 1968. Of course, this conveniently overlooks issues such as segregation, which was then prevalent within the United States.

45   Something of the same argument can be found in John D Kelly & Martha Kaplan's *Represented Communities: Fiji & World Colonization* (University of Chicago Press, 2001): communities are never imagined but derive from colonial divide and rule legacies and decolonisation negotiations. Such legacies are far more important in determining the fate of countries like Fiji than a stubborn resistance to modernisation.

Postcolonialism

Pluralism was one way to account for the state of colonies. But, in the postwar period, the end of colonialism coincided with a remarkable period of global economic introspection that deeply influenced the strategies adopted by developing countries to overcome colonial legacies. The origins of new thinking on development lay in the Great Depression of the 1930s and in the return to long-run theorising about development led by the British economist Maynard Keynes. His stress on state stimulus packages would dominate political responses to recessions well into the next century. They also deeply influenced responses to postwar recovery. The 1947 Marshall Plan and the consolidation of welfare states in Europe are classic examples of this way of thinking. Keynesianism, together with state-driven economic development, shaped the immediate postwar decades, assisted in large measure by a long-lasting postwar boom.

Nonetheless, the Depression weakened faith in market capitalism. Together with the illusion of successful Soviet planning in the 1930s, it popularised the idea that development could be centrally planned. National security demands in the 1930s and 1940s also ensured that state directives took precedence over market signals. The Depression and its aftermath seemed to suggest that only governments could rationally and equitably ration scarce resources and allocate them to ensure national growth in domestic goods, industry and infrastructure. India chose state planning after independence and its decision influenced many politicians in newly independent African and Asian countries also. But, with a closed economy, strong state controls and heavy industry as the motor for growth, India struggled over the next two decades to achieve more than 1.9 per cent annual growth. In part this was because state planning in India dealt with a less wealthy and skilled population. By failing to democratise its economy, India also constrained popular participation in its economy. Western Europe redistributed wealth instead.

National industry was the basis for growth in modernising countries during the 19th and early 20th centuries, and colonies drew on that feature with one significant difference. The successful early industrialisers had used growing surpluses in agriculture to invest in industry; but, in many newly independent countries, no improved agricultural productivity existed to tap into. Instead taxes on food and import tariffs were used to raise the funds needed for industrial investment and for sustaining uncompetitive national enterprises. Struggling farmers soon got the message. They fled the induced poverty of the countryside for the supposed wealth that would come from temporary encampment in urban slums, but there was never enough work and – not unexpectedly – never enough food.[46]

We might ask whether this form of industrialisation was still an appropriate goal in the mid and late 20th century when economies were becoming more globalised, more service-oriented, and a new set of international institutions existed to regulate the global economy and assist with development? To be fair the changed nature of world economies was not obvious to many leaders, and international institutions rarely extended to Third World countries the social and economic privileges increasingly enjoyed by the First World. In part this failure resulted also from entrenched core–periphery ways of thinking, the legacy of decades of imperialism, and it created a crippling global divide that weakened the postwar order. Consequently, struggles for independence, national weaknesses and the exigencies of the Cold War made the state an obvious emphasis for almost all postcolonial governments.

Latin American countries, in contrast, were mostly independent but, like many colonies, their focus on primary export production left them dependent on industrialised countries for markets. The Depression destroyed the value of their products and demonstrated the extent to which terms of trade worked against primary production and reduced their capacity to respond. Raúl Prebisch, head of the UN Economic Commission for Latin America in the 1950s, believed this downward trend in demand for primary products unlikely to reverse. He argued that the best solution for the Third World lay in breaking colonial ties and pursuing import substitution industrialisation (ISI), using high tariffs to protect local industry from the anarchy of the marketplace. In the long term, this patriotic strategy increased the economic role of the state, which began to set domestic prices and wages, grant subsidies and nationalise industries. As a postcolonial strategy, however, ISI did not necessarily encourage economic or political democratisation; if anything it was in tune with the wishes of those who sought to inherit the colonial state

---

46   A Beattie, *False Economy: A Surprising Economic History of the World.* London: Viking, 2009, pp. 48–50. Beattie uses the example of Zambia.

or, in the case of South America, those who already controlled the state and preferred 'cosy, safe monopolies protected by government fiat and regulation to the brutal riskiness of competition'.[47]

ISI was a global response to the new postwar environment, not simply a Third World one. All countries sought to protect their national industries and many rounds of international negotiations would occur before leading industrial countries gradually reduced barriers to trade late in the century. Technological change also made it possible to restructure industry and commerce globally. But, until then, ISI remained attractive to countries seeking to reduce forms of colonial dependence. Prebisch went on to launch the first UN Conference on Trade and Development (UNCTAD) in 1964, which successfully negotiated the general system of preferences that granted Third World countries duty-free access for some manufactured goods into the First World.

Such postcolonial global developments generated optimism during the early postcolonial period. Real development might not only be possible but could also be achieved quickly. Indeed, the United Nations declared the 1960s the Development Decade, as if 10 years alone would be sufficient as long as the hearts and minds of people were captured. But this was also a period of Cold War, and winning hearts and minds served ideological purposes. Within the United States a broad school of development thought emerged known as Modernisation. State driven, it focused on social and political modernisation as well as economic growth, and held that the transition from tradition to modernity could be achieved by adopting a scientific outlook or Protestant work ethic. No consensus emerged, however, as to the means to achieve such a transition. Samuel Huntington believed that dictatorship could be a precondition for growth and democracy,[48] thereby justifying American interests in authoritarian countries like South Vietnam and Iran. Most modernisationists saw the United States as the model of modernity and were comfortable with the notion that development equalled Americanisation. Hence, Third World failures to modernise were due principally to internal factors such as the persistence of tradition, the plurality of societies, or cultural resistance to change.[49] An external agent of change could, however, help offset these internal factors.

---

47   Beattie, *False Economy*, 2009, pp. 12–13.
48   Huntington, *Political Order in Changing Societies*, 1968.
49   For example, see Lawrence Harrison, *Culture Matters: How Values Shape Human Progress*. New York: Basic Books, 2000.

If countries lacked sufficient savings to invest in growth, they might seek foreign capital or aid, which of course added to the mythology of the West as the only dynamic and modern site – the only model for development. But such aid could not be extended to traditional sectors; they were regarded as static and beyond redemption. In fact, this was an inaccurate perception. Modern sectors tended to feed off so-called traditional sectors because they kept costs low and reduced pressures for political change. Appearances of separateness could easily mask its opposite – integration – albeit in a subservient fashion, just as colonialism had recreated traditional systems for purposes of control.[50]

If modernisation theories owed much to colonial thinking, then the group of ideas that briefly challenged it in the 1960s were aligned more directly to struggles for independence. They too captured a single idea, not of tradition as the stumbling block but of external relations first established under imperialism. American economist Paul Baran argued in 1957 that Western capital deliberately kept the Third World backward in order to maintain markets for its surplus production.[51] Hence the Third World came to be systematically underdeveloped, as Andre Gunder Frank expressed it, rather than developed.[52] Dependency theories held that core–periphery relationships deliberately generated underdevelopment in the periphery and that modernity was possible only if those relationships were broken. Thus underdevelopment was not generated internally, as modernisationists claimed, but externally by imperialism, surplus extraction and unequal exchange. The solution lay in cutting old links with the global economy, fostering self-reliance through state-led initiatives such as ISI, and developing new and more equal relationships with the global economy. For political leaders of newly independent countries this approach appealed more than that offered by Modernisationists because it shifted responsibility for the condition of their countries away from internal factors such as class, investment and inequalities to external relationships, both past and present. That it also signified an ahistorical, static and homogenised universal view of societies added to its appeal; it underpinned Third World solidarity.

---

50   Bettelheim (1977) called this process 'dissolution-conservation' and saw the origins of inequality in its impact on productive capabilities. His view contrasted with those who believed disadvantage derived from exchange relations.

51   P Baran, *The Political Economy of Growth*. New York: Monthly Review Press, 1957.

52   AG Frank, 'The development of underdevelopment', in S Chew & R Denemark (eds), *The Underdevelopment of Development: Essays in Honour of Andre Gunder Frank*. Thousand Oaks: Sage Publications 1996.

Inevitably, the costs of self-reliance were high, resulting in inefficient uncompetitive industries isolated from technological innovation and with little emphasis on service and quality, and regimes that paid little attention to democratisation. North Korea's self-reliant hermit state is one of the few surviving examples today. But, for most countries, the result became increased debt, neglected exports and – despite all the rhetoric to the contrary – the penetration of national boundaries by subsidiaries of transnational corporations (TNCs). Nor did preferential agreements that attempted to address the legacies of unequal exchange always assist; instead they confirmed existing economic foci and postponed diversification and other reforms, as Fiji experienced with its sugar trade concessions. Preferential agreements could also become a form of rent-seeking, a Third World entitlement captured by elites with little development to show.

Dependency theories grew out of inevitable postcolonial suspicions of international markets, and former colonial actors, and fears of neocolonialism or renewed subservience. They were allied with postcolonial desires for alternative development that sprung from long-suppressed native energies rather than the dictates of former colonial masters. A natural good now had an opportunity to triumph over an obvious evil. That national isolation or protectionism might stymie growth seemed as inconceivable as capital being simultaneously both progressive and regressive in different places. British communist Bill Warren punctured the dependency bubble in 1980 when he declared underdevelopment the result of imperialism, not capitalism. Certainly colonialism generated path dependencies and class distortions, but decolonisation – he argued – now gave capital the potential to move into the periphery.[53] No better example existed than that of newly industrialised countries (NICs) such as South Korea and Brazil, whose industrial success by the 1980s demonstrated that the Third World was far from homogeneous or fated to mediocrity. By the end of the century, China and India's divergence would finally consume what remained of Dependency rhetoric.

By the 1980s, all theories were open to challenge, in part because of their inconsistencies but also because of experience. When postwar economic expansion finally faltered in the 1970s, recovery as a much more globalised world made nationalist solutions more problematic than they had once

---

53 B Warren, *Imperialism: Pioneer of Capitalism*. London: Verso, 1980.

seemed. Third World solidarity proved weak and new approaches to development emerged that relied less on statist directions than on human agency. Once more, democratisation entered the development lexicon.

The case of the missing national bourgeoisie

A transition to independence invariably implied some form of democratisation. It marked the difference between colonialism and postcolonialism in terms of development goals. In Fiji the colonial state consistently refused to discipline the CSR, even when its officials privately conceded that its actions badly harmed the welfare of the country's farmers. AD Patel pleaded in vain to the Shephard Commission of Inquiry into the sugar industry in 1943 to recognise:

> We growers are also human beings. We also have to meet our social, economic and religious obligations ... We have as much right to be prosperous and happy as anybody in the world, with decent housing and better comforts.[54]

But, on the eve of independence, the state took a different stance, accepting a new award that gave greater weight to the needs of its farmers.[55] For the CSR, the writing was on the wall. A government elected by and responsible to its citizens must have different objectives and priorities than a non-elected colonial administration. CSR decided to leave Fiji rather than adapt and, in 1973, its assets were effectively nationalised. But to whom exactly was the new Fiji Government responsible and to what extent did that responsibility translate into a radically different direction for Fiji's economy?

We noted earlier that, after the Second World War, Fiji's eastern chiefs succeeded in creating a new bureaucracy to service the needs of Fijians, but their success did little to raise the welfare of ordinary Fijians. The same might be said of the colonial state. Its postwar drive to restructure the economy benefited Europeans with resources to invest in tourism. A declining proportion of state loans went to agriculture (40 per cent in 1960, 25 per cent in 1969), with most agricultural and industrial loans

---

54 Farmers' petition to the governor, 16 November 1943, quoted in Lal, *Broken Waves*, 1992, p. 130.
55 The Denning Award changed returns to farmers from 57.75 per cent of gross proceeds to 65 per cent. In 1975, this was altered again to 70 per cent to growers.

going to Europeans (52 per cent) and Indians (34 per cent).[56] Rural Fijians missed out. This created a dilemma for the Fijian elite. It had survived because of the powerful support gained from European businesses, eager for allies in their struggle against competing Indian enterprises and for state support to develop a secure future in tourism. Increasingly during the 1960s, the Fijian elite came to believe that the answer lay in controlling the postcolonial state to facilitate the development of a new Fijian capitalist class, the equal to that possessed by Europeans and Indians. But doing that meant sacrificing, in part, the strategies that were crucial to chiefly success in the past, namely the old racist ideology of the colonial era. At the very least it had to be de-emphasised. The reason was simple: most state resources would continue to come from the export sugar sector. If these were not to be jeopardised, thereby preventing the state financing its Fijian business project, rapprochement with Indians was necessary. Hence the introduction of a new ideology of multiracialism and the new state's symbolic but necessary decision to back cane farmers rather than the CSR in negotiations for a new cane award for the 1970s.

Colonies became independent but economies remained largely neocolonial and dependent. Their states promised the growth of strong local economies to give meaning to independence, a sign that they were moving towards equality with the First World. Yet, despite promising to develop their national capitalists, they were helpless to effect autonomous growth. Few linkages existed between the modern economy and the subsistence activities of the bulk of their population. State policies that funded industrial growth from rural taxes did not help. Taxes simply prevented new businesses from using poor peasants as a market, forcing them instead to focus on export activities that did little to generate internal growth and local participation, or provide for the welfare of the millions that urbanised in anticipation of that growth. Consequently, foreign capital still exerted tremendous sway, despite state rhetoric to the contrary. Herein lay sources for state weakness. Policies that excluded local participation bred instability, with less powerful classes eager for a higher national profile seeking compensation for their weakness by appealing to ethnic, tribal, religious or regional support. Where states found mediating between conflicting interest groups difficult, authoritarianism always loomed as a solution. Such temptation could only be avoided with inclusive social and economic change.[57]

---

56   Sutherland, *Beyond the Politics of Race*, 1992, pp. 114–15.
57   W Ziemann & M Lanzendorfer, 'The state in peripheral societies', *The Socialist Register 1977*. London: Merlin Press, 1977, pp. 143–77.

For many analysts in the immediate postcolonial period it seemed beyond doubt that a central feature of any well-developed economy lay in its ability to act in a self-generating manner. For some that meant not just the establishment of a strong national group of capitalists but also the removal of traditional practices that made impossible the development of integrated economies. But were these unrealistic goals? Could national capital actually represent the national interest? Was the notion of a progressive national bourgeoisie still relevant in a world of internationalised capital?[58]

For two decades scholars pored over contradictory evidence, particularly as it emerged in Africa. Colin Leys argued in 1975 that new Kenyan capitalists had emerged but were still dependent on foreign capital and were unlikely to secure an independent future.[59] Three years later he adjusted his views to provide more scope for the growth of an independent business class, particularly if it continued to receive state protection.[60] But protection for what purpose? To nurture ultimately competitive infant industries or to provide a guaranteed source of wealth for new elites? In 1980, Nicola Swainson also saw possibilities for expansion in association with the state, but still regarded local capitalists as weak and dependent on foreign capital.[61] In the same year, Raphie Kaplinsky argued that no real change had occurred in the Kenyan economy and that what growth had occurred had been due to temporarily high coffee prices, large balance of payments deficits and the movement of international capital out of distribution and into manufacturing and tourism.[62] In 1982, Martin Godfrey agreed: high population growth, an overemphasis on cash crops at the expense of food, a failure to redistribute land and the lack of linkages between import substitution policies and the majority of people prevented any possibility of national economic autonomy. As a result, the Kenyan state in the 1980s looked outside its own borders to fuel growth, but this export focus was hampered by the collapse of the East African community, war in Uganda, competition from Zimbabwe and lack of access to European markets.[63]

---

58   A Phillips, 'The concept of development', *Review of African Political Economy*, 8, 1977, pp. 11–19.
59   Colin Leys, *Underdevelopment in Kenya: The Political Economy of Neo-Colonialism*. London: Heinemann, 1975.
60   C Leys, 'Capital accumulation, class formation, and dependency – the significance of the Kenyan case', *The Socialist Register 1978*. London: Merlin Press, 1978.
61   N Swainson, *The Development of Corporate Capitalism in Kenya, 1918–1977*. London: Heinemann, 1980.
62   R Kaplinsky, 'Capitalist accumulation in the periphery – the Kenyan case re-examined', *Review of African Political Economy*, 16, 1980.
63   M Godfrey, 'Kenya: African capitalism or simple dependency?', in M Bienefeld & M Godfrey (eds), *The Struggle for Development: National Strategies in an International Context*. New York: John Wiley & Sons, 1982.

By the start of the 1990s, a generation after independence, researchers concluded that local capitalists were expanding in former colonies but were not yet capable of accumulating and investing capital independently. But they did gain greater control over the resources of local, foreign-owned enterprises because of shareholdings and directorships. And they did influence state decision-making, even though they were weak and heavily reliant on state assistance (for example, tariffs and monopolies) for survival. Hence their need to exploit internal social differences to garner a stronger political and economic base and thereby secure continued access to the state and its resources.

The size and autonomy of national capital were not the only factors impacting on postcolonial growth. As we have noted, if a state tried to increase revenue to develop industry by raising taxes on its most productive sector, agriculture, it could potentially reduce the very local market needed to expand local commerce and consume industrial products. Both sectors would then be forced to rely on external markets to feed growth, thereby reducing intersectoral linkages and fostering unbalanced development. Favouring capital-intensive industries over small-scale labour-intensive industries could have the same impact. Similarly, encouraging public servants to enter business (with superannuation schemes that matured at 55 years) could also burden the very market their new businesses would depend on to be successful. Clearly, goals of development could be frustrated by the methods used to implement them, as political economist Gavin Williams argued in 1977. They increased foreign control or social inequalities, or both.[64]

In addition, states often squandered their limited resources on luxury consumption for leaders, costly militaries and vanity monuments. Sometimes these activities were paid for by debt, which eventually needed to be serviced and repaid by later generations. Looking back on the first two decades of postcolonialism in Africa, political scientist Martin Doornbos wondered:

> whether the stress on nation-building and national unity at the time [of independence] reflected a genuine desire to create a new 'national' society or whether it constituted the beginnings of an ideological defence of the colonial heritage which had become the state system.[65]

---

64   G Williams, 'Class relations in a neo-colony: The case of Nigeria', in P Gutkind & P Waterman (eds), *African Social Studies, A Radical Reader*. London: Heinemann, 1977, pp. 284–94.
65   M Doornbos, 'The African state in academic debate: Retrospect and prospect', *The Journal of Modern African Studies*, 28: 2, 1990, p. 196.

But, of course, no single outcome was fated. Already signs existed that strong entrepreneurial and middle classes, together with civil institutions, could democratise the state. Whether this meant an insular as opposed to an open outcome remained uncertain.

The postcolonial heritage

Independence in Fiji in 1970 promised a new beginning for all its peoples. Multiracialism, designed to overcome colonial blockages to the joint venture in nation-building, most symbolised that change. As a postcolonial strategy for Fiji, however, it very quickly came undone, although – as we shall see – the fires of race and indigenous paramountcy that quickly ignited after independence obscured its failure. Neither corruption nor extravagance were the cause of this great undoing; rather it was prompted by a fundamental flaw in the country's approach to multiracialism.

Multiracialism sought to respect communal differences rather than transcend them. To that end, Britain accepted a racially based constitution in 1970 as its parting gift to the country. Indians and Fijians were given 22 seats each in a lower house of parliament, with a General Elector grouping of others (including Europeans)[66] holding the balance of power with eight seats, the price for Fijian chiefly acceptance of independence. The exaggerated weighting for this small minority guaranteed Fijian control of any future parliament and denied the Indian demand for a common roll.[67] Thus Fiji's independence parliament comprised a lower house of 27 communal seats (12 each for Fijians and Indians, three for General Electors) and 25 general or open seats. Only general seats enabled cross-voting but for a defined number of communal representatives (10 Fijians, 10 Indians, and five General Electors).[68]

---

66   General Electors included Europeans, 'Part-Europeans', and Chinese. The 1970 Constitution gave 5 per cent of the population control over 15 per cent of lower house seats.

67   In 1970, Fiji's population stood at 530,000, 50.2 per cent being Indian and 45.7 per cent Fijian, Rotuman & Pacific islanders. Under the 1970 Constitution, the remainder – composed of Europeans, Part-Europeans, Chinese and Others – 4.1 per cent of the population, gained 15 per cent of lower house seats.

68   Fijians dominated the 22 members of the appointed Senate or upper house, of whom eight were appointed by the GCC, one by the Council of Rotuma, seven by the Prime Minister and six by the Leader of the Opposition; see R Robertson, 'The parliamentary system', in Walsh, *Fiji*, 2006, pp. 360–83.

While cross-voting represented an improvement on colonial irreconcilability, the concept of multiracialism that underpinned it could only be sustained if all communities believed they shared equally in the prosperity that independence brought. If prosperity failed to materialise or came unevenly, communal difference dictated a competitive zero-sum response, effectively a return to the logic of colonial pluralism. Yet, in Fiji's case, communal competition did not explain the events that unfolded. It was an outcome not a cause. Instead the answer lay within the deliberate failure of Fijian leaders to democratise their own community. In short, they reasserted policies that had already failed to improve the lot of ordinary Fijians and would continue to fail with disastrous consequences for the whole country over the next three decades.

In many respects multiracialism was a charade. Colonialism had locked Fiji's two main communities in political combat and only the threat of independence in the early 1960s forced their respective leaders to reconsider communal configurations. Few changes were anticipated. The farmer organisation, the Maha Sangh, now the dominant partner in the umbrella Federation of Cane Growers Association, lent its support to an Indian-based Federation Party after the 1960 cane strike. In 1965, its now weaker rival and opponent till the end, the Kisan Sangh (which had abandoned the strike in 1960), formed a National Congress of Fiji. A chiefly dominated Fijian Association, formed in 1956 to oppose democratic reform, quickly reorganised once legislative council elections were scheduled in 1963 to give Fijians the vote for the first time. In 1966, the association became the dominant Fijian arm of an Alliance Party, with support also from a smaller General Electors Association and the Indian Alliance, the latter derived from the National Congress. This multiracial appearance had two primary goals: to ensure that any new constitution maintained communalism and to uphold chiefly control over Fijians. In those goals it succeeded; in fresh council elections in 1966, the Alliance Party won 23 seats to the Federation Party's nine and was poised to gain control of the postcolonial state to facilitate its very conservative agenda.[69] Thus a Fijian party, which mirrored the Fijian Administration in makeup, emerged to unite all Fijians within a new expression of the neotraditional orthodoxy.[70]

---

69   A 1965 constitutional conference altered the makeup of the legislative council to enable a form of self-government prior to independence. Fijians had 14 seats, Indians 12 and General Electors 10.
70   Durutalo, 'Of roots & offshoots', 2005, pp. 146–48.

The Federation Party attempted its own multiracial appearance, joining forces with western Viti Levu Fijian dissidents (the National Democratic Party) in 1968 to form the National Federation Party (NFP) and push for a common roll and an elected Fijian head of state. It failed, finally accepting the communal 1970 Constitution on the understanding that it would be reviewed after the first election held under the new Constitution in 1972.

The creation of democratic politics generated a new dynamic within Fiji, and Fijian society in particular, enabling for the first time legitimate political expressions of dissent and hostility to the eastern chiefly elite. Some of this discontent focused on the nature of the postcolonial settlement. Thus trade unionist Apisai Tora's Western Democratic Party sought in 1963 to have Britain shape independence as a simple revocation of cession (i.e. return Fiji to chiefly control) but with western Fiji's rights fully restored. He joined forces with Isikeli Nadala's Fijian Nationalist Party in 1966 to form the National Democratic Party. The mercurial Tora was a survivor and, over the next four decades, he shaped Fijian and west-Fijian dissent, sometimes siding with his eastern opponents, sometimes going it alone. But, in a sense, he would never be alone. As Alumita Durutalo relates, democracy gave postcolonial dissidents the space that Navosavakadua and Ranawai never enjoyed, and they would use it to bring down the postcolonial order that the country's chiefly elite had so carefully constructed in order to maintain their state within a state, the edifice that enabled them to claim to be both multiracial and pro-Fijian.[71]

None of this seemed possible in the heady early days of independence in 1970. Given the size of its sugar and tourism industries, its growth in services during the final decades of colonialism and the production of a small range of consumer products,[72] Fiji gained independence in much better shape than many other colonies. At the same time as Rabuka entered the Royal Fiji Military Forces as a trainee officer in 1968, Fiji's per capita GDP of US$1,200 equalled or bettered that of other small states such as Malta (US$1,400) or Mauritius (US$270). It performed better than many Asian countries such as Thailand (US$330) and Malaysia (US$790), even giants such as India and China (US$105). In fact, Fiji had

---

71   Durutalo, 'Of roots & offshoots', 2005, p. 308.
72   B Knapman, in his 'Afterword: The economic consequences of the coups' (R Robertson & A Tamanisau, *Fiji: Shattered Coups*. Sydney: Pluto Press, 1988, pp. 161–62), lists these as beef, pork, beer, cigarettes, rice, cement and paint.

much to celebrate after independence and, during the next 17 years under Ratu Sir Kamisese Mara's Alliance government, Fiji experienced greater change than it had under colonialism after the Second World War. The economy grew on average 5.6 per cent during the 1970s, with domestic investment comfortably at 20 per cent of GDP. Manufacturing expanded 7 per cent per annum, and tourism's proportion of foreign exchange earnings doubled to an average 34 per cent, almost the same as sugar (down from 60 per cent in the early 1960s), enabling Fiji for the first time to end its dependence on one main product. Actually, tourism's contribution to GDP rose from just 3.5 per cent in 1970 to nearly 14 per cent by the end of the decade.[73] One of Fiji's undoubted economic strengths also derived from its capacity to use local savings, generated principally through its Fiji National Provident Fund (FNPF), to underwrite government deficits. This meant that, although debt was often high (over 40 per cent of GDP), its domestication sheltered government from external currency and interest changes. The downside, however, lay in depleting resources for productive investment in the economy.

Postcolonial governments clearly had different priorities from colonial ones. A new highway linked the western sugar port Lautoka and the airport town Nadi with the eastern capital Suva, opening up new markets for farmers and new prospects for tourism.[74] A new hydro scheme in Viti Levu's centre at Monasavu – once the heartland of old Colo – reduced Fiji's reliance on costly imported fuels. In the western highlands the Vaturu dam provided water to the dry west. New schools and health facilities were developed, and the regional University of the South Pacific (USP) began producing the country's skilled and professional workforce. Agricultural projects increased the production of sugar (particularly at Seaqaqa on Vanua Levu), poultry, corn, tobacco, milk, rice, ginger and timber. Assembly, packaging and small-scale manufacturing plants sprung up to capitalise on new import-substitution policies and a growing urban market. The architecture for postcolonialism had, of necessity, to be different from that required by colonialism.

---

73 S Britton, *Tourism & Underdevelopment in Fiji*. Canberra, The Australian National University, 1983, pp. 157–59.
74 This section draws on 'Shadows of war and revolution' in R Robertson, *Multiculturalism & Reconciliation in an Indulgent Republic. Fiji after the Coups: 1987–1998*. Suva: Fiji Institute of Applied Studies, 1998, pp. 13–14.

It had to be, for development now also entailed coping with an unstable external world. Diversification became a necessary component of Fiji's struggle for survival in a new climate of inflation, price fluctuations and trade uncertainties, yet in Fiji diversification began slowly. Instead Fiji focused on expanding existing activities, often in ways that contradicted its postcolonial desire to generate new national business leaders. Expansion came with foreign capital, against which small local businesses could not compete. Tourism, forestry and poultry industries were all successful examples of expansion that succumbed to the large-scale, centralised and more efficient operations of foreign capital, often in collaboration with the investment companies of the chiefly elite. Where the state did intervene to assist local businesses, to reduce the impact of price fluctuations and to assist with marketing, it created local monopolies; for example, in telecommunications, rice and flour milling and dairy processing, which increased business and consumer costs and took money from government coffers that could have been better employed.

The rhetoric of import substitution was understandable in a newly independent economy, but it raised unrealistic expectations. Fiji's economy was too small to develop a wide range of competitive industries, and protectionism was least likely to generate competitiveness.[75] Instead tariffs protected producers for the local market from import competition. At the same time, a high exchange rate and taxes penalised exporters. Hence, little export diversification occurred. Instead recipients treated tariff largesse not as infant protection but as a cow to be milked for as long as it lasted. When it came to exports, it was always easier to expand sugar production rather than invest in new horticulture ventures. An obvious reason lay in the European Community's Lomé Convention (1976), which paid above world prices for a guaranteed proportion of Fiji's sugar. At least increasing sugar production did not necessitate new and expensive supportive infrastructure. And Fiji's sugar production increased from 361,000 tonnes in 1970 to an all-time record of 502,000 tonnes in 1985. Thus, its share of domestic exports rose over 10 per cent to 80 per cent, providing an undoubted boost to the economy, enabling it to benefit from high sugar prices in 1975 and 1981, protecting it initially from a global recession in the early 1980s and possibly enabling greater domestic stability than might otherwise have been the case. Sugar also

---

75   R Cole & H Hughes, *The Fiji Economy May 1987: Problems & Prospects*. Canberra: National Centre for Development studies, The Australian National University, 1988.

absorbed 40 per cent of all new entrants to the labour market between 1976 and 1980. Thus the labour intensive industry could employ 22 per cent of Fiji's labour force while contributing 16 per cent of GDP.[76] There were costs, however: an overuse of chemicals, the degradation of hilly and marginal lands brought into production, a risk of flooding from increasingly silted rivers, a reluctance to invest as much energy into diversifying agricultural production and providing linkages with other sectors of the economy, and perhaps a false sense of security. Sugar's temporary success made it easier to overlook its associated environmental, social and economic problems.

Other local industries fared less well. Rice production suffered because the state paid poor prices to its farmers and closed down many small but efficient local rice mills. Rewa Milk never met market demand, cocoa production collapsed because of the high margins government marketers demanded, and beef production tended to be poorly managed. Citrus production likewise withered. Targets were often unrealistic, service provision poor, and semi-subsistence farmers unskilled.[77] The development of a clothing export industry became the only exception to this record in the mid-1980s. Modest early success (86 per cent growth throughout 1980–86) built on opportunities provided by Australia and New Zealand in their 1981 SPARTECA[78] trade agreement, which reduced their then-high tariffs on a limited range of goods produced in the Pacific. Some economists believe that these popular postcolonial trade initiatives – sold as helping to address uneven development – actually disadvantaged developing countries, being bureaucratic and costly to exploit. Fiji might have been better off reducing tariff and non-tariff barriers to trade and seeking to become a specialised supplier of competitive goods in niche markets.[79]

---

76   Lomé provided Fiji a market for 172,000 tonnes of sugar at the same price received by European farmers for sugar beet under the EU's Common Agricultural Policy. In 1982, this provided $370 per tonne compared with $192 on the world market; see HC Brookfield, F Ellis & RG Ward, *Land, Cane & Coconuts: Papers on the Rural Economy of Fiji*. Canberra: The Australian National University, 1985, pp. 72–74, 79. All currencies referred to hereafter are in Fiji dollars unless otherwise specified.

77   P Barbour & A McGregor, 'The Fiji agricultural sector', *Pacific Economic Bulletin*, 13: 2, November 1998, pp. 68–70.

78   South Pacific Regional Trade and Economic Cooperation Agreement (SPARTECA). Fiji exported $1 million under SPARTECA in 1985 and $2 million in 1986; see R Chandra, 'Manufacturing in Fiji: Mixed results', *Pacific Economic Bulletin*, 11: 1, May 1996, p. 47.

79   Cole & Hughes, *The Fiji Economy May 1987*, 1988, p. 67.

There were, however, political reasons why Fiji's leaders did not encourage manufacturing. Already the nature of employment in the country had changed since colonial days, most specifically in agriculture. In 1963, 41 per cent of the workforce engaged in agricultural pursuits; by 1984 only 19 per cent were so employed. Much of the difference came from the rise in services provided by government. Its employment proportions rose from 14 per cent to 22 per cent during the same period. This shift posed difficulties for a government heavily reliant on rural support. Did it really want to encourage the growth of an urban working class, potentially disconnected from traditional mechanisms of control and susceptible to union influence? An early example of the impact of such a class was provided in 1959 when a multiracial Wholesale and Retail Workers Union led by Tora and Jim Anthony initiated a wages strike for oil workers in Suva that turned riotous and prompted a renewed effort by Fijian leaders to ensure the racial demarcation of unions. By 1986 some 47 per cent of Fijian wage earners were employed in the public sector, which carried all sorts of risks for a government that regarded unions as harbingers of unwanted class politics or the creatures of Indian politicians. In addition, the shift from agriculture also signalled a small rise in the urban population (from 33 per cent in 1966 to 39 per cent by 1986),[80] which further heightened concerns about employment prospects and rising levels of poverty.

The Alliance government might have handled this new urban pressure well if it had been able to demonstrate rural success. However, urban restlessness grew from rural failure. There was nothing new in this respect. Colonial authorities long struggled to provide some mechanism for change in Fijian communities, but had been stymied by Fijian leaders, who feared the impact of change on their authority.[81] Consequently, colonial planners diverted their attention to the needs of urban centres or the sugar industry. A postcolonial government could not do this so easily, at least not one dependent on rural Fijian votes. It toyed with the idea of an export processing zone in Lautoka in 1981 but, when that received lukewarm donor support, it focused instead on a number of programs designed to raise rural incomes, diversify agricultural output, increase self-sufficiency and reduce urban migration. These were all

---

80   Walsh, *Fiji*, 2006, p. 76.
81   Several early governors (and many colonists) believed that the native system made Fijians lazy, but were wary of change that might spark instability (Robinson, 'The Crown Colony Government', 1984, pp. 43, 57, 99).

noble objectives, and – as historian Asinate Mausio notes in her study of rural development – the Alliance Party could easily have embraced modernity and multiracialism with land and local government reforms, and integrated rural Fijians into the modern economy.[82] But it refused to do so.

In a sense, the Alliance Party still wanted to demonstrate that early colonial critics of the traditional Fijian way of life, such as Alan Burns and Oskar Spate or Fiji's own Rusiate Nayacakalou,[83] were wrong. Fijians could modernise in their own unique fashion. This, after all, was what Mara's postcolonial Pacific Way championed.[84] With heavy government support, the Alliance increased assistance to cocoa projects, cattle and sheep farming, ginger, lime, tea, coffee and fruit processing as a way of diversifying agricultural production. It established a new monopolist, the National Marketing Authority, in 1971 to stabilise market prices for producers and subsidise freight rates. It proposed developing 33 regional growth centres that would overcome regional disparities and provide new rural centres for growth. They all failed.

Undoubtedly a principal cause for failure lay in the Alliance Party's belief that communalism and commercialism could coexist without disruptive tensions. In the case of the 1978 Yalavou beef cattle scheme in the Sigatoka Valley, free Fijian farmers (i.e. non-village-based or 'free' Fijians – *galala*) were settled on 98 200-hectare farms, but local chiefs were given roles on its executive, and eventually they drained the program of resources. Says Mausio, it sought *galala* but embraced tradition. The principle cause for failure, however, derived elsewhere. Australia funded the scheme but repatriated as much as 60 per cent of the value of its aid to pay for experts or technology. The Fiji Government did not make up the shortfall.

---

82   A Mausio, 'Boomerangs & the Fijian dilemma: Australian aid for rural development 1971–1987'. PhD Thesis, The Australian National University, Canberra, 2006, pp. 196–205.

83   OHK Spate, *The Fijian People: Economic Problems & Prospects*. Suva: Legislative Council of Fiji, 1959; AAC Burns, *Fiji*. London: Her Majesty's Stationery Office, 1963; RR Nayacakalou, *Tradition & Change in the Fijian Village*. Suva: University of the South Pacific, 1978; RR Nayacakalou, *Leadership in Fiji*. Melbourne: Oxford University Press, 1975.

84   Mara championed the Pacific Way after the foundation of the regional Pacific Forum organisation in 1971. Graeme Dobell has argued that, in one sense, it described a way by which Pacific elites could 'focus on conversation and consensus, respect for sovereignty and non interference in the internal affairs of neighbours'. 'Characteristically', he added, 'Mara didn't devote much effort to actually defining The Way. The Ratu often didn't see the need to explain things. After all, defining custom too exactly can limit a chief's ability to appeal to "tradition" to deal with a specific problem' ('The Pacific Way wanes', The Canberra Column, *The Interpreter*, Lowy Institute, Sydney, 8 August 2008, www.lowyinstitute.org/the-interpreter/pacific-way-wanes).

Consequently, farmers received insufficient establishment assistance and incentives. Additionally, the scheme was poorly planned and managed, remote and gained little marketing assistance. It possessed no linkages with the wider Sigatoka community.[85]

In contrast, the proposed Vunidawa rural growth centre in Naitasiri sought more specifically to work directly from within existing communal settings, without resort to *galala*. Vunidawa planned to link some 100 villages to supply taro, bananas and *yaqona* (kava) and provide social, commercial and physical infrastructure for a region that included Monasavu. But the scheme never got off the ground, in part because of rivalry between Upper and Lower Naitasiri. According to Mausio, there was also a major contradiction in the way the government delegated responsibility. It wanted to strengthen traditional networks, but did not trust its Fijian provincial councils to engage with villagers or control funding. Instead it used its public service district officers, who did not enjoy the same close working relationship with villages as the provincial councils.[86] Fiji's colonial inheritance of a dual system of governance made all development schemes bureaucratic and ultimately worked against the effective delivery of development assistance. Urban infrastructure projects were always better administered because they possessed no delivery gap. Hence they became more popular with foreign donors. Vunidawa's failure, however, contributed to Naitasiri's lack of infrastructure, and would become a major cause for political tension during and after the 2000 coup.[87]

Mausio argues that the Alliance Party deliberately exploited rural–urban and regional gaps to mask its ethnic preference and desire to promote traditionalism. In doing so, it widened disparities further and produced a spate of failed rural projects. Communal land ownership and village settings restricted profitability and productivity. Because projects were not meant to be disruptive of traditional life, they denied villagers the kind of infrastructure that might have raised living standards and generated economic vibrancy.[88] Most projects were about crop diversification rather than diversifying export processing and, even if successful, would not have addressed Fiji's declining terms of trade. Additionally, they often

---

85   Mausio, 'Boomerangs & the Fijian dilemma', 2006, pp. 186–220, 344.
86   Mausio, 'Boomerangs & the Fijian dilemma', 2006, pp. 222–56.
87   Mausio, 'Boomerangs & the Fijian dilemma', 2006, pp. 327, 348.
88   Mausio, 'Boomerangs & the Fijian dilemma', 2006, pp. 58–59.

focused on semi-subsistence and marginally profitable crops that could in no way deliver the same benefits sugar did to its many Indian farmers. The government would have done better focusing on better paying crops, on plantation production and *galala* participation. But its desire to preserve Fijian orthodoxy as the basis for elite Fijian control undermined its initiatives.

The most successful rural projects were always those that were multiracial and commercial, the best example being Seaqaqa in Vanua Levu. As a rural growth centre, it had the potential to link also with centres at Nabouwalu and Dreketi, the latter being the site of a successful venture that assisted Fiji (with the help of tariff protection) reach 75 per cent rice sufficiency by 1985. Seaqaqa sought to overcome falling sugar production and, from the start, its 837 farmers dealt with a crop that produced better returns. Furthermore, like Dreketi, it involved both Fijians and Indians. Multi-ethnic programs helped expose Fijian farmers to the work ethic and business acumen of Indian counterparts. This is probably the most important benefit of diversity in any society; it widens the pool for skills and knowledge. In low-income countries, however, there are fewer opportunities for gaining from that pool than in higher income countries that are more dependent on skills and knowledge.[89] And less still if governments are fearful of what impact those opportunities might have on their power base. Nonetheless, these schemes demonstrated – to paraphrase Mausio – that the path to sustainable rural development lay in unlocking the economic potential of the rural *vanua* through democratisation and increased integration with the modern economy.[90] Nothing else worked.

The Alliance Party's failure to diversify economic activities had a number of political consequences, as we shall see, but in the first instance, it shifted attention to the role of foreign investment in both fuelling economic expansion and stymieing local growth. In 1979, a USP report revealed that up to 65 per cent of Fiji's annual economic turnover was controlled by foreign corporations. Foreign corporations dominated banking and financial services, insurance, distribution, tourism, gold production and manufacturing.[91] Within a short while, they would also dominate timber, tobacco, chicken, soft drinks and beer production.

---

89   Collier, *Wars, Guns & Votes*, 2009, p. 61.

90   Collier, *Wars, Guns & Votes*, 2009, pp. 81, 331, 334.

91   R Carstairs & R Prasad, *Impact of Foreign Direct Investment on the Fiji Economy*. Suva: Centre for Applied Studies in Development, University of the South Pacific, 1981.

The chicken industry demonstrated the dangers. Between 1977 and 1986 over $1.6 million had been loaned by the Fiji Development Bank (FDB) to chicken farmers, averaging $20,000 per farmer, as part of a strategy for self-reliance and to expand farming, particularly for Fijians. The results were impressive: poultry meat and egg production doubled and imports fell, as they were intended to do. Unfortunately, the dramatic rise in interest rates during the 1980s crippled many farmers, particularly as it coincided with a near doubling of feed costs. Returns on meat and eggs failed to keep pace. When General Foods monopolised the more profitable poultry-processing and feed-production sides of the business, it squeezed farmer returns further. Many farmers went to the wall.[92]

Transnationals also dominated components of the local pine industry in western Viti Levu when the forests that were first planted in the 1950s began to mature. By 1983 there were over 20,600 hectares of hardwood and pine plantations and 10 forestry stations, but conflicts developed between *mataqali* seeking to maximise local Fijian business and employment opportunities (i.e. a more active role in resource development) and the Alliance Party's preference for foreign capital and expertise to create a consolidated efficient industry in which landowners played an essentially passive role. A partnership of eastern chiefs with British Petroleum suggested to many western Fijians a very different motive. For comparable reasons, foreign involvement in tourism, again mostly in western Viti Levu, produced a similar outcome. The majority of tourist shops (91 per cent) were Indian-owned, but foreign businesses took in 72 per cent of all shopping revenue. Similarly, Fijians dominated handicraft outlets (70 per cent) but received only 2 per cent of tourist receipts.[93]

This crowding out of employment opportunities was not felt everywhere. The Australian food and trading company, Burns Philp, gave up copra processing and some of its retail businesses in the 1980s. Similarly, the Australian Carpenter group of companies abandoned manufacturing and contracted work out to cheaper independent local workshops. These changes encouraged a small group of retailers such as RB Patel, Motibhai, Tappoo, GB Hari and Vinod Patel to expand into hardware, clothing,

92   M Chung, 'Ethnic politics and small business: The case of the Fiji poultry industry', *Pacific Viewpoint*, 30: 2, October 1989, pp. 192–206.
93   Carstairs & Prasad, *Impact of Foreign Direct Investment*, 1981.

manufacturing, motion picture and tourism sectors, in some cases assisted by the government through contracts to supply equipment or control airport duty-free outlets. By 1986, local businesses were responsible for 65 per cent of manufacturing output and 64 per cent of value added.[94]

Despite this growth, Fiji's economy remained small, resource-scarce and dominated by foreign capital. What local capital existed was itself dominated by Gujarati businesses that could defend themselves economically and through political patronage. But they were dependent also on an economy that no longer expanded. Undoubtedly, sudden rises in oil prices, falling commodity returns and natural disasters were partly responsible, but the Alliance Party's failure to generate a balanced economy, to ensure intersectoral connectivity, and provide for the country's growing population contributed also. Its linkages with transnational and Gujarati businesses did not always help either, particularly in the highly racialised and expectant atmosphere it had done much to encourage. Critics easily accused it of doing little to increase space for popular economic participation. After all, the economically active population increased by 40 per cent between 1976 and 1986, but employment grew only 12 per cent, which was an effective decline of 8 per cent in the proportion of the economically active population employed.[95] No matter how well it managed the macroeconomic parameters, kept inflation down or managed Fiji's balance of payments, the government's failure to sustain growth would bear political costs.

The costs of failure

Those political costs first emerged in the mid-1970s after a period of relatively high inflation (14.4 per cent in 1974) and global recession following the first oil shock. The high rates of economic growth experienced immediately after independence (6 per cent in 1970, 12.7 per cent in 1974) quickly evaporated and the Alliance government found itself increasingly under attack from Fijians for not doing enough to assist rural Fijians. Western Fijians expressed concern over proposals

---

94   R Chandra, 'The political crisis and the manufacturing sector in Fiji', *Pacific Viewpoint*, 30: 2, October 1989, p. 173.
95   RV Cole, 'The Fiji economy: From go to woe', *Pacific Viewpoint*, 30: 2, October 1989, p. 155. The economically active population increased from 175,785 to 241,160 while employment grew from 70,174 to 79,854.

for the management of pine resources. In part this was a matter of expectations, but it reflected also the lack of clear leadership in many villages, as John Overton and Gerard Ward noted in 1989 when describing the implications of rural change.

> Chiefly hierarchies remained and were respected but this often conflicted with economic realities. Chiefs, large and small, were caught in a dilemma: they wanted to maintain their old power, yet were drawn by the attraction of commercialism (on the land and off) and land rents (which they could pocket). In these non-traditional spheres, they were less bound to share their income with the commoner kin. Commercial agriculture, whether with sugar, rice, beef cattle or copra, touched every corner of village Fiji and the effects included greater materialism and individualism. There is evidence of individual accumulation of land and consequent inequalities ... For the majority of villagers, education, cash cropping, and non-farm employment promised much but usually failed to deliver, and as the gulf between living standards in the towns and the non-sugar countryside began to widen, frustration mounted – frustrations sometimes directed at the chiefly elite but much more commonly at Indians, town dwellers or shopkeepers.[96]

Sakeasi Butadroka best illustrated this transformation. A frustrated small businessman from Rewa and a junior minister in the government in 1972, he criticised its record on assisting Fijians. This was both personal and parochial. His Rewan bus company could not survive competition from established Indian companies. When the Alliance Party chose a Lauan candidate above a local for a by-election in Rewa, he campaigned against his own party and was expelled in 1973, but not silenced.[97] From his seat in parliament he continued to attack, pointedly calling for the expulsion of Indians from Fiji, and launched his own rival Fijian Nationalist Party (FNP) in 1975. Butadroka articulated Fijian discontent, but he did so in zero-sum racial terms. He attacked Indians (not economic failure) as the cause of Fijian 'disadvantage' or 'backwardness'. Butadroka articulated a form of populist nativism, reflecting the continued appeal of divisions and identities that were once fostered by colonialism. But beneath his racial focus lay a less immediately articulated hostility towards eastern

---

96   J Overton & RG Ward, 'The coups in retrospect: The new political geography of Fiji', *Pacific Viewpoint*, 30: 2 October 1989, pp. 210–11.
97   Durutalo, 'Of roots & offshoots', 2005, pp. 172–74.

chiefs and the dominance of Tovata under Prime Minister Mara, the man chosen by Sukuna to succeed him and who had been dutifully accepted by colonial authorities as a future Fiji leader and sent overseas for training.[98]

Butadroka's racial assault resonated, as he knew it would. 'Telling Indians to get out of Fiji was just a political tactic to stir Fijian feelings,' he later conceded disingenuously, 'and so force Ratu Mara to do something about the poverty in Fijian settlements here.'[99] Many Fijians were disenchanted with their inability to benefit from the proceeds of independence. Indians were an easy target for their frustration. After all, Indians dominated the highly visible retail and transport sectors, they held the greatest proportion of white-collar jobs (58 per cent compared with 31 per cent for Fijians), and they dominated professional and managerial positions (70 per cent compared with 17 per cent).[100] This visibility hid the fact that the vast majority of Indians were only marginally better off than Fijians, but that did not matter. Stereotypes fed off what people wanted to see. For Butadroka, the solution was simple: remove Indians and Fijians could fill their places. And that solution had not occurred because the Alliance government connived with Indians through its policy of multiracialism.

In the April 1977 elections, many Fijians responded to Butadroka by failing to vote: a protest by default. Compared with 1972, Fijian participation rates fell 23 per cent to 65 per cent. But an unprecedented 20 per cent also voted for Butadroka's FNP. Alliance support fell 19 per cent. It was enough to unseat the government and, ironically, provide the NFP – with a narrow two-seat majority – an opportunity to demonstrate its leadership credentials. Unfortunately, it too had been damaged by the race debate. Its leader, Siddiq Koya, seen by many in his party as too close to Mara, had been injured by the Alliance Party's refusal to accept the recommendations of a Royal Commission to reduce the communal emphasis of the Constitution.[101] In any case many of his colleagues were all too comfortable with the guarantees communalism offered them and

---

98   Butadroka's antipathy towards Lauans like Mara would grow and, in time, he would argue for Viti Levu's independence from the GCC and the creation of its own council of chiefs. Mara concluded that Butadroka believed only Fijians from Viti Levu should determine what happens on Viti Levu, and that all other Fijians should be declared foreigners like IndoFijians (*fijilive*, 16 October 2000).
99   *Fiji Sun*, 26 December 1986.
100   Sutherland, *Beyond the Politics of Race*, 1992, pp. 151–59.
101   The Royal Commission recommended maintaining ethnic representation at current proportions but sought to make all seats national.

were more concerned that the leader of a Muslim minority now headed a Hindu majority.[102] A common roll would make campaigning more difficult.

Divisions within the NFP also widened over the duration of land leases and the system for measuring land value permitted in a new *Agricultural Landlord and Tenant Act*. These issues greatly concerned all cane farmers who feared the changes would cost them dearly and discourage investment in land. Population pressures on land added further weight to the issue. Additionally, many Indians regarded inequality, in terms of restricted access to public service occupations or to education scholarships, as evidence of their continued status as second-class citizens. They had begun calling themselves IndoFijians during the 1970s to stress their belonging, but IndoFijianness could not fill the void created by the failure of the postcolonial state to foster a national identity or even to recognise the state of IndoFijianness.

When the NFP met after the elections to confirm its leader, dissidents used the opportunity to test Koya's support within the party. In the interim, the Governor-General used the long delay to conduct a constitutional coup, appointing Mara to head a minority government and lead the country to fresh elections five months later. The tactic worked. By September the NFP had split into two hostile factions, and the Alliance Party had won back its Fijian base by stealing the thunder of the FNP, imprisoning its leader for inciting unrest, and reminding voters that if they did not unite around it this time, 'the foreigners' would take over. Thus the Alliance won a massive majority (in large part because of NFP division), and Fiji returned to 'normal'.

But the real lesson of 1977 was not learned. No changes in economic policy resulted and the potential for Fijian dissatisfaction remained as trade deficits, inflation and unemployment grew, poverty became more visible, and a collapse in international commodity prices caused the economy to shrink in the early 1980s. The Alliance had increased educational scholarships to Fijians since the early 1970s, as well as soft loans for business activities through the FDB. It had also established new business ventures through the NLTB's commercial arm, the Native Land Development Corporation. But these activities hardly addressed

---

102 Durutalo, 'Of roots & offshoots', 2005, pp. 178–79.

the gap between rhetoric and reality. The proportion of FDB loans for rural activities fell dramatically in the early 1980s, as did the proportion of loans going to Fijians.[103]

If the Alliance Party thought the race card would enable it to see off any future threat to its political dominance, the 1982 election provided another shock. The NFP had reunited under Jai Ram Reddy and joined forces with a Fijian party based in western Viti Levu, the Western United Front (WUF) led by Nadroga's Ratu Osea Gavidi. It contested the Alliance Party's interference in the nascent pine industry and articulated western concerns at the dominance of the eastern chiefly elite. Fijians wanted to be economically involved, but the nature of Fijian administration made this impossible. Land rentals were considered too low and, in any case, were distributed in such a fashion that they could not form the basis for investment. The NLTB took a massive 25 per cent for administrative costs, 30 per cent went to chiefs, with the remainder distributed to individual *mataqali* members, sometimes numbered in the hundreds if not thousands. To offset this disadvantage, Gavidi had earlier proposed that landowners become partners in a joint venture to exploit their timber resources, but the Alliance denied the proposal, even banning the head of the American company that Gavidi hoped to deal with from entering the country. Gavidi's province rallied behind him and, standing as an independent for Nadroga–Navosa in both 1977 elections, he defeated the Alliance. Other western chiefs soon lent Gavidi their support after a falling-out over the Alliance's costly refit of Bau ahead of a royal visit in 1982. Bau, the Alliance declared, represented 'the whole fabric of Fijian society'. As Durutalo notes, democracy made it much harder for the eastern elite to dismiss troublesome subjects whether those in the west or in Rewa.[104]

The 1982 election was close; the Alliance's 16-seat majority fell to four and the WUF gained two seats. The fallout was swift: Mara accused the NFP of gaining secret funding from Russia, and the GCC called for permanent Fijian political paramountcy. In the heat of parliamentary debate Reddy resigned and the divisive Koya returned as party leader, with shocking consequences for his party, just as its Alliance opponent demonstrated

---

103 The proportion of FDB loans to rural activities fell from one half to one quarter over 1980–85, while loans to Fijians fell from 80 per cent of total value in 1975 to 27 per cent 1980 and to 8 per cent 1985; see Sutherland, *Beyond the Politics of Race*, 1992, p. 143.
104 Durutalo, 'Of roots & offshoots', 2005, pp. 189–96; see also S Durutalo, 'Internal colonialism & unequal regional development: The case of western Viti Levu, Fiji'. MA Thesis, University of the South Pacific. Suva, 1985, pp. 469–70.

an inability to handle difficult economic circumstances. Mara meanwhile began to shore up the position of chiefs within rural Fiji by reintroducing elements of the old Fijian Administration, including proposals for separate village courts. The defection of Tora to the Alliance camp in 1982 gave him an opportunity to tackle the disaffection of western Fiji by proposing major rural development projects in the Sigatoka valley and by rebuilding his party machinery in the west. Mara's efforts to heal the rift with western Fijians were not helped, however, by his government's rejection of a Fijian-owned plywood processing company in favour of a joint venture between an Australian company and an eastern Bau–Kubuna company, nor by the allegations of corruption that hung over his wife's dealing with a *mataqali* that managed royalties from the large Fijian Hotel near Sigatoka.[105] Additionally, in the manner of eastern chiefs, his strategy involved wooing western chiefs back into the Alliance fold, but this strategy brought no guarantee that their more egalitarian subjects would follow them. Indeed, he failed to appreciate that the next challenge to Alliance authority would be of a completely different order and that it would cut across the racial lines he had so successfully reasserted after 1977. The origins of that challenge lay in a sudden deterioration in the state of Fiji's economy and Mara's response to it.

A double whammy hit Fiji after 1981. After a brief boom at the start of the decade, sugar prices collapsed. This coincided with high inflation brought on by a renewed global energy crisis that plunged many economies into recession. Fiji's inflation stood at 14 per cent in 1981 and remained at 7 per cent two years later. Five cyclones and a drought added to the pain of recession in 1983. A harsh budget in 1984 increased tariffs and introduced new taxes. But talk of a possible wage freeze alienated the labour movement, which had been painfully negotiating wage increases since 1982. Strike threats now hovered at the same time that unemployment rose, a teachers' college in Nasinu closed, and graduating education students were denied employment by a polarising Minister for Education, Ahmed Ali. Nonetheless the Fiji Public Service Association (FPSA) successfully pursued its case for wage adjustments at the Tripartite Forum, an organisation of government, business and labour formerly much praised as an example of Pacific consensus-making. No longer;

---

105 An excellent account of this election and its fallout can be found in Lal, *Broken Waves*, 1992, pp. 245–50. See also Michael C Howard's detailed account of pre-1987 political manoeuvrings in *Fiji: Race and Politics in an Island State* (Vancouver: University of British Columbia Press, 1991, pp. 146–206).

the government struck back with an immediate wage freeze in late 1984. The unions left the forum and threatened a general strike. Two cyclones in January 1985 put paid to that tactic, but unions were beginning to cooperate on a scale unprecedented since 1959. Two ethnically divided teachers' unions joined forces to challenge government efforts to employ graduate students on subsistence wages. A Confederation of Public Sector Unions came into existence in April. The government struck back, supporting a Confederation of Blue Collar Workers Unions in mid-1985 and, a year later, gave support to a possible Fijian civil servants' association. By then it had also withdrawn recognition of the Fiji Trades Union Congress, the main labour umbrella organisation. It was too late. In July 1985, the union movement created its own political party.

If Fiji's politicians were growing comfortable with the manipulation of race, they were distinctly uncomfortable with the idea of class. While class was un-Pacific and potentially critical of traditional alignments it was also, above all, damaging to the neat racial compartments they had grown accustomed to working with. Those compartments were themselves social constructions. Clan and provincial loyalties still influenced Fijian thinking, despite colonial and postcolonial pressures to mould a less divisive Fijian identity. Indian experiences of indenture and post-indenture racism combined with the novelty of freedom from continental poverty and prejudice to create IndoFijians, but they too were haunted by religious and linguistic fractures. For both communities facing uncertain change, identity was something to be cherished and never surrendered or lost.

The formation of a Labour Party did not mean that race was out, but it did mean that, for the first time, a political party began to imagine new political alignments that could – no matter how weakly and imperfectly – cut across lines that many people thought were set in stone. To some extent these new alignments reflected changes in postcolonial Fiji: a more urbanised society with an expanding and well-educated middle class. It reflected also an emerging consciousness on the part of some of that class that a focus on race simply failed to address the issues that most affected Fijians and IndoFijians in their everyday lives, particularly the rural and urban poor of both communities who found accessing government services difficult and were the principal victims of low economic growth.[106] Race also failed

---

106   Cole & Hughes, *The Fiji Economy May 1987*, 1988, p. 22.

to acknowledge that, contrary to political rhetoric, both communities were remarkably accommodating and harmonious towards each other, sharing musical traditions and cuisine, and often intermarrying.

We might surmise then that, at some stage, the basic premises of race politics would always be challenged, particularly given that, historically, the most important conflict of interest between the two communities concerned access to land on which increasingly larger and larger proportions of both communities no longer directly depended. Similarly, urbanisation reduced the strict isolation of communities from each other and made possible the development of new relationships at schools and workplaces, and new shared activities around food, entertainment and sport. Of course urbanisation also enabled old distinctions to be reinforced in new forms through schools, clubs, religious practices and political mobilisation. And nothing could immediately offset the colonial legacy of land ownership, which had driven IndoFijians into professions, businesses and skilled employment at a far greater rate than Fijians, whose monopoly of land meant that they rarely faced the same urgency to transform.

Change then was never complete or tidy in its consequences. The modern economy created scope for change but, equally, it provided the setting for new forms of ethnic competition, especially around education, employment and access to state assistance.[107] Nonetheless, postcolonial changes created space for new ways of thinking and action, and nothing demonstrated these possibilities better than the labour movement, in particular unions like the FPSA, which represented all communities in the expanding civil service and helped grow new national and international linkages.[108]

Alliance government responses to the economic challenges of the 1980s placed it on a collision course with unions, which were increasingly concerned at its authoritarianism, its political interference within the public service and its impact on worker welfare. Not surprisingly, given its bruising confrontation over wage increases, the FPSA took a lead role in the formation of the Fiji Labour Party (FLP). President Timoci Bavadra

---

107 Collier, *Wars, Guns & Votes*, 2009, pp. 178–79.
108 See Jacqueline Leckie's comprehensive history of the FPSA, *To Labour with the State: The Fiji Public Service Association* (Dunedin: University of Otago Press, 1997).

and General Secretary Mahendra Chaudhry assumed the same positions in the new political party. Historian Jacqui Leckie notes the importance of the networks that Labour brought to its new political struggle:

> The FLP was not just representative of organised labour and public sector workers … [M]any of the leaders and members of these unions had other networks which drew them to the FLP, such as peace, church and women's groups. The links Chaudhry and Bavadra had formed between urban and rural workers helped to lay the basis for a Coalition being formed between the FLP and the NFP. They both had direct kin connections with the 'western side' of Fiji. Bavadra had served as a medical officer in many rural, as well as urban areas. Chaudhry's strong following in the Western Division drew on FPSA and National Farmers' Union support. Bavadra … as an empathetic and easy going doctor had the support and loyalty of different ethnic communities. When the FLP hit the election campaign trail, Bavadra and Chaudhry brought to it years of working together … Behind these personalities was the energy of numerous supporters and rural/urban, village/white collar connections reproduced among many FLP members.[109]

This was no Fijian Nationalist Party or WUF, defined in the first instance by the peculiar nature of provincial dissent. The Labour Party had the potential for mass appeal and it possessed the organising capacity to reach where no opposition party had previously reached. Would that be enough to break the communalist cage that had constrained political development since independence? Early indications seemed promising.

The Labour Party arrived on the scene at the very moment that both the Alliance Party and the NFP were at their lowest ebb. Five cyclones had devastated the country in 1983 in the midst of its economic crisis. Hospital services were under pressure, roads deteriorating, crime rates and unemployment rising and, everywhere, the realities of poverty were becoming more stark. One in every eight Suva residents lived in 26 squatter settlements, subject to unhealthy crowded living conditions and with no access to utilities.[110] The NFP remained too mired in factional fighting to notice, and the government seemed suddenly unable to manage: education slipped from crisis to crisis, housing funds for the poor disappeared, bus fares increased and minimum wages for textile workers were denied. A World Bank report in 1986 argued that no significant

---

109   Leckie, *To Labour with the State*, 1997, pp. 116–17.
110   *Fiji Sun*, 14 September 1986.

income disparities existed between IndoFijians and Fijians, and that IndoFijians made up the largest component of unemployed and squatters.[111] Labour and the moment were one. It denied zero-sum racial analyses and directly attacked the class bias of the Alliance government, promising a more equitable distribution of wealth. This attack on issues caught the Alliance Party off guard.

Bavadra told an audience in Lautoka that 'the people who have suffered most under the Alliance government are the very people this government purports to champion, the native Fijians', while its leaders 'have amassed huge personal wealth'. No more; the time had come to democratise Fijian institutions like the NLTB:

> The Fijian people therefore should question whether they can continue to entrust their future in such leadership. In a small nation such as ours the country can only progress if all sections work together.[112]

He declared that all Fiji people be called Fijians: 'in spite of our cultural differences and religions backgrounds, we are but one nation'.[113] The Alliance Party hit back, claiming that Labour wanted to take away Fijian constitutional rights and privileges: 'Without a chief, there is no Fijian society', it declared.[114] Alliance stalwart Ratu David Toganivalu declared chiefs 'a force for moderation, balance and fair play ... the protectors of the rights of Indians and General Electors in Fiji'.[115]

Alliance leaders were worried. Labour seemed embarked on unfamiliar territory. Its attacks on Fijian leadership resonated and could potentially win it support from disgruntled Fijians. Journalist Jo Nata (later a participant in the 2000 coup against Labour) set the ball rolling with an article aimed directly at Mara's millionaire status, which had been consolidated since entering office. Mara and members of his family owned shares in a wide number of prominent businesses, farms and islands.[116] Labour drew attention to Mara's involvement with Marella House, a building leased by his family company to the Education Ministry on very generous terms. Labour also attacked the Alliance's close ties with big business, particularly its failure to assist Nasomo people whose land had been used

---

111 *Fiji Times*, 23 June 1986.
112 *Fiji Sun*, 17 November 1986.
113 *Fiji Sun*, 18 February 1986.
114 *Fiji Sun*, 2 October 1986.
115 *Fiji Times*, 9 March 1987.
116 *Fiji Sun*, 2 August 1985.

by Emperor Gold Mining at Vatukoula without compensation. It also claimed that Tovata political dominance was responsible for privileging Lau for education funding. Lau, with 14,000 Fijians, received $1.3 million over three years, the bulk of it directed around Mara's village of Tubou. Ba, with 59,000 Fijians, received only $400,000.[117] 'Under the Alliance, the elite have feathered their own nests,' Labour advertisements intoned, 'while conditions for the rest, particularly the poor and disadvantaged, have got steadily worse.'[118]

Despite being labelled socialist or communist, Labour was essentially reformist. It focused on issues of immediate popular concern: poverty, price rises, the wage freeze, bus fares, garment workers, women's rights, youth and crime. Its proposals for democratising Fijian institutions responded directly to abuses by a privileged few. Its education policies sought to lighten financial burdens on families and develop curricula to produce a more integrated, cooperative and enterprising nation. At the time, local journalist Akosita Tamanisau and I wrote that its 'policies responded with exacting precision to the actual problems confronting a multiracial society still to break free from colonial and postcolonial perceptions of itself and yet desperately searching for a way out of the economic and social straitjacket it found itself confined to'.[119] For these reasons, Labour became an overnight success and quickly assumed the mantel of Opposition, highlighting the plight of workers, the dangers of high levels of poverty and unemployment, and the relationship between Fijian marginalisation and Fijian elite wealth. Hence it sought true multiracialism, a better distribution of the fruits of development, and a more transparent, open and responsible government.

Local body elections confirmed the party's immediate impact but a parliamentary by-election at the end of 1985 quickly brought Labour back to earth. A three-way struggle cost it the chance of success and raised the spectre of the Alliance Party – unused to facing an alert and assertive opposition – winning in the next elections by default and reaping revenge on the upstart labour movement. Koya seemed equally unrepentant and communal. In early 1986, he told a NFP gathering that 'Indians would be finished if they remained disunited'.[120] But Koya's days were numbered

---

117 *Fiji Sun*, 30 March 1987.
118 *Fiji Sun*, 2 April 1987.
119 R Robertson & A Tamanisau, *Fiji: Shattered Coups*. Sydney: Pluto Press, 1988, p. 39.
120 *Fiji Times*, 16 March 1986.

and, in May, he was replaced by party president, Harish Sharma. Still, the NFP remained divided; in November its former general secretary Sharda Nand accused Labour of trying 'to remove Indian leadership and their special position from Fiji politics'.[121] Three NFP MPs left the party and joined Labour.

Nonetheless, against the advice of members, who cherished its multiracial character and feared the impact of NFP internal divisions, Labour leaders formed a coalition with the demoralised NFP in November 1986, but on terms that made it the senior partner. Only three sitting NFP members of parliament were endorsed as candidates. The old NFP rump was furious, but its appeals to IndoFijian communal support gave greater weight to Labour's claim that only radical change could create true multiculturalism. Bavadra called them 'Indian Butadrokas'.[122] The Alliance Party now declared Labour an Indian party, a description that would haunt it in coming years.

The year 1986 should have been good for the Alliance Party. A record cane harvest and new construction and building activities finally enabled the economy to rebound 9 per cent but, after a long period of extremely low economic growth, 1981 to 1985 marked the worst period of economic growth in Fiji's postcolonial history. Average shrinkage of 1.3 per cent represented a far cry from the 9.7 per cent growth experienced for the same five-year period only a decade before. Per-capita income fared worse, declining by 3.1 per cent.[123] In fact, by 1987, average per-capita income stood only 21 per cent higher than in 1970.[124]

Undoubtedly, the shock of the early 1980s contributed to the Alliance Party's paralysis before the unexpected strength of Labour. It did itself no service with the myriad of scandals and abuses of office, which now inconveniently surfaced during election campaigning in March 1987: urban crown land distributed to mates, debts of ministers paid off, donations from businesses to influence policies, the early release of convicted but well-connected felons and rorts over taxi licenses. The list of exposed scandals dragged on unrelentingly. The Alliance was

---

121 *Fiji Sun*, 12 November 1986.
122 Interview, Viseisei, 20 September 1987.
123 BC Prasad & S Kumar, 'Fiji's economic woes: A nation in search of development progress', *Pacific Economic Bulletin*, 17: 1, May 2002, p. 2.
124 S Chand, 'Coups, cyclones & recovery: The Fiji experience', *Pacific Economic Bulletin*, 15: 2, November 2000, p. 122.

unprepared for a campaign fought on issues and not the communal battles of the past. And it was unprepared for Labour's well-targeted advertising that responded daily to new issues as they arose. There had never been a campaign like it in Fiji's history. Unfortunately, there never would be again.

When the results of the elections emerged on 12 April 1987, both the extent of Labour's achievement and its limitations were apparent. Communal seats fell into their all too familiar pattern, although around 10 per cent of Fijians had voted for the Labour–NFP Coalition – a big swing but one that had no impact on communal outcomes. More significantly many voters had chosen to use their three national votes in ways that contradicted their communal vote. Hence, four crucial Suva-based national seats, a region with the largest and most visible concentration of both industrial and unemployed workers, urban youths and squatters swung to the Coalition, largely on the basis of Fijian votes.[125] IndoFijian disenchantment probably helped also. Although it retained 15 per cent of the IndoFijian vote overall, the Alliance Party's South Indian base had been weakened, leaving only Muslims and IndoFijian business leaders to promote the Alliance cause. Crucially, against the wishes of its Indian Alliance, it placed the NFP defector Mrs Irene Jai Narayan as a candidate in the Suva Indian National constituency.[126] Given also the shift in urban Fijian votes, these national seats fell, providing the Coalition a majority of four seats in a new parliament.

The Alliance government, in power for the 17 years since independence, had been banished to the Opposition benches. Mara, its undisputed leader, had been defeated by a political party that he earlier claimed to be a power crazy gang of amateurs who had never run anything, not even a bingo party.[127] Fiji's racial politics had been breached, its colonial inheritance challenged, its postcolonial order shaken. A new era now dawned, but not the one Labour envisaged. It would not be Bavadra who would give shape to that era, but a hitherto unknown Sitiveni Rabuka.

---

125 Overall voter turnout in 1987 stood at 70 per cent compared with 85 per cent in 1982. In Suva-based Indian communal seats, turnout plummeted as low as 60 per cent compared with up to 70 per cent in comparable Fijian seats. Sutherland argues that the low Indian turnout should have favoured the Alliance; the Coalition's win suggests instead considerable Fijian support. The two constituencies with the highest Coalition margins in fact possessed more Fijian voters (Sutherland, *Beyond the Politics of Race*, 1992, p. 180).

126 Lal, *Broken Waves*, 1992, pp. 265–66; BV Lal, *Islands of Turmoil: Elections and Politics in Fiji*. Canberra: ANU E Press, 2006, pp. 68–71.

127 Ratu Sir Kamisese Mara, Radio Fiji Address, 10 April 1987.

2

The great turning

Burning down the house

The new Labour Coalition survived its first test. It did not disintegrate into warring factions as the National Federation Party (NFP) had in 1977. Instead it moved quickly to form the country's most ethnically representative cabinet. Dejected Alliance members retired to nurse their wounded egos, lamenting their loss of free ministerial homes and ministerial salaries.[1] Ratu Sir Kamisese Mara, bitter at his loss of leadership, felt rejected by both Fijians and IndoFijians. 'If only the Indian community had kept faith with me,' he reflected, 'Fiji would have run more smoothly and made greater progress socially, economically and politically.'[2] He hinted that, with the change in government, 'matters of race and religion in Fiji might assume new emphasis over the democratic process'.[3] He was right.

Immediately a faction of Alliance members and supporters formed a shadowy Taukei Movement to test (in their words) 'how Dr Bavadra's Coalition could handle the situation when in power' and 'to force a change in government'.[4] Its leaders included Ratu Inoke Kubuabola, a former head of the Bible Society, Alliance campaign manager in Cakaudrove and originator of the movement's name;[5] Alliance secretary Jone Veisamasama,

1   Ahmed Ali in *New Zealand Listener*, 6 June 1987.
2   *Far Eastern Economic Review*, 28 June 1990.
3   *Fiji Times*, 28 May 1987; *Age* (Melbourne), 18 May 1987.
4   D Robie, 'Taukei plotters split forces', *Dominion*, 7 January 1988.
5   J Sharpham, *Rabuka of Fiji*. Rockhampton: Central Queensland University Press, 2000, p. 98.

also from Cakaudrove, who famously declared that the movement shared the same dedication to its people as Nazis had to Germans;[6] and Mara's son, Ratu Finau.

The Taukei Movement organised roadblocks, rallies and meetings in mid-April and early May, and gathered a petition calling on the governor-general to change the Constitution and protect Fijian leadership. 'National politics and the traditional status of both the Prime Minister and the [Governor-General] cannot be separated,' Kubuabola argued: 'They are inseparable in the Fijian tradition.'[7] Multiracialism had been wrong because it did not give Fijians the predominance they were entitled to as indigenous people. Fijian paramountcy had always been the unwritten agreement since independence:

> We ... took the process of 1970 as an understanding that our special political position and status would be permitted to prevail and we would be allowed to govern our heritage. That understanding was discarded in April 1987 ... hence the need for us to reassert ourselves and regain what must remain ours.[8]

Apisai Tora, now firmly in the ranks of the Taukeists, agreed: 'Upon us is imposed a new colonialism, not from outside but from within our own country by those who arrived here with no rights and were given full rights by us, the Taukei.'[9]

When its tactics failed to rally widespread support, the Taukei Movement began a firebombing campaign to destabilise the new government. It too failed and the momentum appeared to swing away from the terrorists. The new government coped. But, from the very start, Kubuabola had developed an alternative strategy in the person of Lieutenant Colonel Sitiveni Rabuka, the 38-year-old Cakaudrove-born Staff Officer for Operations and Training for the Royal Fiji Military Forces (RFMF), a man desperately in need of a new purpose in life.

---

6   *Auckland Star*, 24 August 1987.
7   *Fiji Times*, 11 April 1991.
8   *Fiji Times*, 27 September 1989.
9   *Fiji Sun*, 21 & 22 April 1987.

Since independence, the 2,600-strong RFMF had grown from a symbolic force of 200 soldiers[10] into a predominantly Fijian force, devoted to international peacekeeping duties and nationally useful both as an employer and trainer of otherwise idle Fijian labour and as a foreign currency earner. Fiji's military had grown in tandem with UN peacekeeping duties, first in Lebanon from 1978 and later in Sinai. By 1987, half of the RFMF served in two infantry battalions overseas. In addition, it possessed 5,000 reservists. Rabuka entered the RFMF as a trainee officer in 1968, and – despite problems with women and managing money – established himself as a potential leader on the eve of the force's rapid growth.[11] That potential bore fruit after 1978 when he served in Lebanon and received an OBE for his service as a commanding officer and, later, the French Legion of Honour. Then came his first setback. Notwithstanding promotion to lieutenant colonel in 1982, he lost his acting role as chief of staff to Jim Sanday. Both men joined the military at the same time. A second setback came in 1985 while Rabuka commanded Fiji troops in the Sinai. Instead of returning in glory, he faced possible disciplinary action for disobeying orders.[12] The incident put his future in doubt; his chances of succeeding the Bauan chief, Brigadier General Ratu Epeli Nailatikau, as commander or replacing his immediate senior, Chief of Staff Col Jim Sanday, now seemed remote. As a commoner he might always play second fiddle to a chief and his record of insubordination could be held against him. Against the advice of his protector, Ratu Penaia Ganilau – both the governor-general and Rabuka's high chief – Rabuka cast around for civil service positions, and even sought to be Police Commissioner in early 1987. Kubuabola's offer created an opportunity he could not resist. He immediately began secretly training some 60 soldiers for 'close-quarter combat'.[13]

---

10   Britain generally only stationed troops in its colonies (except India) if they were required to suppress resistance. Military forces – like Fiji's – were usually small in size, poorly equipped and led by colonial officers.

11   Sharpham, *Rabuka of Fiji*, 2000, pp. 46–55.

12   *Islands Business*, May 1988. He permitted Major Ratu George Kadavulevu Cakobau to return to Fiji for his father's funeral against the army's wishes. Sharpham suggests that Rabuka had been a contender for RFMF Commander, but Mara chose his son-in-law and chief, Ratu Epeli Nailatikau, instead (*Rabuka of Fiji*, 2000, pp. 79–81).

13   E Dean & S Ritova, *Rabuka: No Other Way*. Sydney: Doubleday, 1988, p. 51; see also Sharpham, *Rabuka of Fiji*, 2000, pp. 73–87, 94–106.

While awaiting the final word from the Taukeists, Rabuka arranged a meeting with Mara on a golf course, coming away convinced of his support.[14] With his Commander overseas during the second week of May, Rabuka prepared to arrest all government ministers and MPs at the parliament. Early on Thursday morning, 14 May, he drew up an operations order for the 'Neutralisation of the Coalition Government of Fiji', declaring that 'Our mission is to overthrow the government and install a new regime that will ensure that the RFMF and national interests are protected'.[15] Rabuka had been told by the Taukei Movement leaders that the Coalition planned a wholesale restructuring of the public service and diplomatic corps, and that it would move sideways all senior Alliance-appointed officials. In addition to this radical attack on the Fijian elite, the Coalition intended to adopt a socialist foreign policy, aligning Fiji with Russia, Libya and Cuba, ending the RFMF's roles in UN missions in West Asia, and transforming the military into a multiracial institution. Whether Rabuka believed all this did not really matter; it provided welcome ammunition that could be used nationally and internationally to garner support or weaken opposition. In any case, Rabuka had long distrusted India because of its close links with Russia. Would an IndoFijian-dominated government in Fiji be any different? Conveniently, Rabuka did not think so.[16]

Later that morning Rabuka discreetly entered the parliamentary chamber in civilian clothes. To prevent complications at military headquarters during the next couple of hours, he had sent his immediate superior, Sanday, to an unscheduled meeting with Governor-General Ganilau, well away from the Queen Elizabeth Barracks (QEB) in Nabua. As Rabuka took a seat in the public gallery, former waterside worker union boss, member of the Taukei Movement and new Alliance MP, Taniela Veitata, neared the end of his repetition of a long statement that he had used in

---

14   Sharpham, *Rabuka of Fiji*, 2000, pp. 105–06. Mara always denied this interpretation of their meeting but sometimes sent conflicting messages. He praised Rabuka, telling an Australian journalist: 'I must take my hat off to him, to the courage of the man, I would never have done it myself if I was a soldier. Because I would think I know many of the complications that perhaps will flow. I am thinking of the sugar markets I have established in various parts of the world, the economy built over 20 years and more, and the peace and stability that I built' (*Bulletin*, 26 May 1987). Rabuka also claimed that, on the eve of the coup, Ratu Finau travelled to the Fijian Hotel outside Sigatoka to warn his father of the impending coup (*Daily Post*, 27 December 1991).

15   Dean & Ritova, *Rabuka*, 1988, pp. 60–63.

16   Sharpham, *Rabuka of Fiji*, 2000, p. 74. Long confined within ethnocentric institutions (Queen Victoria School and the RFMF), Rabuka retained a highly dichotomised view of Fiji, despite his military training in Australia, New Zealand and India, and his service in West Asia.

the past to advertise his views. As long as chiefs were in control, he told his fellow parliamentarians in the only novel section of his address, power would never grow from the barrel of a gun. Precisely at 10 am, Ratu Finau opened the chamber doors to a squad of 10 armed and masked soldiers. A back-up team stood outside in the corridor. Other teams fanned out across the city to seize control of telecommunication and power authorities, media outlets and the Government Buildings. Government House, with Sanday and Ganilau deep in conversation, was also secured. By the time Rabuka addressed the media in the afternoon to say that the coup had been designed to prevent the Taukei Movement causing bloodshed,[17] he was confident it had succeeded. All Coalition ministers and MPs in the parliament were arrested and detained at the RFMF's QEB. True, the governor-general – while privately accepting of the situation – initially refused on the advice of Chief Justice Sir Timoci Tuivaga, to endorse the coup publically. Nonetheless, as that public response hit the evening news, Rabuka had already replaced the senior police leadership with officers loyal to him, gained the support of most Alliance politicians, and learned that over 1,000 reservists had arrived at the QEB following a preplanned general call out. And, in the early hours of the next morning, Mara – attending a conference in Sigatoka – agreed to join a Council of Ministers, later telling his fellow chiefs that 'with my house on fire' he had no choice.[18] Everything was going according to plan … well, nearly everything.

The military spectre

Part of Rabuka's confidence lay in the precision of his operation. He had achieved a bloodless coup. A coup d'état is, by its nature, a surgical strike and, therefore, a cheap and potentially decisive way to overthrow the government of a state. This is not to suggest that a coup comes without cost. Economist Paul Collier has estimated that, on average, coups immediately result in a 7 per cent annual loss in national income[19] and Fiji's coup just surpassed that proportion. There would be other ongoing costs but, compared with rebellions or civil war, coups have a decidedly strategic, let alone economic and social advantage.

---

17 *Fiji Times*, 15 May 1987.
18 *Islands Business*, June 1987.
19 Collier, *Wars, Guns & Votes*, 2009, p. 143.

Coups or putsches have a long history around the world, and famous examples during the past 200 years exist in European countries as diverse as France, Germany, Russia and Turkey. However, since the Second World War, the vast majority have occurred in developing countries, a shift that has prompted greater attention to their causes. During the 1960s, when Sub-Saharan Africa joined North Africa, West Asia and Latin America as the leading centres for coups, many modernisationists argued that coups should be regarded positively. This was a time when the United States belatedly sought to justify its support for the military takeover of South Vietnam, then its shining example of modernisation. Of course coups were entirely undemocratic, but it was possible – they argued – that by imposing order and efficiency on chaotic societies the military could in fact make democracy more possible in the future. After all, as disciplined neutral institutions that looked askance at corrupt or ineffective civilian administrations, militaries were prime examples of modernity.[20] The modernising Young Turks and Kemal Atatürk, who eventually prevented the dismemberment of Turkey after the First World War, were an obvious early example, and that image they carefully nurtured and used to good effect in at least four subsequent coups.

But, for reviewers like Nicole Ball, these arguments left many questions unanswered. Who actually makes the decision that the military should intervene? The military themselves, or are strings pulled by other social forces, as we noted in Fiji's first coup? The answer to those questions might vary from country to country; certainly in the case of Turkey the military has been politicised ever since it founded the republic and has portrayed itself as its country's guardian and constitutional guarantor. But strong militaries rarely act alone, as has been demonstrated in recent coups in Thailand, where urban forces allied with the royal family have been the principal beneficiaries of military intervention.[21]

We should also question whether militaries deserve to be labelled modern and efficient. In all likelihood we would never know their effectiveness until they are put to the test in battle, the role they are principally trained and equipped to undertake. Defeat in the Falklands War in 1982 certainly doomed Argentina's junta. Fiji's military prided itself on

---

20   This argument is well analysed in N Ball, 'The military in politics: Who benefits & how?', *World Development*, 9: 6, 1981, pp. 569–82; see also N Ball, *Security and Economy in the Third World*. Princeton University Press, 1988.
21   'A right royal mess', *Economist*, 4 December 2008.

its professionalism, derived in large part from its engagement in trouble spots across West Asia. This was no idle army, poorly paid and brawling drunkenly in public, as occasionally happened in the Philippines or West Africa. But, then again, 1987 was not a war but an unbalanced exercise in might.

Africa provides an interesting comparison. Like Fiji's military, its forces at the time of independence were colonial in origin, small and poorly equipped, dominated by what colonial authorities referred to as 'martial' tribes, with few commissioned officers, and invariably treated with suspicion by independence leaders. Independence necessitated that they be nationalised, and the political intervention this dictated came to be deeply resented. One Kenyan military officer wrote:

> As the military was struggling to attain a national character in order to gain national acceptance, the politicians were becoming more self-seeking, power-hungry and ambitious. Some were out seeking instant wealth for themselves, their friends and relatives. Nepotism became rampant, commonplace and a norm. Others were out experimenting on new and foreign ideologies in the name of African socialism. These were ideologies that had no bearing or relevance to the improvement of the lives of the ordinary man. Some of these governments started openly courting the Eastern bloc for advice and guidance. It did not take the ordinary citizens long to realise that these so-called progressive governments were not delivering the goods fast enough. Corruption had become an accepted way of life. Mismanagement of the economy coupled with sheer incompetence had led to runaway inflation and unaffordable prices. Unemployment and crime rates were on the increase. Yet the greedy get-rich-quick politicians continued getting richer ... In the majority of the coups that have occurred, the military has deemed it a national and patriotic obligation to rescue the country from total collapse and thereby restore lost national prestige.[22]

Major Jimmi Wangome's account above suggests a number of common causes for coups and these too have been examined in detail by Collier and other economists. Economic causes are, in many respects, the most important factors contributing to unease within societies, especially during immediate postcolonial years. Where standards of living and growth rates are both low, the likelihood of coups increases. With regard

---

22   J Wangome, 'The African "neocolonialism" that is self-inflicted'. MA Thesis, Marine Corps University Command and Staff College. Quantico, Virginia, 1985, www.globalsecurity.org/military/library/report/1985/WJ.htm.

to living standards, Collier believes that the threshold is US$2,700 annual per capita income, roughly US$7 per day. Fiji today has a per capita GDP of around US$5,500 but, in 1987, its position was similar in real terms. Growth rates for the 1980s only averaged 1.7 per cent until 1987.[23] Fiji was clearly at risk on the basis of these indices. Contentiously, Collier argues that the distribution of wealth is not a factor, at least not in Africa;[24] nor the nature of governments affected. Democracies and autocracies are all susceptible, with anocracies (chaotic autocratic democracies) most susceptible.

It is low growth and low incomes that are the stand-out features enabling coups to become 'proxies for lack of opportunity other than control of the state'. It is poverty that makes the wealth that can be extracted from minerals and other natural resources (including forests and land) or aid so attractive.[25] Fear that the Coalition would exclude former Alliance cronies from the state trough certainly influenced the thinking of many coup plotters, although Fiji had none of the huge natural resource riches that coup plotters in Africa found so attractive. Nor was Fiji heavily reliant on aid, which in Africa could provide the same attraction as diamonds and make government a target for greed. Aid often comprises as much as 9.9 per cent of African national income, indirectly contributing as much as 40 per cent to all military spending[26] and one third of government expenditures. In Fiji, aid comprised only 4 per cent of GDP in 1986.

Access to natural resource wealth and aid enables governments to avoid taxing their citizens. Taxed incomes in many African countries are as low as 12 per cent of GDP, which has the unfortunate consequence of being 'too low to provoke citizens into demanding accountability', an essential component for establishing democracy and a state capable

---

23   Fiji's per capita GDP stood at US$1,606 in 1986. When adjusted by purchasing power parity, its GDP per capita has averaged from US$6,642 in 1990 to US$8,236 in 2016.

24   This contrasts with D Acemoglu, D Ticchi & A Vindigni in 'A theory of military dictatorships', (*American Economic Journal: Macroeconomics*, 2: 1, January 2010, pp. 1–42, www.voxeu.org/index.php?q=node/1227). They argue that '[g]reater inequality increases the conflict between the elite and the citizens and encourages oligarchic regimes to maintain power by using stronger militaries'.

25   P Collier & A Hoeffler, 'Coup traps: Why does Africa have so many coups d'état?', paper presented at the annual meeting of the American Political Science Association, Marriott Wardman Park, Omni Shoreham, Washington Hilton, Washington, DC, 1 September 2005, p. 19, ora.ox.ac.uk/objects/uuid:49097086-8505-4eb2-8174-314ce1aa3ebb.

26   P Collier & A Hoeffler, 'Grand extortion: Coup risk & the military as a protection racket', Paper presented at the Second Workshop on Political Institutions, Development And a Domestic Civil Peace (PIDDCP), 19–20 June 2006, ora.ox.ac.uk/objects/uuid:ff727e54-408e-4288-a202-cf46a61d7187.

of supplying much needed public goods.[27] Fiji, it should be noted, did possess reasonably well-managed accounts, and taxation represented over 20 per cent of GDP in 1986.[28] Its supply of public goods had extended considerably since 1970. It is worth remembering, also, that Fiji was not so vulnerable that it succumbed to a coup culture immediately after independence.

Nonetheless, there is one important feature that Fiji shared with many African countries: ethnic diversity trumped national identity. Sub-Saharan Africa possesses some 2,000 ethnicities and, while diversity in itself is not a problem, it can be where states have been unable to develop the checks and balances required for a functioning democracy and to foster strong loyalty to the nation among its citizens. Ethnic politics simply deprives electoral competition of its potential to hold governments to account and ensure that governments deliver the national public goods that their citizens desire.[29] Ethnic politics also deprives governments of legitimacy in the eyes of those citizens who are not part of the ethnic community that captures power. And, once in power, governments need only play to their own community in order to survive; thus the nation is weakened further and democracy made ineffective, even dangerous if its outcome is greater confrontation. In fact, from this point, it is only a small step to dictatorship, with the same patronage base and the same temptation to retain power by transferring increasing amounts of wealth to that base.[30]

As Wangome notes, the transference of power to dictators changed nothing: 'more often than not, military regimes have turned out to be more corrupt, oppressive and downright inefficient than the civilian governments they deposed'.[31] Herein lay the real test of modernisationist arguments. Did regime change have positive economic, social and democratic consequences? Except perhaps in the case of the less polarised Costa Rica, where rebels seized power after contested elections in 1948, enacted a democratic constitution and abolished the military, the vast majority of military interventions have been far from benign in their

---

27   Collier, *Wars, Guns & Votes*, 2009, pp. 179, 182.
28   W Narsey ('Just wages & coup impacts', *Fiji Times*, 15 April 2009) claims taxes now comprise 27 per cent of GDP.
29   Collier, *Wars, Guns & Votes*, 2009, p. 73.
30   Collier, *Wars, Guns & Votes*, 2009, p. 61.
31   Wangome, 'The African "neocolonialism"', 1985.

consequences.[32] In Fiji's case, the military coup set the country on a new postcolonial trajectory, although how radical that transformation would be was not immediately apparent, in part because it cloaked itself in Fijian conservatism.

Undoubtedly the most radical and obvious innovation of Fiji's May 1987 coup was the insertion of a new, non-political and non-traditional actor into the political process. The military had not prepared for this role, hence it did not seek to dominate the political process it had transformed, at least not at first. Even when it later did, it could never overcome its own administrative and leadership deficiencies. Consequently, for five years after the first coup, Fiji endured an uneasy standoff between the army and the Fijian elite, who had most benefited from the coup. That standoff ended only when Rabuka seized control of the political process and ruled in his own right. The following eight years of Rabuka government demonstrated once more the dangers of ethnic politics. A tale of electoral manipulation and patronage politics quickly followed, robbing Fiji of transparent and accountable governance and leaving the majority of its people poorer, even those that it claimed held special privileges as indigenous people. Fiji didn't collapse; it simply surrendered to impoverishment in the widest sense of the word.

The insertion of the military into Fiji's politics also had other consequences. It sought financial independence, attempting to model itself on Suharto's Indonesian forces. Economic planners began a fresh push to establish a new urban–industrial base by boosting the infant clothing industry, the success of which depended wholly on preferential access to foreign markets. But, of equal importance for reformers riding an indigenous 'revolution', multiracialism had to go. Affirmative action became the new mantra, but it heralded no revolutionary approach to perceived gaps between Fijians and IndoFijians. Rather, it reinforced the failed strategies of the past – the promotion of a Fijian business class and the reassertion of chiefly control.

---

32   Many coups were conducted under the influence also of the Cold War, such as Park Chung-hee's 1961 coup in South Korea. Unusually for a military-backed leader, Park successfully grew South Korea's economy and, in time, the military withdrew in favour of civilian rule.

There were, however, some differences. Sociologist Steven Ratuva argues that, for Fijians, a focus on specifically commercial activities now increasingly took precedence over communal resource exploitation.[33] Avowedly Fijian post-coup regimes desperately needed to create a sense of difference in order to demonstrate legitimacy and the programs they pursued had of urgent necessity to demonstrate rapid success. Their goose would deliver the golden eggs. With few instruments of accountability untainted by the 'revolution', all the ingredients for economic disaster and frustrated ambitions were being rapidly assembled for future consumption.

There were other unpleasant legacies also. The abuse of human rights, which occurred shockingly during and after the coup, put any return to normality out of reach for a long time. The wounds of 1987 would take a decade to heal and, even then, some wounds continued to fester. Certainly they ended the lingering dream harboured by some citizens of creating a nation out of Fiji. Not surprisingly, increasing numbers of citizens, particularly IndoFijians, emigrated to countries where multiculturalism more effectively provided security and a future. They did not, as Sakeasi Butadroka urged, return to the land of their ancestors. Instead they journeyed to Australia, North America and New Zealand, no doubt where relatives already lived and could provide support. A comparative trickle of a 1,000 emigrants per year in the 1970s settled into a standard 5,000 during the 1990s.[34] In the longer term, emigration profoundly transformed Fiji such that, by 2005, 148,355 citizens or former citizens – 17.5 per cent of its population – lived abroad.[35] Undoubtedly, emigration slowed population growth, helping to minimise some of the more disastrous economic impacts of 1987. But it also drained the country of much needed skills and capital,[36] and ensured that Fiji's bourgeoisie were not so much missing as living elsewhere.

---

33   S Ratuva, 'Addressing inequality? Economic affirmative action and communal capitalism in post-coup Fiji', in H Akram-Lodhi (ed.), *Confronting Fiji Futures*. Canberra: Asia Pacific Press, 2000, pp. 227, 234.

34   These averages disguise considerable spikes: 18,359 emigrants in 1987 and 10,674 in 1988 (D Forsyth, 'Fiji at the crossroads', *Pacific Economic Bulletin*, 11: 1, May 1996).

35   D Ratha & Z Xu (eds), *Migration and Remittances Factbook 2008*. Washington: World Bank, 2008, siteresources.worldbank.org/INTPROSPECTS/Resources/334934-1199807908806/Fiji.pdf.

36   Between 1987 and 1992, Fiji lost 9 per cent of its professional stock, 24 per cent of its administrators and managers, and 11 per cent of its clerical workers of whom 72 per cent were IndoFijians (Walsh, *Fiji*, 2006, p. 56).

The long-term impact of emigration also had political consequences. Dramatically falling IndoFijian proportions meant that the threat of IndoFijian dominance, which Fijian nationalists had exploited to great effect, no longer carried the same weight as before. IndoFijian proportions peaked in 1976 and, by 1986, they were well on their way to losing their near majority status. The coup hastened the process: 48.7 per cent of the population in 1986 became 37.5 per cent by 2007.[37] And, as hundreds of poor IndoFijian farmers lost land leases and flocked to urban settlements, another nationalist myth also crumbled visibly, the myth of Indian wealth. Thus, in the space of a single generation, Fiji moved from a racially diverse or plural society to one fast comprising a single dominant ethnicity. The dynamics of politics began to shift accordingly, subtly at first because the political behaviour of past generations continued as if nothing had changed. But, by 2006, the shift could no longer be concealed, even if political denial continued.

There is one final legacy to be referred to as a guide to reading post-1987 events: successful military coups invariably result in higher spending on military forces. In 1986, the RFMF received $16 million as its operating budget; by 1995, this had increased to $41 million. Admittedly, the military had grown 74 per cent in size by 1995, but the comparison with the $25 million meted out to the police in that year is stark. And it did not take into account the military's failure to live within its budget. In fact, between 1986 and 1996, it annually overspent its budget by an average $23.5 million.[38] Such excessive expenditure impacted on the state's provision of public goods, on state indebtedness and most assuredly on economic growth. Together they contributed to further discontent and instability, with damaging human consequences, although just how damaging would not become apparent in Fiji's case until much later.

Three long-term consequences of Fiji's troubled postcolonial development strategies give some indication exactly where dangers lay. First, Fiji's failure to break free of racialised and elite-oriented economic strategies meant that it increasingly possessed a large pool of disaffected youth. In 1986 youth (15 to 24 years) comprised 8 per cent of the population; by 2007 19 per cent.[39] Why were they disaffected? Wadan Narsey provides one

---

37   Walsh, *Fiji*, 2006, p. 101; www.statsfiji.gov.fj/.
38   *Fiji Times*, 30 October 1996. The military expanded from 2,100 troops to 3,650 during this period.
39   Fiji Bureau of Statistics, *2007 and 2009 Population Census of Fiji*. Suva: Fiji Island Bureau of Statistics, June 2012.

possible answer. Child dependency ratios are much higher for Fijians than for IndoFijians; only 4 per cent higher in 1976, but 62 per cent higher by 2007. Larger families mean, among other things, a poorer lifestyle, fewer resources for education per child, higher school dropout rates and fewer skilled entrants into the workforce.[40]

Second, under-employment and unemployment – especially in long-neglected rural areas – resulted in unprecedented urbanisation (from 39 per cent in 1986 to 51 per cent by 2007), much of it centred on the capital, Suva, where there were also insufficient jobs and houses to go around. This created a new political risk which Alan Beattie sees as a direct consequence of urbanisation:

> When it comes to exerting political power, those within rioting distance of [government] have a better means of making their grievances known than do equally disgruntled peasantry muttering into their gruel as they go about their miserable rural lives … miles from the capital.[41]

At 24 per cent, Suva's proportion of the country's population was no more than that of many other capital cities, but it is growing rapidly and as it does 'the incentive for rural flight towards the city increases, and so does the political imperative to keep the urbanites happy'.[42]

The third consequence derived specifically from the politicisation of the military. Having engaged in a coup once, the military could more easily take the step on subsequent occasions; first blood, as it were. Indeed, the successful outcome of a first strike might well create the expectation that future strikes would produce similar responses. In other words, the nature of the first political response to military action sets the scene for future action. Importantly when those political reactions are favourable, they essentially legitimise violence as a means for change, with consequences that go far beyond the military, especially if political violence is civilianised among growing numbers of disaffected urban youth. This is the coup trap and its reality hit Fiji very quickly after the overthrow of the Bavadra government.

---

40   W Narsey, 'Fiji's far reaching population revolution', 21 March 2010, www.usp.ac.fj/fileadmin/files/schools/ssed/economics/Wadan_Narsey/Media_articles/2010_C____Fiji_s_population_revolution.pdf.

41   Beattie, *False Economy*, 2009, pp. 50–51.

42   Beattie, *False Economy*, 2009, pp. 50–51. By 2007, Greater Suva encompassed one third of Fiji's population and by 2016 produced 40 per cent of Fiji's GDP, according to the Asian Development Bank (*Fiji Times*, 15 December 2016).

The coup trap

After 14 May 1987 the army became the obvious elephant in Fiji's political space, although it was not seen this way at first. Rabuka's coup appeared less a military coup than an elite coup and, very quickly, the governor-general tried to put his own stamp on it. He was not going to accept whatever Rabuka instructed him to do. This was the start of a remarkable showdown between the old elite and the new faction within politics. The showdown would continue for the next five years until Rabuka emerged triumphant as leader of a new establishment party endorsed by the chiefs.

Rabuka delivered the governor-general a list of mostly Alliance personnel who would form a Council of Ministers. Ganilau appeared to accept this, and swore in Rabuka as head of government on the Sunday after the coup, but changed his mind on the advice of the Chief Justice. Rabuka attempted unsuccessfully to prevent further meetings between the governor-general and the justices, and retreated to his barracks to rally his troops. He released his Coalition hostages. But the governor-general was only one man; on Tuesday 19 May, the Great Council of Chiefs (GCC) met to deliberate on the political crisis facing the country. The Taukei Movement organised a riot during its second day of deliberations, using waterside workers to demonstrate 'Fijian' anger at the governor-general's position. In fact, sporadic acts of violence continued during much of the week; buildings were burnt, homes broken into and people assaulted. On the third day, the movement presented a petition to the GCC calling for Fijian political paramountcy or the declaration of a republic.[43] As Ganilau arrived to address the GCC, crowds outside the Civic Centre booed. It was not an auspicious moment for the governor-general, who had come with a compromise: he would provide amnesty for the coup makers, dissolve parliament, select a council of advisors, investigate constitutional change, and take the country back to elections. The GCC agreed.

Rabuka told the crowds, 'I will not accept any solution to the political problems facing the country that will destroy the aim of the coup'. Later he told journalists, 'I will remain in control so as to stop rioting, the very thing I tried to avoid by staging the coup'. The governor-general 'will be serving my purpose if he remains in office although he is powerless to

---

43   Draft, 'Portions of the Constitution to be amended', GCC submission.

enforce his office'.[44] The 19 members of the new Council of Advisors were mostly from the Alliance Party but nine were also members of the Taukei Movement.[45] Ganilau was in an invidious position and Brij Lal argues, 'Had he resisted the pressure to endorse the coup, he might have been isolated, his candidature for the title of Tui Cakau [the highest title within the Tovata confederacy] placed in jeopardy, and the Fijian polity possibly split. This was the price of loyalty to the Crown, and Ganilau was not prepared to pay it'.[46]

Ganilau now took Fiji on an uncertain journey. While its economy sharply contracted and trade sanctions bit hard, the military and the Taukei Movement ran amok. Ganilau had promoted Rabuka to colonel at the same time that he assumed authority, but the reward brought no compliance from the army. Rabuka claimed to possess his own 'revolutionary' committee and promised to declare a republic if he did not get his way.[47] He developed a new relationship with sympathisers within the Methodist Church hierarchy, certain that they could provide a wider support base than the Taukei Movement if such support was needed in the future.

The RFMF now also rapidly expanded; Rabuka aspired to build an 8,000-strong standing force.[48] He sent officers overseas to seek new training facilities and to purchase weapons and helicopters. Two patrol boats were purchased for the naval squadron and key military personnel entered senior positions within the public service. A campaign of arrests harassed political opponents and unionists, and intimidated the populace. The entire staff of Morris Hedstrom, a large department store in Suva's CBD, was threatened with arrest when the wife of the new Police Commissioner complained of discrimination when given a smaller plastic bag (they were being rationed) for her purchases than other customers. The intimidation coincided with a massive increase in crime. Gangs of youths terrorised families and isolated communities. Shops and homes were looted, sometimes by thieves dressed as military personnel. Such

---

44   *Fiji Times*, 22 May 1987.

45   It also included three civil servants, one former military commander, one IndoFijian Methodist, and Bavadra and his deputy. The last three refused to join.

46   Lal, *Broken Waves*, 1992, p. 278. A journalist later argued that Ganilau's initial resistance nearly caused a rebellion in Cakaudrove (*Evening Post*, Wellington, 19 May 1988).

47   *Fiji Times*, 13 June 1987.

48   Sharpham, *Rabuka of Fiji*, 2000, p. 142. The RFMF stood at 5,000 by the end of 1987, a near doubling of size.

incidents became increasingly violent. A 10-year-old girl had her arm partially severed when she was attacked with a machete outside her school. A Lautoka shopkeeper was stabbed to death during a robbery. Soldiers beat a detained man unconscious at their barracks and, after two weeks in a coma, he had to be sent to New Zealand for urgent treatment.

Fiji's season of madness continued unabated until August, by which time economic realities demanded more reasoned responses. Hotel occupancy rates fell to 20 per cent. Garment exports lay on the wharves, the industry crippled by trade bans enforced by Australasian unions. Cane farmers protested by delaying the harvest. The Fiji Sugar Corporation (FSC) called their bluff and shut all mills until mid-July. In late June, the Fiji dollar devalued 17.75 per cent. Government departments were directed to cut expenditure by 20 per cent and civil servants received a 15 per cent salary cut, although the military ignored the rulings. By August its expenditure already exceeded its budget by 42 per cent and it laid plans to develop its own farms, to fish, and to engage in inter-island trade. It would become self-reliant.

Post-coup politics were equally challenging. The GCC met again in July and flexed its muscles. It rejected Mara's proposal for minimal changes to the Constitution, arguing instead for a parliament dominated by Fijians (at least 56 per cent of seats), with all Fijian seats filled by nominees of provincial councils. By the time a Constitutional Review Committee reported in August, this proposal had been amended to allow Fijians the vote, but only on the basis of provincial constituencies. There would be no urban constituencies for Fijians, a move that appeared to deny the Taukei Movement future influence. They protested, threatening to burn Suva and declare a republic. Unexpectedly, Rabuka rebuked them.[49] The path he trod had suddenly become more unpredictable. Political hostility to the coup increased. Newspapers became more daring in their opposition to the chaos generated by both the military and the Taukei Movement. The Coalition, partially recovered from the shock of May, began an improbable campaign to win the hearts and minds of Fijian villagers in Viti Levu.[50]

---

49 *Fiji Sun*, 20 July 1987.
50 Labour stalwart Simione Durutalo observed of Labour's Operation Sunrise: 'Indigenous Fijians are not fooled by such gimmicks'. Its very existence is 'an unspoken admission that the party sponsoring them treats commoner Fijian interests and aspirations as merely an appendix to their main concern elsewhere' (*Fiji Times*, 9 February 1992).

The real game changer, however, came with a High Court ruling in August. It agreed that the governor-general's dismissal of parliament might be illegal and declared that the matter be heard in court. In response, Ganilau announced that he would form a new caretaker government and urged the Alliance Party and Coalition to reach accommodation. Talks were held for three weeks during September, amidst a Taukeist firebombing campaign in Suva that ended with the mass breakout of prisoners from Naboro prison. The Coalition knew that court action might not ultimately produce the political outcome it wanted. The Alliance, for its part, feared losing control to extremists. Compromise now seemed the best way forward for the two political parties. A final meeting was held, safely outside of Suva at Deuba (Pacific Harbour) on 23 September 1987, which decided on a caretaker government, derived equally from the two parties and led by Ganilau. The ensuing Deuba Accord intended for the government to tackle both the economic crisis and constitutional review in the spirit of bipartisanship and begin a process of national reconciliation.

On the eve of the accord's implementation, Rabuka decided 'to resume executive authority'. His second coup on 25 September overthrew the governor-general and established a military government composed largely of Taukeists and nationalists. To prevent legal complexities, he declared Fiji a republic on 7 October and sacked the judiciary. To deny his opponents a forum, he closed all media outlets (except Radio Fiji). To consolidate his support among Methodists, he introduced a Sunday Observance Decree which banned sport and trading on Sundays. To help with security he introduced a night curfew. Precision is the hallmark of a military leader and Rabuka prided himself on his organisational skills. But, as Mara had noted earlier, Rabuka always had a tendency to overlook the long-term consequences of his actions. He had told the governor-general that he would support the Deuba compromise,[51] but fell under the sway of the Taukeists who had set up their own intelligence operation in the Ministry of Information. His exclusion from the Deuba talks annoyed him and its outcome mocked his coup. Having done the deed for a second time, however, Rabuka wavered. He wanted the chiefs on side again. The Taukeists found it difficult to get Rabuka to focus on a republic.[52]

---

51   P Thomson, *Kava in the Blood: A Personal & Political Memoir from the Heart of Fiji*. Auckland: Tandem Press, 1999, p. 179.
52   Robbie Robertson, Interview with Ratu Meli Vesikula, Melbourne, 9 August 1989.

The second coup was psychologically more difficult for Rabuka. His first coup had been against what he saw as foreign control of the country by people who did not respect Fijian custom. 'I am a commoner and to see my high chief being accused of corruption with no proof,' he complained in May: '[T]he language used against [Mara] I will never accept nor would any right thinking Fijian.'[53] By October his views were more tempered. 'A lot of people say that chiefs should not participate in politics because in politics you might be subjected to some adverse comments that are unbecoming to your status,' he now argued: 'This is the same sort of thing here.'[54] Better to have commoners ruling; he could speak with them on the same level.

Nonetheless, Rabuka was no revolutionary. It disturbed him that few chiefs had congratulated him on his second coup. They had always opposed breaking links with the Crown, even if the Taukeists, who dominated the reformed GCC, sometimes swayed them otherwise. As a result, Rabuka tried once more to get Ganilau and Mara on side. He met with the Deuba parties to get their agreement, but Timoci Bavadra refused to play ball.

Mara disagreed with Rabuka's assessment of the role of chiefs. Chiefs have always been involved in politics, he argued; they could not remain aloof from it.[55] Mara flew to England to have the Queen sanction his and Ganilau's continued role, hoping this might be sufficient to pull Fiji back from the abyss, but without success. He was denied an audience with the Queen and, to make matters worse, against his own advice, Ganilau gave up the fight and resigned his office just as the Commonwealth met. No reason now existed for the Commonwealth not to suspend Fiji's membership. The chiefs had lost control, twice in the space of one year. Mara's wife had called Rabuka their 'brave hearted champion';[56] no longer. They saw themselves as moderates; they regarded their self-interest as altruism. When Ratu Meli Vesikula, an ex–British army major from Verata who served as spokesperson for the Taukei Movement, had delivered copies of his Movement's constitutional proposals to Mara and Ganilau, they looked on him with contempt and said there was no way he was going to get away with such a proposal.[57] Now it looked like he might.

---

53   *NZ Herald*, 19 May 1987.
54   *Islands Business*, October 1987.
55   *Fiji Times*, 3 October 1991.
56   *Fiji Times*, 2 November 1995.
57   Robertson, Interview with Vesikula, 9 August 1989.

Rabuka formed his own Council of Ministers in which 17 of its 24 ministers were from the Taukei Movement. Vesikula was one of them. He had served in Ireland and Cyprus and had firm ideas about what needed to be done: 'What we have to do is apply a force that will stun the people ... That force will have to be applied by the military or a hardline civilian government. In my experience the military option is nearly always the best ... That is the set piece I hope to have played out in Fiji.'[58] The abolition of trade union rights marked a first step in this direction. Butadroka was also there as Minister for Lands, a ghost from Mara's past, wanting above all to make up for lost time. Crown land would immediately return to Fijians and Fijians would receive first option on the sale of freehold land. If such radicalism helped doom the Council of Ministers, then its inability to turn the country around economically sealed its fate. The economy continued its spiral downwards: a further devaluation (15.25 per cent), looming bans on flights to Fiji, and even threats to deny Fiji sugar export rights.

Rabuka had left the positions of president and prime minister vacant, claiming he would withdraw once the positions were filled.[59] Some on the Council, like Butadroka and Vesikula, were suspicious of his intentions and objected to Mara's return; but Rabuka insisted that Mara would restore Tovata's prominence.[60] Rabuka began to undo the more draconian aspects of his military government, restoring union rights, allowing newspapers to operate freely, ending the curfew, re-establishing a judiciary, and promising to reduce the size of his forces. The scene was set for fresh meetings with Mara and Ganilau and, on 5 December, the now self-promoted Brigadier Rabuka returned power to them as prime minister and president respectively.

In effect, Rabuka restored the Alliance government but in a very different and potentially unstable form. Had its leaders learned wisely from the events of the past year? Had they finally understood that, for all the anti-IndoFijian venom of their supporters, they actually faced a people deeply unhappy with the consequences of development for them under Alliance rule, a people now perhaps with a new champion in the military? Rabuka later argued that 'Fiji had not become a fully independent country between 1970 and 1987 ... until I took over the government, declared Fiji

---

58 *Far Eastern Economic Review*, 8 October 1987.
59 *NZ Herald*, 14 November 1987.
60 Robertson, Interview with Vesikula, 9 August 1989.

a Republic and handed the leadership over to the Bose Levu Vakaturaga (Great Council of Chiefs)'.[61] How would post-coup Fiji differentiate itself from the immediate postcolonial era that had ended so suddenly and sharply?

A new trajectory for Fiji?

In February 1990, Navitalai Naisoro, one of the self proclaimed 'New Fijian' economic managers appointed after the coups, told students at the University of the South Pacific: 'My hope is that one day instead of seeing the greenery of sugar cane fields, we see the greenery of well-engineered factory complexes.'[62] As permanent secretary for trade and commerce, Naisoro was the public face of a self-declared radical redirection in Fiji's economic policies. Given the rapid contraction in Fiji's economy (nearly 8 per cent in 1987), Naisoro understood that Fiji had to do something dramatic to attract the attention of foreign investors: 'We realised that if we were to survive in the long term, the solution lay with the export sector.'[63] That signal came in December 1987 in the form of tax free zones (TFZs), a policy lifted from the Alliance Party's aborted Ninth Development Plan (1986–90).

The idea had been mooted first in 1981 but, with the rise in garment production during the 1980s from small local tailoring businesses that tapped into the protected home market and survived on the basis of family labour and low wages, it quickly developed traction.[64] By the mid-1980s, standards of production had improved sufficiently for garment producers to attract the interest of Australasian distributors. Fiji's lower wages provided Australasian manufacturers who were prepared to move offshore or contract work out an opportunity to compete with Asian exporters who now entered their formerly protected markets. Australasian governments were determined to make manufacturing internationally competitive, and slashing import duties or ending import licensing became important

---

61   *Fiji Times*, 28 April 1992.
62   'Reflecting on the Fiji experience and USP', *University of the South Pacific Bulletin*, 23: 4, 2 March 1990, p. 2. This section draws in part on R Robertson, '"The greenery of well-engineered factory complexes": Fiji's garment-led export industrialization strategy', *Bulletin of Concerned Asian Scholars*, 25: 2, 1993, pp. 31–41.
63   R Callick, 'Fiji grasps for a bonanza', *Australian Financial Review*, 30 November 1988, p. 13.
64   Chandra, 'The political crisis and the manufacturing sector in Fiji', 1989,' p. 48; production rose 81 per cent during 1986 alone.

means to that end. Fiji's wages were not low compared with most Asian wages, but Fiji's advantage lay in its ability to gain duty-free entry into Australia and New Zealand through the South Pacific Regional Trade and Economic Cooperation Agreement (SPARTECA). Australia had also created a special sampling quota for the Pacific during the early 1980s and, in 1991, added an Import Credit Scheme that enabled Australian companies to source textiles from Asia, dye and print them in Australia, export the cloth to Fiji to be assembled into finished clothing, reimport them duty free, and then use the import credits gained to finance more purchases from China.[65] Protectionism was not yet dead.

During 1986 the garment industry employed 1,500 workers, twice as many as during the previous decade, which comprised 11 per cent of all manufacturing workers, although only 2 per cent of the national work force. Exports were worth nearly $5 million, only 1.6 per cent of all exports, but growth had been achieved rapidly. Nonetheless, the garment sector remained difficult for the government to promote, particularly in the run-up to an election. It generated controversy because of its poor conditions of employment. Wages, at an average of 74 cents an hour, were half those in other manufacturing industries.[66] Employers warned that higher wages would cripple the industry before it could expand. The government agreed. It twice lowered the minimum wage for garment workers. During the 1987 election campaign, Labour had alleged that garment manufacturers made donations to the Alliance Party to secure the enforcement of these lower-than-minimum wages.[67] The post-coup government, desperate to make a difference, promoted the industry with much greater vigour.

Since TFZs were costly to introduce and could not be established quickly, the government permitted individual workshops to be declared tax-free factories (TFFs). Workshops that exported 95 per cent of their production (later reduced to 70 per cent) received 13-year exemptions from company tax, as well as duty-free entry of raw materials and equipment. The results were impressive. By early 1991, 104 TFFs employed 9,327 persons (10 per cent of total paid employment), 78 per cent being in garment

65   P Cawthorne, 'Fiji's garment export industry: An economic and political analysis of its long term viability', Faculty of Economics & Business Working Paper, University of Sydney, 2000, p. 4.
66   C Slatter, 'Women factory workers in Fiji: The "half a loaf syndrome"', *Journal of Pacific Studies*, 13, 1987, pp. 55–56; W Narsey, 'What's the plight of women garment workers', *Fiji Sun*, 10 November 1985.
67   *Fiji Times*, 27 March 1987.

and footwear factories, the remainder in food and related industries. Garments alone earned $130 million in 1991 and, at 20 per cent of exports, became the second highest earner of foreign exchange after sugar, representing over 7 per cent of GDP. Little wonder Naisoro described the rate of change as 'breathless':

> Now people are thinking of takeoff again. But the really important ingredient is devaluation plus the fact that we don't have a democratic government ... Businessmen don't care about the voting structure.[68]

Devaluation, deregulation, privatisation and foreign investment quickly became the catchwords of the post-coup regime. According to the new Minister for Finance, former Native Land Trust Board (NLTB)-technocrat Josevata Kamikamica, Fiji had become too reliant on state-oriented development. The coups permitted Fiji to 'sever the apron strings which tied us to inherited colonial characteristics'.[69] By means of the corporatisation of selected government enterprises (pine, fisheries, shipping, shipyards, post and telecommunications), the abolition of import licensing, tariff and excise reductions, and the expansion in TFFs, Kamikamica hoped to transform Fiji into a new entrepôt, the South Pacific's version of Singapore, South Korea and Taiwan.

Such hope was never based on realities. The success of East Asia's 'little tigers', in particular South Korea and Taiwan, grew out of the experiences of war. They suffered unprecedented destruction, including that of their traditional leadership structures. This opened the way for stronger states, reformed bureaucracies, and for change that was fuelled in large part by massive Cold War military expenditures and aid that continued for more than two decades. In their wake came Japanese investment. Thus South Korea and Taiwan were able to sustain growth rates of 10 to 12 per cent during the 1960s and 1970s and, by the 1980s, begin investing their surpluses into the regional economies of East Asia. Much of the wealth generated also came to be reinvested back into communities, resulting in growth with equity, sustained over several decades and boosting the capacity of East Asia's economies to plan and develop.[70] Growth with equity is democratisation. It channels resources into infrastructure, education and health. It enables greater popular participation in economic growth, and it raises the quality of life for its

68   *Islands Business*, February 1989.
69   *Fiji Times*, 3 June 1989.
70   R Stubbs, *Rethinking Asia's Economic Miracle*. London: Palgrave Macmillan, 2005.

citizens. This democratisation began to spill over into the political sphere by the end of the 1980s, perhaps demonstrating economist Amartya Sen's claim that democratisation represented the most important universal commitment of the 20th century, the only way to widen circles of social capital, bridge divides, and develop modern societies.[71]

Nothing similar happened in Fiji. The 'Fijian revolution' by 'New Fijians'[72] did not place Fiji on such a trajectory. It did not mark a fundamental break with colonial or postcolonial characteristics. Despite all the hype of heralding a new era of prosperity, TFFs offered labour little more than poor wages under less-than-perfect working conditions. The government refused to pressure employers to provide greater national benefits from its hastily prepared scheme. Since no local value-added preconditions were stipulated and little in the way of local raw materials utilised, much-needed linkages back into economy were never developed. No textile industry emerged to stimulate growth, as happened in Mauritius. Certainly it provided many women, the bulk of the workforce, an alternative to domestic employment, but its poor remuneration ensured that few benefits spilt over into the community beyond the injection of subsistence wages. While the government created a special training school to up-skill garment workers, it gave insufficient funds for it to be effective. Consequently many employers simply imported skilled Asian labour instead, which came, at one time, to comprise over 10 per cent of the garment labour force.

Accordingly, TFF success needs to be highly qualified. It managed to continue expanding for most of the 1990s, using temporary access to US and European markets to reduce its overwhelming dependence on Australasia. By 2000, garment exports had risen to $333 million, an astonishing 33 per cent of exports and nearly 12 per cent of GDP. The industry employed close to 20,000 employees. But Fiji possessed none of the aid or market access advantages that proved so important for East Asian growth. Neither was it as galvanised by external threat and domestic transformation. TFFs were highly market vulnerable. Access depended on preferential agreements that were constantly revised as countries like Australia and New Zealand ended import licensing and reduced tariffs

---

71   A Sen, *Development as Freedom*. Oxford University Press, 1999.
72   *Islands Business*, February 1989.

while seeking ways to soften the blow for its own manufacturers.[73] As tariffs fell, so did Fiji's cost advantage against cheaper and more competitive Asian countries. Its factories were comparatively small and lacked the scale economies of its competitors. Its less productive labour force remained largely unskilled and, as a consequence, poorly paid. Thus Fiji neglected the very base required for moving into better paying, high-end niche markets based on design and brand, and – as we shall see later – neglected opportunities to exploit the international linkages tourism brought, as Fiji Water did so successfully after 1997. The garment industry never became anything more than an export industry designed to soak up surplus labour.

Part of the problem also lay in the nature of investment within the industry. In 1999, Pamela Cawthorne found that 64 per cent of 110 garment factories were partially or wholly foreign owned.[74] Of them, 21 per cent were owned by Asian companies that came to Fiji simply to get around American quota restrictions on their own countries. They were highly mobile minimalist operators, often bringing their own labour with them, and demonstrated little interest in diversification or establishing linkages with the rest of the economy. Australian and New Zealand producers made up 34 per cent of foreign ownership, and set up in Fiji also only as long as trade preferences made it worthwhile. The majority of foreign producers brought no sophisticated technology with them. If anything, SPARTECA discouraged such investment, first because its 50 per cent rule of origin forced manufacturers to source capital goods and raw materials from Australasia rather than from cheaper Asian suppliers and, second, because its 50 per cent local content rule could only be met by maximising labour costs. It made no sense to become more technologically efficient. Thus the very scheme designed to assist Pacific countries to grow manufacturing capacity conspired to frustrate its development within the Fiji economy. It never escaped its dependency on trade preferences and, to Cawthorne, bore all the hallmarks of maquiladora industries along the US–Mexican border. Without investment in new technology, productivity remained low, wages failed to rise, living standards stagnated or declined, and

---

73   Thus, SPARTECA could be seen as a strategy more for the benefit of Australasian manufacturers than for Pacific producers. In this respect, SPARTECA is similar to the EU Lomé Convention's Sugar Protocol, created in 1975 to ensure a steady supply of sugar to Tate & Lyle's refineries in Britain (R Grynberg, 'The WTO incompatibility of the Lomé Convention trade provisions', Working Paper 98/3. Canberra: Asia Pacific Press, 1998, p. 13).

74   Cawthorne, 'Fiji's garment export industry', 2000, pp. 5–14; this section draws heavily on Cawthorne's analysis.

a rejuvenated manufacturing sector within Fiji failed to burn brightly. With changes to SPARTECA and an end to quota access into the United States early in the next century, the garment flame dimmed.

TFFs may have replaced the postcolonial emphasis on import substitution but, as enclaves within the domestic economy, they shared features all too similar with colonial strategies. Both sheltered and protected industries linked with export demand and both frustrated value-adding capabilities and industrial sophistication. With an education system reeling from cutbacks and with a growth strategy intent on denying skills and creativity, Fiji seemed stubbornly intent on excluding long-term growth factors such as human capital. In addition, labour-intensive industrialisation failed to promote capital-intensive growth. Not surprisingly, Fiji's leaders divided on the value of TFFs. Apisai Tora reportedly bragged to an Australian businessman at the start of the strategy, 'This place is ripe for carpetbaggers. You had better get your guys over here if you want a slice of the action'.[75] Some members of the Fijian elite did invest in garment factories, but others were less enthusiastic. Rabuka worried about its political consequences. 'Who needs overseas investors?' he quipped in 1993.[76] Foreign investment of this kind invariably meant greater urbanisation and expanding working classes. These classes were less trusted after the 1987 elections. They and the capitalism they drew strength from created loyalties and aspirations that did not coincide with those of traditionalists. 'The political logic,' economist Roman Grynberg wrote, 'is that a nation of barmen and chambermaids is to be preferred over that of factory workers.'[77]

Something of the same logic applied also to new economic strategies for Fijians although, in the post-coup atmosphere, they were never so described. Fijian development strategies had been largely passive, replicating existing lines of authority, and using communal activities to raise funds invested in provincial companies controlled by chiefs. Sociologist Steven Ratuva has described this as communal capitalism, and it drained rural communities of valuable resources for which there were no returns at the community level. The beneficiaries were chiefs and the bureaucrats who staffed Fijian institutions.[78] One might have thought that, after 1987, this disconnect

75   SL Malcomson, *Tuturani: A Political Journey in the Pacific Islands*. New York: Poseidon Press, 1990, p. 129.
76   *Fiji Times*, 3 June 1993.
77   *Fiji Times*, 27 August 1994.
78   Ratuva, 'Addressing inequality?', 2000, pp. 230–31, 245.

with communities would have been better appreciated. It was not, with the result that the only change after 1987 lay in the intensification of a strategy already found wanting.

Ordinary Fijians might have expected more. After all, the coups had been launched in their name, and perceived socio-economic disparities were always high on the list of official justifications. Indeed, the post-coup regimes did seek to create the impression that they were now addressing disadvantage with both urgency and determination. Affirmative action became the new mantra and, in 1988, a Fijian Initiative Group comprised of senior Fijian technocrats (including the head of the Fiji Development Bank (FDB) and future prime minister, Laisenia Qarase) released a nine-point plan for advancing Fijian economic development. But, instead of addressing disadvantage directly, the plan proposed revitalising communal capitalism and its associated Fijian bourgeoisie. It proposed loaning $20 million to Fijian Holdings Company Ltd (FHL), an investment company begun in 1984 to invest provincial and Fijian institutional funds into established companies such as Basic Industries (a cement manufacturer), Carlton Brewery, and Burns Philp. The plan also proposed a unit trust and a compulsory savings scheme for Fijians. It called for enhanced government concessions to Fijian businesses (21 years tax free), minimum levels of Fijian ownership in resource-based industries and Fijian ownership of a daily newspaper. It requested administrative reform and innovation within the Fijian Affairs Board (FAB), which was responsible to the GCC for the performance of the Ministry of Fijian Affairs.[79] Aside from the establishment of a Unit Trust, a management advisory service within the FAB, and government ownership of the *Daily Post* newspaper, the most dramatic outcome of the nine-point plan concerned FHL.

From the FAB, FHL received $20 million of government funds as an interest-free loan, enabling it to massively increase its investments in Fiji-based companies such as the Merchant Bank of Fiji, the Denarau tourist project outside Nadi, Fiji Sugar Corporation, Motibhai (a duty-free retailer), Goodman Fielder Watties (food producers principally involved with chicken production), and the Suva Stock Exchange. Total assets increased from around $5 million in 1987 to over $36 million in 1994, by which time the company paid dividends of up to 20 per cent from

---

79   Fijian Initiative Group, *Nine Points Plan*. Suva, 1988.

annual profits of $3 million. As Ratuva argues, FHL performed well by any stretch of the imagination but, at the end of 1991, it became a private company with the ability to manage funds from private Fijian investors.[80]

That change was not publicised until allegations were made in 1993 that some 26 well-placed bureaucrats and their business associates possessed more shares than institutional investors. Some of those shares had been purchased with government-subsidised loans from the FDB. Accusations of insider trading flew furiously,[81] perhaps unfairly, but the contrast between private and institutional beneficiaries was unavoidable. Of course, unlike private investors, Fijians who contributed to provincial investments did not benefit directly from institutional investments. Most earnings went to pay for provincial bureaucracies. Ratuva notes:

> The change in status of the [FHL] was primarily a result of lobbying by the ethnic Fijian elite who dominate its private company share ownership, and who want greater control over their investment and the dividends it paid. Moreover, this emerging ethnic Fijian bourgeois class had found a new ally: with the foreign and local non ethnic Fijian bourgeoisie in whose companies the [FHL] had purchased equity. Thus, the new ethnic Fijian bourgeoisie has been able to use affirmative action policies in order to promote its own interests through state subsidised capital accumulation.[82]

Success outside the FHL was harder to gauge. Smaller investment companies like the Suva-based Gaunavou Investments tried with less success and capital to emulate the FHL. The FDB began a soft-loan scheme for Fijians in 1989 that, over the next four years, increased funds available to Fijians by over 300 per cent. Unfortunately, Fijians were often encouraged to invest in areas where competition from established companies was stiffest. A classic example was the FDB's attempt to organise small-scale Fijian retail activity through its Equity Investment and Management Company Limited or EIMCOL, which established nine small supermarkets after

---

80   Ratuva, 'Addressing inequality?', 2000, pp. 240–41. By 2017 the FHL Group held assets worth $492 million, its pre-tax profits stood at $19.4 million, and it returned 0.35 cents per share to its investors. Its star performers were Basic Industries, Pacific Cement and the RB Patel Group (*Fiji Times*, 1 February 2017).
81   *Fiji Times*, 19 May 1993; 22 May 1993.
82   Ratuva, 'Addressing inequality?', 2000, p. 246.

1989. All had collapsed by the end of 1993, due in large part to poor location (often close to established supermarkets), inadequate feasibility studies and inappropriate management training.[83]

Investment in taxis produced a similar outcome. Most prime taxi sites were already allocated, leaving only the less profitable outer urban sites available for Fijian operators. The government attempted to get around these difficulties by denying new permits to IndoFijians, but even this could not prevent unacceptably high arrears on loan repayments. In 1995, funding for taxis ended. At the small business level, where institutional support might have helped most, affirmative action failed Fijians. This complaint had been common before 1987; even Rabuka had argued in 1988 that the FDB only helped well-off people.[84]

The problem with the nine-point plan lay not in its ambition to extend Fijian participation in business but that it was presented as something that would benefit all Fijians when, clearly, it could not. Part of the problem lay with government's refusal to debate policy. Provincial councils never publically complained when government decisions impacted on their businesses or on large employers in their districts as, for example, when Air Pacific shifted its head office from Suva to Nadi or when the government deregulated the dairy industry, cut beef tariffs, and granted licenses for imported chickens. Wadan Narsey lamented a public culture of silence.[85] Few government ministers appreciated that, if the culture of silence extended also to institutions defending Fijian rights, there was little chance of popular decision-making or accountability in development.

Reliance on modern bureaucratic versions of the Fijian *vanua* as solutions proved equally as deceptive as the nine-point plan. Rabuka believed bureaucracies would lay 'the golden egg' for Fijians but, instead, they seemed only to promote dependence and empty shells. Rabuka attempted to create his own 'golden egg' in late 1987 by making the Army Auxiliary Unit a supplier of essential commodities and a monopoly marketing agent for producers in the outer islands. He seized four Marine Department and two Fisheries vessels (the latter donated by Japan) for the purpose. He claimed that Fijians could not compete without such infrastructure. But the unit did nothing to alter the pattern of trade for outer islanders.

---

83   *Fiji Times*, 13 November 1992.
84   *Fiji Times*, 25 November 1988.
85   *Fiji Times*, 6 May 1997; 24 December 1996.

Khaki capitalism effectively only substituted one group of traders for another and, in the process, restricted local initiative further. The unit's agricultural activities had a similar effect, undercutting the value of goods produced by villagers for sale in urban markets. Eventually this thinly veiled attempt to develop an independent economic base for the military collapsed under the weight of corruption and incompetence, having achieved little for the people it championed.[86] Rabuka went back to raiding government coffers instead.

The NLTB, perhaps the most important Fijian institution, encapsulated the bureaucratic mentality after 1987 as much as it had before. It centralised control of all Fijian land and, for the privilege, the 250-strong bureaucracy earned 25 per cent of all rentals (reduced to 15 per cent in 2001), 10 per cent of royalties, as well as regular contributions from government towards a wages bill it never seemed able to constrain. Additionally, it found managing its vast estate (30,000 leases on 42,000 hectares for 16,000 *mataqali*) and transaction records difficult. It failed to publish annual reports for most of the 1990s, and eventually conceded in 1998 that, with accumulated losses of $4.3 million, it was close to bankruptcy.[87]

Part of the NLTB's problem was the near divine status that many Fijian leaders bestowed on the goose. 'To abolish the NLTB,' declared its former manager Jo Kamikamica, 'would mean the demise of Fijian society and the basic stability we enjoy today.'[88] Yet many *mataqali* members were dissatisfied with the service they received, in large part due to their inability to mobilise rental proceeds for development purposes. The shares that chiefs received were sometimes utilised for *mataqali* and village development, but often they also became the basis for clashes between *mataqali* over claims to highly lucrative chiefly titles.

Land as a resource bears some similarities with natural resources in terms of its impact on communities. *Mataqali* members were not the only ones who regarded it as their golden egg; increasingly the guardian NLTB leased land or approved logging without consulting land owners. Members of *mataqali* in the catchment area of the Monasavu dam spent

---

86   Robertson, *Multiculturalism & Reconciliation*, 1998, p. 161. Its Commander, Esala Teleni, would figure prominently again after 2006. See Schumpeter, 'Khaki capitalism' (*Economist*, 3 December 2011) for an analysis of similar military activities globally.
87   Robertson, *Multiculturalism & Reconciliation*, 1998, p. 165.
88   *Fiji Times*, 17 June 1992.

years seeking compensation for the loss of their land and its resources, and eventually resorted to blocking access to the power station in 1998 to get the government to begin negotiations. This was old Colo, the 'bush constituency' that Rabuka reportedly considered too demeaning to visit during a by-election the previous year.[89] Its anger would be felt in future years but, for many Fijians, such outcomes epitomised the downside of bureaucratic development. It transferred few skills, it removed responsibility and often all knowledge of development, and it denied people direct access to resources or involvement with their investments. Above all it prevented local initiative and produced powerlessness.

Some Fijians sought consolation in religion. By the mid-1990s, 15 per cent of Fijians belonged to Pentecostal religions and cults such as the New Life Centre, the Assemblies of God, the Christian Mission Fellowship and the Apostles Gospel Outreach Fellowship International. At Kalabu, the Kelekeletabua cult collected $25 and a *tabua* from members and promised them six containers of cash in return. In Ba, the one-time rebels of the 1960s, the Bula Tale or Dra ni Lami, maintained a commune of 300 people dedicated to peace, non-violence and non-competition, and survived by operating small businesses in the west. Other groups like the Spiritual Congregation of the Poor and the Fiji in Every Home movement sought to reconcile people to their poverty.[90]

Frustration also encouraged the ideological quick fix that was promised by ethno-nationalists. Scapegoating IndoFijians received new impetus during the late 1990s as nearly 3,300 of some 11,000 30-year sugar cane leases negotiated under the *Agricultural Landlord and Tenant Act (ALTA)* in 1977 came up for renewal. It provided an ideal opportunity for the NLTB to direct attention away from itself by claiming that Fijians would receive more satisfactory returns if IndoFijian farmers paid higher rents on shorter leases. Rents normally comprised up to 6 per cent of the unimproved capital value of the land, but the actual amount varied according to the quality of the land in question. A review in 2001 quoted rents at $54 per hectare for marginal land and $480 per hectare for class I land. This equated to an average 3.4 per cent of the gross value of production, which the NLTB claimed was inadequate and far below

89   *Review*, July 1997.
90   Robertson, *Multiculturalism & Reconciliation*, 1998, p. 166; *Sangharsh* (Suva), October 1995; *Fiji Times*, 5 March 1996; *Daily Post*, 5 June 1993.

international norms.[91] To drive home the point, it advocated that leases not be renewed, hoping to force government to introduce new legislation in its favour. In 2000, it introduced a fee for considering new leases, and encouraged landowners to charge goodwill for new leases equivalent to one year's rent,[92] perhaps as a way of increasing *mataqali* returns without impacting on its own income. Journalist Jo Nata argued in 1997 that the goodwill of Fijians had not been recognised in the past and that the time had come to share as much as 50 per cent of farmer income with landowners.[93]

At some point reality had to sink in. Rents were low because much of the land farmed was of low quality, but rents still represented an average 45 per cent of net returns. On high quality land, rents comprised 23 to 27 per cent of net returns. Furthermore, once goodwill payments were accounted for, the real average rent was more like 10 to 14 per cent of the gross value of production, a proportion similar to that in Europe, South Africa, and Australia,[94] although not the high 60 per cent in parts of India that was sometimes quoted approvingly by critics who conveniently overlooked its impact on Indian productivity and farmer welfare. But, then again, feudalism might have been precisely the intent.

Vitogo villagers near Lautoka rented out 400 hectares for $30,000 but they believed that the land earned $540,000 and in 1997 decided that the time had come to engage in farming themselves.[95] The desire to become commercial farmers or to extend communal gardens to accommodate village populations undoubtedly impacted on decisions not to renew leases. Between 1997 and 1999 only 26 per cent of leases were actually renewed to sitting tenants. But the realities of farming were often forgotten in the heat of debate. Economists Padma Lal and Mahendra Reddy demonstrated that the average net return to sugar cane farmers in 2001 was $842 per hectare, in total $3,500 per annum, below Fiji's then average $3,889 per capita income.[96] However, economics did not decide the issue.

---

91   P Lal, H Lim-Applegate & M Reddy, 'Fijian landowners and IndoFijian tenants have their cake and eat it too', *Pacific Economic Bulletin*, 16: 1, November 2001, pp. 109–10.
92   P Lal & M Reddy, 'Old wine in a new bottle: Proposed sugar industry restructuring and land conflict in Fiji', *Pacific Economic Bulletin*, 18: 1, May 2003, pp. 82–85.
93   *Fiji Times*, 28 January 1997.
94   Lal, Lim-Applegate & Reddy, 'Fijian landowners and IndoFijian tenants', 2001, pp. 111, 114.
95   *Fiji Times*, 20 January 1996.
96   Lal & Reddy, 'Old wine in a new bottle', 2003, p. 85.

Back in 1997 the general consensus had politics driving decision-making. There were suggestions that chiefs, not commoners, were 'instigating the non-renewal of leases' in order to take the opportunity to regain control over land.[97] Mara had equated land ownership with economic power in 1991 and suggested that only the flexing of economic muscle would sustain political power.[98] Similarly, the then Minister for Primary Industries, Koresi Matatolu, argued in 1993 that 'to ignore the relationship between tenancy and political power would be to misunderstand the 1987 Fiji coup'. He wanted Fijians to take over the sugar industry completely by 2000.[99]

The NLTB drove responses to these pressures after 1987 and created a special taskforce to examine leases under Marika Qarikau, who would later become its general manager. In 1996, he declared that sugar cane farmers should be prepared to lose their leases, but no government before 1999 seriously considered what to do with farmers who lost their livelihoods, or what might happen to the land no longer leased to farmers. The NLTB thought farms should be restructured for Fijians and the industry mechanised to enable large-scale farming, but believed no decision was yet needed since most leases did not expire until the next century.[100] Forward planning was not the NLTB's strength. It did not seem to consider that rents should be used effectively to provide capital for rural Fijians to launch themselves into new commercial activities. Nor did it think the expertise of existing tenants might assist the industry in the future. Instead it envisaged another bureaucracy to train landowners and plan large-scale cane farming. In any case, an indecisive government provided little assistance. Although prepared to let individual *mataqali* decide future land use, it left them tied to the demands of the NLTB.

Such uncertainty had tremendous consequences for the sugar industry. Listening to the comments of Fijian politicians and bureaucrats, you could easily be excused for not appreciating that this was an industry that in 1989 comprised 35 per cent of all merchandise exports by value, contributed 12 per cent of GDP, employed over 23,000 cane growers, directly impacted on the livelihood of at least a quarter of the population, and – because most inputs into the industry were domestic – possessed

97   *Fiji Times*, 3 & 6 March 1997.
98   *Pacific Islands Monthly*, December 1991.
99   *Fiji Times*, 15 May 1993; *Review*, November 1994.
100   *Fiji Times*, 20 January 1996; 26 February 1997.

a multiplier effect greater than most other sectors. Despite fluctuating world prices, the higher EU prices for fixed quotas (often 2.5 times world prices for half Fiji's production or 200,000 tonnes of sugar, the equivalent of 5 per cent of GDP) provided the Fiji economy a degree of certainty that it would otherwise have lacked.

Certainly high sugar prices following the coups enabled its economy to bounce back much faster than expected, not that this was always appreciated. Former senator and Taukeist Jona Qio argued in 1987 that any collapse in the sugar industry would affect only IndoFijians; Fijians could always survive in their villages.[101] This was surely prejudice masquerading as economic analysis. After all, many Fijians were deeply involved in the industry, even as farmers. In short the health of the industry affected everyone, directly or indirectly. But such ignorance proved powerful nonetheless. It reinforced ethnic separation and it drove neglect of an industry that would in any case have faced tremendous challenges, not least because a limited waiver of World Trade Organization (WTO) rules for Lomé preferences in the mid-1990s made the future of its European market extremely uncertain. Being predominantly labour-based, a condition perpetuated in order to maximise employment, the sugar industry lacked the efficiencies of mechanised farming. Most farms were small, on average devoting only 4.2 hectares each for cane-growing, of which some 75 per cent was planted with more labour-effective but less productive ratoon crops.[102] Low farmer morale compounded these structural problems. With leases unlikely to be renewed, farmers invested less in their land, further reducing productivity. Low investment impacted on other sections of the industry also. Rail linkages and milling facilities deteriorated. Milling delays added further to declining sugar quality. Drought during 1997 and 1998 reduced output. This was an industry now in serious decline.[103] By the end of the decade its contribution to GDP had fallen to 7 per cent, its share of exports to 22 per cent.

---

101 *Fiji Sun*, 19 July 1987.
102 Lal, Lim-Applegate & Reddy, 'Fijian landowners and IndoFijian tenants', 2001, pp. 107–08.
103 Cane sugar content fell 50 per cent during 1970–95 due to cane-burning prior to harvesting, and transportation and milling deficiencies. Ageing mills required greater capital outlay than the industry could afford. A Catch-22 situation existed: in 1997, for example, 62 per cent of cane was deliberately burnt as growers sought priority for milling after a cyclone ravaged the crop. Sugar production subsequently fell 24 per cent and cost the industry $40 million in lost earnings. Investment in mills, rural road and rail networks, and in farming practices declined (*Review*, June 1998).

Much the same circumstances faced agriculture in general with its share of GDP falling 6 per cent to 16 per cent between 1988 and 2000, despite being the country's main source of employment. Nearly 6.5 per cent of GDP came from subsistence agriculture, which, agricultural economists Paul Barbour and Andrew McGregor argued, was a hidden strength, helping to keep food imports down.[104] Its proportion of agriculture grew from 30 per cent to 40 per cent during this period, reflecting also the difficulties facing most commercial sectors of agriculture. Deregulation clearly impacted on rice, tobacco and meat production, but it also forced producers to take more responsibility for what they produced and how they produced it, if they wished to meet the increasingly exacting standards of importing countries. This was particularly the case for horticultural export crops such as ginger, taro, kava and papaya, which grew rapidly after 1987. Perhaps in recognition of this potential, the government partially reversed deregulation in 1997 with the introduction of a commodity development framework to increase capital expenditure for agriculture over a four-year period, support failing businesses such as Yaqara Beef, upgrade services and research, and subsidise inputs such as seeds, fertilisers and tools. Unfortunately, it also proved an attractive way to buy votes.

Like sugar cane, agriculture suffered from uncertainty over leases and farm sizes that made efficiencies difficult to achieve. Barbour and McGregor noted that 60 per cent of farms occupied only 7 per cent of farm land and were usually no bigger than three hectares. Fifty per cent were *mataqali* owned. Just 2 per cent of farms occupied 40 per cent of farm land. Many of these farms also suffered from land degradation due to overgrazing, steep slopes and excessive use of chemicals. Agriculture also suffered from underinvestment. Lending to agriculture declined from 19 per cent of loans in 1989 to 12 per cent in 1996. Despite tax concessions being offered in 1996 for food exporters, few farmers took advantage of them. They faced disincentives: a third currency devaluation in 1997 pushed up input costs (especially for animal feed), high interest rates discouraged lending, and the longstanding poor state of rural education and entrepreneurial skills depressed opportunities further.[105]

---

104 Barbour & McGregor, 'The Fiji agricultural sector', 1998, pp. 65–66. This section derives from their analysis.
105 Barbour & McGregor, 'The Fiji agricultural sector', 1998, pp. 73–78.

Agriculture and manufacturing showed no sign of the dynamism that coup-makers promised after 1987. No new trajectory emerged to boost Fiji's economic wellbeing or to transform the lives of the very people leaders claimed were disadvantaged. Even where opportunities existed to redress past unequal arrangements, they were neglected or sabotaged. In late 1987, the military government secretly supported lower gold royalties for the Vatukoula mine, thereby surrendering much-needed income.[106] Although Fiji's economy appeared to rebound strongly in 1989 with 12 per cent growth, largely on the back of strong sugar production, it never achieved high growth in subsequent years. With poorer sugar production and declining world prices, GDP growth managed 5 per cent in 1990; in 1991 only 0.4 per cent. New investments in manufacturing slowed. Only tourism expanded, with arrivals increasing from 258,000 in 1986 to 287,000 by 1993, mostly from Australia, the United States and New Zealand, but also from Europe, Japan and Korea. This expansion continued throughout the 1990s, reaching 410,000 arrivals during 1999. Accordingly, its share of export receipts – only 25 per cent in 1980 – rose to 30 per cent in 1990 and to 38 per cent in 2001. Its share of GDP followed a similar trajectory, rising from 11 per cent in 1980 to 20 per cent in 1990 and to 25 per cent by 2001.[107]

In many respects tourism remained the sole bright spot in the economy, absorbing some 40,000 employees, nearly 12 per cent of the labour market. Maintaining market share, however, was not easy in a highly competitive and volatile market, and seesawing occupancy rates tended to discourage much-needed new investment. Only in the late 1990s did significant investment begin, particularly in large-scale integrated resorts such as Denarau, west of Nadi, although Fiji continued to attract a growing number of five-star resorts for holiday-makers willing to pay for luxurious exclusion. As we will examine later, however, in terms of tourism's multiplier impact on the economy, its notorious leakage rate (approximately 60 per cent) – which no post-coup government seemed willing or able to address – significantly reduced its overall economic value compared with sugar. Garment manufacturing was similarly inflicted.

---

106 Gold royalties were limited to 2.5 per cent of adjusted chargeable income rather than 5 per cent of actual gold value. This meant, for example, that in 1993 Fiji received only $1.7 million in royalties instead of $23 million (*Fiji Times*, 30 October 1996).
107 PK Narayan, 'A tourism demand model for Fiji. 1970–2000', *Pacific Economic Bulletin*, 17: 2, November 2002, pp. 103–04.

Partly because of these difficulties, post-coup governments pushed ahead with more liberal economic policies than their predecessors, deregulating previously protected industries and reducing tariffs by as much as one third by 1995. But strange echoes from the past haunted Fiji's 'new trajectory'. During 1991 Mara drew up plans for a state-owned oil importing company, a Fiji National Petroleum Company, which would purchase crude oil directly from Malaysia, rather than through Australian oil subsidiaries, and refine it in Singapore. The plan reflected Mara's growing hostility towards Australia since 1987: 'The Australians and New Zealanders … prefer not to understand our minds' unlike Asians, he argued.[108] He wished to 'better control [Fiji's] principal source of energy and also provide potential for further development'.[109] Critics thought one source might not in fact be better than an existing three in terms of security of supply or cost. But Mara seemed determined to return to the state monopoly days of the 1970s and to create in the energy sector a national monopoly similar to that established for the sugar industry. That it could become yet another golden egg for the state (or whoever controlled the state) to harvest certainly worried Pacific leaders whose countries imported their oil from Fiji.

Tax reform did make it through the political morass, in particular a value added tax (VAT) of 10 per cent introduced in mid-1992, but proved impotent to rescue Fiji's economy. Fiji needed investment, but funds for investment were in short supply. In the late 1970s, Fiji invested the equivalent of one quarter of its GDP, over half of which represented private investment, enabling real GDP growth rates over 5 per cent per annum. Following the coups in 1987, investment fell considerably, comprising only 11.4 per cent of GDP during 1996–99, of which only 38 per cent came from private sources. Savings similarly fell from 27 per cent of GDP

---

108 *Fiji Times*, 4 December 1991.
109 K Mara, *The Pacific Way: A Memoir*. Honolulu: University of Hawai'i Press, 1997, pp. 222–23. He wrote: 'The oil oligopoly's contribution to, or involvement in, the Fiji economy, outside its own immediate infrastructure, is virtually non-existent. There is not a single blending plant, or even a joint move by the oil companies to establish an oil refinery here. It appeared that whatever profits had been made over the years have been regularly repatriated out of the country. Developing countries, when moving into manufacturing and industry to complement their agriculture, find that control of their energy sector becomes more and more crucial in determining the direction and pace of economic advancement.' The scheme, although never implemented, cost Fiji taxpayers some $12 million.

in 1980 to 10 per cent in 1999. GDP growth rates slumped accordingly, growing only 0.2 per cent on average between 1986–90, 0.8 per cent 1991–95, and 1.5 per cent 1996–2000.[110]

It was a miserable result for the new trajectory Fiji's post-coup mandarins had declared would transform Fiji; instead a rapid increase in poverty became one of its early consequences. In 1977, 15 per cent of Fiji's population lived in poverty, with rural people recording the highest proportion (21.4 per cent). By 1991 the national poverty rate had nearly doubled to 29 per cent; by 1997 it had climbed further to 34 per cent. In that year, rural households again fared worse at 42 per cent (IndoFijians 47 per cent, Fijians 39 per cent) compared with 24 per cent for urban households (IndoFijians 26 per cent, Fijians 23 per cent).[111]

Fiji's economy failed to grow and poverty escalated. What caused this outcome? Certainly Fiji's economy remained externally dependent as before, although its sources of dependence were more diversified than before, and the potential remained to grow more value-added forms of production. Fiji's relatively high levels of education, its use of English as a working language, and its central position in the Pacific served to reinforce these potentials. Yet this did not happen. Mauritius, whose per-capita GDP had been slightly less than Fiji's in 1980, had more than doubled its per-capita GDP 20 years later; Fiji's increased by only 11 per cent.[112] Only two factors accounted for this difference – political instability and the corruption it generated. For this, the coups were almost entirely to blame.

---

110   Prasad & Kumar, 'Fiji's economic woes', 2002, pp. 2, 13; W. Narsey, 'The struggle for just wages in Fiji: Lessons from the 2009 wages councils and the continuing coups', the Rev. Paula Niukula Lecture, University of the South Pacific, 15 April 2009, p. 8.

111   BC Prasad & J Asafu-Adjay, 'Macroeconomic policy & poverty in Fiji', *Pacific Economic Bulletin*, 13: 1, May 1998, pp. 50–51; W Narsey, 'Truth behind our poverty', *Fiji Times*, 10 June 2007; W Narsey, 'Incidence of poverty & the poverty gap in Fiji: Unpalatable facts for ethnocentric parties', *Pacific Economic Bulletin*, 23: 2, November 2008, p. 72. Narsey argues that the proportion of the population in poverty could have been as high as 36 per cent by 1991 and that rates declined marginally in subsequent years.

112   Narsey, 'The Struggle for Just Wages in Fiji', 2009, p. 9. Fiji's real per capita GDP stood at US$1,800 in 1980, that of Mauritius US$1,600; by 2000 Fiji's was US$2,000 compared with Mauritius's US$3,800.

Political instability

Mara's restoration as prime minister at the end of 1987 did not restore the status quo ante, nor did it bring stability. This part of Fiji's history is largely forgotten today, overshadowed by more recent events. Undoubtedly Fiji's culture of silence has also meant that these events are effectively lost to those born since 1987, nearly half Fiji's population today. For them, Rabuka is the ageing former politician who for most of the past decade has stood outside of the political system; impotent, discredited and given to repeating shallow apologies. But, in 1987 and in subsequent years, he represented something very different, as Ganilau's then permanent secretary Peter Thomson recounted:

> [A] new generation of Fijian leaders … had tasted power after the first coup and no doubt saw the Deuba Accord as a scotching of their ambitions; it was in the fever of millenarianism that they stood the best chance of advancing their careers. This younger generation had now sat around the same executive tables as the Fijian leaders whom they had previously held in awe, and saw that they could foot it with them. A changing of the guard was underway.[113]

Of course, Rabuka represented a lot more than just a younger generation; he represented the insertion of a new actor into the political scene – the military. Often during this period, there were similarities with his later status – the reflective outsider looking in – but the big difference after 1987 lay in his belief that he was now the ultimate king-maker. This belief both shaped and shook Fiji politics for five long years and delivered prolonged instability. It ended only when he decided to assume the crown himself.

Mara's so-called 'interim' regime faced instability from the start. This derived from both the military and remnants of the Taukei Movement. Little over a month after assuming office, Mara faced his first test. Three Taukeists seized Radio Fiji on 22 January 1988 in expectation that the military would help them drive out the Tovata leaders (Mara and Ganilau) and install Bauans instead. Rabuka – a subject of Tovata – not surprisingly declined the invitation but, in February, his officers were again approached by Taukeists unhappy with his decision to return power to Mara. Rabuka, now brigadier general, had attached conditions to his handover, the most

---

113 Thomson, *Kava in the Blood*, 1999, p. 179.

important being the adoption of a new constitution. To that end the military had proposed a 67-seat parliament with 36 Fijian seats, reserved posts for Fijians, and continued observance of new Sunday laws. Once in office, however, Mara seemed unwilling to acknowledge these demands. Instead he announced plans to reduce the size of the GCC,[114] to make the British (and former Fiji) Queen the Tui Viti (the Kubuna title first claimed by Cakobau as part of Bau's designs on the whole of Fiji), and to review the Sunday ban. On Sunday 12 March, Rabuka's soldiers occupied Suva, ostensibly to enforce the ban but, in reality, to demonstrate displeasure at Mara's proposals. In late March, senior military officers wrote to Mara and Ganilau that they were deeply concerned at the delay in producing a new constitution. The 'two elderly gentlemen' had failed to honour their agreement at the time of the handover. 'The only factor left now between the indigenous Fijians and oblivion is the FMF [Fiji Military Forces],' they declared, calling on the chiefs to step aside and allow the military to introduce its preferred constitutional changes.[115] The Taukei Movement leaked the document to the press, forcing Rabuka to abort his behind the scenes pressure and publicly pledge full military support for the interim administration.[116]

A more potent means to influence the course of events fell into Rabuka's lap in May 1988 when Sydney customs officers discovered a container holding 12 tonnes of weapons awaiting shipment to Lautoka. The shipment had been organised by Mohammed Kahan, a Fiji-born British citizen whose contradictory and implausible explanations variously implicated the Coalition, the Taukei Movement, Mara and even Rabuka in his conspiracy. The discovery of an earlier shipment of weapons that actually reached Lautoka undetected in April allowed Rabuka to declare 'a foreign sponsored attempt to destabilise the country' and demand from the government an Internal Security Decree (ISD) with sweeping powers of search and arrest.[117] The decree ended any hopes to which Fiji's citizens might have clung that a return to civilian government would restore respect for legal process. Already since the start of 1988, critics such as Bavadra's former spokesperson Richard Naidu and lawyer John Cameron had been ordered out of the country; so had this author.

---

114 The plan was to reduce the GCC from 154 members to a more manageable 56.
115 Unsigned Military Document, OPS FMF, 30 March 1988, pp. 2, 6.
116 *Fiji Times*, 22 April 1988.
117 *Age*, 2 June 1988; *Fiji Times* editor Vijendra Kumar was regularly hosted at the Nabua barracks. For more details on this section, see Robertson, *Multiculturalism & Reconciliation*, 1998, pp. 43–70.

In Suva, protestors at the anniversary of the first coup were arrested and gassed in their cell. When newspapers highlighted police treatment of the 'Democracy 18', they were threatened with closure. In fact journalists and editors regularly found themselves 'questioned' in the early hours of the morning, as did several university academics. Literature academic Som Prakash was assaulted and tortured for 15 days for critically reviewing Rabuka's biography, published earlier that year.[118]

The ISD now permitted far worse. Raids were conducted on farms and homes in the west to search for missing weapons, often on the basis of anonymous opportunistic tip-offs. Over 40 homes in Suva were raided in August, and supermarkets were also targeted because the military assumed that 'wealthy' IndoFijians had sponsored the arms shipments. Lawyers who protested the treatment of their clients were similarly harassed. Soldiers badly beat an Australian tourist passing the Nabua barracks for acting 'suspiciously'. They detained an accountant from the Ministry of Finance who queried army expenses.

The increasing and bizarre responses of the military accompanied a new wave of attacks on IndoFijians. Temples were burnt or vandalised, homes stoned and vehicles belonging to IndoFijian unionists and former politicians attacked. Many of these attacks were organised by the Taukei Movement, which by this time had split into two factions, one supportive of the Mara government, the other keen to promote communal tensions in order to precipitate another military coup. That latter faction now imploded, literally. One of its prominent members, Jone Veisamasama, a former Alliance general secretary (ironically also a foundation member of the Labour Party), fatally shot himself, by accident, with a pen pistol, one of a number of Lebanese imports circulating among members of his faction. His death resulted in the arrest of colleagues for arms violations and a saga that would continue to resonate for more than five years, with damaging consequences for Rabuka. Vesikula, the former Taukeist spokesperson, chose this moment to renounce the Movement and join forces with his former foe, Bavadra.

While conspiracies abounded and the interim government sought to limit human rights abuses, Rabuka became increasingly frustrated. In August 1988, he attacked the government for failing to produce

---

118 S Prakash, 'Return to theatrics', in S Prasad, *Coup & Crisis: Fiji – A Year Later*. Melbourne: Arena Publications, 1988, pp. 98–104.

the much-anticipated new constitution. It was 'getting back to the old ways of taking things easy' and acting as if 'they were elected into government'. 'I don't know whether a coup is the answer,' he mused.[119] But the government had been discussing a constitution, in fact one very similar to the proposal Mara had earlier submitted to the GCC, only to see it ungraciously rejected. Additionally, in September, the government proposed putting it to a special Constitutional Inquiry and Advisory Committee (CIAC) that would also receive public representations. Undoubtedly this process would push back even further the implementation of a new constitution, but it also had immediate implications for the ISD and the military if public meetings were to be encouraged to discuss constitutional proposals.

Foreign governments clearly thought the ISD should go. Angered at Australasian criticisms, Rabuka refused to meet Australia's Foreign Minister, Gareth Evans, in October 1988 and warned that he would close Australian banks in Fiji if Canberra kept 'poking its nose in our affairs'.[120] Equally worrying to the interim government was Rabuka's attack on the FDB for failing to do enough for ordinary Fijians. Rabuka drove home his point by sending troops to occupy a chicken farm whose nationalist Fijian owner faced eviction for loan arrears to the FDB. He even visited striking workers at Tropik Woods in the west, although he offered no support. The President sought to placate Rabuka, promoting him to major general, while the cabinet decided that the time had come to confront Rabuka and relax the ISD. An angry Rabuka told his troops on 'Republic Day' that he could not afford to demobilise them until the government stabilised; to others he hinted that another coup might be forthcoming. On 17 November, the interim government finally called his bluff and suspended the ISD. In protest, Rabuka brought 300 soldiers in full combat gear to conduct 'normal security operations' around Suva's Government Buildings.

In practical terms the ISD achieved little. Few illegal weapons were collected, and those found were old and in poor condition. In all likelihood Kahan's shadowy militia was a figment of his imagination[121]

---

119   *Fiji Times*, 11 August 1988.
120   *Australian*, 12 & 18 October 1988.
121   In total, 21 people were arrested and all were either cleared by the courts or discharged after pleading guilty to possessing weapons without a licence. Kahan was arrested in London but escaped extradition because his offence was deemed to be political rather criminal and because he could not be guaranteed a fair trial in Fiji.

but the events convinced the military that, at the very least, it had to improve port security. More importantly, the ISD provided the military with an opportunity to remind the people of Fiji that they should never forget the coups of 1987. It also demonstrated that Rabuka's struggle with the interim government was far from over, although for now it seemed to have the upper hand and sensed that the time was right to pursue constitutional reform through a process of its own choosing.

The cabinet proposed a 71-member single house of parliament, with four members appointed by the Prime Minister, eight nominated by the GCC and the remainder elected from strictly communal constituencies. Its recommendation, which described Fiji as 'a sovereign democratic republic' dedicated to the teachings of Jesus Christ, went in November to the CIAC chaired by a former RFMF Commander, Col Paul Manueli. Over the next few months Manueli's committee received 588 submissions on the cabinet proposal, but the outcome was far from certain. Mara had already told his own Lau Provincial Council that if the process failed, the military would take over.[122] In May the following year, Rabuka and his chief of staff, Colonel Jioji Konrote, presented Mara and Ganilau a 44-page document recommending a military resumption of power once the interim government's two-year term ended. Konrote allegedly told the leaders, 'This is our country and we are not going to compromise nor settle for anything less than absolute political domination'.[123]

When the CIAC released its recommendations in August 1989, it had clearly departed from the cabinet's proposal. It restored a bicameral parliament, giving the House of Representatives 69 seats: 37 for Fijians (30 provincial, seven urban), 27 for IndoFijians, one for Rotumans and four for General Electors). The President would appoint a 34-member Senate (24 chiefs, one Rotuman, nine others). In March 1990, the GCC reduced the urban Fijian vote to five seats and took one seat from the western Ba province, giving the three freed-up seats to the eastern strongholds of Lau, Cakaudrove and Tailevu. In July, these amendments were promulgated without further public scrutiny, much to the consternation of the International Commission of Jurists, which slammed

---

122 *Fiji Times*, 20 October 1988.
123 *Fiji Times*, 26 September 1989.

it as 'a military constitution … as bad as the apartheid laws in South Africa' and designed to perpetuate rule by an 'oligarchy of Fiji chiefs and their associates'.[124]

It worried critics that decisions taken by the Supervisor of Elections could not be challenged in court, that a president could suspend the Constitution for up to six months and govern under emergency rules, that Fijian institutions were no longer subject to scrutiny from the ombudsman and that a simple majority of parliament could overturn the Constitution's fundamental freedoms. A Group Against Racial Discrimination (GARD), composed mostly of university staff and students, protested at Suva's Howell Road Sangam temple during Diwali on 18 October 1990 by burning copies of the Constitution. The interim government declared their action treasonous and directed the police to lay charges. But, before police could act, five soldiers from the Special Operations Security Unit abducted physicist and GARD member Dr Anirudh Singh, tortured and beat him for 11 hours, repeatedly smashing his hands with a crowbar.[125]

Elsewhere, criticisms of the proposed Constitution were surprisingly muted. Australian Prime Minister Bob Hawke declared it the best that could be hoped for at the moment,[126] sentiments that many in Fiji endorsed, no matter how reluctantly. The *Fiji Times* later editorialised that 'after the traumatic military coups of 1987, the Constitution offers one way out, a path back to parliamentary democracy'.[127] Only India protested strongly, in part also because Fiji had expelled its ambassador in October 1989 for questioning whether it was religion or Indianness that motivated temple attacks. But parliamentary democracy still seemed a long way off to many journalists, especially after Mara's attack on them as being out of control and irresponsible. His Information Minister threatened

124   Fiji Independent News Service, *Fiji Situation Report*, Sydney, 13 November 1990.
125   Ultimately, seven protestors, including Singh, were charged with sedition and unlawful assembly, but the charges were eventually dropped in December 1992. The soldiers who attacked Singh were fined and received 12-month suspended sentences. There were, however, other consequences. The soldiers' leader was forced to return from a stint as a member of a UN observer team in Kuwait in 1991 when Singh protested his involvement to the United Nations. In October 2007, the High Court awarded Singh nearly $800,000 as compensation for his ordeal. See also Singh's account in *Silent Warriors* (Suva: FIAS, 1991).
126   *Age*, 3 October 1990.
127   *Fiji Times*, 15 February 1992.

newspapers with a registration system if they did not toe the line.[128] In fact, even while the CIAC's recommendations were being considered, another coup was in the making, this time within the Methodist Church.

Rabuka had introduced the Sunday Observance Decree as means to draw Methodists to his anti-IndoFijian cause and replace the faded Taukei Movement.[129] His desire to declare Fiji a Christian state served the same goal, often expressed after 1987 as hostility to the presence of temples and mosques. On 15 October 1989, 17 members of the Lautoka Methodist Youth Fellowship, dressed in their Sunday clothes and clutching bibles, sang hymns while they firebombed mosques and temples in Lautoka.[130] Members of the cabinet visited Lautoka four days later during a day of protest to try and heal wounds, but clearly they were unprepared to tackle the religious sentiment that lay behind the attacks. After all, the coups had been bathed in religious sentiment. Rev. Tomasi Raikivi had hosted the initial Taukei Movement meeting with Rabuka prior to the first coup. The secretary of the Bible Society, the Baptist Ratu Inoke Kubuabola, acted as the go-between. Rabuka was a lay preacher who, years later, still argued that his coups were divinely ordained.[131] For these men, the Sunday Observance Decree demonstrated a difference around which Fijians could rally to protect the objectives of the coups. Thus, when the interim government relaxed the decree in May 1988 to permit farm work and picnics, Methodists protested in Suva.

But not all Methodists. The former Methodist communications secretary, Rev. Akuila Yabaki, rejected the way in which Taukeists had turned two separate issues – Fijian nationalism and the Sunday ban – into a desire for 'Fijian domination in all aspects'.[132] The Methodist President, Rev. Josateki Koroi, did all he could to prevent church resources being used to support the goals of the coups. 'The Sunday Decree is not Methodist and

---

128 *Pacific Islands Monthly*, February 1990.
129 S Tarte, 'Fiji: 1989 in review', *Contemporary Pacific*, Fall 1990, pp. 358–61. The decree remained in force until October 1995.
130 *Islands Business*, November 1989.
131 Rabuka wrote, 'for me 14 May was the only convenient day for my plan in 1987. That the day coincided with Israel's Independence Day, and the first arrival of Indian workers into Fiji – I have often wondered – whether it really was a coincidence and not divine design. I made the Declaration of our Republic at midnight on 6 October 1987 to coincide with the date of the Yom Kippur War and for Fiji to start its new journey on October 7, "7" being the number serious students of theology and God associate with our Creator' (S Rabuka, 'Divine intervention', *Fiji Times*, 26 October 2008).
132 A Dropsy, 'The church & the coup: The Fijian Methodist coup of 1989', *Review 20*, September 1993, p. 50; *Islands Business*, February 1989.

is not Christian,' he declared, 'and is not scripturally sound.'[133] But he faced formidable forces within the church led by his own general secretary, Rev. Manasa Lasaro, and the Bauan chief, Rev. Ratu Isireli Caucau. When the interim government further relaxed the ban in October 1988 to permit limited taxi and bus services, Lasaro and the old nationalist Butadroka organised some 70 road blocks around Suva on 18 December in protest. Rabuka intervened and the roadblocks were lifted, but Lasaro remained unrepentant. 'So much has been taken away from us,' he argued, 'and we are now left only with our faith which we will fight to the death to keep.'[134]

Koroi now moved against Lasaro, suspending him from his position as secretary general. It made little difference. On Christmas Day, fresh roadblocks were erected, but this time police arrested 150 protesters, including Lasaro. All were charged with illegal demonstration and conditionally discharged. Lasaro turned on Koroi. With the support of nearly three quarters of the church's divisional superintendents, he suspended the church's constitution on 3 February 1989, barred Koroi from his office, and replaced him with Caucau. Thrice the High Court declared the church's actions illegal and twice the rebels ignored its ruling. 'Any constitution can be amended or added to if there is a need,' Lasaro's lawyer declared.[135] History was on their side; so too the authorities. Mara, Ganilau and Rabuka visited Lasaro in April to receive a petition protesting the court's ruling and demanding that the Sunday ban be strengthened. Meanwhile church officials plotted their own revenge on Koroi, organising ex-prisoners to rape Koroi's wife in front of her husband at their Deuba house. At the last moment, the church social worker charged with executing the plan backed out.[136]

The rebels hoped to legalise their actions at the next Methodist annual conference, now only months away. In preparation Lasaro apologised to the High Court in mid-April and permitted Koroi to return to his office. Lasaro's next actions, however, nearly prevented him from attending the vital conference. In July, he participated in a protest in Labasa against Sunday cane-harvesting and milling and earned a jail sentence of six months for breaking the terms of his earlier release. Rabuka flew to

---

133 *Fiji Times*, 21 December 1989.
134 *Age*, 20 December 1988.
135 *Fiji Times*, 30 March 1989.
136 *Review, The News & Business Magazine of Fiji*, August 1996.

Labasa in early August 1989 and released all 57 protestors on compulsory supervision orders. Thus Lasaro was able to attend the conference and retain his position as general secretary. Caucau became president. The Methodist coup had been legitimised.

Rabuka had additional reasons to strengthen his relations with the Methodist Taukeists. In April 1989, Mara hinted that he would resign at the end of his term as interim prime minister and Rabuka saw this opportunity for advancement as his due. 'I'm not an ordinary commander,' he declared, 'I'm not an ordinary servant of the government.'[137] He saw himself in historic terms: he alone had helped Fijians claim their manifest destiny and made Fiji truly independent.[138] Mara's announcement now promised an end to the uncertainty that had hung over his future since 1987. His officers quickly drew up a plan for succession, which Rabuka passed on to Ganilau and Mara. The military would institute a 15-year government based on what they called Fijian Democratic Socialism. It would neutralise the Coalition, abolish unions, reintroduce censorship, evict Australian businesses and seek alternate Asian markets, close the Indian embassy, and replace common law with customary law.[139] When the press obtained copies of the plan in late September, Ganilau moved quickly to quell uncertainty. He requested Mara stay on for a second term, but the Prime Minister made it very clear that he would do so only if Rabuka agreed to certain conditions: 'I cannot carry on with him doing what he is doing now.'[140] Rabuka had to decide whether to return to the barracks as a non-political military commander or leave the military altogether and become one of two deputy prime ministers. A third option existed also – Rabuka could remain in cabinet as military commander but would have no responsibility for police and immigration.

Rabuka chose to leave cabinet and remain Commander. Accordingly, Mara reshuffled his cabinet and reduced its military personnel. Rabuka smarted at having his hand forced. 'Power can only be taken from us,' he reminded government in early 1990, 'when a constitution is approved.'[141] If Mara had thought that taking Rabuka out of cabinet would reduce tensions, he was soon disappointed. In late June, the Fiji Nursing Association went on strike, demanding night-time transportation for

---

137 *Pacific Islands Monthly*, August 1990.
138 *Fiji Times*, 28 April 1992.
139 *Fiji Times*, 26 September 1989.
140 *Australian*, 29 September 1989.
141 *Fiji Times*, 23 January 1990.

members who feared the increased dangers of assault in post-coup Suva. The interim government declared the strike illegal and were about to shut down their pickets when Rabuka unexpectedly joined them. Jubilant public sector unions threatened to broaden the strike nationally, and the government backed off, humiliated. A buoyant Rabuka announced his desire to be prime minister in order 'to finally realise the objectives of the 1987 coups':

> The new constitution lays down the machinery for the attainment of the objectives; whether we actually achieve them or not depends on who is running that machinery ... A lot of people are saying 'You started this, you've got to finish it'.[142]

Labour's Mahendra Chaudhry, now head of the National Farmers Union (NFU), saw an opportunity to expand his union's influence among cane farmers. Unless the government suspended its newly imposed growers' award, his members would refuse to harvest cane. After six weeks of intense standoff, the government relented and amended the award, confirming the NFU as the new voice of farmers.

Chaudhry's success impressed Rabuka; perhaps less hostile relations with the unions might gain him advantages. In February 1991, he visited Vatukoula, where miners sought recognition for their union from the Emperor Gold Mine. He sympathised with their plight and hinted that Fiji might not participate in the forthcoming (and ultimately abortive) peacekeeping force on Bougainville if Fiji's workers were similarly treated by multinational mining companies.[143] Additionally, he supplied tents and food to squatters removed from land set aside for Fiji's new tax-free zone.

Union restlessness provided fresh opportunities for Rabuka during 1991. A national economic summit in May that year proposed sweeping changes to industrial laws, including the removal of union immunity from prosecution for illegal strikes, raising the basis for recognising unions (from 50 to 66 per cent of membership), and abolishing wages councils. The NFU sprung into action, urging its members to strike if they did not receive the exact sugar price forecast the previous year. This was a ruse, designed to force the government to call an election for the Sugar Cane Growers Council, a large and expensive consultative body that the NFU

---

142 *Age*, 21 July 1990.
143 *Pacific Islands Monthly*, May 1991.

now wished to dominate. Aware that a showdown loomed, Mara sought to neutralise those critics who could do him most damage. In mid-April, he proposed that Rabuka re-enter the interim government as deputy prime minister. Because he wished to weaken further the unpopular Sunday Observance Decree, Mara also proposed that Lasaro join as minister for youth and sport.

At first Rabuka accepted the offer, but when Lasaro refused he reconsidered. He would only enter if he could remain military commander. 'There is no guarantee in politics ... not like the army,' he mused.[144] A cabinet proposal to cut the military budget confirmed his suspicions. Soldiers around the world are similar, Rabuka had earlier told his biographers: 'We belong to a very exclusive club and we all feel that we are just being used by politicians.'[145] Now he sent his own ultimatum, informing Ganilau that he should either become prime minister or deputy prime minister, minister for home affairs and commander. Mara rejected both options, and pushed ahead with two anti-union decrees aimed at the sugar and gold industries. Chaudhry called for dialogue, but the government had already determined its course of action. Ganilau toured Labasa cane fields in June 1991 and declared that the army would be used to assist with the harvest if a strike went ahead. Rabuka contradicted him. His soldiers would not cut cane. 'This government is made up of overpaid people who sit on their laurels and wait for something to happen before they react,' he declared. It should resign. If it failed to, and he assumed control again, he would simply be repossessing the authority he had bestowed on the two chiefs at the end of 1987. It would not be a third coup, merely a restoration.[146] To emphasise his seriousness, Rabuka called up his army reservists.

An angry Ganilau informed him that the new Constitution now superseded any powers he once possessed, and his actions tarnished the reputation of the RFMF. Rabuka lost his nerve. Mara and Ganilau, both chiefs, refused to melt away, and he – the commoner – did not really want another coup. He was simply disillusioned he later told a visiting television crew.[147] Nonetheless, the actions of its one-time foe emboldened the labour movement; it called for a general strike on 16 July.

---

144 *Fiji Times*, 25 May 1991.
145 Dean & Ritova, *Rabuka*, 1988, p. 83.
146 *Fiji Times*, 8 June 1991.
147 *Fiji Times*, 24 June 1991.

Having defused one crisis, the President had no wish for another to undo his work. Ganilau asked Rabuka to rejoin the government. Sensing the government's weakness and seeking to gain from his back down, Rabuka publicly committed to leaving the military and joining the government but only if the warring parties reconciled. 'This is not the time for childish one-upmanship,' he declared after arranging for Chaudhry and Ganilau to meet.[148]

Chaudhry agreed to call off the general strike and the sugar boycott and Ganilau promised to suspend the decrees and convene an all-industry conference to discuss sugar issues. A reluctant government had little choice but to cave in. In the New Year, however, Ganilau was less than gracious, condemning unions for pursuing confrontation and threatening the economy. 'They have often ignored the realities of a multicultural society and attempted to impose their will by coercion and threats,' he argued with no hint of irony, 'Their actions serve only to emphasise the things that divide us and make no contribution towards solving our problems.'[149] Behind the scenes, moves were afoot to expel Chaudhry from the Fiji Trades Union Congress. Of course, the union movement was indelibly associated with the government's old Coalition foe, which many ministers blamed for the mess Fiji was in. Minister for Labour Taniela Veitata had earlier slammed every effort by unions to overturn anti-labour legislation as 'an act of war'. Now he saw it as 'direct interference in the sovereignty of this nation'. His colleague, Kubuabola, believed the labour movement should be treated like a hostile foreign power seeking to overthrow a legitimate government.[150] Undoubtedly they were angry at the power some unions possessed, and were in no mood to assist less powerful unions, even those predominantly Fijian in membership. Hence the interim government refused to cave in to the Vatukoula strikers and to pressure Emperor Gold Mining to attend conciliation talks.

Taukeists were also angry. At a protest march shortly after the back down they declared – also with no apparent sense of irony – that Rabuka's deal represented 'an open invitation for others to break the law of the country and seek presidential reprieve and pardon'. Butadroka claimed that 'the only solution to the problems facing the country was the full repatriation

---

148   *Fiji Times*, 12 July 1991.
149   *Daily Post*, 1 January 1992.
150   *Fiji Times*, 1 May 1989; 25 June 1991; 5 April 1989.

of Indians to India'.[151] But the nationalists and the government were powerless. The union movement had won a major victory and in doing so protected itself from annihilation.

Nonetheless, some Coalition members felt uneasy. 'The FLP will run into trouble sooner or later if it treats the General as a strategic ally,' Simione Durutalo warned his colleagues.[152] His words proved prophetic but, despite the disaster the confrontation seemed to present to the government, it at least emerged with a completed road map for elections in the following year and Rabuka safely out of the army. This brought the government greater security than it had enjoyed since 1987, but only because the road map implied that the mantle had already passed to new aspirants and, in particular, Rabuka. He had bowed finally to pressure, although in a way that saved face and augmented the new image he wished to present, that of the man of action concerned for the welfare of the people, no matter how much the political instability he generated reduced their wellbeing.

Raiding the nest

Rabuka's political career now began in earnest. To secure the future he felt sure was his due, he had to seize control of the new Fijian party, the Soqosoqo ni Vakavulewa ni Taukei (SVT), established by the GCC in early 1991. Success was by no means assured, in part because Mara had other plans. But even Mara misjudged the problems that provincially based electorates could create for Fijian politics. He wanted his Finance Minister, the former NLTB head Josefata Kamikamica, as his successor. To assist his campaign, Kamikamica's Tailevu province proposed on 30 October that the former Alliance politician Ratu William Toganivalu become president of the SVT. But, at the last moment, Rewa province also proposed its paramount chief, Mara's wife, Ro Lady Lala Mara. Between them they inadvertently split the anti-Rabuka vote, allowing him to assume the party's presidency. 'Those defeated in elections should take it in their political stride, accept the defeat and move out gracefully,' he lashed out at his critics.[153] This was 1991, not 1987.

---

151   *Fiji Times*, 15 July 1991.
152   *Fiji Times*, 16 August 1991.
153   *Fiji Times*, 6 November 1991.

Rabuka had won round one, but Mara still backed Kamikamica as his preferred successor and forced Rabuka to step down as a minister, claiming that members of political parties were inappropriate in an interim government.[154] Rabuka faced a challenging task, recreating a unified party for Fijians who were now politically divided into rival provinces and aware that the Constitution's majority guarantees excluded the need for Fijian political unity. In many respects he was the right man for the job. He was a commoner. Despite Fijian respect for tradition and for chiefly leadership, Fijian society had changed substantially since independence. Commoner Fijians no longer believed chiefs automatically took precedence, even if many chiefs failed to recognise their shift in thinking. The events of 1987 demonstrated the importance of the transition. Rabuka led his coups to preserve the predominance of Fijians, not just the role of chiefs. He was no radical, but he was a commoner, and that in itself spoke volumes for the kind of society emerging in Fiji, one potentially more transparent and democratic than in the past. This is what made Fiji's politics so interesting in 1992. The post-coup Constitution might have ensured a Fijian majority in parliament, but it did not dictate who would govern. Of course an even more important issue loomed: could a newly elected government provide Fiji the stability it had lacked since 1987 and which it desperately needed in order to recover and prosper?

Not surprisingly, the first post-coup election in late May 1992 proved very different from earlier elections. The Constitution's communalisation of electorates made politicians unresponsive to popular concerns. Communalism effectively meant a separate general election for each community, with only one community having the capacity to rule. IndoFijians lacked that capacity. No longer united within a coalition, they were bitterly divided between Labour and the NFP. In part the coups caused this falling-out. The NFP now regarded its former coalition with Labour as a mistake. Personnel changes contributed also to changing political perspectives. Labour's affable Fijian leader, Bavadra, had died in November 1989 and with him went the party's emphasis on multiculturalism. So too the clarity of focus that Labour displayed during the 1980s when popular issues dominated its political agenda. Social problems might now be far worse, but they were not subjects on which it could challenge the interim government's likely successors.

---

154 This was not entirely personal. Mara asked Apisai Tora to leave in June 1991 when Tora formed the western-based All Nationals Congress (ANC), a purportedly multiracial political party designed to fight for a separate Fijian western confederacy.

In fact, communal demarcations minimised such challenges. Without national seats requiring cross-voting by different communities, nothing existed to make multiracial perspectives politically advantageous. Labour would more likely find itself up against the NFP, not the SVT. The SVT was indisputably a Fijian party. The NFP regarded itself an IndoFijian party, its 1987 multiracial experiment having been a failure.[155] Only Labour continued to claim a multiracial face; it appointed Bavadra's widow, Adi Kuini Vuikaba, as his successor to emphasise continuities. But tensions over leadership and election strategies forced Vuikaba out in early 1991. Her replacement, Mahendra Chaudhry, made matters worse. Chaudhry transformed Labour into an avowedly IndoFijian party, with its base in the rural cane belt. Although they never acknowledged the shift in strategy, Chaudhry and his colleagues occasionally let slip their new priorities, declaring Labour 'the representative of the Indian community'. They blamed the Constitution for the transformation: 'In this kind of racial electoral system, how else can you operate,' Chaudhry argued[156] and Labour politician Krishna Datt dismissed Labour's past strategy as a fragile 'facade of multiracialism'.[157] The Constitution made it easy to avoid self-examination.

Consumed by the politics of participation, Labour's transformation was not immediately obvious in 1992. Ever since the new Constitution had been promulgated, Labour agonised over the message it would send if it participated. At first Labour believed it should deny the Constitution legitimacy. It would hold its head high and boycott elections.[158] But a boycott could be disastrous if it surrendered the IndoFijian vote to the NFP, a party that many Labour members characterised as right wing. It would also mean – as the late Simione Durutalo argued – a return to 'the pre 1981 era when ethnic based parties dominated politics in Fiji'.[159] Not surprisingly, he and other Fijians in Labour became increasingly disenchanted at the direction their leaders were taking and resigned in protest at the party's insistence on a boycott.

---

155   *Pacific Islands Monthly*, March 1991; this was the assessment of Dr Balwant Singh Rakka, NFP President.
156   *Review*, September 1994.
157   *Daily Post*, 28 January 1994; *Review*, February 1994.
158   When the NFP announced its intention to participate, Kubuabola declared it 'tacit recognition of the Constitution' (*Fiji Times*, 30 July 1991).
159   *Fiji Times*, 9 February 1992.

Internal disarray cost Labour dearly. It could easily have accepted both perspectives and maintained its boycott but formed political fronts to fight the elections on its behalf. Instead Chaudhry took Labour to the brink of disintegration before bowing to popular pressure on the eve of the elections by suddenly declaring that Labour would conduct its boycott from within parliament, not outside it. In the subsequent elections it won only 13 seats, all rural NFU strongholds, and lost its urban seats to the NFP, which gained the remaining 14 Indian seats, although with narrow margins. Labour's transformation was now fully exposed.

Of course the real focus of the 1992 elections lay on the 37 Fijian seats. Here Rabuka's SVT won 30 seats, with the remainder going to Ratu Osea Gavidi's Soqosoqo ni Taukei ni Vanua (STV) in Nadroga–Navosa (one seat), Butadroka's Fijian Nationalist Party (three seats), and two independents in Ra.[160] Although Rabuka had overwhelming support from among his own MPs to claim the prime ministership, he still needed coalition partners to secure a parliamentary majority. Behind the scenes, Kamikamica (with the support of only nine SVT MPs) managed to cobble together enough votes from the NFP and General Voters Party (GVP) to mount a serious challenge to Rabuka's ambitions. Rabuka rallied Butadroka's Nationalists and Gavidi to his cause and used them to woo Labour. Chaudhry believed an opportunity now existed to force Rabuka to review the Constitution, revoke the labour decrees, scrap the VAT and begin discussions on land leases. Success would restore Labour's relevance. Rabuka agreed to consider them.

Rabuka's last-minute lobbying won him the position he had for so long coveted. 'This time it's legal,' he told his supporters and although he claimed he was there for all people, not just Fijians, it soon become apparent – as he admitted two years later – that he could not deny his Fijian heritage and 'turn on the universal prime minister picture'.[161] 'Rabuka overthrew democracy violently,' one magazine noted. 'He now presides over a facade of democracy.'[162] Opportunities did exist to move beyond authoritarianism but, ironically, it would be Rabuka's backroom manoeuvring that ensured continued political instability. Butadroka expected to be rewarded for his efforts on Rabuka's behalf. Chaudhry

---

160 The General Voters Party won all five General Elector seats and Paul Manueli the sole Rotuma seat. Tora's ANC won no seats.

161 *Islands Business*, July 1992; *Review*, September 1994.

162 *Islands Business*, July 1992.

also expected movement on his log of claims, although Rabuka denied conceding anything. Rabuka's problems did not end there. Many of his colleagues made constant comparisons between him and Mara and continued to regard Kamikamica as the rightful heir, particularly as Rabuka quickly stumbled from crisis to crisis and constantly reshuffled his cabinet like a deck of cards.

In part, Rabuka's difference lay in his commoner status; it enabled journalists and parliamentarians to speak more freely than they had under Mara. 'To those who might not appreciate the fact that a commoner is now leading the nation,' Rabuka later remarked, 'all I can say is that they must prepare themselves because in the future there will be more and more like me.'[163] In fact Rabuka could draw on a long history of commoner activity in politics that went back to Apolosi Ranawai. Bavadra had been a commoner, Kamikamica also. Fiji's substantial postcolonial strategy had been to create a strong middle class, a goal that potentially conflicted with provincialism, tradition and chiefly power, all elements strengthened in the new Constitution. But political instability derived more immediately from two sources, the first being Fijian disunity. MPs owed their allegiance to their province, not their party. To maintain support, Rabuka had either to appease provinces or buy off MPs, sometimes both. Hence his unprecedented 27-member cabinet, which included three GVP members (the price for its support), and two independents. The second source of instability derived from Rabuka's links with the Nationalists.

Butadroka's FNP had helped secure Rabuka the crucial numbers for the prime ministership. In return it wanted seats in cabinet, but the GVP made the Nationalists' exclusion a condition for its support. Consequently, the FNP sought compensation of a different kind. Butadroka's campaign manager, Tony Stephens, had been imprisoned in 1988 for possessing pen pistols. He had been a shareholder in Viti Marketing (Fiji) Ltd, the company established as the economic arm of the Taukei Movement. In jail, he and former politician Fred Caine planned the creation of a vast business in logging and rural banking. By 1991 they had allegedly arranged a loan of US$200 million from Kuwait to finance their venture, but to obtain it they had first to pay an upfront commission of $980,000. Stephens had a longstanding compensation claim for $30 million against the government for his arrest, and saw Rabuka's election as an opportunity

---

163 *Review*, April 1994.

to fast-track matters. With Butadroka and Gavidi, he pressured Attorney-General Apaitia Seru, to accept an out-of-court settlement of $980,000 in cash and $9 million in assets. Rabuka advised his Attorney-General to look seriously at the agreement. Seru signed it. Only when the Finance Minister, Paul Manueli, learnt of the request, did the deal collapse. Three days later, in late September 1992, a copy of the deed fell into the hands of the Opposition and, in the uproar that followed, Seru resigned and the government appointed a commission of inquiry to investigate the affair.

Rabuka attempted to distract the nation from the debacle by suddenly proposing in December the formation of a government of national unity. The Nationalists and many chiefs denounced the proposal, as did Kamikamica's faction within the SVT. Even Chaudhry, who had initially discussed the plan with Rabuka, went cool on the idea, especially after his party lost a by-election to the NFP in May 1993. Chaudhry wrote to Rabuka reminding him of his promises immediately after the election. When Rabuka did not reply, he led his colleagues out of parliament in protest. Labour's disaffection would have mattered little except it followed a cabinet reshuffle designed to reduce its size and drop poorly performing ministers. One of those was Ilai Kuli who, as Minister for Information and Broadcasting, had failed to resolve longstanding problems associated with Fiji Post and Telecommunication's transition to a public enterprise. His province, Naitasiri, promised revenge.

Similar problems confronted the top-heavy Ports Authority, where one of the leaders of the Taukei Movement ran the union and convinced the Minister for Transport to stop privatising stevedoring. Veitata, the former dockworkers' union boss, parliamentarian, and Taukeist became its chairman.[164] Equally damaging were revelations in mid-May that, by using soft loans from the FDB and the National Bank of Fiji (NBF), private Fijian companies owned by cabinet ministers, bank and provincial officials, even senior FHL managers, now owned more shares in Fijian Holdings Ltd than provincial councils or their *tikina*, for whom the company had originally been established. Government supported embourgeoisement, but did not wish to defend a heavily subsidised business against allegations of insider trading, especially since it could never be a vehicle for empowering the mass of Fijians.

---

164   PAF's accumulated reserves of $10 million in 1989 had morphed into a $22 million deficit by the end of 1993.

The FHL case was not the only Fijian institution to embarrass the post-coup government. Given the greater emphasis on indigeneity after 1987, many part-Fijians sought to change their identity. In some instances there were clear political and economic advantages in doing so, as in the case of businessman and Rabuka ally, Jim Ah Koy. Many nationalists and others disagreed, however, and called for all Fijians to be vetted, effectively for purity. In June 1993, a report commissioned by the GCC recommended the removal of 36 people from the Fijian land register, the Vola ni Kawa Bula (VKB),[165] on the basis that they were not Fijian enough.

Fijians had achieved the paramountcy many of their leaders had for so long craved and now, under the leadership of one of the architects of that paramountcy, they seemed suddenly to lack any clear strategy as to how they might achieve their vision of prosperity. If anything paramountcy under Rabuka brought only disgrace and disunity. Butadroka wanted all Fiji's resources on land and sea to be distributed to ordinary Fijians (*tauvanua*), not the state, and he wanted the abolition of all colonial bureaucracies, including the NLTB.[166] He proposed a new Viti Levu Council of Chiefs to offset the influence of Lau and Cakaudrove. The release in July 1993 of the report[167] by former Supreme Court justice, Sir Ronald Kermode, into the Tony Stephens scandal added further to Rabuka's woes. It condemned ministerial conduct and concluded that, on the basis of available evidence, the Prime Minister among others had committed criminal offences. But, with the Taukei Movement still hovering in the background and the Methodist Church openly supporting Rabuka, opponents felt uncomfortable using issues of propriety to confront his government. Instead they chose the 1994 budget, which did little to compensate producers for lower tariffs, raised government debt, and reduced Fiji's capacity to invest. Dissident backbenchers led by Kamikamica saw their opportunity to bring down the government and joined the opposition to vote against the budget. It was a grave miscalculation.

---

165 The 1990 Constitution restricted the use of 'Fijian' to people enrolled on the VKB, a colonial register begun in the early 20th century to record land ownership by patrilineal means. In many respects the use of this register contradicted the more flexible practices adopted by *mataqali* or *yavusa* when dealing with *vasu* (those with maternal ties). Traditionally ancestry had little to do with determining Fijianness. Fijians tended to be very receptive people. Nonetheless, the VKB continues to record the letter 'B' for 'bastard' alongside the names of children born out of wedlock (*Fiji Sun*, 7 December 2016).

166 *Pacific Islands Monthly*, April 1993.

167 'Report of the Commission of Inquiry into the Deed of Settlement dated 17.09.92 between Anthony Frederick Stephens and the Attorney General of Fiji', Parliamentary Paper 45. Suva: Government Printer, 1993.

Kamikamica thought the President would resolve the issue by appointing a new prime minister. Instead Mara, now acting president as a result of Ganilau's terminal illness,[168] accepted Rabuka's advice to dissolve parliament and call fresh elections. During the campaign that followed, Rabuka portrayed Kamikamica and his supporters as traitors handing Fijian rule to the IndoFijian opposition. 'Are we so lacking in honour and integrity ... to our community,' he asked the GCC in December, 'that we are prepared to be giving away that national control of our future and destroying that which we now have?'[169] Rabuka's appeal to the objectives of 1987 enabled him to contain Kamikamica's rebellion to two provinces and marginally strengthen his hand. Kamikamica's new party, the Fijian Association Party (FAP) won five seats only – in Lau and Naitasiri. Kamikamica lost his own Tailevu seat. Gavidi and the Nationalists were similarly defeated. Rabuka received 61 per cent of the Fijian vote which gave him 31 Fijian seats; with two independents and four GVP members he secured a narrow majority. The GVP did well out of Rabuka's dependence on them. As a recognised minority, General Electors gained access to FDB soft loans, taxi and chicken-import licences, and assistance for small businesses. Their MPs sat in cabinet.

'A saving grace of what has turned out to be a largely failed constitution,' one magazine speculated, 'is that it tends to concentrate tensions within ethnic communities rather than intensifying strains between them.'[170] Again Labour found itself competing with the NFP for the spoils and, on the basis of its failed deals with Rabuka, lost badly, gaining only seven of its former 13 seats. A rejuvenated NFP demanded constitutional talks, but Rabuka was in no mood for change. 'Apartheid here in Fiji is a necessary evil for the moment to try and gain some semblance of balance,' Rabuka told journalists, 'I know Fijians are not willing to compromise much of what they have written into this Constitution.'[171]

But racial compartmentalism also meant that threats to Rabuka's position would always come from Fijians, not marginalised IndoFijians. Victory brought Rabuka no respite, as he quickly learned upon announcing a new lean cabinet comprising only 12 ministers. Dumped ministers, particularly Taukeists disinclined to allow Rabuka sole ownership of 1987, set about

---

168 Ganilau died on 16 December 1993. Mara succeeded him in early 1994.
169 *Weekender*, 17 December 1993.
170 *Pacific Islands Monthly*, January 1994.
171 *Review*, April 1994; *Age*, 1 March 1994.

to remind him that he was not invincible. In March 1994, Kubuabola and five former ministers accused Rabuka of being morally unfit for office because he had had an affair with a journalist in late 1993. Again Rabuka outsmarted his detractors. At a SVT caucus he offered his resignation, which was not accepted. Inevitably news of the confrontation leaked.[172] But, unlike Kamikamica, Kubuabola and his colleagues had no intention of bringing down Rabuka's government; they sought only to bargain for a share in the spoils of victory.

Unfortunately, those spoils were little in evidence in the wider community. If anything, the lacklustre performance of the government worsened. Government debt had increased 25 per cent since Rabuka's first election, most of it raised locally, thereby starving the domestic market of investment funds and inflicting low growth and high interest rates on the country. Once thriving economic sectors faced stagnation. The potential loss of preferential markets threatened Fiji's highly uncompetitive sugar industry.[173] Local content regulations restricted garment-industry growth. Rabuka did nothing to address these issues, claiming that Fijian issues should come first.[174] Accordingly, he decided that local chicken growers and producers should now compete with US imports licensed only to Fijians on a provincial basis.

A flat economy provided no basis for raising Fijian expectations, or for solving problems of crime, unemployment and rapid urbanisation. The army's solution was to extend cadet training to some 20 secondary schools; the government's to establish a rural National Youth Training Scheme based at an expensive farm at Navua purchased from the chairman of the FDB and FHL;[175] and that of Fijian chiefs to reimpose their discipline on villages by resurrecting colonial powers abandoned in 1967. Judicial apartheid would now be added to economic apartheid. 'On the one hand

---

172   Jo Nata's *Weekender* newspaper hinted at morality issues in Rabuka's cabinet, but gave no names. The news and business *Review* revealed the whole story at the start of April. Not to be outdone, the *Weekender* promised a special issue on the 21 women Rabuka had had affairs with since leaving the military. Police Commissioner Isikia Savua and then Electoral Commissioner Qoriniasi Bale spoke with Nata and the issue never appeared (*Weekender*, 2 April 1994; *Review*, April 1994).

173   Economist Roman Grynberg warned Fiji of the dangers in May 1994. Nearly one third of Fiji's cane farmers produced less than 100 tonnes of cane, and Fiji's harvesting rate equalled half that of Mauritius, and one eighth that of Australia's prior to mechanisation (*Review*, June 1994).

174   *Fiji Times*, 17 September 1994; *Review*, September 1994.

175   The scheme eventually morphed into VitiCorp, but it fared poorly and required a constant injection of government funds. In 2005, it restructured and eventually leased all its land for agricultural purposes, its Navua farm to the Fiji National University (*Fiji Sun*, 1 September 2016).

government encourages individualism through its business incentives,' one journalist noted, 'while on the other it attempts to enforce traditionalism and collectivism through a legal system.'[176] Mara acknowledged that no traditional means existed to assist the urban poor; Rabuka, however, blamed IndoFijians for imbalances in the distribution of wealth: 'As long as this happens I cannot guarantee ... that there will not be another coup in this land [or] bloodless like mine.'[177] Meanwhile, the largesse of the FDB and NBF towards favoured Fijian clients continued until the National Bank collapsed in late 1995 owing over $220 million or nearly 9 per cent of GDP.

The problems facing the NBF were longstanding. Formed in 1976 from a savings bank, the NBF almost immediately found itself hostage to the fortunes of one of the country's longstanding trading companies, Stinson Pearce Holdings Ltd, when it loaned $2.7 million to the company in 1978. Not only did the loan lack sufficient security, it breached banking regulations that no more than 25 per cent of a bank's equity be loaned to a single borrower. At the time the NBF possessed only $500,000 in capital, and the Minister for Finance was none other than the former head of the company, Sir Charles Stinson. In 1984, the NBF gained a formal regulatory exemption, which it apparently understood applied to any subsequent transaction. As Grynberg, Doug Munro and the late Michael White note in their outstanding study of the NBF, 'all the problems of nepotism, corruption and appallingly weak public administration that developed in Fiji and the NBF after the coups were already there well before 14 May 1987'.[178] The coups, however, enabled those problems to escalate out of control.

It began with the military appointment of Visanti Makrava, the manager of a small branch, as the NBF chief manager. He began a massive expansion program that saw staff numbers treble to 600 by 1993, market share double to 30 per cent, deposits and loans quadruple to $420 million and $287 million respectively, and foreign exchange earnings double to $3.7 million. By 1993 Makrava had apparently turned a loss of

176 *Fiji Times*, September 1994.
177 *Fiji Times*, July 1994; *Australian*, 17 June 1994.
178 R Grynberg, D Munro & M White, *Crisis: The Collapse of the National Bank of Fiji*. Suva: USP Book Centre, 2002, p. xxiii. The Stinson debt eventually exceeded $6 million.

$5.3 million in 1987 into a $2.2 million profit, and was set to embark on a new range of financial services in a joint venture with the Malaysian National MBf.[179] In reality the bank was insolvent.

A Reserve Bank of Fiji (RBF) report in 1991 estimated that the NBF possessed problem loans worth eight times its paid-up capital of $9.6 million, not the 50 per cent recommended by the World Bank,[180] and its problems only got worse. In 1993, when the government began domesticating foreign debt, many larger depositors like the national superannuation scheme (Fiji National Provident Fund (FNPF)), shifted their funds out of the NBF into higher yielding government bonds. The resulting liquidity problem, however, did not prevent the bank from increasing its lending and, by 1993, it was wholly dependent on overnight borrowing from the RBF to survive. By 1994 its loans totalled $332 million, 21 times its paid-up capital of $15.75 million.[181] The RBF, the Auditor-General and cabinet all knew of the NBF's difficulties but did nothing. 'If I open my mouth,' Makrava later said, 'half the government goes, including the leader.'[182] In fact, nothing better illustrated Wadan Narsey's 'culture of silence', as Grynberg, Munro and White explain:

> NBF board members were all government appointees, part of Fiji's 'carousel' of financial elite that shifted from the board of one statutory body to another. These are trusted individuals in a small society with a limited number of individuals able to perform such roles. The trust stems from the willingness of these individuals if not to remain silent in the face of malfeasance, at the very least to be consistent in erring on the side of their patrons. A small society generates only a small number of individuals who are technically competent enough to sit on such boards. But the number of such posts is almost as large as would be found in a large society, and appointments to such positions are determined by a handful of politicians. Those unwilling to live by the code of silence and compliance towards those in a position to grant such patronage find themselves excluded from the lucrative carousel of board positions.[183]

---

179 Grynberg, Munro & White, *Crisis*, 2002. p. 10. The National Mbf MasterCard exposed the NBF through its credit-line facility to a debt of $25 million (see Robertson, *Multiculturalism & Reconciliation*, 1998, pp. 139–41).

180 Grynberg, Munro & White, *Crisis*, 2002, p. 12. The World Bank also recommends that problem loans should be no more than 10 per cent of all loans.

181 Grynberg, Munro & White, *Crisis*, 2002, p. 75.

182 *Fiji Times*, 2 August 1995.

183 Grynberg, Munro & White, *Crisis*, 2002, pp. 137–38.

The scandal became public when an audit of the NBF leaked to the press. In fact, the press, particularly the *Fiji Times* and the *Review*, were pivotal in exposing the scandal. The *Review* had earlier been threatened with deregistration over its publication of Rabuka's affair in 1994; now both papers were threatened with Malaysian-style licensing laws to ensure that they remained respectful of Pacific cultural sensitivities and did not denigrate Fijian business acumen.[184] Makrava did not help. He declared that his sole purpose had been to 'achieve the goals of the coups for Fijians and Rotumans'.[185] Rabuka remained unrepentant: the media had launched a 'campaign to discredit Fijian leaders, senior Fijian civil servants and Fijians in positions of responsibility [in order to] show us as incapable of governing our own country with any sense of fair play'.[186] More realistically, the *Review* noted, 'The NBF debacle is, if nothing else, symbolic of the failure of racism'.[187]

The repercussions of the NBF collapse were immense and, as a way forward, it was split into two banks, with the viable portion eventually sold to the Australian Colonial Group for just under $10 million in 1998. The bad debts were accumulated into a separate entity and funded by the issue of government bonds. Stabilising and restructuring the NBF in this way created a sudden contraction in money supply in 1996 and a rise in interest rates, which helped precipitate a recession that lasted until 1999, in part because it coincided first with drought and later with the Asian financial crisis. Government debt increased by 41 per cent as a consequence. Most of the funds used in the rescue came from the FNPF, which closed time deposits and decreased lending to businesses in order to raise its government securities holdings by 23 per cent.

But the icing on the cake for the government came in 1998 when it sold the state's 49 per cent stake in Fiji's telecommunications monopoly – the Amalgamated Telecom Holdings Ltd (ATHL) – to the FNPF for $253 million, nearly four times its estimated commercial value. As Grynberg describes the transaction, the FNPF effectively exchanged assets then earning 8 per cent per annum for assets returning only 2 per cent, with the possibility of even lower returns when ATHL lost its

---

184 *Review*, December 1995. The government did review media legislation in 1996, but the commissioned report recommended against any restriction on media freedom. For a full account of the media and the NBF, see Grynberg, Munro & White, *Crisis*, 2002, pp. 48–71.

185 *Review*, January 1996.

186 *Fiji Times*, 12 December 1995.

187 *Review*, August 1996.

monopoly status. The Minister for Finance, responsible also for the FNPF, saw no conflict of interest. ATHL was privatised to pay for the NBF debacle and Fiji's pensioners paid the cost. Twenty per cent currency devaluation in early 1998 helped lower the cost of public debt further and enabled the government to increase public expenditure ahead of a general election in the following year.[188] The fiasco would cost Rabuka and his SVT party dearly, but no one was ever convicted over the affair. The director of public prosecutions at the time later conceded that her under-resourced office was subject to intimidation and personal attacks.[189] Makrava retired for the rest of his short life to a new mansion built in Rotuma.

Rabuka might have weathered the storm better had the NBF collapse not been accompanied by so many other scandals. The FDB was itself under the spotlight, with some 20 per cent of loans unrecoverable. Its profit fell 83 per cent in 1996 and required the injection of $120 million through promissory notes and bonds. Return on equity remained at only 0.72 per cent. Additionally, its EIMCOL supermarket scheme had collapsed owing $2.7 million. The RBF lost $18 million in foreign exchange earnings in 1995 and allegations of corruption and mismanagement at the Housing Authority forced its chief executive to resign. The Fiji Broadcasting Commission required an injection of $1.4 million to stay afloat. Rumours had the secretive NLTB in debt to the tune of $16 million dollars by 1996 while, on the waterfront, a disastrous post-coup decision to build a large cruise ship for half its actual cost burdened the government with litigation and costs in excess of $12 million. Senior public servants overdrew on shares in the Fiji Public Service Credit Union at the same time as its travel agency accumulated debts over $1 million. The Public Trustee illegally lent over $2 million. The Methodist Church failed to account for over $1.5 million received from the Poverty Alleviation Fund for squatter resettlement, and itself faced bankruptcy at the start of 1996.[190]

---

188   The NBF's collapse cost taxpayers $615 million in today's terms (*Fiji Sun*, 12 July 2017). Grynberg, Munro & White, *Crisis*, 2002, pp. 99–126.
189   High Court Judge Justice Nazhat Shameem; *fijilive*, 21 March 2007.
190   Robertson, *Multiculturalism & Reconciliation*, 1998, pp. 141–43.

Reset

By 1998 broken shells littered Fiji's landscape. Fortune seekers were still out there but the eggs they coveted were often damaged or – worse – stripped of their contents. Plans were afoot to exploit new resources, a huge copper mine in Namosi or wealthy Chinese migrants seeking refuge from the Chinese takeover of Hong Kong. Some Fijian politicians coveted land as the ultimate nest egg. If IndoFijian leases were not renewed, Fijians could completely control the sugar industry. Sociologist Ropate Qalo thought Rabuka rode a tiger he could no longer control: 'Everyone had to be paid off and now they are asking for their pay.'[191] Grynberg also believed that Fiji's politicians possessed a cargo cult mentality; wealth would simply flow in, all Fiji had to do was sit and wait. No restructuring, no pain, all gain.[192] But, with little to show, the once fiercely Taukeist government looked lost.

The drift had begun early in Rabuka's second term, well before the scandals. Against Methodist protests, Rabuka finally ended the Sunday ban on 12 October 1995 and sought greater authority over his cabinet with regular reshuffles. 'Called by God to lead this nation,' Rabuka brooked no dissent but, increasingly, he ruled from a position of weakness.[193] Poor oversight resulted in the SVT's Tailevu MP, Adi Samanunu Talakuli, being twice disqualified for failing to meet the new Constitution's citizenship laws. Her terminally ill successor was himself disqualified on a technicality after election. Increasingly sensitive to criticism, the SVT tried unsuccessfully to muzzle an elderly columnist and it still maintained a blacklist of persons banned from Fiji. 'In a situation so politically fluid, nothing seems to be moving in Fiji,' the *Review* reflected:

> With an economy that is rapidly going to the cleaners: escalating crime, rising unemployment compounded by the mass exodus of skilled workers and trade union movement looking for a scrap, Fiji is [again] looking down the barrel of a gun.[194]

Rabuka retreated into religious symbolism. He prayed for forgiveness before 4,000 people at the National Gymnasium and again on national radio in late 1996. In February 1997, he attended a four-day Festival

---

191 *Review*, March 1996.
192 *Fiji Times*, 19 January 1995.
193 *Australian*, 1 August 1995.
194 *Review*, June 1996.

of Praise in Suva. It did not save him from criticism. The *Review* accused him of presiding over a 'Lost Decade'[195] during which Malaysia's per-capita GDP had doubled to US$3,890 and South Korea's trebled to US$9,700. Fiji's rose only 20 per cent to US$2,140 and much of that meagre rise came from a statistical aberration caused by the massive outflow of over 40,000 people, many with the skills needed for economic growth.[196]

Indeed, Fiji's growth strategies seemed bent on denying skills and creativity, and its preferential market access for garments, sugar and fish failed to generate production efficiencies. Furthermore, poverty escalated with urbanisation, but the government remained unwilling to generate urban jobs for fear of antagonising its rural provincial political base, yet another disastrous consequence of the 1990 Constitution. But it could hardly deny the social costs. Forty per cent of housing estates were overcrowded and had poor sanitation. Seventeen per cent of families were headed by an unemployed person. Crime rates soared but, unlike the military, the police force remained constantly constrained for funds. Fiji's rate of diabetes stood at twice the international rate, while the medical system groaned under the weight of poor infrastructure and planning and the loss of trained staff. Government contributed only 2.9 per cent of GDP to health in 1996 and, yet, the Health Department managed to underspend its budget. Primary school dropout rates increased more than seven-fold during the 'Lost Decade', even after 1992 when school education became progressively free. The quality of education also declined; suggestions that students did better in multicultural environments did not sit easily with the message of Taukeism.[197]

In fact, Taukeism sat uncomfortably with just about every economic reality confronting Fiji in the late 1990s. This was no easy conclusion for men like Rabuka to concede. Only in 1993 he had told the GCC that the 1990 Constitution was the ultimate guarantee of a Fijian future.[198] The economic disasters that had followed now suggested otherwise. Perhaps a constitutional review, required by the Constitution, might enable multiracial cooperation to stem the economic haemorrhaging, or at least buy time. The possibility existed because in March 1995, after much delay, a Constitutional Review Committee (CRC) – chaired by

---

195   The *Review* declared the post-coup decade a 'Lost Decade' in May 1997.
196   *Review*, April 1997.
197   Robertson, *Multiculturalism & Reconciliation*, 1998, pp. 153–61.
198   *Weekender*, 17 December 1993.

New Zealand's former governor-general Sir Paul Reeves and comprising expatriate academic Brij Lal and former parliamentarian Tomasi Vakatora – began its investigations. It toured the country and consulted widely and, in September 1996, submitted a lengthy and detailed report calling for a return to mixed communal and national parliamentary seats, with twice as many national seats.[199] There were many reasoned criticisms of the report, particularly of its reliance on the Australian alternative vote system as a means to promote moderation and cooperation between parties. Wadan Narsey, who had earlier written that constitutional racism was counterproductive to Fijian interests,[200] argued that a list (proportional representation) system would most encourage cooperation out of self interest: the more votes, the more seats.[201]

Rabuka urged caution, but his SVT colleagues were livid. Nonetheless, having embarked on the path of reform, it was much more difficult for the SVT to reject the Reeves report than it had been for Mara when the country's first Constitution had been reviewed in 1975 following post-independence growth. The Constitution then was new and the two main ethnically based parties were content to maintain the ethnic status quo. Rabuka however operated in a climate of decline and the mere existence of the CRC raised expectations that something might be done to address a constitution that many non-SVT politicians saw as deeply flawed. Consequently, when the issue came before a parliamentary select committee, it recommended a compromise of sorts: a mix of seats but with twice as many communal seats as the CRC recommended.

Rabuka added his own twist – multi-party government. Parties that received more than 10 per cent of the vote would be entitled to proportional representation in cabinet. Communalism would still exist but it would be tempered by national seats and multi-party government. Possibly only the inclusion of the CRC's social justice and affirmative action provisions

---

199 P Reeves, T Vakatora & BV Lal, *The Fiji Islands: Towards a United Future*, Report of the Fiji Constitutional Review Commission, Parliamentary Paper 34. Suva: Parliament of Fiji, 1996.

200 These articles were published in the *Fiji Times* on 29 July, 31 July and 1 August 1995. Narsey reminded readers that the 1990 Constitution – with its massive rural bias – discriminated against Fijians as much as IndoFijians. Ethnic constituencies and traditional structures discouraged ability and decision-making in the national interest. No basis for fears of Indian domination now existed. Proportional representation alone would ensure a Fijian majority and avoid international condemnation.

201 *Fiji Times*, 2 November 1996.

swayed the SVT,[202] and Rabuka was keen to downplay the novelty of the new Constitution. Fijians were now the country's majority population; they no longer needed racially exclusive constitutional clauses to retain power. Such clauses affected Fiji's international standing and denied it membership of the Commonwealth.[203] Nonetheless, the GCC tried unsuccessfully to reduce the number of national seats further, and baulked at the idea of reducing the voting age from 21 to 18. In the end, it could only deny Vakatora the opportunity to promote to provincial councils – especially those opposing it[204] – the new Constitution that would come into effect in mid-1998.

Rabuka was in a hurry to create multi-party governance ahead of the next election, but the NFP refused to share government under the terms of the 1990 Constitution. It accepted, however, the idea of working with Rabuka in the future, and its leader, Jai Ram Reddy, sealed the accommodation by becoming the first IndoFijian to address the GCC in June 1997. He seconded Rabuka's bill to amend the Constitution. 'We want to convert what [has become] a political culture of confrontation into a culture of cooperation,' he declared.[205] The next month, Rabuka's 10th cabinet reshuffle created a multi-party cabinet of sorts, with members of the FAP rejoining, albeit briefly.[206] It was not quite what Rabuka had wanted, but it added to the atmosphere of change and the expectation of economic benefits that he hoped would offset his party's dismal performance in office.

But Fiji was in no shape to reap an immediate economic dividend from its constitutional amendments. It had dawdled for too long on many fronts, especially land. The onset of the Asian economic meltdown in mid-1997 and a long dry summer exacerbated the pain. Drought destroyed one third of the cane belt and reduced sugar production by 45 per cent, wiping

---

202 *Fiji Times*, 4 July 1997. This was the view at least of journalist Sophie Foster. The Constitution included a Bill of Rights, a Human Rights Commission, Freedom of Information legislation and a Compact of Understanding incorporating indigenous rights. It provided women equal citizenship rights for the first time and made sexual discrimination illegal. In addition, future parliaments would now contain sector standing committees to provide a form of backbench check on executive power.
203 *Fiji Times*, 15 May 1997.
204 Eight of the 14 provinces opposed the new Constitution.
205 *Australian*, 11 June 1997.
206 Kamikamica saw the opportunity to secure stronger representation for the FAP by standing in opposition to the SVT. Hence he ordered his members out of cabinet, but his Lauan members refused to leave. Provincial representation made unity hard to maintain for all Fijian parties. Kamikamica died shortly after in August 1998.

2.5 per cent from Fiji's GDP. Tourists abandoned Fiji for cheaper Asian destinations; so too did Australasian garment importers. Twenty per cent devaluation in early 1998 to lower the cost of debt received little support, even from tourist operators and garment manufacturers.

Dissident Fijian politicians planned to scuttle Rabuka's new era. Apisai Tora formed a Party of National Unity (PANU) to fight the SVT in Ba province. In Vanua Levu, Lasaro's Methodists formed the Veitokani ni Leweni Vanua Vakaristo Party (VLV) to reintroduce the Sunday ban and declare Fiji a Christian state. A worried Rabuka had his cabinet declare loyalty to the SVT, but ministers remained deeply troubled by the prospect of a new political landscape in 1999. A multi-party cabinet threatened greater competition for cabinet posts and preaching multiculturalism meant surrendering the racial card to Butadroka's nationalists or the VLV.

Had Rabuka taken the country down a false path in 1987? On the eve of new elections, he could hardly concede as much. 'I have never had any regrets,' he declared.[207] If fault existed, it lay in the divisive 1970 Constitution or in the Alliance's failure to address Fijian issues after 1977.[208] He still believed in communalism, and used support for multi-party governance as a device to provide the semblance of power sharing while maintaining Fijian communal power. Reddy recognised the limitations. 'My great fear here is that we could all again polarise into our separate racial groups,' he cautioned.[209] Timoci Bavadra had recognised the problem in the mid-1980s:

> Our future political stability rests ... on how well our present past and future leaders lead, accountable to the modern world, not relying on tradition and culture to make their race an exception to the laws of political logic or economic gravity.[210]

The great turning in Fijian politics after 1987 had been ephemeral. In its wake came a new wave of seekers for the golden eggs they believed their birthright and, this time, Rabuka would become one of their early victims.

---

207 *Fiji Times*, 14 May 1998.
208 *Fiji Times*, 14 May 1997.
209 *Fiji Times*, 24 August 1998.
210 *Fiji Times*, 14 May 1997.

3

Redux: The season for coups

The 1997 Constitution could have presented Fiji with the opportunity to determine for itself a very different future. Indeed, Sitiveni Rabuka introduced it by declaring that 'It is not enough that we should accept our collective presence in Fiji as simply one of coexistence. We should accept each other as belonging together as one people and one nation'.[1]

Beyond the level of rhetoric, however, little changed. Fiji's citizens did indeed gain a new national name; they were to be known as Fiji Islanders after the new name for the country. The term 'islander' held a different meaning for many people on Viti Levu (i.e. non-mainlanders) and was not widely accepted. Others believed its sole purpose was to sidestep the reality that one constructed ethnicity – Fijians – still held for itself the name of the country. Hence Fiji remained 'a nation of separate identities', sociologist Satendra Prasad argued, its political structures and institutions emphasising and feeding off 'the separateness of those identities'.[2]

The Constitution, however, did restore some measure of equality to the country's IndoFijians, perhaps the only sign of change to emerge from Fiji's long post-coup decade. There were now 25 open seats in which candidates and voters were not demarcated along ethnic lines. Unfortunately, these seats represented only 35 per cent of the total lower house seats available compared with 48 per cent before 1987, with the

---

1   *Fiji Times*, 24 June 1997.
2   S Prasad, 'Civic challenges to Fiji's democracy and the CCF's agenda for the next decade', in Arlene Griffen (ed.), *With Heart and Nerve and Sinew: Postcoup Writing from Fiji*. Suva: Christmas Club, 1997, p. 356.

majority still strictly divided along communal lines (23 Fijian, 19 Indian, one Rotuman and three General Electors). In addition, the political parties that contested the May 1999 election remained stubbornly divided along communal lines and the size of electorates perpetuated longstanding patterns of inequality. Fijian communal electorates held on average nearly 8,500 voters, IndoFijian electorates 10,500, and general electorates 4,600. Within the Fijian and IndoFijian electorates there were also huge variations. Urban Fijians, for example, comprised some 45 per cent of all Fijians in 1999, but received only 26 per cent of Fijian seats. Provincially based open seats were more evenly distributed but, with an average 17,500 voters, they vastly exceeded the size of communal seats.[3] Fiji's revised democracy still did not enable votes of equal value.

This should not have surprised; Rabuka never intended Fiji's return to multiracialism to be revolutionary. He wanted only for his proposed alliance with the National Federation Party (NFP) to demonstrate to all Fiji Islanders a transformed polity and thereby restore the Fijian Soqosoqo ni Vakavulewa ni Taukei (SVT) as the country's natural rulers in the 1999 general election. But many Fijians did regard the Constitution as revolutionary. Rabuka had dramatically overturned one of the important goals of his 1987 coups, namely the primacy of Fijian communalism, and they abandoned his party in droves. Sixty-two per cent of Fijians voted instead for Fijian minor parties like the Veitokani ni Leweni Vanua Vakaristo Party (VLV), Party of National Unity (PANU), the Fijian Association Party (FAP) and Butadroka's reformed Nationalist Vanua Tako Lavo Party (NVTLP), some of which, like the VLV and the NVTLP, opposed the new Constitution and power sharing, and called for the reinstatement of Fijian paramountcy.

The Constitution also introduced a new way to record people's voting intentions. Voters were told that preferential voting would encourage parties to cooperate before elections. The SVT's alliance with the NFP signalled such cooperation and so, too, did the Fiji Labour Party's (FLP) coalition with PANU. But preferential voting also introduced distortions. Voters had two choices. They could either vote for a party's choice of candidates (above the line) or independently select their own preferences (below the line). The second option presented unfamiliar difficulties. The long list of candidates for each electorate so confused

3   C Walsh, *Fiji*, 2006, pp. 360–63.

many voters that nearly 9 per cent of all votes in the 1999 election were invalid. Additionally, because most voters chose the simpler above-the-line voting option and accepted the preference deals that parties had worked out, outcomes were heavily dependent on how well parties had thought through the implications of their preference allocations. Many had not; some minor Fijian parties were so estranged from the SVT that they put Rabuka's party last, fragmenting the Fijian vote and denying the SVT its goal of representing and maintaining Fijian unity. The FLP more strategically swapped preferences to exclude its rivals, privileging the nationalists and VLV ahead of the SVT and especially the NFP, which it still regarded as its chief rival for the IndoFijian vote.

Had results been determined by proportional representation, a new era might well have come into being. Instead preferential voting condemned the SVT to only eight seats instead of 15, and the NFP to the indignity of losing all its seats instead of gaining 10. This cost Fiji the opportunity to develop a meaningful and strong multi-ethnic Opposition. Instead Labour – which focused its campaign on cost-of-living issues rather than constitutional nirvana – won the election with 37 seats. Proportional representation would have awarded it only 24 seats. The parties with which it formed a People's Coalition similarly benefited from the distortions wrought by preferential voting. PANU won four seats instead of two and the FAP 11 instead of seven, although the VLV picked up three when it could have gained seven under a more representative system of voting.[4]

Nonetheless, the persistence of post-1990 intra-communal rivalries, not electoral flaws, now most impacted on Fiji. Four days after the elections, Mahendra Chaudhry told Radio Navtarang talkback listeners that 'the NFP was the biggest enemy of the FLP and it was only fair that enemies be treated with contempt'.[5] Not surprisingly, the new constitutional era quickly became mired in the same destructive politics that had doomed Fiji's postcolonial development. Within seven years, it would be gone, swept away by yet another military intervention, and this time Rabuka would be little more than an ineffectual bystander.

4   Walsh, *Fiji*, 2006, p. 362.
5   *Fiji Times*, 11 April 2008.

Wheels within wheels

Constitutionally, the SVT had the right to cabinet places, as it passed the 10 per cent threshold for power sharing. But Fiji's political parties were in no mood to be conciliatory, especially Rabuka's SVT, whose share of the Fijian vote had collapsed from its high of 66 per cent in 1992 to 34 per cent in 1999, leaving it with only eight seats in the 71-seat parliament. Fijians still dominated the legislature but were now members of rival parties, many of whom joined the People's Coalition government as a demonstration of their opposition to the SVT. Never in Fiji's postcolonial history had an establishment party been so devastated in an election.[6] Nonetheless, the SVT wanted more than just its three constitutionally guaranteed cabinet seats; it demanded four specific posts. Chaudhry refused to negotiate and denied the SVT any role in cabinet. It proved a costly mistake. Including the SVT within government might have calmed the political climate and strengthened support for the new Constitution. Instead Chaudhry encouraged his opponents to resurrect the very politics of ethnicity that Labour had long sought to overcome. Nor did Rabuka challenge his decision. Instead he declared his party the official opposition and retired from politics to chair the Great Council of Chiefs (GCC).[7]

His successor, Ratu Inoke Kubuabola, one of the founders of the Taukei Movement in 1987, reportedly told the SVT's management board that 'people must be prepared to shed blood and die to get rid of the Chaudhry government'.[8] His strategy to woo disaffected members of rival Fijian parties into a grand alliance proved, however, to be less confronting. At first it seemed to have much going for it. Although PANU appeared a natural ally for the Labour Party given that members of both had a long association with western Fiji and its struggle against marginalisation orchestrated by eastern chiefs, PANU's leader, Apisai Tora, lost his seat because Labour ran a candidate against him and later denied him a seat in the Senate. Similarly, the VLV and FAP's rationale for cooperation with Labour evaporated with Rabuka's departure from the political scene.

---

6   This section draws on the chapter 'Mayhem and mutiny' in R Robertson & W Sutherland, *Government by the Gun: The Unfinished Business of Fiji's 2000 Coup* (Sydney: Pluto Press, 2001, pp. 1–49).
7   Alternatively known as the Bose Levu Vakaturaga or BLV.
8   Jone Dakuvula statement, www.fijihosting.com/pcgov/docs_o/jd_defending_speight.htm, 2 November 2000.

Within the FAP, this change soon saw members of the eastern Tailevu province seeking control of the party from Adi Kuini Vuikaba, both the widow of Labour's 1987 Prime Minister, Timoci Bavadra, and a former Labour leader. But the grand coalition was not to be. The VLV wanted the SVT to admit its past mistakes, particularly its failure to declare Fiji a Christian state and retain the Sunday ban.[9] And the FAP dissidents procrastinated. Hence the SVT's political manoeuvring came to nought. Instead Labour's incompetence drove opposition to assume new forms outside the political arena.

Chaudhry was much to blame for this. From the very beginning of his prime ministership he fell out with the media, especially the major English daily, the *Fiji Times*, whose expatriate editor he tried to deny a work permit. When the newspaper responded with stories critical of government policies, Chaudhry overreacted and threatened to license the media into reporting more favourably. Despite having relished anti-government press during its years in opposition, Labour seemed suddenly to have morphed into the very authoritarian master it had long railed against. As one commentator later noted, Chaudhry's behaviour diverted public attention from Labour's laudable attempts to reduce the cost of living: 'Every condescending smirk in response to even perfectly reasonable questions were duly recorded and broadcast on the 6pm [television] news.'[10] It did not help that he also made questionable appointments; his son became his personal secretary and an inexperienced politician his information deputy. Neither had the skills nor the temperament to woo the media, and both became issues of controversy themselves.

Nor did it not help that Labour had inherited a declining economy, with 30 per cent of Fiji's people living in poverty, 20 per cent of its children malnourished, and cities congested with over 50,000 squatters.[11] Labour wanted to create a more caring state, to introduce a social wage with improved social services and infrastructure, and to halt the process of privatisation begun after the 1987 coups. It also wished to reverse the decline in rural infrastructure, to improve roads and upgrade educational facilities for all Fiji's citizens. Thirteen years after Bavadra, it still officially regarded itself as a multiracial party. Above all, it saw itself as a people's

---

9   *Review*, February 2000, p. 14.
10   Nesian, 'The forces coalesce', *Croz Walsh's Blog – Fiji the Way it Was and Can Be*, crosbiew. blogspot.com.au, 31 January 2010. The website is operated by Crosbie Walsh, a former professor of Development Studies at the University of the South Pacific.
11   *Review*, December 1999, p. 28.

party, not a party for elites. And it was the first opposition party to have survived beyond the formation of government. Hence its belief that criticism, particularly from the press, so early within its term of office was misplaced.

Nonetheless, Labour's critics believed it 'tackled too many well entrenched interests too quickly'.[12] Its attack on privatisation upset Fijian corporate interests who regarded it as an important avenue for Fijianisation. Its welfare measures were similarly received. Reducing interest rates from 11 per cent to 6 per cent for low-income homebuyers financially compromised the Housing Authority. Other commentators wished for more debate, believing that the removal of consumption tax (VAT) from medicine and food, instead of introducing specifically targeted poverty-reduction programs, advantaged the well off more than the poor. They saw a government bulldozing its way ahead rather than seeking to build consensus.

Indeed, many changes did needlessly engender resentment. Labour's attack on expatriates in the name of localisation challenged vested foreign interests for little gain. Similarly flawed was its axing of Fiji's Intelligence Service and its refusal to renew Police Commissioner Isikia Savua's contract beyond two years. Decisions about the mahogany industry also created resentments. At stake were some 52,000 hectares of rare plantation mahogany – variously valued at between $136 million and $500 million. Unlike the less valuable, fire-prone and poorer quality pine forests in western and northern Fiji, these high-quality stands lay in Viti Levu's damp central and eastern provinces of Tailevu, Namosi and Naitisiri. Like the Alliance Party in its dealings with western landowners over pine 20 years before, Labour antagonised their chiefs by not consulting with them on a preferred partner for mahogany milling. More dangerously it upset a plan by Fijian businessmen to profit from their links with one processing tenderer. The controversies engendered by these issues, together with allegations about the misuse of ministerial entitlements and the treatment of some Fijians in the public service, began to take their toll politically. Labour had clear goals but it found communicating them

---

12   Rowan Callick, 'No ready way out of Speight's big hole', *Australian Financial Review*, 24 July 2000.

difficult and it did poorly in municipal elections in late 1999. 'If we are not careful with the little things we're doing,' conceded Deputy Prime Minister Tupeni Baba, 'it will blow up in our faces.'[13]

In the end, the land issue most damaged the Coalition in the eyes of its opponents. Rabuka's government had failed to resolve what would happen when some 40 per cent of the country's farm leases began expiring (one third of these before 2005). Many Fijian landowners wanted their land back. They had expanding families to accommodate or they wanted to farm themselves. Some believed that they did not benefit sufficiently from leasing land to warrant tying themselves to a new round of 30-year leases. If leases were to continue, they wanted them based on the market value of the land rather than its unimproved value and the lease period reduced. Neither response addressed the issue of land degradation, which was encouraged by short-term leases, nor the difficulties that Fijians faced obtaining loans for farm development.

But land always involved more than landowner demands. It also involved thousands of tenant farmers, most of them IndoFijians, who might at any time find themselves landless and unemployed. And it involved Fiji's collective economic welfare. Whatever happened to leases, Fiji had to ensure that it continued to earn vital foreign exchange from the productive use of its land. Any government would find these issues difficult to resolve. For this reason, President Kamisese Mara – while endorsing Labour's manifesto as good for Fijians – warned Chaudhry to give himself at least two years to win the confidence of Fijians before tackling the thorny issue of land.[14]

Instead, Labour immediately proposed extending existing 30-year farm leases and establishing a land use commission with a broad brief to address, among other things, the poor state of rural infrastructure. The Native Land Trust Board (NLTB), which administered all leased Fijian land, bitterly objected to losing its monopoly. Its officials began a campaign at provincial and village levels to frustrate the government's goals. It portrayed the Land Use Commission as 'a Trojan horse for a land grab and for emasculating the NLTB' and demanded that the NLTB be privatised to remove it from government interference.[15] Labour's failure to

---

13   *Fiji Times*, 20 December 1999.
14   *fijilive*, 30 April 2001.
15   Dakuvula, pcgovt.org.fj, accessed 2 November 2000; *Fiji Times*, 2 November 2000, p. 1.

build consensus now weakened its belated efforts to depoliticise the issue. The NLTB's counter strategy amounted to nothing less than a 'scorched earth campaign against Chaudhry'.[16] It did not help that Labour's public relations efforts focused almost exclusively on an English print media that it simultaneously argued was part of an orchestrated destabilisation campaign.[17] Unfortunately for the Coalition, the land issue exploded at the very moment it introduced constitutional amendments, most of which derived from changes that the SVT had failed to enact in 1998. This convergence handed the SVT a new weapon to destroy the Coalition – a civil disobedience campaign against Labour's attempts to weaken Fijian institutions by mounting what it purported to be an Indian takeover.[18]

Pressure on the Coalition now assumed new forms.[19] In April 2000, Tora announced the resurrection of the Taukei Movement to fight against the Coalition's land schemes and reforms. Its first rally in Lautoka on 20 April drew few protestors but, in Suva eight days later, 8,000 supporters turned out. This time a wider number of Fijian parties helped in the organisation, including a new Indigenous Foundation headed by FAP politician Ratu Timoci Silatolu. The development alarmed Tora's brother-in-law, Savua. The government should listen to the grievances of the Taukei Movement, he warned. The police may not be able to cope with more protest. Chaudhry dismissed his concerns and told him not to interfere in politics.

The sudden escalation in tension, together with the re-emergence of the Taukei Movement, sent shock waves through Fiji. Both the Australian High Commissioner and the US ambassador urged Chaudhry to act

---

16   Dakuvula believed that the NLTB had no interest in resettling evicted farmers or ensuring that farming continued. Its objective was simply to return land to Fijians regardless of the cost (Dakuvula, 'More land gossip from the grassroots', *Citizens' Constitutional Forum*, ccf.org.fj, 2 May 2001). Some Coalition members later alleged that the NLTB hatched the coup in conjunction with Fijian Holdings Ltd, one of whose senior executives planned to be its public face (pcgovt.org.fj, accessed 18 May 2000).

17   Minister for National Planning, Ganesh Chand quoted, *Fiji Times*, 21 December 1999, p. 3.

18   Dakuvula, pcgovt.org.fj, accessed 2 November 2000.

19   Behind the scenes, this might always have been the case. Commodore Bainimarama, the new RFMF Commander, claimed the old nationalist – Sakeasi Butadroka – demanded on the day after Labour assumed government that he launch a coup. Coup plotter Maciu Navakasuasua claimed that at the same time two Fijian businessmen, one heavily involved in the 1987 coups, and some Fijian politicians drew up a plan to shut down the Lami power station and use a mob to force a military intervention led by Colonel Filipo Tarakinikini. Fiji's future deputy prosecutor, Peter Ridgway, argued that plans had been drawn up for a coup in April 2000 based on a similar scenario of a breakdown in law and order. They did not go ahead because the plotters were unable to access the explosives and weapons required (Graham Davis, 'Fiji – democracy by the gun', *Sunday*, 7 May 2006, Nine Network; *Fiji Times*, 19 February 2003, and *Fiji Sun*, 12 January 2006).

cautiously. So, too, did many Labour sympathisers. It made more sense to create an atmosphere of stability and to address issues such as poverty and education rather than inflame ethnic tensions.[20]

But Chaudhry ploughed on regardless and his second deputy, Vuikaba, came to his defence. 'Decisions of the nation's leaders should be respected,' she argued: 'Leaders should be left to implement what they thought was right.'[21] This was not what many less autocratically inclined Labour members wished to hear. David Pickering, Deputy Leader of the Opposition, suggested an alternative solution: 'replace Chaudhry with his deputy [Baba] and do the whole country a favour'.[22] Some members of the Coalition came to the same conclusion. They were alarmed at Chaudhry's casual disregard of the dangers facing his government. When the NVLT, now led by the political outsider Iliesa Duvuloco, announced a rally in Suva on 19 May to petition the President to dismiss the Labour government, abrogate the Constitution and return all freehold land to Fijian ownership,[23] Home Affairs Minister Joji Uluinakauvadra promptly proclaimed a ban on further protest marches. Unfortunately Chaudhry overruled him, prompting Coalition dissidents to escalate their plans for his removal.[24]

Kubuabola also finalised an end game. The SVT plotted a motion of no confidence with FAP dissidents Silatolu and Ratu Tu'uakitau Cakanauto, the man tipped to replace Vuikaba as leader of the FAP. Whether an attempt to regenerate a Grand Fijian Alliance or, more simply, to prompt Coalition dissidents to move rapidly towards their goal, the SVT's strategy heightened a growing sense of crisis. Kubuabola later insisted that he had no interest 'in overthrowing a government that was

---

20   See comments of Dr Anirudh Singh (*Fiji Sun*, 4 May 2000), constitutional lawyer Yash Ghai on the Social Justice and Affirmative Action Bill, and journalist Tamarisi Digitaki ('Dangerous tinkering', *Review*, April 2000, p. 17).

21   *Fiji Times*, 10 February 2000.

22   *Fiji Times*, 4 May 2000.

23   The petition also called for the country's official name 'Fiji Islands' to revert to Fiji (*Fiji Times*, 1 February 2003).

24   Chaudhry would be permitted to celebrate one year in office until 20 May but would be replaced by Deputy Prime Minister Tupeni Baba in the following week. This theory was forwarded by FAP's Viliame Volavola, the Coalition's Minister for Urban Development and Housing (*Fiji Times*, 23 May 2000) and Australian High Commissioner Sue Boyd (*New Zealand Herald Online*, 21 August 2000). The later interim prime minister, Lai Qarase, also claimed to know of 'rumblings within the Coalition' and thought that a planned vote of no confidence had a good chance of succeeding (*Review*, August 2000, p. 11). Other Labour Party officials denied the rumour (*Fiji Times*, 23 August 2000, p. 3). Chaudhry approved the march on 26 April 2000.

self-destructing,'[25] but it was clear that, by mid-May, there were many overlapping conspiracies afoot, so many in fact that it became difficult to distinguish them. Within these kava-infused wheels within wheels, coup whispers gained volume.

Indeed, FAP research officer Inoke Sikivou became so alarmed at what he heard that he started holding regular meetings with Special Branch officers.[26] Third Battalion (3FIR) Commanding Officer Lt Col Viliame Seruvakula, who had sent intelligence operatives into the field after the elections, began regular briefings on the political situation with military HQ in late 1999. By May 2000 intelligence reports suggested an imminent coup, but Seruvakula lacked firm details and names, and sometimes suspected he was deliberately being fed false information.[27] Undoubtedly the patchwork of ad hoc and loosely connected conspiracies and their fluid membership also made detection difficult. Yet, if Fiji's military leaders were awake to the possibility of political disruption, who among them took the lead? Not military commander Voreqe (Frank) Bainimarama who, on the eve of his departure on 12 May to a UN peacekeeping conference in Oslo, appeared relaxed about possible threats. 'Well, you guys had better be prepared,' he warned his officers.[28] But the military were anything but prepared. In this they were not alone.

---

25   *Review*, June 2000, p. 11.
26   Inoke Sikivou, interview, *RFMF Board of Inquiry Report into the Involvement of the First Meridian Squadron in the Illegal Takeover of Parliament on 19 May 2000 and the Subsequent Holding of Hostages until 13 July 2000 (BoI)*, 24 October 2000, p. T654. The Board of Inquiry was held in the months immediately prior to the November mutiny, but its report never became public. Subsequently, 3FIR Commander Tevita Mara leaked the report after he fell out with Bainimarama and fled to Tonga in 2010. He alleged that Bainimarama refused to speak to the board and ordered all copies of its report destroyed. The report is posted on his web site at www.truthforfiji.com/uploads/8/4/2/3/8423704/1st_meridian_report_rfmf_opt2.pdf. It is divided into two parts, each numbered separately. To identify the separate sections referred to here, page references for the Findings are preceded with an F, Transcripts of interviews with a T.
27   *BoI*, pp. T938–T939.
28   *BoI*, p. T944; testimony of Lt Col Viliame Seruvakula. Ratu Tevita Mara later alleged that Bainimarama knew about the coup but took no steps. The President had questioned the wisdom of departing Fiji at such an unsettled time, but Bainimarama insisted in order to distance himself from it ('Fiji's dictator Frank Bainimarama's truth revealed', www.truthforfiji.com/uploads/8/4/2/3/8423704/fijis_dictator_frank_bainimarama_revealed.pdf, 17 December 2011, p. 3). Tarakinikini made a similar claim in an affidavit in 2005 (*Fiji Times*, 16 April 2005). These views are based solely on the 'convenience' of his absence or on his role as commander (he was responsible; he must have known). Seruvakula, however, who claimed that Rabuka seemed at the time to be the one most aligned with Ligairi, harboured no such suspicions about Bainimarama. It is unlikely that he would have protected Bainimarama from the rebels on his return to Fiji if he believed Bainimarama was in cahoots with them (*BoI*, pp. T939–940). Later in 2005 he claimed that the colonels Jone Baledrokadroka and Tarakinikini were among the senior officers behind the coup (*Fiji Times*, 2 March 2005).

Fracturing the postcolonial state

In fact the key to the events that unfolded lay very much with the military, and demonstrated the dangers inherent in the highly bureaucratic and centralised colonial-heritage state that Mara and later Rabuka had both done so much to construct but could do little to prevent unravelling. In the end both would suffer personally as a result.

Indeed, the attempted coup, which took place on Friday 19 May 2000, drew heavily on Rabuka's first coup for inspiration. But this copycat coup had two striking features that set it apart: first, it was poorly planned and, second, it stunned Fiji's main ruling institutions, which responded in confused ways.

Undoubtedly, the initial 'coup de farce' would have collapsed but for the later improvisations of two very important recruits, former British Special Air Service (SAS) Warrant Officer Ilisoni Ligairi, and the man who unintentionally became the public face of the coup attempt, George Speight.

Ligairi joined the British Army in the early 1960s and served in Ireland, Saudi Arabia, Kenya and Oman as a member of the SAS. He retired to Fiji in 1984 where, some three years later, he served as Rabuka's security advisor before becoming founding Commander of a 70-man antiterrorist Counter Revolutionary Warfare Unit (CRWU)[29] that Rabuka established as a palace guard to protect his 1987 coups. It was a spectacular promotion for a man who had only ever been a non-commissioned officer and had never received officer training.

Regarded as a specialist elite, nearly half the CRWU's personnel were drawn from Ligairi's (and Rabuka's) Vanua Levu, a reflection of its origins following the 1987 re-establishment of Tovata political dominance. It trained apart from the rest of the army and jealously retained its guardianship ethos. During the 1990s it allegedly engaged in covert operations, spying on politicians such as Vuikaba as well as unionists, cane farmers, business people, NGOs and diplomats. It even spied on NZ military forces engaged in joint exercises with the Republic of Fiji

---

29   The CRWU was renamed the First Meridian Squadron in 1999 and placed under the command of Lt Penaia Baleinamau. It was later claimed that the CRWU had never been gazetted as a unit within the RFMF; in all probability was an illegal entity (*Fiji Times*, 31 July 2003).

Military Forces (RFMF) in 1996.[30] The 60-year-old Major Ligairi fostered its guardianship role. Every year members of the unit trained on Rabuka's Valavala estate on Vanua Levu, 73 kilometres north of Savusavu and celebrated the 1987 coup anniversary with him. Although the unit underwent changes after Ligairi's retirement in 1997, it possessed no clear organisational structure or standard operational procedures. Intelligence operatives, who rarely trained with the rest of the unit and remained close to Ligairi, dominated its leadership. Ligairi officially answered to the RFMF Commander but, in reality, he headed what amounted to a private army 'with its own agenda'. It was doubtful, the RFMF's subsequent board of inquiry into the events noted, if the Commander was ever privy to any CRWU activity.[31] In all probability, Ligairi and his close intelligence operatives alone planned the simple repeat of Rabuka's May 1987 coup, a task made all the easier when Bainimarama brought Ligairi back at the end of April 2000 as a training advisor to assist the CRWU protect international delegates at the forthcoming African Caribbean Pacific (ACP) conference in Suva.[32] The unit's training officer, Captain Shane Stevens, later told the RFMF's board of inquiry that, had Ligairi not been there, the CRWU would not have launched the coup.[33] The board agreed, but rooted home most of the blame for the coup to the RFMF for allowing one man so much power, especially one it considered so ill-equipped to be a director and planner.[34]

One of the CRWU's intelligence operatives was 36-year-old Sergeant Vilimoni Tikotani. Described to the board of inquiry as arrogant and boastful, 'Commander Bill' Tikotani bragged to journalists soon after the start of the coup of his own role in its planning.[35] Fired up from his visit to Rabuka's estate and the following celebratory *yaqona* (kava) session on Sunday 14 May, he 'saw the opportunity to execute the coup when the

---

30 These charges were made by the prosecution during the court martial of CRWU soldiers (*Fiji Times*, 30 & 31 July 2003).

31 *BoI*, pp. F37, F47.

32 *BoI*, p. T876; testimony of Lt Col Filipo Tarakinikini. The African Caribbean Pacific (ACP) grouping came into existence at the same time as the ACP–EU Lomé Convention in 1975 and existed to strengthen the voices of otherwise disparate former colonies in their dealings with the European Union (EU). Its Suva conference was charged with producing a successor agreement to the Lomé Convention.

33 *BoI*, p. T1002. Baleinamau also regarded Ligairi's role as pivotal (p. T64).

34 *BoI*, p. F47.

35 Mary-Louise O'Callaghan & Christopher Dore, 'Shadowy figures thicken the plot', *Australian*, 24 May 2000; Dore wrote of Tikotani 'madly waving his cocked handgun around at reporters with a deranged smile on his face, exclaiming his prowess and detailing the planning that went into the coup' ('Just another day in paradise', *Australian*, 27–28 May 2000, p. 24).

nationalist protest march was approved'. As NVTLP President Viliame Savu later acknowledged, 'all attention by the security forces would be on the march while there would hardly be any focus placed in Parliament'.[36] Thus, on his return to Suva the very next day, Tikotani contacted the NVTLP's Peceli Vuniwai and provided the one crucial element that all the various conspiratorial groups lacked, confirmation of military involvement. Said Savu, 'we assigned Navakasuasua and Peceli Vuniwai to work with them' in order to hastily prepare an indigenous fight-back against the policies of the Labour government.[37] Clearly the initiative was not entirely Tikotani's, Ligairi was the special ingredient. 'When they told me this thing is set, I just asked, "Who's this? Who's that?"' Ligairi later disingenuously recalled: 'And then I say, "OK, go ahead".'[38]

On the Tuesday, Ligairi informed some of his officers to be on standby for the Friday march,[39] in what capacity they were not told. Even the conspirators seemed uncertain. At a meeting in Colo-i-Suva the next day, Tikotani, Vuniwai and Maciu Navakasuasua, a mining-explosives expert and participant in earlier abortive post-election conspiracies to bring down Labour,[40] discussed assassinating Chaudhry but decided, instead, for the event that would coincide with Duvuloco's NLTV march on Friday 19 May. On the 18th, a small cache of weapons was smuggled into parliament and hidden in the FAP photocopy room in preparation. Other weapons were smuggled out also on the Thursday.[41] Selected CRWU soldiers were told they were to protect VIPs if the march turned violent; others were purposely kept in the dark.

---

36 This proved all too true. The police, however, were also totally unprepared for the march's descent into rioting. Its Riot Squad, based in Nasinu, could not attend the crisis, allegedly because its bus had been diverted to pick up Police Commissioner Savua's son from Yat-Sen School (*Fiji Sun*, 2 September 2004).

37 *Fiji Sun*, 22 September 2005.

38 'Cyclone George', *ABC*, 15 November 2000, www.abc.net.au/4corners/stories/s198296.htm.

39 *BoI*, p. T449; testimony of Lt Charles Dakuliga.

40 Davis, 'Fiji – democracy by the gun', 2006.

41 *BoI*, pp. T451–2. Dakuliga and others were concerned at the instructions they were given and returned their weapons to camp.

Navakasuasua also drafted the media-savvy Speight to be their spokesperson.[42] The 44-year-old would-be corporate star, son of a senator and closely ally of the businessman and former SVT politician Jim Ah Koy, had spent most of his early life overseas, studying in the United States and working in Australia. His political and business connections in Fiji promised a privileged future after he returned in 1998. In little over a year he became one of Fiji's most senior forestry executives, poised to reap lucrative rewards from processing plantation mahogany. But that world crashed when the Rabuka-led government lost office. His chairmanship of Fiji Hardwood Corporation Ltd and other directorships ended and he was charged with currency offences. In the weeks prior to the coup the frustrated Speight held discussions with Duvuloco and lobbied the FAP to overthrow the Coalition government, even joining in on discussions at its parliamentary rooms.[43] At 8.45 am on Friday 19 May he met up with Tikotani and Ligairi, allegedly for the first time, at the School of Maritime Studies in Laucala Bay.[44] Together they agreed to proceed with their coup that day, although how exactly still remained fluid. According to Savu, the CRWU soldiers wanted to 'shoot to kill' if necessary but were convinced instead to focus on taking hostages.[45] Navakasuasua also alleges that Speight wanted first to seize Mara, but a quick phone call that

---

42 Although termed a 'Part-European', George Speight had Fijian family and a Fijian name, Ilikimi Naitini, which he rarely used. Later attempts to shroud Speight's actions in Fijian mythology claimed his surname meant 'the coming of the end' (Jone Luvenitoga, 'The vision', *Sunday Post*, 14 March 2004). But Fiji's rigid racial compartmentalism could work against him. Thus Rabuka's public mocking of Speight's claims to be a champion of indigenous rights: 'I am still waiting for him to make his announcement in Fijian' (*fijilive*, 21 May 2000). However, 'Few thought to question George Speight's origins', according to Madraiwiwi, 'or his new found commitment to the indigenous cause'. Instead they were persuaded by the rhetoric and vision that he would restore to them control of their destiny (Madraiwiwi, 'Ethnic tensions and the law', 2004).

43 *BoI*, pp. F24; T654, testimony of Sikivou. Allegedly Speight also met with Police Commissioner Savua and Rabuka at JJ's Restaurant in downtown Suva on 18 May (*fijilive*, 19 December 2002). On the same day, Speight and Savu allegedly also met with members of the NLTV, FAP, the Taukei Movement and the SVT, including Jo Nata and Silatolu, in the SVT office as they were discussing the march and finalising the petition. They informed the group of the coup. A further briefing was held at 6 pm (*Fiji Times*, 5 December 2002, 9 & 19 February 2003).

44 Tikotani claims he met Speight for the first time on Wednesday 17 May (Dore, 'Just another day in paradise', *Australian*, 27–28 May 2000, p. 24), although Navakasuasua seems to suggest it may have been the Thursday when they lunched or dined at Duvuloco's home (*Fiji Sun*, 20 & 21 September 2005).

45 *Fiji Sun*, 22 September 2005. Savu claims that Jim Speight wanted to oust Mara at the same time as Chaudhry (*fijilive*, 19 July 2004).

morning to the Presidential Palace soon established Mara's unavailability. His private secretary, Joe Browne, would receive the marchers' petition instead.[46]

Back in the parliamentary complex, other FAP conspirators were busy working the phones. At 8.45 am Sikivou overheard Silatolu claiming that he would be prime minister by the end of the day.[47] Fifteen minutes later at CRWU headquarters, Lt Penaia Baleinamau briefed his unit to prepare for a VIP protection exercise and then left for the School of Maritime Studies. Speight's brother, Jim, an Australian citizen, took additional weapons from the CRWU armoury in his vehicle. By 10.30 am the two Speights, Tikotani, Navakasuasua and three CRWU soldiers were preparing to enter parliament while Ligairi headed for the RFMF camp to rally the troops. All were confident that the military would back them;[48] so confident in fact that the small group was woefully unprepared. They possessed few weapons, inadequate plastic ties to secure their targets, and no food and refreshments. No detailed plan had been drawn up, no rehearsals undertaken, no duty rosters produced and, once the small team burst into parliament and declared their intentions at 10.45 am, they seemed not to know what to do next.[49] They constrained an IndoFijian cleaner mistaking him for Chaudhry's bodyguard, who wisely used the confusion to slip out of parliament with a group of visiting students.[50] Observers witnessed no clear command structure. They believed the unidentified men were waiting for instructions from someone; who that

---

46   *Fiji Sun*, 27 October 2005. Browne claims that a member of the NVTLP approached him on the Thursday, requesting a written undertaking that Mara would receive the petition in person (*fijilive*, 3 June 2001). Fiji still technically refers to the former colonial governors' building as Government House. But it has become the Presidential Palace in all but name since 1987.

47   *BoI*, p. T655.

48   *BoI*, pp. F24; T655, testimony of Sikivou; T397, testimony of Speight; Bainimarama statement (*Fiji Sun*, 22 March 2006). Savu argues instead that there were seven CRWU soldiers and five NVTLP members who entered parliament (*Fiji Sun*, 20 September 2005).

49   *BoI*, p. T919, testimony of Adi Kikau.

50   *BoI*, p. F41.

might have been produced much press speculation.[51] Poseci Bune, leader of the VLV and the man who had dashed Speight's corporate aspirations, recalled Speight telling his captives between phone calls (to Duvuloco, then leading his 50,000 strong march to the Presidential Palace)[52] that 'we would be surprised' when the real leader arrived. Finally, at the end of one call, he suddenly turned and said, 'I think he is going to be late. Well, I'll have to take over from here'.[53]

Between them, Ligairi and Speight would recast this hastily planned and clumsy coup into a revolution designed to send shock waves through the very community it purported to serve. Indigenous Fijians, they argued, were weary of marginalisation by Indians, one of whose sons – for the first time in Fiji's history – now headed the country's government. Consequently, Ligairi assumed that Fijians would readily accept Chaudhry's departure from office. But, after Ligairi arrived at the Queen Elizabeth Barracks (QEB) in Nabua to rally support, he quickly discovered that assumption flawed.

---

51   Police Commissioner Isikia Savua became the favourite (*fijilive*, 24 August 2000), in part because he was deemed missing in action at the time and because the police had developed no action plan for the rally. Wadan Narsey later reported a would-be prime minister backing out prior to the swearing in of the new rebel government when his brother rang to say, 'Get the hell out of there; the army is no longer with you'. He reportedly told the Speight group he was going home to freshen up and never returned ('Fiji's cancerous conspiracies of silence', narseyonfiji.wordpress.com/2012/03/18/fijis-cancerous-conspiracies-of-silence-5-november-2011-on-blogs/, 5 November 2011). After Savua resigned in 2003 to become Fiji's ambassador to the United Nations, his successor, Andrew Hughes, believed he had enough evidence to charge Savua with treason (*Fiji Times*, 8 June 2004). No charges were ever laid. Chief Justice Tuivaga investigated Savua's involvement later in the year and cleared him. But the report was never made public. A letter from Speight to that inquiry did surface; in it he denied Savua's involvement (*fijilive*, 17 May 2001). Navakasuasua claimed instead that former Col Savenaca Draunidalo, then Public Service Commissioner, had been the intended leader and was waiting in the nearby Holiday Inn but backed out after the march degenerated into looting (Graham Davis, 'The camera doesn't lie', 15 June 2011, www.grubsheet.com.au/the-camera-doesnt-lie/). Lt Col Meli Saubulinayau told the board of inquiry that Draunidalo had warned Tarakinikini of the coup the night before it occurred (which perhaps accounts for the latter's unexplained frantic calls to the CRWU the next morning). Draunidalo rang the acting commander, Col Alfred Tuatoko, the next day to say that he was returning to the RFMF barracks. Tuatoko ordered the gates shut, fearing that Draunidalo might try to assume command (*BoI*, p. T889).
52   Vodafone later revealed that Speight was in constant contact with journalist and FAP member Jo Nata and Silatolu on 19 May (*Fiji Times*, 12 December 2002). Prosecutor Peter Ridgway claimed Speight called Duvuloco, Nata and Silatolu constantly from the early hours of 19 May, and frantically used his mobile in the final 10 minutes before 11 am (*fijilive*, 11 March 2003).
53   scoop.co.nz (NZ parliamentary website), 18 Aug 2000. According to Savu, at this point the whole scenario changed. Speight made the mistake of taking control and deviated from the plan. At this stage they still believed that they had full military backing (*Fiji Sun*, 20 September 2005).

To begin with, most senior officers who met with him did not understand what had happened. They suggested using the CRWU to put down the coup, but Ligairi told the Land Force Commander and acting RFMF Commander, Col Alfred Tuatoko, 'We are there'.

'What do you mean, "We are there?"' Tuatoko responded.
'I and some of the boys', Ligairi replied.

'The sad thing was,' Tuatoko's chief of staff Lt Col Samueli Raduva later recalled, 'the very unit that was planned to take the counter security measures [necessary for such an eventuality] … was the unit that carried out or used the events of May 19th'.[54]

Ligairi had now to buy time. 'We don't want a confrontation,' he stressed, telling Tuatoko that he had only intervened two hours earlier to control the situation. And he quickly volunteered to accompany Tuatoko to brief President Mara, who obligingly directed them not to escalate the situation with confrontation.[55] But, by then, the situation itself had escalated. Duvuloco's march had morphed into a $30 million orgy of looting and violence in downtown Suva in the early afternoon. On his return from visiting the President, Tuatoko briefed his officers: 'These are the pillars that we are going to work on: no confrontation, no bloodshed, everything within the law, solidarity for the RFMF.'[56]

But the pillars provided little guidance for officers wanting to know if the CRWU should be allowed to continue drawing on weapons and food from the barracks, or indeed whether CRWU troops should be allowed to join their colleagues in the parliament. Tuatoko clearly did not want the military to turn on itself. Yet, from the very beginning, it did. On the evening of 19 May, at the same time as Mara declared a state of emergency, Seruvakula intervened to prevent soldiers burning down the CRWU HQ. And he worked with Captain Shane Stevens to hide the remaining CRWU weapons and set up checkpoints around their complex. But his efforts to cordon off the parliament on 20 May in preparation for a counterattack were frustrated. During an emergency meeting of senior officers that same day, Lt Col Filipo Tarakinikini – the Logistics Unit's chief staff officer – and Raduva 'lectured' him about the plight of Fijians and told him that

---

54   *BoI*, p. T846.
55   *BoI*, p. T935, testimony of Tuatoko.
56   *BoI*, p. T847, testimony of Raduva.

regarding the crisis as a hostage situation was a Western perspective.[57] Such views echoed those held by the rebels for obvious reasons. Lt Col Metuisela Mua, formerly head of the Fiji Intelligence Service, told the board of inquiry that the army relied on imported principles. It sought to apply a military solution to a political problem. He believed it should have used Fiji's indigenous protocols, which he called the best reconciliation system in the world.[58] Obviously Tuatoko's pillars could not hold for long, but they held long enough for Ligairi and Speight – now bereft of military support – to re-engineer their coup into a very different beast, one which sought to remove Fijian leaders whose preparedness to deal with Indians as equals had – they believed – cost Fijians political leadership.

What began as a simple copy of Rabuka's first coup[59] also had a second striking feature: the stunned and confused responses of Fiji's main ruling institutions. Many of Fiji's leaders were deeply implicated in various plots to bring down the new Labour Prime Minister following his election or at least sympathised with that goal. In addition, the President, the GCC, and the Fiji military forces, among others, were all willing participants in and beneficiaries of the 1987 coups. Having acquiesced once, their hands were tied. 'We approve of the cause, but not the means,' they nervously and frequently intoned,[60] a mantra that all too often implied support. Col Savenaca Draunidalo certainly believed so, telling the board of inquiry that, when the Commander said 'We support the cause', he meant that the military should develop strategies to make it happen.[61] So too Speight: the military would say 'we support what you have done, we support the reason but we can't say much about the method; apart from that we are behind you'.[62]

---

57   *BoI*, p. T946, testimony of Seruvakula. At his later court martial, Stevens claimed that Tuatoko, Raduva and Tarakinikini had permitted the continued transfer of CRWU weapons and ammunition to parliament on 19 May. When Bainimarama returned, he directed that they be brought back. Altogether 309 weapons went to parliament (*fijilive*, 26 September 2002).

58   *BoI*, p. T376, testimony of Mua.

59   When Rabuka arrived at parliament on 19 May hoping to act as a mediator, he asked Speight why he did it. Speight responded, 'What do you mean asking me that question; only two people here did this thing, only you and me. You did not complete it; I will complete it' (*BoI*, p. T739, testimony of Volavola).

60   This section draws on R Robertson, 'A house built on sand', *Time* (Sydney), 24 July 2000, p. 16; and Robertson & Sutherland, *Government by the Gun*, 2001, pp. 1–4. The latter contains a detailed account of the coup in 'Mayhem & mutiny – the 2000 crisis', pp. 1–49.

61   *BoI*, p. T862.

62   *BoI*, p. T402.

In May 1987, Rabuka had launched his coup to remove 'an Indian dominated' Labour government that had won office from the long-serving Ratu Mara just one month before. Mara rushed immediately to Rabuka's side and was restored – eventually – to the prime ministership. Fijian paramountcy returned and with it the dominance of an eastern chiefly elite. Thirteen years on, the 80-year-old Mara was halfway through his second five-year term as president. Rabuka, the commoner who had succeeded him as prime minister for seven years until defeated by Chaudhry, now headed the GCC, ostensibly in order to maintain control.[63] This supreme Fijian institution had also rushed to endorse Rabuka's coups in 1987, bestowing on the commoner life membership of the chiefly council. In return a new Constitution in 1990 bestowed on the GCC the power to appoint members of the Senate and to choose Fiji's president. Later it was rewarded with a secretariat of its own. In addition, the Council's main investment company, Fijian Holdings Ltd, profited greatly from Rabuka's affirmative action policies, as did many of its individual shareholders.

Rabuka's own former institution, the military, also benefited from the coups. Its official size had nearly doubled since 1987[64] and, during most of the 1990s, the country's leaders turned a blind eye to successive blowouts in the annual military budget. Now members of one of its more highly politicised units were holed up in parliament with over 43 hostages. Thus compromised, the military found it difficult to resolve the situation decisively. It did not storm parliament; nor did it cordon parliament off. 'Let us not use the universal template of the army coming in to restore order,' Rabuka advised: 'There are friends and relatives in there. The army would think twice about going in.'[65] Draunidalo warned the officers' think tank advising the Commander that even setting up checkpoints around the parliament could endanger life. That its officers may not have supported either the Chaudhry government or Speight counted for little when there was no one prepared to take control and end the situation.[66] This generated an 'atmosphere of distrust' in which

---

63 *BoI*, p. T954, testimony of Rabuka.
64 Stewart Firth and Jon Fraenkel note that, by 2005, the RFMF comprised 3,137 staff and 767 reservists, the latter down from nearly 2,000 prior to the 1987 coups ('The Fiji military and ethno-nationalism: analysing the paradox', in J Fraenkel, S Firth & BV Lal (eds), *The 2006 Military Takeover in Fiji: A Coup to End All Coups*. Canberra: ANU E Press, 2009, p. 120).
65 *Age* (Melbourne), 23 May 2000, p. 14.
66 *BoI*, pp. T952–3, testimony of Rabuka.

many soldiers found it useful 'to hedge their bets', as Tarakinikini put it.[67] Thus officers who proposed action were often viewed with suspicion, an outcome not lost on the rebels holed up in parliament. They constantly rang them at the QEB, offering inducements for their support or threats if it failed to be forthcoming. And they sought to divide the military. Tarakinikini (a founding officer of the CRWU) and Col Ulaiasi Vatu (Strategic HQ) – both supportive of the cause but not the method – were publically promoted as new heads of the RFMF by the rebels and found their loyalties suspected as a consequence. In the long term, their military careers suffered.[68] Lt Col Jone Baledrokadroka, chief staff officer Operations at Land Force Command, believed that, had Speight alone headed the coup, there might have been less contention and military uncertainty. He was seen as a nobody, a part-European businessperson and beneficiary of Rabuka's cronyism. But the military had no such doubts about Ligairi and, if alleged backers such as Draunidalo had actually come forward, the coup would have gained much more credibility.[69]

A kind of psychological warfare now began, its goal to divide and paralyse the RFMF, and its effects on trust between officers would be long-lasting. The ambitious and frustrated Tarakinikini became an easy target. His efforts to promote the reorganisation of the RFMF in the 1990s had achieved little. Bainimarama had denied him leadership of the CRWU in 1999 and of security for the ACP conference in 2000. He was on leave and sitting an MBA exam at the University of the South Pacific (USP) when the coup took place, but quickly volunteered to act as a negotiator. 'I could see through these guys,' Tarakinikini told the board of inquiry, 'I could see the lies they were spinning in the name of the indigenous Fijian cause and especially George Speight when he came on, I could see the line he was coming on, I had to match him … if I did not step in … the situation was going to deteriorate not by design but by inactions.' As a spokesperson for the RFMF, the highly personable and articulate

67   *Fiji Times*, 16 April 2005.

68   *Fiji Times*, 16 April 2006. In 2003, the military claimed that Tarakinikini met with the Police Commissioner and a senator at a Nadi eatery one month before the coup (*fijilive*, 9 February 2003). During the later mutiny trial, one CRWU soldier claimed the Naitasiri chief and future senator, Ratu Inoke Takiveikata, believed that both Tarakinikini and Baledrokadroka had been assigned tasks by the rebels on 19 May that they had not executed (Evidence of Sgt Manoa Bonafasio, *fijilive*, 4 July 2003). Col Vatu died in 2004, still distressed at the aspersions cast on his character. Tarakinikini, who resigned from the military in 2001 and left Fiji with government approval for a UN peacekeeping role, never cleared his name. The military declared him a deserter in 2003.

69   Jone Baledrokadroka, 'Sacred king and warrior chief: The role of the military in Fiji politics', PhD Thesis, The Australian National University, Canberra, 2012, pp. 147–48.

Tarakinikini proved effective. Although his goal was to establish rapport with the rebels in order to prevent bloodshed, he also became dangerously effective as an official counter to Speight: 'I knew all along what they were trying to do, they were really trying to undermine me and when they knew that it was not going to work then they came out and started accusing me of being with them … in order to … pull the rug under my feet.' Once the rebels knew that the army would not support them, 'their tactics then was to try and put in the Trojan horse inside the RFMF to try and break us from within'.[70] To some extent it worked. Bainimarama allegedly told Tuatoko not to trust Tarakinikini and Raduva.[71]

Complicating matters also were divisions between serving officers and reservists. The presence of many reserve officers, particularly Rabuka, created discomfort among some serving officers. But this discomfort paled in comparison with the army's physical inability to act. Despite Rabuka's largesse while in office, the RFMF lacked equipment, weapons and vehicles to support domestic operations.[72] Even the weapons it possessed were poorly managed. The CRWU kept its own armoury but the RFMF possessed no master register. What records it did keep were woefully inadequate.[73] When the police belatedly requested its assistance to deal with the rioting and looting that broke out in downtown Suva at 1 pm following the NVTLP march, the military lacked sufficient vehicles to send its soldiers into the city. It tried to hire buses, but most of the city's buses were busy taking children from their rapidly closing schools. Hence soldiers did not arrive on Suva's streets until 6 pm, three hours after the initial request and well past the time when they could be most effective. If the intention of the riot had been to stretch Fiji's forces during the coup, the rebels did not have to try too hard.

That both the Commander and chief operations officer were overseas probably did not assist the RFMF either, but without contingency planning and training to deal with a national crisis, it is doubtful that their presence could have made much difference.[74] Of course many officers

---

70   *BoI*, pp. T869–871, testimony of Tarakinikini.

71   *BoI*, p. T1003, testimony of Captain Shane Stevens.

72   *BoI*, p. F51.

73   *BoI*, p. F58. This probably accounts for the discrepancy between RFMF records of weapons missing after the coup and CRWU claims. The CRWU claimed it took 131 weapons from its armoury and returned them. The RFMF maintained that 25 were missing, but it is possible that the CRWU never possessed these weapons; the difference being explained by poor records (*BoI*, pp. F58, 67). By 2002 the number of weapons missing had been officially reduced to 13 (*Fiji Times*, 14 March 2002).

74   *BoI*, p. T886, testimony of Lt Col Meli Saubulinayau.

had long been aware of the RFMF's deficiencies but felt constrained by the vision of their leaders. Plans to reorganise the institution had lain dormant for years with the result that its many parts such as HQ FMF, HQ Land Force and Strategic HQ were disconnected, although restructuring in late 1998 brought these together as Strategic HQ and Land Forces HQ.[75] Additionally, too many rapid promotions in the past conspired to create tensions over how the institution was run, and much of this came to the fore after 19 May[76] and focused on the Commander himself.

Commodore Josaia Voreqe Bainimarama had served with the Fiji Naval Squadron since its inception in 1975 and replaced Ratu Epeli Ganilau as commander in March 1999, when the latter left – unsuccessfully – to enter politics as part of Mara's VLV challenge to the SVT. Many senior officers, perhaps feeling that they were more deserving, resented that their commander was a naval officer; moreover an officer who lacked the combat experience and Sandhurst training of the colonels. One even argued, 'That is where the whole thing starts'.[77] Bainimarama had not taken kindly to this reception and posted perceived dissidents to the military's Strategic Headquarters in Suva, away from the QEB in Nabua suburb.[78] 'We now operate [more] like a gang than a military force,' Tarakinikini told the board of inquiry.

Rent by internal division and constrained by its ethnic identity, the RFMF dithered as the coup evolved. Many of its officers refused to commit, leaving their troops confused.[79] Fijians confronted Fijians as never before. Their leaders no longer acted as a united political force. Mara and Rabuka had never trusted each other and their differences

---

75   A Defence white paper proposed restructuring in 1997 but, with the SVT in turmoil, in its final year and the Labour Party disinterested once in office, little came of it (Baledrokadroka, 'Sacred king and warrior chief', 2012, pp. 92–94).

76   *BoI*, pp. T833–4, testimony of Co JM Waqanisau; T875, testimony of Tarakinikini.

77   *BoI*, p. T834, testimony of Waqanisau. Baledrokadroka suggests that the Tovata Ganilau sought a malleable commander not linked with the rival Bauan dynasty such as Colonel Administration Quartermaster, Lt Ratu George Kadavulevu (Baledrokadroka, 'Sacred king and warrior chief', 2012, pp. 229–30), who Col Dr Senilagakali claimed had approached him two months before the coup to ask Mara to step down as President (*BoI*, p. T839). Lt Col Etueni Caucau claimed that there were rumours of an internal coup against Bainimarama in April 2000, resulting in his security being strengthened (*BoI*, p. T898).

78   Baledrokadroka, 'Sacred king and warrior chief', 2012, p. 247.

79   *BoI*, p. T946, testimony of Seruvakula.

now resurfaced.[80] Given how quickly events unfolded, Mara possibly believed that the military's slow reaction meant that it was colluding with the coup-makers.[81] Certainly, many provincial chiefs saw the attempted coup as an opportunity to redress long-perceived inequalities within the community; others saw it as a chance to consolidate a new and more radicalised Fijian leadership. Ligairi played to all these divisions.

Hundreds of supporters flocked to the parliament to act as human shields in case the military decided to attack. Ligairi organised them into fighting units. By threatening to stir the rumblings of commoners, Ligairi sent a strong message to all chiefs: commoners would take over if necessary. Ligairi's transformation of the forces within the parliamentary complex, however, created tensions that he found difficult to control, although this was not always obvious to outsiders at the time. He headed the military wing, which – with the addition of more CRWU soldiers and reservists – soon comprised over 56 soldiers. By the end of May he had established an intelligence and operations centre, a logistics cell, as well as duty and weapons rosters.

Speight headed the political wing, a fluid group that grew strongly due to the army's failure to blockade the parliament. Politicians, former soldiers, public servants, Methodist ministers[82] and chiefs assembled at the parliament, ostensibly to find out what was happening but in many cases to participate in what they undoubtedly viewed as a transformative event. The former intelligence chief, Metuisela Mua, provides a useful example. He went into parliament within hours of the coup, joined in an early

---

80   In April 2001, Mara somewhat belatedly revealed that he found Rabuka's 1987 coups 'disgusting'. He added that in his seven years in government, Rabuka showed that 'he couldn't run an office' (Mara, interview, *Closeup*, Fiji TV, unofficial transcript on pcgovt.org.fj, accessed 29 April 2001). Sir Vijay Singh later revealed that Mara had told him both Rabuka and Savua were behind the coup (*fijivillage*, 18 August 2006). It did not help that when Rabuka first visited Mara on 19 May, he requested that Mara appoint him as commander (*Fiji Times*, 8 July 2004).

81   Baledrokadroka, 'Sacred king and warrior chief', 2012, pp. 148–49.

82   Methodist President Rev. Tomasi Kanailagi wrote to Speight on 16 June: 'we must not let Fijians fight among themselves or the Indians will have the last laugh'. He promised them a divine pardon for their actions (*Fiji Times*, 20 June 2004).

meeting, and eventually became part of Speight's team.[83] Negotiations were a key activity for this wing and a special negotiating room was established alongside the ops room, symbolically located above where the bulk of hostages were held.[84]

But the key innovation remained the *vanua* wing; its formation was a direct result of military inaction, in particular its failure to storm parliament during the first weekend of the crisis. That failure enabled the rebels to encourage hundreds of ordinary Fijians to flock to parliament and organise them loosely into provincial groups that provided a veneer of traditional legitimacy. Such groups were publicly marched around the parliamentary complex and sometimes sent out to attack police or soldiers. Ligairi bragged that his new soldiers would soon be better than the military.[85] They got one opportunity to prove themselves on Sunday 28 May. Led by CRWU soldiers, over 500 rebels slipped into Suva, firing at the Presidential Palace en route. There they trashed the offices of Fiji TV, which had aired a program ridiculing the rebels, in particular Speight and Duvuloco. During the rampage, a ricocheting bullet killed a police officer. A security officer also died from heart failure. Both deaths destroyed the notion that the rebels opposed confrontation. Indeed, they secretly plotted to escalate violence by destroying both the Presidential Palace and Suva in order 'to show Ratu Mara that even though he was the head of government and in total command of the Army, Police and Civil Service … the *vanua* was much stronger than him'. A group of hymn-singing women would lead the *vanua* and rebel soldiers on a destructive march to the capital. However, rain thwarted their plans.[86] But the events of 27 May were not the first foray outside parliament.

---

83   *Bol*, p. T370, testimony of Mua. Others, like Simione Kaitani, would later claim that they were only volunteering their skills to assist Fiji in a difficult situation. Kaitani claimed his skills lay in conflict management (Wansolwara, August 2005) although, in 2003 on FTV's *Closeup*, he admitted sedition and inciting people with hate speech (Thakar Ranjit Singh, 'Shame on our banana republic', *Fiji Sun*, 18 April 2006). Many others would make similar claims when later charged. The future Tui Cakau, Ratu Naiqama Lalabalavu, used his chiefly status to justify his presence at the rebel takeover of the Sukanaivalu Barracks in Labasa while Ratu Josefa Dimuri claimed he wanted only to facilitate talks between rebels and loyalists (*Fiji Times*, 29 January 2005).
84   *Bol*, p. T754, testimony of Lt Ratu George Cakobau.
85   *Bol*, p. T754, testimony of Lt Col VS Volavola.
86   *Bol*, pp. T736, T738, testimony of Volavola. Maika Qarikau, the NLTB head who shortly began circulating a 'Deed of Sovereignty' to entrust Fiji to the rebels, allegedly concocted the plan.

Early Sunday morning, 21 May, CRWU personnel in two vehicles journeyed across Viti Levu on the Queens Road to snatch Bainimarama as he returned from Norway. Alert to their intentions, Seruvakula sent 30 troops to meet their commander and they prevented the would-be kidnappers gaining access to Nadi airport, quickly spiriting Bainimarama along the longer northern and eastern Kings Road route to Suva instead.[87] On Friday 26 May, Speight and 20 armed men strode out of parliament and confronted troops who had replaced police outside the parliamentary complex. The next day 200 rebels and supporters challenged 10 soldiers in a shootout at a checkpoint that injured three soldiers, one rebel and a British journalist.[88]

The rebels' descent into violence and death made many CRWU soldiers uneasy; some even contemplated returning to their barracks.[89] But the *vanua* felt emboldened. They demanded their own weapons and swore at Ligairi when he refused.[90] Leadership of the *vanua* now became difficult. Speight and Duvuloco clashed over who should head it; Speight wanted only chiefs in such a role, Duvuloco believed he was best suited.[91] Difficulties over *vanua* leadership, Silatolu claimed, 'distracted us from resolving the issue with the military'.[92] Those difficulties, however, went far beyond leadership. The *vanua* was unruly. Looting, drunken parties, gang rapes and orgies conflicted with the disciplined order Ligairi wished to project.[93] But it had its uses also; across Fiji, isolated IndoFijian communities were terrorised or their homes looted and razed. The military 'won't rise up against its own people', Speight taunted.[94]

Speight played his part, too, holding court in the parliamentary complex with his supporters and engaging with international and local media. Unlike most politicians in Fiji and the rarely seen Commander, he was articulate and comfortable with the media – too comfortable, according to some journalists. They felt that their presence 'aided the rebel leader's

---

87   *BoI*, pp. T940, T888, testimony of Seruvakula and Saubulinayau.
88   *fijilive*, 09 February 2003; Tikotani was tried in 2003 for the shooting.
89   *BoI*, p. T467, testimony of Warrant Officer A. Waqaniboro.
90   *BoI*, p. T852, testimony of Raduva.
91   *BoI*, p. T395, testimony of Speight. There were other divisions among the rebels. Navakasuasua claims that Nata was never trusted because he was Lauan. The coup was by and for Viti Levu. Hence their later support for Samanunu as prime minister rather than Qarase (*fijilive*, 7 March 2003). Of course this view disregards Ligairi's central role and goals.
92   *BoI*, p. T392.
93   *BoI*, p. T736, testimony of Volavola.
94   *Fiji Times*, 2 June 2000.

propaganda fire … gave him political fuel'.[95] They were not alone. Many Fijian leaders who flocked to parliament were concerned to promote their particular Fijian brand; none wished victory to accrue solely to the political outsider.

Rabuka, ever eager to demonstrate that he was still the man for the moment, called for a meeting of the GCC on 23 May, hoping to seek independent resolution of the crisis. He had not supported the rebels as they hoped, but at least seemed prepared to negotiate, and negotiations kept the situation fluid. Hence the nervous rebels released 11 of their hostages hoping to maintain the initiative and reduce the risk that Bainimarama might launch an attack. They were buoyed by the independent visits of GCC members and their messages of support. An emboldened Speight declared Bauan chief Ratu Jope Seniloli president, with Silatolu his prime minister, and swore in a raft of ministers.[96] On Ligairi's recommendation, he mischievously selected Vatu as his military commander and Tarakinikini his chief of staff. When the GCC met, it clearly wished to side with Speight but could not overlook Mara's opposition. As a compromise it endorsed Mara as president but called for an advisory council of rebel leaders and chiefs to oversee constitutional changes. Rabuka's attempt at a resolution through the GCC had failed.[97] 'Democracy, we have always stated, [is] a foreign flower,' Rabuka reflected. It should be amended to suit local circumstances.[98] The rhetoric of 1987, however, did not now sit well with the remade statesman. Although he had never fully apologised for his coups, he began to find comparisons between his and Speight's actions difficult to stomach. Rebel confidante Simione Kaitani declared that they

95   David Robie, 'Coup Coup Land: The press and the putsch in Fiji', paper presented to the Journalism Education Association Conference, Queensland, 5–8 December 2000, p. 9. Some even wondered 'how much of the coup and its twists and turns was the product of the media itself' (Michael Field, 'Farewell to Coup-Coup Land', *Fiji Times*, 8 August 2000).

96   Speight contacted Seniloli at 4 am on 19 May and invited him to watch the action from the parliamentary gallery. He didn't but, the next day, Speight invited him to be president (*Fiji Times*, 8 July 2004). Ratu Tua'akitau Cakanauto advised his FAP colleagues not to accept these cabinet posts because the 'whole thing's illegal'. 'I will not lead you down the road that I can't lead you out of,' he told them to no avail (*Fiji Times*, 1 July 2004).

97   Robert Norton believes that Rabuka's hand may have been weakened by his need to keep Deputy Chair Adi Litia Cakobau – a strong Speight supporter – onside ('The changing role of the Great Council of Chiefs', in Fraenkel, Firth & Lal, *The 2006 Military Takeover in Fiji*, 2009, p. 105).

98   *fijilive*, 25 May 2000.

wanted immunity from prosecution 'like Rabuka got in 1987'. 'There is no other way,' Speight mocked.[99] 'It is unfortunate, but … the present [coup], just as mine, can probably never be justified,' Rabuka admitted.[100]

Mara quickly acted on the GCC's recommendations, dismissing both the Coalition government and parliament, but refused to place any rebels on a council of advisors or discuss amnesty until all hostages had been released and weapons returned.[101] Speight immediately upped the ante, calling for both Mara and the Constitution to go. He was buoyed by the arrival of a small group of reservists under Major Joseva Savua, the Police Commissioner's brother. Other soldiers continued to slip into the parliamentary complex to lend their support to the soldiers already there.[102] Speight felt more confident than at any time during the previous weeks; hence the forays outside the complex and the traditional Fijian welcome given to the GCC's negotiating delegation. Its leader, Ratu Epeli Kanaimawi, told the rebels:

> From now on, Fiji should be ours; we should lead so that other races can be safeguarded. [S]urely they will be happy. But Leadership should be in the hands of indigenous Fijians; [there's] no difference from what you have done from what the Council desires.[103]

It was a different story when the Military Advisory Group's Col Jeremaia Waqanisau arrived in parliament as part of a military *vanua* 'to cool things down' and prepare for negotiations to release the hostages. At that meeting Kanaimawi allegedly took the opportunity to berate the army.[104] Not surprisingly these early discussions went nowhere. Despite initially agreeing to the GCC's compromise, the rebels denied they had done so when they next met formally with the military. 'I have never seen people who can lie in your face,' Tarakinikini observed; 'it is unbelievable.'[105]

Speight's attack on the Presidential Palace that weekend clearly demonstrated where his focus now lay. That he held Mara's daughter, Adi Koila Nailatikau, as a hostage added to the pressure he felt able to

---

99   Mary-Louise O'Callaghan, 'Rabuka legacy: Rule by the gun', *Australian*, 26 May 2000, p. 1. *No Other Way* was the title of Rabuka's 1988 biography.
100   Interview with Jana Wendt, *Dateline*, SBS, 31 May 2000.
101   *fijilive*, 28 May 2000.
102   The board of inquiry estimated that at least 67 soldiers were stationed in the parliamentary complex (*BoI*, p. F66).
103   *Fiji TV*, 18 December 2006.
104   *BoI*, p. T827, testimony of Col Waqanisau; pp. T879–880, testimony of Tarakinikini.
105   *BoI*, p. T879.

exert. And he announced a new march on the Palace. The military feared
inaction. With the situation rapidly deteriorating, a mob poised to storm
the Presidential Palace and capture the President, and negotiations going
nowhere, it desperately needed to force Speight to release the hostages and
return its weapons. It feared anarchy. 'Our role changed when the then
Commissioner of Police declared that the police could no longer contain
the upheaval,' Bainimarama later argued.[106] Necessity now demanded
that the military produce a 'situation-saving' device[107] to replace 'non-
confrontation' with 'tightening the noose' in order to 'unhinge' the
rebels.[108]

That device proved also to be the military's default position – a coup.
On Monday 29 May at 9 am, Mara held a meeting with Ganilau, Rabuka,
Bainimarama and Special Branch Director Berenado Daveta (standing
in for Savua) to discuss who might act as prime minister in a council
of advisors.[109] The lack of adequate security at the Presidential Palace
deeply troubled Mara's secretary Joe Browne. He rang Seruvakula and
they discussed an option to take Mara to safety on a naval vessel in Walu
Bay. Only the next day did Browne learn that, shortly after his hasty
evacuation, Mara had been visited by another delegation comprising
Bainimarama, Rabuka, Ganilau and Savua. They asked him to step aside
as president in order to allow the military to assume control. Mara felt
betrayed. The military were meant to support him. He informed them
that he would never return as president.[110] The military eventually took
him to his Lakeba home in the Lau islands, although not before rebels

---

106   *Fiji Times*, 1 February 2004. In 2006, Bainimarama restated the importance of Savua's position:
'when the coup happened, the police were helpless and could not do much. And that was when the
military stepped in to take over' (*Fiji Times*, 4 December 2006).

107   *BoI*, p. T849, testimony of Raduva.

108   *BoI*, p. T862, testimony of Dr8unidalo. Tarakinikini regarded the military takeover as a way to
'unhinge' the Speight Group (*BoI*, p. T872). On 29 May, he was part of a delegation that told Speight
that since the military had now 'fulfilled what we want', the hostages should be released (*BoI*, p. T349)

109   *Fiji Times*, 16 November 2006. Browne claims that Ratu Joni Madraiwiwi had been offered
the position but refused to accept an unelected position. Rabuka volunteered to be prime minister
instead. Dr Senilagakali also claims to have been approached for the role but recommended Qarase
(*fijivillage*, 7 December 2006).

110   Joe Browne, interview, *fijilive*, 1 May 2001. Sir Vijay Singh later wrote that Mara confided
in him that he stepped down from office for fear of the fate of his daughter if he did not (*fijilive*,
17 August 2006). Family members believe that Mara's health deteriorated after his removal. Both he
and his wife died within three months of each other in 2004.

allegedly attempted to assassinate him on the vessel.[111] Later that evening, Bainimarama told the nation he had taken over and abrogated the Constitution because it did not permit a framework to resolve the crisis and encourage Speight to release the hostages. The subsequent board of inquiry thought this action wrong. The RFMF had again failed in its role and mission to preserve the sovereignty and stability of Fiji.[112] The future Attorney-General, Aiyaz Sayed-Khaiyum, later observed that the military's 'erroneous' belief that removing the President temporarily could help it re-establish law and order led to the tragic departure of 'one of the very few people who could have provided true national leadership'.[113]

Many senior officers concurred. The military's sudden takeover did not prevent hundreds of supporters continuing to stream into parliament or members of the rebel *vanua* committing random acts of violence with impunity. Nor did Bainimarama's promise to include rebels in an interim government win Speight's endorsement.[114] He wanted his own Taukei civilian government in power instead. In desperation Bainimarama sent a large army delegation to parliament buildings on 31 May to explain his intentions. But the very next day, when he met Speight for the first time, he compromised. The GCC would decide if the government should be a military one or Speight's. When Bainimarama told his officers what he

---

111 There remains much confusion over this event. Ratu George Kadavulevu claims that initially Rabuka was sent to advise Mara of the military plans and request that he not accept the plan in order to save face (*BoI*, p. T857). Saubulinayau claims that Mara feared he was under arrest when he was moved to the vessel (*BoI*, p. T890, testimony of Saubulinayau). Later, confronting Bainimarama, Savua and Rabuka, Mara told them that they had just given Speight what he wanted (pcgovt.org.fj, accessed 1 May 2000). At the board of inquiry Tikotani denied leading an assassination attempt (*BoI*, p. T339) and Mua alleged that Special Branch invented the threat to Mara and his family in order to give the military an excuse to remove them (*BoI*, p. T380).

112 *BoI*, p. F51. Tarakinikini claims that they should have got better advice (*BoI*, p. T879), advice that apparently came from Alipate Qetaki, according to the director of the Army Legal Service, Lt Col Etueni Caucau (*BoI*, p. T896). But two judges and Chief Justice Sir Timoci Tuivaga drafted the decree that abrogated the Constitution. Col Dr Jona Senilagakali believed the military should have invoked the Public Emergency Regulations instead and put the Constitution aside (*BoI*, p. T842).

113 A Sayed-Khaiyum, 'Political support and the law', *Fiji Times*, 13 January 2005. Sayed-Khaiyum argued that the military action did not amount to treason. The President agreed to step aside and did not formally resign until 15 December 2000. Although the Commander had no authority to abrogate the Constitution (it was formally reinstated) and the legal advice he received was unsound, the courts accepted that other military actions were justified in law and that it had acted solely to preserve national security. As Justice Gates argued on 15 November 2000, Mara did not resign on 29 May and the Constitution stayed in place. Bainimarama had acted on the basis of the doctrine of necessity to secure the safety of the state but had no genuine desire to remove the Constitution. Hence the decree abrogating it was unconstitutional (Verenaisi Raicola, 'Doctrine of necessity', *Fiji Times*, 29 March 2006).

114 'I'm telling the military to back off,' Speight retorted, 'The military came in at the twelfth hour. They have effectively performed a coup and I find that quite ironic' (*bbc.co.uk*, 31 May 2000).

had done, they objected. They were not prepared to place the country's future in the hands of an institution already tainted by close links with Speight. They would not surrender the military's role as guardian of the nation and they would not give in to a terrorist.[115] 'What is now happening to us is a moral recession,' Tarakinikini told the nation that evening, 'the very core of our existence is being challenged.' The rebels 'will threaten and they will try and destabilise and fragment our community so that we become vulnerable, and we will play into their hands if we succumb to tactics of fear'.[116]

Intervention by the colonels, however, did not produce the certainty they craved. If anything it confirmed to the rebels the success of their tactics. After increasingly violent *vanua* attacks on both the military and civilians in early June, and with IndoFijian refugees fleeing marauding gangs roaming across Tailevu and Naitasiri, former intelligence boss, Metuisela Mua, warned that they had plans to target the military across the country if it did not cave in.[117] Support for the rebels seemed to be building; the President of the Methodist church even assured them of a divine pardon.[118]

A desperate and disillusioned military now accepted an offer by Ratu Josefa Iloilo, the Tui Vuda and Mara's former Vice President, to host talks between the rebels and the military at his Muanikau suburban residence. But the talks dragged on, with the rebels constantly changing their demands. An initial agreement collapsed when they demanded they keep their weapons for future protection. Not surprisingly, the army wearied but, short of launching an attack on parliament, could do little. 'The paucity of leadership in the country is staggering,' the *Australian* journalist Christopher Dore observed. Mara had vanished, Rabuka sulked in his office, and Bainimarama had not spoken publically for two weeks. His Military Council, dominated by two former commanders

<hr />

115 *Bol*, pp. T829–830, testimony of Waqanisau. The colonel believed that these negotiations were not well handled. The army had no fall-back position and gave too much away. And Bainimarama should not have been directly involved. Ratu Tevita Mara later alleged that Bainimarama only changed his stance when Waqanisau challenged him at the meeting and called Speight a terrorist. The officers present clapped (Mara, 'Fiji's dictator Frank Bainimarama's truth revealed', 2011, p. 14).

116 Murray Mottram, 'Speight meets his match', *Age*, 5 June 2000, p. 15.

117 David Hardaker, interview, *7.30 Report*, ABC, 12 June 2000. That police vehicles were allegedly used to transport cattle and produce from IndoFijian farms at Muaniweni, Nausori, further weakened public faith in its police.

118 Rev. Tomasi Kanailagi wrote on 16 June 2000: 'we must not let Fijians fight among themselves or the Indians will have the last laugh', *Fiji Times*, 20 June 2004.

(Rabuka and Ganilau) had 'never emerged from the shadows'. Even the GCC seemed to have vanished from sight, its liaison committee mired in conspiracies with the rebels. And, in the parliament, the scheming continued, with rebel leaders bickering over 'whose coup it really is'. 'No-one in Fiji,' Dore wrote, 'has the slightest clue about how to end the political crisis.'[119]

But all was not as it seemed. Behind the scenes Bainimarama attempted to regain the confidence of his officers. On Tuesday 4 July, he announced the formation of a new interim government headed by the former senator, CEO of the Fiji Development Bank and managing director of the Merchant Bank, the 59-year-old Lauan Laisenia Qarase.[120] He and a new 18-member, all-male cabinet would introduce a new constitution together with a new deal for Fijians, amend land leases along lines favoured by the NLTB, and return Fiji to elections within two years. The message to the rebels was clear; the Fijian bureaucratic establishment was once more in charge. It was a message they read, however, as a declaration of war. These people never 'fought for the cause of the takeover', Ligairi declared. They had failed Fiji in the past and would do so again.[121] 'We didn't carry out the coup to provide an opportunity for the military to come in and run the government,' Speight pronounced: '[T]hat's not the objective of the coup and they don't seem to accept that.'[122] As if to drive home their point, 80 rebel soldiers under the command of Ligairi's grandson, Lt Rupeni Vosayaco, and 500 supporters seized control of the Sukanaivalu Barracks outside Labasa, the capital of Vanua Levu. Two hours later in Suva, 200 rebels and soldiers clashed outside parliament. One rebel died.

---

119 *Australian*, 29 June 2000, p. 10. The Military Council comprised Rabuka, Ganilau, Tuatoko, Vatu and Major-General Jioji Konrote.
120 Baledrokadroka claims that this outcome was forced on a reluctant Bainimarama by the colonels, in particular Tarakinikini. The Military Council had wanted the former governor of the Reserve Bank and vice chancellor of USP, Savenaca Siwatibau to be prime minister, with Nailatikau as his deputy, but Siwatibau refused. Consequently the Military Council chose Qarase (rawfijinews.wordpress.com, 17 April 2009). In an interview in 2007, Bainimarama claimed Qarase's appointment had been an impulsive decision: 'I was busy with George Speight's issues one particular morning in 2000, then somebody asked me whether I was looking for a pm. They said they have Qarase, I said OK. Well, who is Qarase, he was a banker; so let's go for him … We made a hell of a mistake back then' (*fijilive*, 18 September 2007). In 2006, Dr Senilagakali claimed he had been approached to head an interim government but advised Bainimarama to appoint Qarase instead (*fijivillage*, 7 December 2006).
121 *Fiji Times*, 6 December 2000.
122 *fijilive*, 4 July 2000. Allegedly on the same day Rabuka urged Seruvakula to remove Bainimarama as commander. Seruvakula refused (*Fiji Times*, 16 November 2006).

The next day, when the army responded by finally imposing an exclusion zone around the parliamentary complex, Speight taunted its leadership. Chiefs will call on Fijians to leave the military and 'As that takes place over the next few days, I'm sure Commander Bainimarama will find himself in command of an army that has no men'.[123] These were not idle words. On Thursday 6 July, some 400 Naitasiri villagers marched on the military barracks at Nabua amid rumours of an uprising. In the Naitasiri highlands, rebels drugged soldiers guarding the Monasavu power station and cut power to Suva. The soldiers were taken hostage. Macuata chiefs in Vanua Levu demanded Bainimarama step down, and the paramount chief of Naitasiri – Ratu Inoke Takiveikata – demanded a president elected by the GCC who would choose his own interim administration. The military caved in, finally signing the Muanikau Accord on Sunday 9 July at Iloilo's residence in front of 500 hymn-chanting rebel supporters and a despondent Bainimarama. 'We don't want to shed blood amongst ourselves,' the Naitasiri-born Tarakinikini conceded.[124]

Despite promising to 'surrender' and release their hostages, the amnestied rebels were in no mood to end their campaign of civil disobedience. But they had now to convince the country's chiefs that Fiji's future lay in their hands. Roadblocks sprang up around Fiji. One hundred and fifty rebels led by one CRWU soldier seized Korovou in Tailevu. Villagers took over the Savusavu and Seaqaqa police stations in Vanua Levu, and Labasa came under attack; so too the Nadi and Vanuabalavu airports, the army base in Lautoka, the police station and fish cannery in Levuka on Ovalau, tourist resorts on Turtle and Laucala islands, and a mineral water plant in Rakiraki. Fiji Telecom workers went on strike. Landowners and disgruntled employees occupied Road Transport offices in Suva and Lautoka, and prisoners rioted at Naboro prison. The former journalist and now rebel Jo Nata bragged, 'Suva is almost under siege; the whole nation is in chaos … is that what you call holding a gun to the chiefs' heads?'[125]

But not all chiefs required convincing. The deputy chair of the GCC, Adi Litia Cakobau, called a special meeting of 200 district and provincial chiefs (Bose ni Turaga) prior to the GCC's deliberations, and her sister, Adi Samanunu Cakobau, Fiji's ambassador to Malaysia, flew back

123 *SBS*, 5 July 2000.
124 *fijilive*, 7 July 2000.
125 *Australian*, 13 July 2000, p. 7.

to chair it. Designed to increase pressure on the GCC, the meeting recommended that Iloilo be president, the rebel 'President' Ratu Jope Seniloli his vice president, and the leader of the GCC negotiating team – Ratu Epeli Kanaimawi – prime minister of a new 22-member cabinet containing at least 11 rebels. When the GCC met on 14 July it accepted the first two demands but left it to Ratu Iloilo to determine the makeup of the new cabinet. Satisfied, the rebels released their remaining hostages. But when Iloilo announced the next day that Qarase's administration would remain intact, Ligairi unleashed his 'dogs of war' for another round of destruction. Iloilo did not turn up to swear in his new cabinet on 19 July. Ligairi and Speight took their rebels out of the shattered parliamentary complex that had been their home for the past 62 days and moved to the Kalabu Fijian School, 12 kilometres from Suva in Naitasiri territory, looting on their way. From this base they would fight for lasting influence and power.

Ligairi and Takiveikata now pressured Iloilo to accept a new set of demands that included replacing Qarase with Adi Samanunu as prime minister. Her support for the rebels can be seen as another chapter in the long struggle between the Cakobau and Mara families and between Kubuna and Tovata for ascendancy within Fiji, a struggle that introduced a useful dynamic for the rebels in the already fractious relationship between Fijian provinces and between old centres of power. Iloilo agreed to include more rebels in the cabinet but, when he met with the rebels, Speight threatened further instability if he failed to deliver.[126]

With the rebels out of parliament and their hostages released, Bainimarama now had more room to manoeuvre. Another initiative of the colonels (in particular Tuatoko, Tarakinikini and Baledrokadroka) assisted also. They had established a special Force Reserve Unit (FRU) or Task Force Group in late June to directly confront the rebel *vanua*. Comprising 3rd Battalion soldiers stationed in Nadi and Lautoka, as well as Suva's Engineers, it made the Engineers HQ at the QEB its base.[127] Securing Naboro prison, where prisoners had taken wardens hostage

---

126 *Sydney Morning Herald*, 27 July 2000. This was a confusing period of claim and counterclaim. Four paramount chiefs and one public servant apparently threatened instability if Iloilo failed to appoint Samanunu (*fijilive*, 6 April 2004). Bainimarama later alleged that six politicians met him in the FHL boardroom and requested that he overthrow Iloilo (*Fiji Times*, 25 August 2005). Poseci Bune claims that, when Iloilo looked like appointing Samanunu as prime minister, Qarase requested Bainimarama remove the President (*fijilive*, 3 August 2003).

127 Baledrokadroka, 'Sacred king and warrior chief', 2012, pp. 170–73.

under instruction from the rebels, became its first successful operation on 17 July. Thus, a much more confident Bainimarama moved to frustrate the Speight group's political manoeuvres. On 26 July, he rushed to the Presidential Palace and told Iloilo to 'get a prime minister of our choice or else lose the army'.[128] That same evening, the FRU quietly arrested Speight en route to Kalabu. At 6 am the next morning, Day 70 of the crisis, the FRU took the rebels at Kalabu by surprise and rounded them up. Sporadic outbreaks of violence occurred in retaliation around the country, mainly in Vanua Levu, and by the time the FRU recaptured Labasa's Sukanaivalu Barracks at the start of August and swept through the Viti Levu highlands around Monasavu, an uneasy calm had descended over the country, punctuated only by distrust, fear and loathing. 'No one is the winner here,' Raduva told the board of inquiry a month or so later, 'we are all losers.'[129]

Nearly 500 rebels and their supporters across the country were arrested, many of them resentful at the beatings they received from their captors. Most civilian rebels were charged only with minor offences and were quickly released on lenient bail terms, but key perpetrators like Duvuloco, Speight and Ligairi were quarantined on the small Nukulau Island near Suva. Investigations were also begun into the activities of hundreds of citizens during the crisis, among them the Police Commissioner, who was forced to stand aside pending an investigation by the Chief Justice, himself under public scrutiny for advising the military on its seizure of power. Tarakinikini lost his post as army spokesperson and soon left, disillusioned, to a UN peacekeeping post in New York.[130] Bainimarama also found himself under attack when he admonished chiefs for instigating division and hate among Fijians, and the High Court declared the Muanikau amnesty he had negotiated invalid. Stung, Bainimarama hit back when President Iloilo left for medical treatment in Sydney. He would never accept the rebel Seniloli as acting president and threatened a new military takeover.[131] In the uproar that followed, Rabuka offered to serve as president and the target of loathing shifted again.

---

128 Tony Parkinson, 'The rebels had military chief in their sights', *Age*, 3 November 2000.

129 *BoI*, p. T855.

130 After the mutiny Tarakinikini was suspended from duties but no evidence of collusion with the mutineers could be found. He resigned in 2001, citing mistreatment from Bainimarama (*Fiji Times*, 27 February 2002).

131 Saubulinayau observed that, while the events of 19 May helped bring the army together again, suspicions about officer loyalties always lingered, and resurfaced once things cooled down (*BoI*, p. T888).

At the QEB, the CRWU soldiers smarted at their treatment. They felt ostracised; they did not take to their new commanding officer and were convinced that the army planned to disband the CRWU, despite the fact that most of those remaining (the majority) had stayed away from parliament, unlike their intelligence operatives and raw recruits.[132] They were now placed within the 3rd Battalion, but were permitted to continue using CRWU offices and barracks. The rebels among them shared similar feelings. 'We felt betrayed by Bainimarama,' Serupepeli Dakai declared.[133] Bainimarama claimed to forgive them, but they were still being arrested and charged.[134] The return of weapons created considerable angst, in part because RFMF records were hopelessly inaccurate but also because, when soldiers did return weapons, they were promptly charged.[135] Yet, in many respects given the enormity of what had happened, the RFMF treated them leniently. At a special ceremony on 26 October, Captain Shane Stevens – now the CRWU's second in command – formally sought the military's forgiveness. Bainimarama accepted the request, and agreed to release the rebel soldiers into the custody of their families until the law took its course. A board of inquiry would be held. He even praised them for securing the safety of their hostages and containing 'the rowdy and abusive' *vanua*.[136] But he also confirmed the demise of the CRWU.[137] The soldiers were stunned. Revenge became the new order of the day. They hid weapons in preparation. Stevens had already been sought out twice by Takiveikata, the Naitasiri chief who wanted Bainimarama

---

132   *BoI*, p. T1004, testimony of Stevens.

133   *fijilive*, 3 November 2000.

134   *BoI*, p. T936, testimony of Tuatoko. Other coup conspirators felt the same. Maciu Navakasuasua, who ended up incarcerated on Nukulau with Speight, claimed that failed politicians, church ministers and corrupt businessmen who 'talked us into taking part' in the coup had simply used them 'to fulfill their political agendas'; they accepted positions in the interim government and 'turned their backs on us as we were thrown into jail' (*Fiji Sun*, 22 August 2015).

135   *BoI*, p. T1008, testimony of Stevens. At his court martial Stevens claimed the military fabricated the non-return of weapons in order to justify their violence in pacifying rebel areas in Kalabu, Monasavu, Ra, Tailevu and Vanua Levu (*fijilive*, 26 September 2002).

136   scoop.co.nz, 31 October 2000.

137   Baledrokadroka, 'Sacred king and warrior chief', 2012, pp. 184–85. Baledrokadroka argues that discontent at Bainimarama's leadership resurfaced with the disbandment of the CRWU. Bainimarama had already begun to move officers who potentially threatened his leadership, including those in Strategic HQ, out of the QEB. But there was also the simple fact the Bainimarama had come from naval ranks and lacked the Sandhurst training of Stevens, Vatu and Tarakinikini. Victor Lal and Russell Hunter claim that the mutiny was the CRWU's revenge for Bainimarama's betrayal; he had ordered them to conduct the coup in the first place ('Details of the death of CRWU soldier Selesitino Kalounivale revealed', www.coupfourandahalf.com, 19 March 2012).

removed for dumping the Muanikau Accord and for the military's treatment of civilian rebels at Kalabu, Monasavu and on Vanua Levu.[138] Now Stevens had grounds for action. Bainimarama later reflected:

> I never thought they would be swayed with the lie that the RFMF had lost the trust of the *vanua* and that the *vanua* only trusted the CRWU because of what they stood for in May 2000. And so if the CRWU wanted the trust of the *vanua* to be returned to the RFMF, then they should take leadership of the army. Only then would the *vanua* be there for them.[139]

One week later, on Thursday, 2 November, the CRWU mutinied.

It was a bloody and confused affair.[140] Led by the once loyal Stevens, 40 CRWU soldiers, many reportedly intoxicated,[141] seized weapons and took over the Officers Mess, Bainimarama's office and administration complex, the national operations centre and the armoury in the early afternoon. They wanted hostages; above all they wanted Bainimarama. In the process they executed three unarmed loyal soldiers. Again their planning was meagre; the whole operation was designed simply as a repeat of 19 May, this time at the QEB on a day when many soldiers were out training and at a time when Bainimarama would be lunching in the Officers Mess. An unsigned fax ordered Vodafone to shut down army mobiles. A coded message over Radio Fiji told Naitasiri, Tailevu and Rewa provincial organisers to get as many human shields into the camp as possible. Two hundred men gathered at Takiveikata's Wailase farm in preparation.[142] The rebels planned to negotiate for the release of their colleagues on Nukulau, establish a Taukei civilian government, and replace Bainimarama.

Within hours the operation collapsed. The mutineers were unable to secure ammunition for the weapons they seized and had to make do with a more limited range of standard issue weapons. They botched the attack on Bainimarama and the senior command. Instead of employing stealth, they 'brazenly assembled at the camp ground, conspicuous in

---

138 *fijilive*, 17 September 2010. This was revealed in Takiveikata's trial in 2010. He was given a life sentence in 2007 but released on appeal in 2008. On retrial in 2010 he received a seven-year sentence.

139 *Fiji Times*, 14 March 2006.

140 See also 'Mayhem and mutiny' in Robertson & Sutherland, *Government by the Gun*, 2001, pp. 40–49

141 Mara, 'Fiji's dictator Frank Bainimarama's truth revealed', 2011, p. 15.

142 Evidence presented at Takiveikata's trial, *Fiji Times*, 12 & 17 November 2004. At his trial, Stevens claimed that Takiveikata gave orders to Tarakinikini and Vatu to 'secure' the RFMF HQ on 2 November (Jone Dakuvula, 'The unresolved issues at stake over the commander controversy', *Asia-Pacific Network*, 30 January 2004).

their black 'T-shirts' and green pants, and fired 'warning shots as they dispersed towards their targets'.[143] Bainimarama and his bodyguards narrowly escaped through a nearby cassava patch. Nor did they consider how the wider army might be neutralised. In point of fact, elements of the Third Fiji Infantry Regiment returned from field exercises in Nadroga Province in the late afternoon and joined forces with Baledrokadroka who, with Raduva, Lt Col Solomone Raravula (the CO Engineers), and Lt Col Silivenusi Waqausa, rallied the FRU at the Engineers complex and merged them with raw engineer trainees. When the loyal troops learned of Takiveikata's plot to bus in human shields, they closed the camp gates. At dusk they quickly mounted a counter offensive.[144]

Within two hours the battle for Nabua was over. Eight soldiers lay dead, five of them CRWU soldiers arrested in Suva after the mutiny began and allegedly beaten to death while detained. In addition, 28 soldiers were injured and stray bullets hit two civilians.[145]

---

143   Shailendra Singh, 'The thin line', *Review*, December 2000, p. 15.
144   Baledrokadroka provides the best account of the mutiny currently available.
145   One of many unsolved crimes emanating from the 2000 coup, the deaths in custody, continue to haunt the military to this day. Immediately after the mutiny, the wife of one dead soldier claimed that her husband – who had not participated in the mutiny – had been taken to the barracks after the event. In March 2001, the police announced that they were investigating the five deaths as murder. All the dead soldiers had been arrested outside of the QEB and kept at the Central Police Station in Suva. They were later taken to the barracks where they died (*Fiji Times*, 26 March 2001). Nothing came of these investigations, although they were reopened again in 2005. Bainimarama has consistently denied ordering the deaths (*Fiji Times*, 8 February 2003), even of knowing about the investigation (*Fiji Times*, 2 January 2007). In April 2006, the widow of one soldier won $24,000 in compensation under the *Workers Compensation Act*. During a civil suit against the RFMF in 2007 by three former CRWU soldiers, who had been taken by soldiers after surrendering at the Nabua police station and beaten at the Vatuwaqa rifle range, Baledrokadroka, then chief of operations, claimed that tensions raised by the mutiny probably lay behind the spontaneous assaults (*fijilive*, 17 October 2007). Bainimarama, who had surrendered one of the CRWU soldiers from the naval base to the police, made a similar claim to journalist Graham Davis in 2007: 'I think they were just bashed up by the [loyalist] soldiers because they got pretty peeved. I think that is an understatement. You know they'd been part of the RFMF for 10, 20 years and all of a sudden one day they turned around and shot people up. Do you expect our guys to go and kiss them on the cheek? Let's be real about the situation … These guys came to kill people. They came out to kill, so if they died in the process I'm not going to cry about it' (*Fiji Times*, 2 January 2007). In 2011, after escaping Fiji, Ratu Tevita Mara claimed that some 60 CRWU soldiers were tortured and held at Korovou prison ('Fiji's dictator Frank Bainimarama's truth revealed', 2011, p. 15). The issue never really died, despite later police claims that Bainimarama had been cleared back in 2003 and that the Police Commissioner confirmed this in 2004 and sought to mislead people by claiming to reopen the case in 2006 (*fijivillage*, 15 February 2007). The issue resurfaced yet again when pictures of the five battered bodies circulated on dissident websites after 2012 (www.fijileaks.com/home/bloody-2-november-2000-the-day-bainimarama-wanted-mutinous-soldiers-punished-some-innocent-thirteen-years-ago-kicked-to-death-police-wanted-to-question-him-before-coup). Warning: this website contains graphic images.

In February 2015, Opposition leader Ro Teimumu Kepa tried to reopen the issue by calling on police to complete their investigations (*Fiji Times*, 20 February 2015).

Military victory over the mutineers brought no peace. Instead it intensified recriminations. Rabuka became one of its early victims. Since 1997 Rabuka had been fêted internationally for bringing Fiji back from the abyss he had driven it to. He had been honoured with the Solomon Islands dispute to resolve. But the year 2000 proved difficult for Rabuka. Each time 'the Statesman' inserted himself into the dramas around him, he created suspicion, not respect. Mara had accused him of conspiracy; Speight and Ligairi of betrayal. Now Bainimarama charged him with treachery. During the mutiny he came to the barracks uninvited just as the military counterattack began. He threatened to put on his uniform and return as commander if the assault team did not withdraw. He criticised the Commander's leadership. He left with one of the rebels in his car. Bainimarama suspected Rabuka was trying to buy time until the human shields arrived under the cover of darkness. 'He really confuses the army, that man,' Bainimarama declared.[146]

Rabuka told it differently. Having flown in from Savusavu, he was lunching at a function with business executives when his personal assistant informed him of the mutiny. At 1.15 pm he first called Colonel Seruvakula of the 3FIR, and then Home Affairs before speaking to a number of people at the camp. One of the rebels asked him to mediate because he disapproved of the mutiny. Rabuka also spoke with one of the hostages. At this point he decided that he was needed. But he got there too late. Baledrokadroka refused to speak with him. The orders for a counterattack had been issued.[147]

Rabuka denied any part in the mutiny.[148] He did not approve of the rebels' goals. 'We should allow ourselves to evolve into a vibrant society of mixed races, [a] multi ethnic, multi racial, multi religious society,' he declared: 'Those who are trying to drag us back into the era of the dinosaur … hopefully will quickly be called to their graves.' Meanwhile he would

---

146 *Fiji Times*, 9 November 2000; Singh, 2000, p. 15. In 2006, Seruvakula alleged that on 2 November 2000 Rabuka tried to convince him to remove Bainimarama as commander. Both he and Bainimarama also alleged that Rabuka made a similar request earlier in July when the hostage crisis ended (*Fiji Times*, 11 November 2006).
147 *fijilive*, 7 November 2000; *Fiji Times*, 3 March 2004.
148 In late 2006, Rabuka was found not guilty of inciting mutiny, but the long police investigation cost him his appointment by the Qarase government as Fiji's ambassador to the United States.

continue to work for a new Fiji: 'I cannot let the flame that inspired me to work towards the 1997 Constitution … burn out.'[149] But the knives were out for Rabuka. In March 2001, the GCC dumped him as their chairman.

Bainimarama also came under scrutiny. Although his dramatic retreat from the Battle of Nabua and alleged refuge at the naval base caused him to lose face and left him traumatised, he strongly believed that everything he had done during the course of 2000 had been designed to foster stability and reconciliation among indigenous Fijians.[150] He had assumed authority on 29 May to protect the President and save Fiji from descending into anarchy. He had refused to raid parliament for fear that the deaths of innocent or naive Fijians would produce an even greater backlash against the army. He had backed Qarase's interim regime because it alone promised Fijians a clearly articulated direction. And he had managed to hold the RFMF together, despite its officers' ideological differences and the lack of respect many showed to him as commander because of his naval background.

But Bainimarama's actions did not always accord with international conventions, let alone satisfy Fiji's other communities. IndoFijians in particular felt excluded; so, too, did many business people. The new Qarase regime planned to reintroduce a Taukeist Constitution, an act that potentially threatened international retaliation and the loss of important markets for Fiji's products. Its chaotic approach to land use and its support for the Taukeist demands of the NLTB additionally threatened Fiji's agricultural production and a new wave of rural refugees. Yet for many people, including Fijians, a sense of déjà vu left most disillusioned. Thirteen years of patience and consensus-building had seemingly come to nought. Fiji's politics lay shattered and its economy teetered on the abyss. The 2000 coup had cost Fiji well in excess of $1 billion (equivalent to the government's total annual budget) and $300 million in damage to infrastructure and lost government revenue alone. The parliamentary complex, which Rabuka had built in 1992 to mark a turning point in

---

149 *Review*, October–November 2000, p.17.
150 Baledrokadroka believes that Bainimarama's bodyguards were sufficiently armed to have made a stand at the Officers Mess; instead, by abandoning the Officers Mess, Bainimarama lost an opportunity to boost the morale of his troops. His unprepared bodyguards told the later court martial, however that they had almost exhausted their ammunition by the time they fled (*Daily Post*, 27 February 2002). And Bainimarama did not quit the QEB. He came to the Engineers HQ prior to the final assault but was advised to go the Stanley Brown Naval Base for his safety (Baledrokadroka, 'Sacred king and warrior chief', 2012, pp. 190, 194).

Fiji's democracy, lay shattered. Over 10 per cent of the paid workforce had lost their jobs as the economy shrank an astonishing 12 per cent. Hotel occupancy rates plummeted 80 per cent, while Fiji's large garment industry lost nearly one quarter of its 20,000 workers. According to one estimate, 40 per cent more people lived in poverty than when the crisis began.[151] Fiji's postcolonial economic transformation – Sutherland noted in 2001 – had never been accompanied by the kind of popular economic participation that enabled political stability. Now, in the face of sharper class and rural–urban inequalities, there was every reason to believe that politicians would once more defend themselves by resorting to racial scapegoating.[152]

Reclaiming the goose

Laisenia Qarase presented the grandfatherly face of Fijian nationalism. Portrayed as a neutral public servant, he was anything but disinterested. After his election as prime minister in late 2001 he boasted of his centrality in the development of affirmative action programs for Fijians since 1985 when he had returned from a study tour of Malaysia. He wanted a 20-year strategic plan for Fijian economic growth, a review of Fiji's Constitution, the transfer of state lands to the NLTB, and Fijian ownership of fishing waters. He damned existing land leases as 'statutory fraud' and claimed Fijians were subsidising the sugar industry through unfair rental agreements. His agenda would dominate Fiji politics for the next six years, and encourage many former rebels and nationalists to claim that Fiji's bureaucratic elite had at last started to make the 2000 coup a success.[153] Yet, instead of driving Fijians towards nirvana, it brought them back to where they had been under Rabuka in the mid-1990s, fractious and floundering. Fiji's peoples had to learn how to live together and to use their diversity as the basis for united strength.

For most of his six years in office, Qarase chose to address this need with silence, despite the fact that his reassertion of Fijian paramountcy – which he presented as the only solution available to Fiji – posed many threats,

---

151   *fijilive*, 23 October 2000; 17 February 2001; *Review*, August 2000, pp. 19–20; Joseph Veramu, Fiji Community Education Association President, scoop.co.nz, 5 February 2001.
152   Robertson & Sutherland, *Government by the Gun*, 2001, p. 141.
153   This was the view of Tailevu CAMV MP, Samisoni Tikoinasau, Speight's brother (*fijilive*, 16 May 2002).

not least to Fijians themselves. 'If Indians are forced to leave Fiji,' Mara told his Lau Provincial Council in late 2000, 'the next group of people will be islanders who have made a living in Viti Levu.'[154] Indeed, the more Fiji moved towards the kind of traditional *vanua* politics Mara warned of, the more divided the *vanua* became. Identity has a habit of becoming exclusive, while targets of envy shift. Rabuka noted how even moderate provincial successes created jealousy in other provinces, and encouraged self-pity.[155] Fijians really needed to come to terms with their own history and their modernity. The past offered no justice or direction to the thousands of Fijians who had abandoned the poverty of their villages for the poverty of urban slums. Nor did it assist them to come to terms with the reality of Fiji's multiracialism and multiculturalism. It offered no guide for the future.

Nor did Qarase's interim government. Its blueprint for Fijian development advantaged the Fijian middle classes, not the disaffected masses that had fuelled the CRWU rebellion. Education, which Bainimarama believed essential for Fijian development, received no boost in the first Qarase budget. Government grants to secondary schools halved and, although it set aside special funding for Fijian education, not a cent reached Fijian children if they went to multi-ethnic schools, as so many urban Fijians did.[156]

Although aware of these divisions, neither Bainimarama nor Qarase could suggest anything other than reconciliation to resolve internal Fijian divisions that had already created so much strife and misery. But how might reconciliation be achieved? Bainimarama conceded that Fijian unity existed only during periods of opposition to IndoFijians, but such an acknowledgement was hardly a strategy for Fijian reconciliation, let alone national healing.[157]

Nonetheless, Qarase created a Ministry of Reconciliation and launched a National Council for Reconciliation and Unity in late November 2000. Promisingly, it proposed the educational integration of Fiji's communities,

---

154 *fijilive*, 16 October 2000.

155 *Fiji Times*, 2 December 2000.

156 In May 2001, Qarase finally released a blueprint for Fijian education, detailing a much needed $8.4 million injection of capital into Fijian educational infrastructure. But it was a technocratic response only and did nothing to address the concerns of the Education Commission, whose report remained hidden from public scrutiny.

157 *Fiji Times*, 12 November 2000.

racial parity in the military, and a new national identity. But no strategy ever emerged to deliver such outcomes.[158] For the present, Qarase could only plead that Fiji's peoples be more forgiving of each other. 'One needed to forgive unconditionally before attempting reconciliation,' Qarase told the National Tourism Forum in December 2000, 'because unity was impossible without forgiveness.'[159] Forgiveness included Speight. 'There are so many people with much worse records who got away free right around the world,' he declared.[160] Rabuka agreed. He told the Cakaudrove Provincial Council that the courts should consider reconciliation as part of the endeavour to unite the people of Fiji and give sentences accordingly.[161]

Qarase's permanent secretary for reconciliation, Col Jeremaia Waqanisau, who had told the board of inquiry that unity and reconciliation might prove illusory,[162] declared investigations into the coup an obstacle to reconciliation.[163] The dropping of charges 'for lack of evidence' against four rebel leaders held on Nukulau encouraged this line of action. 'If Fiji is to go forward,' declared one of the freed rebels, 'the reconciliation process must start on Nukulau' where the rebels' leaders were quarantined. Perhaps for this reason the Suva Magistrates Court permitted Speight and Ligairi to register as candidates in the August 2001 election. Reconciliation presented itself to the public service too. On the Chief Justice's recommendation, Savua was reinstated as Police Commissioner in November. In May 2003, a public service inquiry also cleared Adi Samanunu of any wrongdoing. Her sister, Adi Litia Cakobau, told the Senate in the following year that all political prisoners must be released. 'To criminalise freedom of expression is to criminalise democracy,'

---

158   *Fiji Times*, 26 February 2001. It also planned a special program in 2002 to prepare young chiefs for leadership.

159   *Fiji Times*, 8 December 2000.

160   Mark Chippendale, 'Qarase sees a future of affirmative action', *Sydney Morning Herald*, 19 February 2001.

161   *fijilive*, 16 November 2000. Reconciliation was presented as a uniquely Fijian response and, according to one participant at a workshop convened by the Constitutional Commission in 2012, involved spending a lot of money so chiefs could say sorry, even in 2003, for the 1867 killing of Christian missionaries in Naitisiri.

162   *BoI*, p. T836. Waqanisau claimed that 'I do not think we will achieve any unity, I do not think we will achieve any reconciliation, I do not think so if we continue as we are … Whilst there are people who actually needed to pay for whatever acts they committed, I think what we need to do now is rebuild RFMF and I do not think we can rebuild the RFMF after bashing each other up first'. Waqanisau, a former force commander of UN Forces Lebanon, resigned from the army in 1997 to become Commissioner Western and, in 2003, became permanent secretary for Home Affairs.

163   *fijilive*, 8 November 2000.

she declared, adding that the blueprint was not enough to correct the historic injustices done to Fijians; the 1997 Constitution 'is a time bomb and must be changed before time pulls the trigger'.[164]

There were dangers in this ethnocentric approach to reconciliation. A disillusioned Seruvakula left the command of the Third Fiji Infantry in March 2001 and, with three other officers, began service with the New Zealand Defence Forces before heading to Afghanistan with the United Nations. New Zealand's High Commissioner, Tia Barrett, publicly condemned Fiji's apparent reluctance to bring to justice 'those responsible for the upheaval … despite the wealth of information available'.[165] His country offered the director of public prosecutions (DPP) legal assistance but he declined the offer. In early December, some of the hostage takers at Monasavu received suspended sentences.

Mara warned the Lau Provincial Council that 'The reconciliation that has been undertaken today will be worthless if investigations into the coup do not reveal the truth behind [its] staging'.[166] Many Fijians agreed, including the army's legal officer, Lt Ilaisa Tagitupou. 'Justice was necessary,' he said, 'because reconciliation was not appreciated.'[167] Interim deputy prime minister Ratu Epeli Nailatikau took a more principled stand.

> Unadulterated greed and the unbelievable arrogance as was shamelessly displayed by chiefs and people alike on May 19 will not bring about paramountcy in this day and age.

Justice had to come before reconciliation, he declared, contradicting Qarase.[168]

Nailatikau's wife – Adi Koila – who had suffered imprisonment in the hands of the rebels in parliament, agreed. When in October 2004, Qarase attempted to draw a line under reconciliation by having two coup participants – Ratu Naiqama Lalabalavu and Ratu Jope Seniloli – undertake a traditional *matanigasau* ceremony for forgiveness before himself and the President during a special Reconciliation Week, Adi Koila declared the exercise pointless given that it was directed at two main beneficiaries of the coup, one of whom she accused of having ordered

---

164   *fijilive*, 10 December 2003.
165   scoop.co.nz, 27 November 2000.
166   *Fiji Times*, 14 December 2000.
167   *Fiji Times*, 15 January 2001.
168   scoop.co.nz, 20 December 2000.

the burning of her father's Seaqaqa cane farm in July 2000. Why had her recently deceased parents not been so honoured? They would both be still alive were it not for the coup. Why were other coup participants like Kubuabola, Rabuka and Savua being honoured with diplomatic posts? Like her father before her, she believed reconciliation worthless if no one knew who had been behind the coup.[169]

Because Fijians could not agree on how to resolve the issues dividing them, the danger existed that they would simply muddle on without substantially changing anything. And that, some Fijians believed, carried the even greater risk of endless repetitions, endless violence and endless misery. 'Unless we nip it now,' one of the authors of the 1997 Constitution – Tomasi Vakatora – presciently stated, 'this mentality will continue.'[170]

In the wake of Speight and Ligairi, Fijians faced a dilemma that they could not resolve. Old ideas concerning paramountcy dictated that reconciliation among Fijians came before anything else. But reconciliation was never going to be possible until Fijians came to terms with their own diversity. And that meant understanding that the old politics of the *vanua* could no longer serve Fiji's multicultural *vanua* and the international context in which it now existed. It also meant understanding, as the former Labour minister Ema Tagicakibau wrote in 2004, that the 2000 coup 'did not break the rules of the *vanua* but of the law. The law must take its course, not for vengeance, but to set a high standard of behaviour to which everyone must aspire'. This, she believed, was the only way to stop Fiji's coup culture.[171]

To many chiefs, however, such an understanding amounted to capitulation. When they met again in late April 2001, they signalled that they wanted more chiefs in a future parliament and the level of debate in such a parliament to reflect the status due to them as chiefs. Further, they wanted Fijian representation (nominated in the first instance by chiefs) restricted to provincial representation.[172] The ghost of 1990 was still clearly present, but now faced a more fraught environment. Vanua Levu

---

169 *Fiji Times*, 23 October 2004. The former Speaker of the House, Militoni Leweniqila, also believed that all the hostages should be compensated (*Fiji Times*, 6 May 2005). The intention had been for the apology to be given also to FLP members but the party refused to attend, fearing ulterior political motives (*Fiji Sun*, 12 February 2005).
170 *Fiji Sun*, 1 September 2000.
171 'The politics of forgiving', *Fiji Times*, 23 October 2004.
172 *fijilive*, 27 April 2001.

rebel Ratu Jo Dimuri signalled where opposition might lead. Provincial councils were captive to the Fijian chiefly elite, he argued. They had long suppressed the voices of ordinary Fijians and 'were to blame for the outbursts of Fijians'. Provincial councils should be replaced by *mataqali* (clan) and *yavusa* (district) meetings instead.[173]

Qarase, who desperately wanted to plug the gap left by Mara's departure and Rabuka's loss of power, had no time for such nonsense. Democracy, he warned, could be dangerous if it undermined the very communal values that defined Fijian identity. Instead he proposed strengthening the chiefly system and granted $20 million to make the GCC financially independent, drafted constitutional changes to place it under presidential rather than parliamentary control, and planned a new administration complex for the GCC.[174] But his responses came too late. The events of 2000 effectively placed the chiefly system on trial and, over the next 10 years, its political role would be destroyed.

This was a surprising outcome for those who believed that the events of 2000 had least reasserted Fijian paramountcy. But paramountcy derived from too many interests and too many power manoeuvres to enable the emergence of stable political consensus. From the very moment of the coup, disunity generated its own self-serving momentum and rationalisations. It drove the Chief Justice to accept the army's abrogation of the Constitution and to deny legitimacy to anyone who questioned his judgement. It drove the Constitutional Review chairman, Asesela Ravuvu, to declare that 'Politics must come before the law and legalities'. It drove Qarase to argue that the treason that succeeds is not treason.[175] And it drove Bainimarama to defend his abrogation, even when the High Court in November 2000 ruled it illegal and called for the reinstatement of the dismissed parliament. 'It's no use moving towards democracy if we can't settle the security problem,' he warned.[176] But, as Vakatora acknowledged, without democracy there is only dictatorship.[177]

---

173 *Fiji Times*, 4 May 2001. Leweniqila later declared them unelected representatives not qualified to speak on politics (*Fiji Times*, 6 May 2005).

174 *Fiji Times*, 23 October 2004. Ro Pateresia Vonakua, the paramount chief of Naitasiri's Waimaro district and Ratu Jope Seniloli's sister-in-law, declared that no one could break the law with impunity, regardless of the cause they held dearly or their rank.

175 Charles Sampford, 'Dare to call it treason', *Overhere.com*, May 2001.

176 Singh, 2000, p. 15. In Lautoka, Justice Anthony Gates first declared the abrogation of the Constitution illegal, condemned the actions of senior judges who assisted the military commit illegal acts, and resisted the Chief Justice's efforts to transfer constitutional cases to Suva.

177 *Fiji Times*, 1 September 2000.

By March 2001 Bainimarama had changed his mind. He accepted the High Court's ruling that his actions in abrogating the Constitution had been illegal;[178] so too – reluctantly – did a divided GCC. It reappointed Iloilo president and advised him to hold fresh elections under the 1997 Constitution. Having ended the threat of a commoner revolt in 2000, Fiji's elite had no wish to surrender to the old parliament the power it had since gained. By one account Bainimarama had not wanted Chaudhry back for fear that he might frustrate confirmation of a general amnesty for military misdeeds committed during 2000.[179] Hence he reluctantly accepted the court's decision, and Iloilo dismissed Chaudhry and his government and dissolved parliament. Qarase now returned as caretaker prime minister with the same cabinet as before. So too Ravuvu's Constitutional Review Committee, pursuing – according to the Citizens' Constitutional Forum's (CCF) director, Rev. Akuila Yabaki – the same 'illegal objective of George Speight'.[180] Nothing it seemed had changed, except that all parties – including Labour – now agreed to an early election.[181] Both Qarase and Bainimarama urged Fijians to unite behind one party. Only by this means could Fijian paramountcy be assured, meaning that the Fijian establishment would not lose out as they had in 1999. This concern lay behind Qarase's focus on Fijian reconciliation and unity throughout his years in office. 'Calling for unity only among Fijians makes a mockery of national reconciliation and national unity,' the Catholic Archbishop

---

178 At the start of 2001, Bainimarama and Colonel Ratu George Kadavulevu allegedly told Iloilo in the presence of Qarase and some of his cabinet that the military would support a government of national unity drawn from the former parliament if the Court of Appeal upheld the High Court ruling (*Fiji Times*, 20 January 2001). In March, Qarase told the Court of Appeal that he would respect its ruling and help return Fiji to constitutional government, but engineered the GCC decision that retained his incumbency (Dakuvula, 'The unresolved issues', 2004).

179 Baledrokadroka, 'Sacred king and warrior chief', 2012, p. 214. In 2003, Bainimarama declared that the military did not reinstate Chaudhry because 'there would have been physical casualties, mayhem and strife; things would have gone straight downhill' (Sandra Gebhart, 'The role of the military in a democracy: civil–military relations in Fiji', in *Background Paper on the RFMF and Fiji's Defence Policy*, CCF papers submitted to the Defence Review Committee, October 2003, p. 63). From a defence perspective this is the more likely reason for Bainimarama's decision. Of course Chaudhry had also advised the President to hold fresh elections although not all his party agreed with his advice. An amnesty bill was eventually tabled in parliament in 2004 but the government's coalition partner, the Conservative Alliance, refused to ratify it, claiming that the interests of the military's victims also needed protection (Dakuvula, 'The unresolved issues', 2004).

180 *fijilive*, 3 May 2001.

181 Tupeni Baba claims that after the High Court ruling, the Labour Party did want the old parliament recalled and Chaudhry knew he no longer had party support as leader. Hence he advised the President to dissolve the interim government and hold elections (*fijilive*, 22 April 2006).

Petero Mataca wrote: 'Instead it speaks loudly and clearly of Fijian nationalism and discrimination against non-Fijians ... We need leaders who can rise above racial politics and work for the common good of all.'[182]

Yet, by mid-2001, as Qarase feared, the fallout from the coup left Fiji more divided politically than before. Indeed, it appeared as if the divisions of 1999 were repeating themselves. At the same time that the GCC formally abandoned the SVT as its official party, rebel Macuata and Cakaudrove supporters split from the SVT to form a new Conservative Alliance Matanitu Vanua (CAMV). Poseci Bune left the VLV to join PANU, which itself split, with Apisai Tora forming a rival Ba Kei Viti (BKV). In May, former Deputy Prime Minister Tupeni Baba left the Labour Party to form his own party and join a preference sharing Moderate Fijian Coalition with Vuikaba's FAP faction, Mick Beddoes' United Generals Party, and Rabuka, who had also abandoned the SVT. Even the precocious NVTLP split, its rump reuniting with its one-time rival – the New National Party – as a Taukei Civilian Forum. Melanesian members deserted the United Generals Party, declaring themselves unhappy with their leader's support for the restoration of democracy.

Meanwhile several provinces formed their own parties (Naitasiri offered a Citizen's United Party) or proposed their chiefs as provincial candidates, in both instances arguing that no Fijian candidates should challenge them. Lau put its weight behind Qarase who, in May, launched his own Soqosoqo Duavata ni Lewenivanua (SDL or People's United Party), backed it was alleged by Fijian Holdings Limited[183] and supported by the Tailevu faction of the Fijian Association Party. Naitasiri's Turaga ni Qaranivalu, Takiveikata, became its vice president. Certainly 12 caretaker ministers and Qarase hoped that the SDL would be their vehicle to electoral success. Even before the formation of his party, Qarase was on the campaign trail dispensing funds for villages, roads and schools across the country. But, like other Fijian leaders, Qarase understood that success also depended on how voting preferences were distributed. A government analysis of the 1999 election claimed that the SVT would have won if Fijian parties had directed preferences to it instead of the Labour Party.[184] Hence the rash of umbrella organisations formed – the Moderate Fijian

---

182 P Mataca, 'Churches must preach unity', *Fiji Times*, 9 February 2005.
183 pcgovt.org.fj, accessed 18 May 2001.
184 *fijilive*, 21 May 2001.

Coalition, the Nationalists' Taukei Civilian Forum, and the SVT's Fijian Political Forum. In mid-May, the Methodist Church tried to bring the rival coalitions together and have all major Fijian parties share preferences.

Despite efforts to unite all Fijian parties under a single political umbrella, Fijians remained deeply divided over the meaning and the legality of the events of 2000: 'We have tried the illegal and unjust route on many occasions and we, the indigenous people, continue to pay the price for our recklessness,' lawyer Tupou Draunidalo warned towards the end of 2000. The ball, she believed, was now firmly in the hands of the military: 'Fiji will emerge from this mess when the FMF takes its role as the ultimate guardian of the State and Constitution more seriously ... You reap what you sow'.[185] The Citizens' Constitutional Forum (CCF) agreed. In May 2001, it legally challenged the President's failure to recall parliament.[186] Qarase dismissed its members as 'zealots of constitutionality' and declared that 'the welfare of people come before the rule of law'.[187] But the pressure told on the Chief Justice and he resigned.

As Sutherland and I noted that year, the August 2001 elections fell too much under the shadow of the 2000 coup to enable dispassionate debate on strategies and outcomes.[188] The Labour Party fought for the restoration of its government, the SDL for the continuation of its interim administration and policies, and the Conservative Alliance for the legitimisation of the 2000 coup. The results reflected that polarisation. Former People's Coalition partners like PANU, FAP and VLV were routed. So too the new BKV and the once dominant SVT. Fijians rallied behind Qarase's SDL which won nearly all Fijian seats, except for five in Vanua Levu and one in Tailevu (Speight's) that were taken by the Conservative Alliance.[189]

---

185 *Fiji Times*, 15 December 2000. Her stepfather, Dr Timoci Bavadra, had been one of the May 1987 coup's first victims, while her father – Col Savenaca Draunidalo – had been implicated in the 2000 coup.

186 Eventually justices Ward and Barker ruled that, while the CCF's case was valid, the President had had no alternative given the Labour Party's divisions and the lack of a government-in-waiting. Elections had already been held. They could not turn back the clock.

187 *fijilive*, 14 May 2001. The Qarase regime also pressured the CCF by deregistering it as a charitable trust (*fijilive*, 23 April 2001).

188 Robertson & Sutherland, *Government by the Gun*, 2001, pp. 141–42. The analysis in the next five paragraphs also draws on Sutherland's 'Postscript' in that volume.

189 Additionally, the NLUP won two seats, the GVP one, the NFP one (later lost on a recount to the FLP), and independents two. Although in custody, Speight was permitted to contest the seat in Tailevu but was expelled from parliament for non-attendance in December 2001. He remained incarcerated on Nukulau Island. His brother, Samisoni Tikoinasau, assumed his place instead.

With 31 seats and 51 per cent of the Fijian vote, Qarase was the clear winner and he immediately set about forming government in partnership with CAMV.

By heralding a third period of post-independence Fijian political domination and segregated economic development, rather than the start of a new era of multiracial cooperation, Qarase – like Mara and Rabuka before him – portrayed elite Fijian interests as synonymous with those of ordinary Fijians and declared their primacy above all other interests. For that reason Sutherland and I concluded our study of the 2000 coup and its aftermath by stating that 'it was too early to forecast an end to government by the gun in Fiji in the long term'.[190]

But we also detailed what we believed Fijians could do to put the indigenous question behind them and take Fiji forward.[191] First, we argued that Fijians needed to understand that the causes of their disaffection lay within their own communities. The notion of Fijian paramountcy made this task more difficult; it enabled a Fijian elite to dominate on their behalf and reject the kind of open environment that might assist Fijians to achieve their potential. Unfortunately, pursuing the idea of Fijian political unity has always produced its opposite, not to mention marginality, victimhood and eventually dictatorship.

Second, we believed that indigenous identity should not be claimed at the expense of national identity; 'calling everybody by the same name is a first step in overcoming legacies of colonialism and moving forward'.[192] We recommended that everyone be accepted as Fijian[193] after the name of the nation, and that those who up until then had claimed the national name for themselves be called the Taukei. But we also recommended recognition of people's multiple identities and heritages as a way of discouraging the stereotyping associated with exclusive identities.

---

190 Robertson & Sutherland, *Government by the Gun*, 2001, p. 142.
191 'Addressing the indigenous question' and 'Building the nation', Robertson & Sutherland, *Government by the Gun*, 2001, pp. 132–39.
192 Robertson & Sutherland, *Government by the Gun*, 2001, p.133.
193 Adi Litia Cakobau would clearly not have agreed. In 2003, she attacked IndoFijians at USP who used the journal *Fijian Studies* to include 'Indian' matters, calling their action an insidious form of 'ethnic violence', even 'an act of ethnocide' (*fijilive*, 10 December 2003).

Third, we urged that indigenous institutions be transparent and accountable, that they be democratised and work to empower their people, not act like fiefdoms above the law. Such fiefdoms were among the root causes of Fiji's contemporary misadventure.

Fourth, we contended that affirmative action had done little to assist Fijians not already in advantaged positions; had it been otherwise then the *vanua* of 2000 might never have presented as Ligairi's 'dogs of war'.

We ended our study by arguing that the challenge facing Fiji was not the absence of indigenous paramountcy as so many Fijian nationalists asserted. Fijians were politically dominant but such dominance brought them neither wealth nor unity.

> Similarly, the challenge is not to do with the incompatibility of democracy with tradition. Democracy is needed more than ever to ensure indigenous wellbeing. Nor is it even the impossibility of harmony in plural societies. Pluralism takes many forms and is just as capable of enriching societies as creating the basis for division.[194]

Instead the real challenge lay – as the authors of Fiji's 1997 Constitution had earlier recognised – in citizens understanding 'that what is good for their neighbours must ultimately be good for them as well, when difference and diversity are seen not as sources of division and distrust but of strength and inspiration'.[195] Ligairi and Speight had demonstrated for a second time what could happen when that challenge was denied. Unfortunately, Qarase would now demonstrate how much harder the challenge would become each time it is rejected.

The post-2000 regime of Laisenia Qarase rebuilt the Fijian establishment party that both Mara and Rabuka had lost before him and, like the government under them, did little for ordinary Fijians. Its much-vaunted affirmative action policies in education benefited only Fijians who attended Fijian-run schools. For the majority, who increasingly dominated the rolls of non Fijian-run primary and secondary schools, there was no assistance.[196] Many of these students were among the most disadvantaged Fijians, residing in squatter settlements and poor households. Of course Fijians

---

194 Robertson & Sutherland, *Government by the Gun*, 2001, pp. 138–39.
195 Reeves, Vakatora & Lal, *The Fiji Islands*, 1996, p. xix.
196 *Fiji Times*, 22 February 2007. The remainder of this section draws on Robbie Robertson, 'Coups & development: the more things change, the more they stay the same', in BV Lal & G Chand (eds), *1987 and All That: Fiji Twenty Years Later*. Lautoka: FIAS, 2008, pp. 27–41.

were not the only ones in this situation. Despite government attempts to argue that Fijians represented the most disadvantaged population in the country, increased IndoFijian depopulation of the countryside after 2000, the greater presence of IndoFijian beggars on the main streets of urban centres, the growth of IndoFijian peri-urban squatter settlements, and official statistics all suggested a more complex story.[197] Poverty and disadvantage afflicted every community.

Although the maintenance of ethnic forms of discrimination as the basis for affirmative action became increasingly tenuous, the rationale for all Fijian-first policies pursued since independence never varied. Too much had been invested in them for Fijian parties to simply disown them, a fact that Speight knew only too well in 2000. 'I've stepped in to stop the Indians or any other migrant culture achieving in this country what the Europeans have achieved in Australia and New Zealand,' he declared.[198] Prime Minister Mara had similarly promoted the primacy of Fijian interests and employed the racial card. In 1987, he put loyalty to the Fijian cause ahead of democracy and the law, and had been reinstated as prime minister and gone on to become president as a result. Although in 2000 he declared that 'armed intervention and attempted coups are not the way to reach political and economic goals,' his willingness to sack Prime Minister Chaudhry said otherwise. This was not lost on many soldiers in the RFMF. In July 2000, the Labasa mutineers declared themselves 'soldiers of the *vanua* first and Government later'.[199] The legal support offered to both the President and military commander by members of the judiciary to circumvent constitutional procedures, and the subsequent actions of

---

197 Even the SDL's *Strategic Development Plan (SDP) 2007–2011* concedes this; about 36 per cent of Indians lived in poverty, 33 per cent of Fijians. The more significant difference lay in the nature of employment: 26 per cent of Indians were engaged in subsistence activities compared with 43 per cent of Fijians (*SDL Government Paper to the National Economic Summit*. Suva, 2006, pp. 6–7). Demographic changes also made sustaining the Indian dominance argument difficult. In 1976, Indians made up 49 per cent of the population. In 2006, they most likely comprised only 37 per cent. If current emigration trends continued, by 2022 Indians might comprise only 25 per cent of the population.

198 The former Constitutional Review Committee chair, New Zealander Sir Paul Reeves replied: 'I keep hearing again and again that they must not allow what happened to the Maori in New Zealand to happen to us. My response to that is this. Maori lost land and social structures but at the same time the Maori today are showing much more creativity and real effort to rectify their situation than I detect what Fijians are doing' (*Fiji Times*, 23 September 2000, p. 2).

199 *fijilive*, 30 January 2003.

the military all suggested the viability of extra-legal actions for the Fijian cause. If institutions do not observe the rule of law, Draunidalo observed, 'there is nothing to ground the citizen to observe the rule of law'.[200]

Chiefs and Christian leaders were similarly swayed by the Fijian cause, among them Takiveikata, the paramount chief of Naitasiri, one of two provinces that were deeply implicated in both the coup and subsequent military mutiny. 'Fijians do not know much about democracy and free living,' the SDL Vice President declared: 'They need to work with laws and regulations to keep them in order. Fijians would be better off if colonial rules were activated. This would keep Fijians in their villages.'[201]

Qarase expressed the same sentiments when he laid forth his blueprint in July 2000 to revamp the colonial Fijian Administration and to make the GCC more independent of government. In the following years, he delivered on his promises. By 2006 a massive multimillion-dollar headquarters for the GCC took shape on the Nasese foreshore, close to the scene of the 2000 coup, and built with funds originally set aside for Fijian development projects. Qarase's assurance that the government would henceforth pay the operating costs of the NLTB similarly promised more income for the chiefs. His conversion of Rabuka's earlier $20 million loan to Fijian Holdings Ltd into a grant secured the privatised wealth of its principal beneficiaries.

In order to appease the nationalists behind the coup, Qarase (like Chaudhry before him in 1999) rejected the constitutional power-sharing requirement to bring Labour into a multi-party cabinet (parties with over 10 per cent of seats were entitled to a similar proportion of cabinet seats). That Labour did not contest his decision probably indicated the extent to which both parties saw non-cooperation in the more ethnically

---

200 *Fiji Times*, 15 December 2000, p. 7. The problem, however – as Madraiwiwi later noted – is that many Fijians see the rule of law as a foreign concept that subverts their way of life. Hence indigenous rights 'can only be secured by force'; 'However, the problem with this state of affairs is that force and political power are notoriously fickle instruments. They are subject to whim and fancy and are dependent on the inclinations of those who wield authority. In comparison the rule of law in its reliance on systems, laws and regulations is a far more reliable instrument and shield' (Madraiwiwi, 'Ethnic tensions and the law', 2004).
201 *Fiji Times*, 26 August 2000, p. 2.

polarised post-coup political environment as in their long-term interest. Hence Qarase formed a coalition with the CAMV in 2001, the party that supported the coup's perpetrators and their goals.[202]

Qarase's nationalist credentials were similarly enhanced by determined support for ministers charged with criminal offences during the coup,[203] his continued backing of the rebel Seniloli as vice president, by his dogged pursuance of a constitutional review twice declared illegal by the courts, and by his presentation to parliament in 2005 of a Reconciliation, Tolerance and Unity (RTU) Bill that, among other things, held out the promise of amnesty for persons involved in the 2000 coup, if not an end to all coup prosecutions. In the final year of his first government, Qarase introduced a Qoliqoli Bill to enable coastal villagers to earn revenue from the sea, just as they did from the land. Later he also promised an indigenous claims tribunal and a review of the foundational colonial document, the Deed of Cession. Some critics believed that the latter intention amounted to a rewriting of history to suit his nationalist agenda.[204]

Qarase's SDL government clearly saw itself as a government working in the interests of Fijians rather than that of the whole nation. Its Foreign Minister, Kaliopate Tavola, declared in 2002 that 'Democracy is a foreign imposition [that] does not sit well with traditional hierarchies,'[205] echoing the claim by nationalists in 1987 that democracy was a foreign flower unsuited to Fiji's soils. Democracy here meant a system of transparent governance open to the equal participation of all citizens and working in the interests of all citizens, as Qarase recognised back in 2000.

> We all welcome democracy in laying importance on the equal rights of individuals, their equality before the law, and a system of government and leadership based on the consent of the people, and not on divine right or status at birth. But in the long run, it will also serve to undermine chiefly status and authority in our traditional society. And the collective value systems that bind us together.[206]

---

202 In early 2006, CAMV was merged into the SDL to better maintain Fijian political unity ahead of fresh elections.

203 These included Ratu Naiqama Lalabalavu, Simione Kaitani, Ratu Rakuita Vakalalabure and Isireli Leweniqila.

204 S Shameem, 'The assumption of executive authority on December 5 2006 by Commodore JV Bainimarama, Commander of the RFMF: legal, constitutional and human rights issues', Fiji Human Rights Commission, Suva, 3 January 2007, p. 12.

205 *Daily Post*, 16 August 2002.

206 *Fiji Times*, 12 October 2000.

The SDL believed such governance impossible as long as Fijians were disadvantaged.[207] Disadvantage had generated political and economic instability in the past and, until it was addressed, no 'Western'-type democracy could be possible. Rather, government had to be first and foremost composed of Fijians because, as Qarase reminded voters ahead of the 2006 election, only Fijians could be depended upon to secure Fijian interests.[208]

But, if Qarase believed that he had inherited the mantle of Mara and Rabuka, he was tragically mistaken. The post-coup environment after 2000 certainly shared many features with that pertaining after 1987. Fijian paramountcy had been reasserted. Politically Fijians appeared to be united although, until 2006, the SDL's hold on majority Fijian support remained tenuous. But the crucial difference lay with the military and, in particular, with its Commander, the importance of which seemed constantly to elude the Prime Minister. Given the country's history of military intervention, this response is puzzling but can possibly be explained by Qarase's belief that Bainimarama – lacking Rabuka's charisma and public profile – would be malleable and that, ultimately, his interpretation of Fijian paramountcy would make the difference. In the end, however, his faith in paramountcy as the primary driver of Fiji politics proved his undoing, just as it had for Mara and Rabuka before him. This time the trigger was not an adverse electoral result but Bainimarama's anger at Qarase's unwavering support for individuals involved in the 2000 coup and his clumsy attempts to remove the Commander from office in 2003 and after. That anger was slow in manifesting itself publicly. Until then, as one journalist noted, Bainimarama 'rarely encroached on the political arena'.[209]

Some military officers believed that they only ever intended Qarase to lead a group of public-spirited individuals until such time as elections could be called. Thus Baledrokadroka described the interim government as a creature of the military, albeit a military traumatised by and divided over

---

207   This view is reflected also in its *Strategic Development Plan 2007–2011* (p. 2), and in press comments by Qarase and investor Ballu Khan that 'the widening wealth divide between Indians and Fijians had given rise to a coup culture' (*Fiji Times*, 25 & 26 February 2007).

208   Such thinking also pervaded his handling of relations with the military later in the year. Qarase insisted that his dispute with the military was 'an indigenous problem', not a national one, and that it should be dealt with by the GCC as the paramount indigenous body (*fijilive*, 9 November 2006). That body promptly claimed it was a Tailevu problem, and unsuccessfully asked Bainimarama's province to deal with it. National issues, Bainimarama argued, should be addressed through proper parliamentary and democratic channels, not the Fijian administrative system (*fijilive*, 1 November 2006).

209   *fijilive*, 9 April 2003.

the events of 2000. Nonetheless, the military did provide a mandate to the interim government to improve Fijian wellbeing and tied its survival to the military as the guarantor of national security.[210] Hence Bainimarama began to see himself as a kingmaker. By winning an election is his own right, however, Qarase believed that he had trumped the power Bainimarama held and began acting independently of the military's goals. In itself this was unproblematic but, with former rebels and their supporters having charges dropped, given reduced sentences or released early from jail, with Qoriniasi Bale – a disbarred lawyer and former senator – now a powerful attorney-general, and with revelations emerging of vote-buying from Ministry of Agriculture funds during the 2001 election, a cold war – as Brij Lal has termed it[211] – between Bainimarama and Qarase gradually unfolded late in 2001 and became increasingly public, especially between 2003 and 2006 when many coup prosecutions were finalised and the networks of conspiracies that lay behind the 2000 coup were momentarily exposed to light.[212]

With the exception of Speight, who was sentenced to death in 2002 but had his sentence immediately commuted to life, most of the coup conspirators received light sentences. Stevens also received life but his CRWU comrades (including Tikotani) were more fortunate and served six years; Nata, Silatolu, Savu, Ligairi and Jim Speight served only three years, Vuniwai and Navakasuasua two years, and Duvuloco 1.5 years.[213] Takiveikata went through a number of trials and appeals from 2004 and eventually received a seven-year sentence.[214] But their fellow travellers generated more controversy, particularly those with the political and chiefly associations that epitomised the shadowy forces at work behind the scenes. They were seemingly protected. Kubuabola and Savua were posted overseas. Ratu Rakuita Vakalalabure, who had appeared to serve

210   Baledrokadroka, 'Sacred king and warrior chief', 2012, pp. 212–13.
211   BV Lal, 'Anxiety, uncertainty and fear in our land: Fiji's road to military coup', in Fraenkel, Firth & Lal, *The 2006 Military Takeover in Fiji*, 2009, p. 22. The Agricultural Assistance scam came to light in 2002 and involved $25 million used mostly for vote buying. Permanent Secretary for Agriculture Peniasi Kunatuba, and three of his staff, were eventually jailed, the former for four years in 2006. At his trial Kunatuba claimed that the purpose of the scheme was to assist the interim government establish itself as a credible government and gain popular confidence (*Fiji Times*, 12 October 2006). After 2009 he allegedly became Commissioner of Corporate Services as part of a Yellow Ribbon rehabilitation program (www.coupfourandahalf.com, 22 July 2012).
212   In a Legend FM radio interview in late 2007, Bainimarama indicated that he had considered a coup against Qarase in 2001 (exactly when he did not say). It did not happen because the military decided to give Qarase a chance 'to mend his ways' (*Fiji Times*, 6 December 2007).
213   www.coupfourandahalf.com, 20 February 2002, 19 February 2003.
214   www.coupfourandahalf.com, 25 November 2004.

as one of Speight's legal advisors, became Deputy Speaker and remained in office until a four-year sentence made his role untenable. Qarase pointedly refused also to take action against colleagues such as Lands Minister Ratu Naiqama Lalabalavu and Sports Minister Isireli Leweniqila when they were charged, on the grounds that they were innocent until found guilty.[215] All had participated in the parliamentary drama. The same reasoning applied to Seniloli, the Vice President, who accepted a presidential role under Speight. Although eventually jailed for four years in 2004, he remained Vice President. Seniloli had offered to resign, but his offer had been refused for fear of weakening the position of Qarase's other ministers. In the end, Seniloli served only three months of his sentence before being released for health reasons on a compulsory supervision order and allowed to resign.[216] Such orders invited suspicion or derision. Vakalalabure was similarly released early in 2006. Lalabalavu served only 10 days in 2005 and returned to a ministerial post. Kaitani, who publically admitted sedition in 2003,[217] became Minister for Information shortly after. The Methodist Tomasi Kanailagi, who had pledged support for the coup, became a senator; so, too, did Apisai Tora, although he was jailed for eight months in 2005.

Clearly such leniency helped maintain the SDL and CAMV alliance, but it also flowed from Qarase's belief that forgiveness assisted reconciliation between Fijians and would make possible stronger racial unity ahead of future elections. His party also held that a blanket pardon would most help Fiji move closer to reconciliation with IndoFijians. 'Let bygones be bygones' became the new mantra.[218] Bainimarama opposed such leniency, seeing it as a recipe for further instability. 'Fijians only respond to the stick from us,' he reputedly told the Police Commissioner.[219] Aware that Bainimarama's hard line most jeopardised his plans, Qarase looked for ways to remove the Bainimarama thorn during 2002. In March, he nominated him to become the UN force commander in Kuwait, promoting him to rear admiral in order to boost his prospects. But despite a November interview in New York, Bainimarama was unsuccessful in being appointed. Next Qarase offered him a diplomatic posting but, by now, Bainimarama

---

215 *fijilive*, 12 June 2003.
216 *Fiji Times*, 23 June 2004. The lawyer and former High Court judge, the Bauan Ratu Joni Madraiwiwi, replaced him at the start of 2005.
217 He was later acquitted on a technicality.
218 Dakuvula, 'The unresolved issues', 2004.
219 Victor Lal, 'Bainimarama's behind-the-scenes backers were in the judiciary', www.coupfour andahalf.com, 24 May 2012.

had tired of manipulation and resolved to make his concerns public. In March 2003, incensed that the Attorney-General had approached the President to reduce sentences or pardon CRWU rebels, he very publically warned that some politicians wanted to destabilise Fiji.[220]

The two former allies in the reconstruction of Fiji in 2000 were now increasingly determined to pursue contradictory goals. Qarase, through his RTU amnesty proposals, planned greater leniency for coup perpetrators and their fellow travellers. He and his party saw the RTU Bill as a litmus test of their support for indigenous causes.[221] Qarase believed that customary obligations entangled most Fijians in the events of 2000.[222] They should not be treated as criminals but as political actors. Accordingly, he would create a commission, whose members he would appoint, to conduct hearings, sometimes in secret. This commission would have power to grant reparations (funded by the state) and recommend amnesty to individuals, even if they refused to acknowledge guilt and were prepared to reoffend. In addition, an amnesty committee could direct courts to end prosecutions and wipe criminal records clean. CCF's Jone Dakuvula believed its sole intent was to allow certain individuals to stand for parliament. 'Deep down, contrary to his words,' Dakuvula added, 'the PM [Prime Minister] and his colleagues still believe that the overthrow of the Coalition government in 2000 was justified.'[223] Lawyer Aiyaz Sayed-Khaiyum declared the proposed RTU Bill unconstitutional. It would duplicate the work of the police. It would strip power from the DPP. It was not in Fiji's long-term political and economic interests. It would weaken social stability and national security.[224] Graham Leung, President of the Fiji Law Society, maintained also that it threatened the rule of law and the independence of the judiciary and would undermine military discipline. Wadan Narsey added investor confidence to that long list of weaknesses in Qarase's legislation, noting that it would do nothing to discourage future crime.[225]

220　Dakuvula, 'The unresolved issues', 2004; *Fiji Sun*, 14 April 2005.
221　Ratu Joni Madraiwiwi, 'Making the right choices', keynote address to the 34th Annual Congress of the Fiji Institute of Accountants, Sofitel Resort Spa, 23 June 2006. '[Is] there any purpose served by the Bill in light of the divisions it has caused?' he asked.
222　*Fiji Times*, 5 May 2005.
223　*Fiji Sun*, 28 August 2005.
224　*Fiji Times*, 1 June 2005.
225　Wadan Narsey, 'Great concept, bad reality', *Fiji Times*, 31 May 2005.

Despite all the jargon about restorative justice and the uniqueness of the Fijian condition, Fiji had ample experience of reconciliation and its pitfalls, as Edwina Kotoisuva of the Fiji Women's Crisis Centre noted in early 2006.

> Reconciliation is a great thing and ideally if reconciliation does take place the offence should never be repeated. But the reality is that the offence is likely to occur again without proper intervention that is targeted at changing the man's behaviour … [R]econciliation, as it exists within the cycle of abuse, is almost meaningless because it is supported by most people and structures in society who are willing to place the lives of women and children on the line for a mythical concept of family life.[226]

For a patriarchal elite this was a comparison too far, and soon the debate degenerated into personal attacks.

Commissioner of Police Andrew Hughes, who had been drafted in from the Australian Federal Police to reprofessionalise the police force after Savua's departure in 2003, opposed amnesty on the understandable grounds that it would interfere with ongoing police investigations and prosecutions. Earlier he called the rebels 'domestic terrorists'; now he wanted his own commission, one that would inquire into their activities. 'How can you reconcile something when you don't know what occurred,' he argued; 'who do you forgive and what are you forgiving them for?' But Qarase refused. If investigations are ongoing, why have an inquiry?[227] Many of Qarase's colleagues were blunter. Senator Mitieli Bulanauca declared that people who do not want to be part of the reconciliation process should leave Fiji.[228] When Bainimarama attacked the RTU Bill's amnesty proposals, claiming that they were designed to promote the ethnic cleansing of Indians and to garner rural Fijian votes, Tora taunted him brutally: step down and let 'a real army man take over to restore military honour'.[229]

---

226 Edwina Kotoisuva, 'When reconciliation is unjust', *Fiji Times*, 11 January 2006.

227 *Fiji Sun*, 25 August 2004; 25 & 26 August 2006. But, in mid-2005, he made that task more difficult by refusing to extend the contract of the expatriate public prosecutor, Peter Ridgway, who had been most involved in the post-coup cases.

228 *Fiji Times*, 23 October 2004. The Minister for Lands expressed similar sentiments on introducing the Qoliqoli Bill: if hoteliers did not like it they could invest in another country (*fijivillage*, 13 August 2006).

229 *Fiji Sun*, 2 July 2005; *Fiji Times*, 25 August 2005.

The military spoiler

Bainimarama's opposition generated increasingly personal attacks. Jioji Kotobalavu, the long-serving CEO of the Prime Minister's office, later reminded him that the 2000 coup involved not only the illegal takeover of an elected government but the removal of a president. Bainimarama concentrated on one aspect of the coup alone, he warned, not 'total justice', not 'the illegal abrogation of the Constitution, which he was responsible for'.[230] The message was clear. Everyone had skeletons in their cupboards, including the Commander, who knew only too well that parliament had failed to approve amnesty for the military and that the police continued to investigate the deaths associated with the mutiny. The government was not going to bow easily to the military. Bainimarama 'is a person who suffers from insecurity', Kotobalavu declared in 2004, 'and has a tendency to behave like an autocratic dictator'.[231]

Certainly, government now faced a much more pugnacious Bainimarama, one prepared to purge his senior officers in order to stay on top and to challenge political leaders who disregarded his authority or who failed to give him and his military the respect that he believed they deserved. It helped of course that Bainimarama's vision for the military placed it at the very centre of Fiji, obliged to uphold the wellbeing of the country in addition to its defence and security duties. That this vision, inserted into the Taukeist 1990 Constitution, had been repealed in 1997 did not trouble him given that Qarase's Government had also brushed aside so much of the 1997 Constitution. The events of 2000 and Bainimarama's growing distrust of Fijian communal and political leaders quickly transformed the military 'into an agent of partisan national politics'.[232]

Surprisingly, Qarase appeared to take the loyalty of the military for granted. He sought to reduce the court martial sentences of Labasa soldiers found guilty of mutiny. He even planned to halve the size of the RFMF and not renew Bainimarama's five-year contract as commander. Bainimarama became aware of these machinations and laid his own plans. He recalled all soldiers guarding state officials and asked his officers to pledge support to

230 *Fiji Times*, 10 January 2005.
231 *Fiji Post*, 21 March 2004.
232 Baledrokadroka, 'Sacred king and warrior chief', 2012, pp. 294–95. In addition, the highly partisan Directorate of Army Legal Services probably fed Bainimarama's incorrect interpretation of the status of constitutional clauses relating to the military (Baledrokadroka, 'Sacred king and warrior chief', 2012, pp. 252–53).

him. He called on the government to resign if it did not back the military. He increased military briefings with the President. In June 2003, he announced that he wanted his contract renewed in the following February and received endorsement from opposition politicians.[233] But not from Permanent Secretary of Home Affairs Jeremaia Waqanisau; his very public denunciations of Bainimarama served only to make himself a target for military hatred.[234] Also in Bainimarama's sights were Waqanisau's two deputies, former major Dr Lesi Korovuvala and Penijamini Lomaloma. He suspected both of trying to influence the President to reduce sentences. In August, Bainimarama recommended that the three senior home affairs officials be removed from office. Nothing happened. Instead the Attorney-General allegedly sought to bypass the President by seeking legislation to establish a parole board. By this means he alone could make recommendations for pardons and reduce sentences.[235] Meanwhile the political attacks on coup investigations continued. In June, the GCC discussed a Tailevu proposal to close all investigations and issue a general pardon. In December, Adi Litia Cakobau called on the Senate to release all political prisoners and cease coup investigations.[236]

An angry Bainimarama told his officers in December 2003 to prepare to take over government if it chose not to reappoint him. They urged him to desist, sending a copy of their advice to the Home Affairs Minister. Qarase probably read this to mean that Bainimarama did not enjoy the full support of the military and that a coup was unlikely.[237] But, to ease tensions, he agreed in January to reappoint Bainimarama as commander for a final five-year term. Bainimarama was not mollified. He took revenge on his senior officers. Those who refused to pledge personal loyalty to him were purged at the start of 2004.[238] Indeed, as political scientist

---

233 Wainikiti Bogidrau, 'Checkmate: why the army and state went head-to-head', *Review*, 1 July 2003; Dakuvula, 'The unresolved issues', 2004; *Daily Post*, 8 May 2003; *Fiji Times*, 6 June 2003.
234   Dakuvula, 'The unresolved issues', 2004. Allegedly Waqanisau recommended that Bainimarama's contract not be renewed because the military had overspent its budget by $20 million in 2003 (*Fiji Times*, 23 March 2003).
235 Dakuvula, 'The unresolved issues', 2004. As the chair of the Prerogative of Mercy Commission, the Attorney-General already possessed similar powers.
236 Dakuvula, 'The unresolved issues', 2004. *fijilive*, 26 September 2003.
237 Victor Lal & Russell Hunter, 'Smuggled papers show Bainimarama's lust for power', *New Zealand Herald*, 25 February 2012. The text appeared in the press in April 2004 (*Fiji Sun*, 7 April 2004).
238 They were Kadavulevu, Tuatoko, Raduva and two chief staff officers from Strategic HQ – Lt Col Akuila Buadromo and Commander Timoci Koroi. Baledrokadroka claims that Bainimarama demanded they draw up plans for a takeover, claiming that legal channels to effect his reappointment would take too long. Tuatoko argued that the Commander should not use the RFMF in this way to have his contract renewed (Baledrokadroka, 'Sacred king and warrior chief', 2012, pp. 218–23).

Jon Fraenkel later noted, 'Each subsequent spat served also as a loyalty test'.[239] Qarase saw an opportunity to settle the dispute once and for all. In mid-July, he successfully advised the President to hold a commission of inquiry into Bainimarama's purportedly treasonous activities but, the very next day – after a visit from Bainimarama – Iloilo suddenly reversed his agreement.[240] Defeated, Qarase sent Waqanisau to Beijing as an ambassador.

Bainimarama gave as good as he got; he demanded that the government transform its economic policies, educate people on the problems associated with coups, and end corruption. Much like Rabuka in 1987, he envisaged the military assuming new roles in commerce and politics and, in 2004, launched his 'Military for Life' concept, which immediately took form as a successful bid for engineer reservists to build Telecom satellite stations in 87 villages. Such initiatives, Bainimarama believed, were desperately needed for a RFMF 'on the verge of burning out as it continues to work with insufficient resources'[241] and as it sought to staunch the exodus of seasoned personnel. Indeed, by mid-2005, some 1,000 Fijians were serving as soldiers, guards and drivers in Iraq and Kuwait and over 2,000 were members of the British military forces.[242] But a lack of resources most explained the military's constant overspending of its budget. Some was due also to inadequate controls over the purchase of goods and services and to the increased roles that the army played in maintaining domestic security and assisting with disaster relief. Additionally, peacekeeping duties were a real budget killer because, as operations increased, so did the proportions of monies spent on salaries and allowances, from 51 per cent in 1977 to over 80 per cent in 2002. Dagney Fosen argues that Fiji's governments consistently failed to reimburse the military adequately for its duties, with the result that its administration, logistics and equipment

---

239   Baledrokadroka, 'Sacred king and warrior chief', 2012, pp. 218–23, Jon Fraenkel, 'Fiji's December 2006 coup: Who, what, where and why?', in Fraenkel, Firth & Lal, *The 2006 Military Takeover in Fiji*, 2009, p. 46.

240   *Fiji Times*, 24 July 2005. According to one account, Bainimarama used his knowledge of an attempt in late 2001 by businessmen close to Qarase to remove Iloilo from the presidency to sway the President to drop the investigation (Wainikiti Bogidrau, 'Inside a palace coup', *Fiji Times*, 25 June 2005).

241   *Fiji Sun*, 23 October 2004.

242   Nic Maclellan, 'Fiji, the war in Iraq and the privatization of Pacific Island security', *Australian Policy Forum*, Nautilus Institute, 6 April 2006. Some recruiters were of deep concern. In one instance as many as 15,000 villagers paid a recruiter a registration fee of $150 just to be listed for work opportunities. Often this money came from church or village development funds. But, if realised, the benefits were lucrative. Remittances, valued at $200 million in 2005, surpassed sugar and garments in earning Fiji foreign exchange.

needs suffered dramatically.[243] Perhaps a small country like Fiji could never afford such a comparatively large military. Since 1978 its share of the government budget had jumped from 2.8 per cent to over 7 per cent in 2000;[244] in post-coup years proportions were even higher. Although various reviews had been held to restructure and reform the military, most of them – like attempts to audit RFMF finances in the years after 1987 – came to nought. Only in 2006 did Fiji finally recognise that it had created a beast it could no longer control.

The warning signs had been there since 2003 and they emerged again in 2005 when the government pressed ahead with its RTU Bill, despite fresh military opposition. This time the military employed new tactics, placing ministers under surveillance and, in some instances, allegedly stalking them. When the RTU Bill was read in parliament in June 2005, military officers filled the public gallery. A leaked report suggested it planned to remove the government if the Bill passed. The government responded by docking Bainimarama's pay for exceeding the military's budget, and tit-for-tat allegations raged in the months ahead.[245] A furious Bainimarama threatened to relocate his HQ into the home affairs section of Government Buildings in December and challenged both Home Affairs Minister Josefa Vosanibola and his CEO Korovuvala to come to the barracks and sack him. The head of the Public Service Commission, Anare Jale, threatened police retaliation should Bainimarama move against home affairs officials, and Police Commissioner Hughes put the newly formed Police Tactical Response Unit on standby.[246]

Bainimarama denied threatening anyone but maintained that the military now no longer recognised the minister and was answerable to no one.[247] But he began preparations, allegedly telling his senior officers on Sunday

---

243 Dagney Margrete Fosen, 'RFMF in Fiji's defence policy', in CCF, *Background Paper on the RFMF*, 2003, pp. 11–14. Fosen notes that the military contributed to its budgetary problems; it was over ranked by some 333 personnel (CCF, *Background Paper on the RFMF*, p. 26).

244 CCF, *Background Paper on the RFMF*, p.10.

245 Journalist Wainikiti Bogidrau argued that, because the government knew that the President would side with Bainimarama over the RTU Bill, it organised for the GCC to send a delegation to deliver a truce with the military. Nothing came of it. When the President later called Qarase to brief him and the Vice President on the Bill, he bluntly told him to drop it ('Inside a palace coup', 2005).

246 Set up in 2005 to replace the anti-terrorist functions of the CRWU on the recommendation of the 2000 Military Board of Inquiry and 2004 Security and Defence Review, it built on the foundations of the 1973 Police Mobile Force and Special Patrol Group. Based in Nasinu, it eventually comprised 138 staff and operated as a SWAT team. Bainimarama closed it down on 2 February 2007 (*Fiji Sun*, 6 February 2007).

247 Serafina Qalo, 'Champion of rights or lawbreaker?', *Fiji Times*, 16 March 2006.

8 January 2006 that he intended to take over the government. The next day he told them to rescue him if he was arrested. Jokapeci Koroi, Labour's longstanding President, informed Fiji TV on 11 January that 'I think he should do it because we are waiting, the Labour Coalition government, we are waiting to complete what we started in 1999 and 2000'.

> I know a lot of people will disagree with me … I am not saying that I support it but you don't know what kind of takeover he is going to do and I have a feeling its not going to be like in the 2000 and 1987 coup, no![248]

It was a stunning performance for those of us watching it. It hinted at collusion between Labour and the military, something that only a few years ago would have seemed impossible. Here was a party that had twice been felled by military interventions apparently welcoming another.

Back at the QEB the newly appointed Acting Land Force Commander Col Jone Baledrokadroka probably drew similar conclusions. The next day he and two colleagues warned a surprised Commander that what he proposed was treason and he should resign. Instead Bainimarama rallied his officers and demanded Baledrokadroka's resignation, accusing him of plotting a mutiny.[249] He then escalated the tension, stationing three naval vessels in Suva Harbour purportedly to protect the President. A hastily convened National Security Council met as the police erected roadblocks in Suva. Perhaps fearing resistance, Bainimarama pulled back. Vice President Ratu Joni Madraiwiwi, who had replaced the convicted former Vice President Seniloli in early 2005 and increasingly acted as president due to Iloilo's worsening health, got Qarase and the Commander together in February to produce an agreement that bound Bainimarama to normal civil service processes for airing grievances. In return Qarase agreed to take on board military concerns with the RTU and Qoliqoli bills.[250]

---

248 www.coupfourandahalf.com, 28 July 2011.

249 *Fiji Times*, 16 January 2006; see also Steven Ratuva, 'Officers, gentlemen and coups', *Fiji Times*, 25 January 2006. Fearing Bainimarama would move against him, Baledrokadroka closed access to the QEB on 12 January and sent two officers to Strategic HQ to inform the Commander he would not resign. Bainimarama accused him of threatening a mutiny and stood him down, pending a court marshal. Baledrokadroka eventually fled to New Zealand, and later successfully undertook a doctorate at ANU in Canberra before joining the UN Development Program.

250 Journalist Robert Keith-Reid argued that Madraiwiwi was under pressure to get Bainimarama to moderate his anti-government rhetoric or else he would be forced to accept Qarase's request for the Commander's dismissal, an action that would not be easy. That same month Iloilo indicated he wished to retire but the military refused to countenance it ('Fiji's simmering election pot', *Island Business*, April 2006). Consequently, the GCC reappointed Iloilo and Madraiwiwi for new five-year terms.

The agreement did not survive. By March the planned fortnightly meetings between the two leaders were on hold, and Bainimarama again started issuing public statements ridiculing the government. Once more the Home Affairs Minister pressed for his removal and again the President did nothing. Bainimarama taunted the government, withdrawing the security detail for the Prime Minister and challenging the government to sack him.[251]

If anything, Baledrokadroka's resistance forced Bainimarama to plan more carefully the steps he might undertake should his bluff be called. In February, he had the military's legal office draft two letters in preparation for a takeover. By accident they fell into the hands of Commissioner Hughes. The first – addressed to the Vice President – detailed Bainimarama's complaints against the government. The second – citing the doctrine of necessity – outlined a legal justification for military action. Hughes allegedly showed these to the Australian High Commissioner who informed the American ambassador, Larry Dinger. Dinger thought it clear that Bainimarama would remove the government if it continued on its current course. At the end of February, Hughes met Bainimarama to dissuade him from such action. But the Commander was in no mood for turning. He reiterated his dismay at Qarase's consistent leniency towards the rebels and their supporters. The army should have retained power in 2000, not surrendered it.[252]

The two men met again in the following month, this time to discuss another of Bainimarama's concerns: the danger the Police Tactical Response Unit posed to the military's monopolisation of weapons in Fiji. In 2005, the unit had purchased 123 pistols and 30 submachine guns to replace obsolete weapons and enable its members to be properly equipped for peacekeeping missions. Bainimarama argued that the consignment had been for the military, while Hughes maintained that he armed the police only to meet criminal threats, not to encourage Fijians to confront Fijians. The two agreed to continue talking.[253] Again Bainimarama was under pressure to pull back. The Vice President had

---

251 *Fiji Times*, 18 & 20 March 2006.

252 Victor Lal, 'Bainimarama's behind-the-scenes backers', 2012; evidence based on embassy correspondence obtained by Wikileaks. American cables described Bainimarama as an 'erratic, sometimes violent leader, thin-skinned, often defensive and insecure, and prone to be wildly excessive in his reaction to criticisms' (Philip Doring, 'US cables reveal the brutality of Fijian regime', *Age*, 27 August 2011).

253 *Fiji Sun*, 17 March 2006.

released legal advice that refuted the military's longstanding claim to a constitutional role in politics. The DPP was about to make a decision on police investigations into the deaths of CRWU soldiers during the 2000 mutiny. And, increasingly, civil society organisations and politicians were joining forces to condemn his destabilising actions. SDL director Jale Baba, clearly not a disinterested observer, restated his party's opposition to Labour's renewed call for an independent inquiry into the events of 2000. 'We cannot let the nation be held ransom by events of the past,' he argued: 'A commission of inquiry can be regressive in terms of nation building by opening up old wounds and scars.'[254] But Bainimarama would have been less prepared for the responses of some nonaligned forces. Angie Heffernan, coordinator of the Pacific Centre for Public Integrity, and Virisila Buadromo, the executive director of the Fiji Women's Rights Movement, declared that it was 'now time for the military to step back and let Fiji's constitutional and democratic processes work'. One cannot 'break the law to protect the law', they pointed out.[255]

Elections were now due in Fiji, but the census – used for redistributing seats and last held in 1996 – had been postponed because of the elections. Normally this might not be of major concern but, since 2000, the number of IndoFijians emigrating had more than doubled. This reduced the FLP's chances of winning an election in its own right, especially in open constituency seats. Redistribution might also reduce the number of closed communal seats it could contest.[256] Obviously, Labour had no desire to insist on a census prior to elections, and the SDL – which believed it could win if it maintained Fijian unity – urgently sought a fresh mandate to dangle before Bainimarama.[257] Bainimarama, however, remained undaunted. He faulted the government for holding elections without first conducting a census and escalated his campaign against it.[258]

---

254 *Fiji Times*, 24 March 2006.
255 *Fiji Times*, 24 March 2006.
256 Estimates suggested that the IndoFijian population had fallen from 49 per cent to 38 per cent of Fiji's total population between 1986 and 2004 (20,720 citizens – mostly IndoFijians – had emigrated since 2001) while the number of registered voters had fallen nearly 10 per cent, the electoral impact of which was compounded by rapid urbanisation (*Islands Business*, April 2006).
257 Despite 13 parties fielding 270 candidates and 68 independent candidates, the potential for ethnic division remained high. With the economy slumping and western Viti Levu as fractious as ever, Qarase had no reason to suppose that he could deliver Fijian unity. Hence his desire for Fijian parties to share preferences. To this end, veteran politician Tomasi Vakatora brought together a Grand Coalition of Fijian parties in early 2006 (NAP did not join) and Qarase finalised the union of CAMV and the SDL.
258 In fact, the stronger argument for delaying the elections lay in the inadequate time that the Electoral Office had for preparation. The week-long polling got off to a chaotic start on 7 May with inadequate ballot papers at polling stations and inaccurate rolls.

Although Labour appeared to align itself with Bainimarama in January 2006, Bainimarama did not rise to the party's public bait. He had no wish to ally himself too closely with a party that he damned in the past. In any case, he had developed strong links with his former commander, Ratu Epeli Ganilau, and his new National Alliance Party (NAP) and anticipated its success in the 2006 election. In March, he told the *Fiji Times*: 'The RFMF, and I as its head, have no particular political affiliation, nor do we support a party.'[259]

Nonetheless, in the lead up to the May elections in 2006, Bainimarama sent his soldiers into villages as part of a Truth and Justice Campaign against the SDL.[260] On the same day as parliament dissolved, Bainimarama led 200 troops in camouflaged gear with military vehicles armed with machine guns through the streets of Suva. 'We have taken it upon ourselves to be the watchdog of this nation for the simple reason that the same group of people who had a hand in the events of 2000 seem to be back,' Bainimarama later argued. 'The RFMF is all powerful and it has outlived a lot of governments and people,' he warned.[261] In an echo of the younger Rabuka, his new Land Force Commander Colonel Pita Driti dismissively declared that 'Politicians are politicians, but we are professionals'.[262]

By the time of the Truth and Justice Campaign, however, Bainimarama's drive against the SDL had begun to assume different characteristics. When the scandal surrounding the SDL's agricultural policies first erupted, Chaudhry had suggested that the 2001 election might be illegitimate as a consequence. According to Baledrokadroka, a commonality of interest now drove Chaudhry and Bainimarama together, and it added a new feature to Bainimarama's rhetoric.[263] Qarase's affirmative action bills had always been used to demonstrate his dangerous links with former rebels. Affirmative action itself had never been questioned. Now, however,

---

259 *Fiji Times*, 14 March 2006. Journalist Maika Bolatiki claimed that Ganilau had formed the NAP 'as revenge for his removal as chairman of the GCC by the Government' (*Fiji Sun*, 28 February 2005).
260 That this military campaign was covertly funded from the $1.5 million received from Telecom did not seem to jar with its anti-corruption message (Baledrokadroka, 'Sacred king and warrior chief', 2012, p. 248).
261 *Fiji Times*, 27 March & 10 October 2006. Lawyer Richard Naidu made essentially the same observation of the Rabuka government 10 years before: 'Every time I look forward, I see what I am supposed to have left behind … In the hazy background the same movers and shakers still move, shake and fix' (A Griffen, *With Heart and Nerve and Sinew: Postcoup Writing from Fiji*. Suva: Christmas Club, 1997, pp. 358–59).
262 *fijilive*, 1 November 2006.
263 Baledrokadroka, 'Sacred king and warrior chief', 2012, p. 224.

ethno-nationalism came to be projected increasingly as denying Fiji's peoples equality. The importance of this shift would not become fully apparent until much later, but in 2006 it was sufficient to enable the military to win new allies from among the IndoFijian population and to present itself as progressive, multiracial and modern in outlook. Importantly it forced Qarase to reconsider his attitude to power-sharing, although not with immediate effect.

Brij Lal believes that the 2006 election drove the tussle for power between Qarase and Bainimarama underground.[264] Certainly the media blitz of campaigning smothered it, but with the sniping continuing – fuelled by lazy political rhetoric – it never strayed far from people's minds. Qarase told his party faithful that all Fiji's coups had been directed against the FLP and he could not guarantee that the same would not happen again if Labour won. Bainimarama retorted that this time his army had prepared for such eventualities.[265] Rabuka entered the fray, declaring that 'Fijians must unite and hold on to political leadership in their homeland'.[266] Qarase variously informed rallies that only a Fijian prime minister could understand the concerns of Fijians, that the prime minister must be Fijian, and – just ahead of polling – that if Labour won, Fijians would lose their lands like Maoris in New Zealand.[267] Tupeni Baba, formerly of the FLP and now a SDL candidate, and Viliame Savu (NTLP) both also warned of instability if a 'foreigner' was elected.[268] When the *Fiji Post*, partially owned by the SDL, argued on the eve of polling that the reform and downsizing of the military had to begin with Bainimarama, the military placed an advertisement in Fiji's dailies saying 'that any attempts to remove the Commander will not in any way deter or stop the RFMF as an institution promoting truth and justice and the values of good governance'.[269]

Nonetheless, the electoral outcome provided a fresh opportunity for contemplation. Enveloping Bainimarama's bugbear – the CAMV – within the SDL enabled Qarase to regain office with an outstanding 80 per cent

---

264 Lal, 'Anxiety, uncertainty and fear', 2009, p. 26.
265 *Fiji Sun*, 2 May 2006. He had earlier declared the organisers of the SDL and CAMV as 'a threat to national security' (*fijilive*, 24 February 2006). The outbreak of rioting in Honiara, capital of the Solomon Islands, in mid-April brought forth memories of Suva in 2000.
266 *Fiji Sun*, 23 February 2006.
267 *Fiji Times*, 24 March & 4 May 2006; *fijilive*, 30 April 2006.
268 *fijilive*, 29 April & 1 May 2006.
269 *Fiji Sun*, 7 May 2006.

of the Fijian vote (45 per cent of the total vote). It was, however, a one-seat majority and dependent on compliant independents for a working majority. Labour under Chaudhry similarly won 83 per cent of the IndoFijian vote (and 38 per cent of the total vote).[270] Thus a much more politically polarised Fiji finally emerged, despite all the intentions of the 1997 Constitution. Qarase had railed against the Constitution's power-sharing provisions during the election campaign and was expected to act as he had in 2001, shutting Labour out. But he changed tack on regaining office and offered Labour nine substantial portfolios within a multi-party cabinet. Possibly he planned to fracture the Labour Party while muting military criticism. If so, then an overly confident Qarase needlessly complicated matters by simultaneously vowing to curb the Commander. Predictably Bainimarama hit back, threatening martial law if the SDL continued to fight the army.[271]

The sudden emergence of multi-party governance garnered unexpected widespread support. Labour stalwart Krishna Datt told parliament that 'We must arrest the vicious cycle of adversarial conflicts that have polarised our people [if we are to] unleash the creative potential of our people and restore their dignity … Without them we have no creativity, productivity and growth, no culture, no identity, no nation and no government in the true sense of the word'.[272] Vice President Madraiwiwi similarly presented multi-party cabinet as a 'unique opportunity to develop new paradigms and ways of doing things'. In contrast 'for most of the period since 1987', he declared, 'we have been governed largely by indigenous Fijians with little pretence at involving the other communities who call this place home'.[273]

---

270 The EU considered the elections well conducted, despite some shortcomings. Of registered electors, 88 per cent turned out (compared with 78 per cent in 2001) and invalid votes stood at 9 per cent (11 per cent in 2001) (*fijilive*, 21 September 2011). A massive education program preceded the elections and registration processes were much improved. This time only 11 seats were decided on preferences compared with 29 in 2001. Two independents – Robin Irwin (NE General) and Joji Konrote (Rotuma Communal) – gave the SDL a working majority. The United People's Party (UPP) – in alliance with Labour – only gained two seats, but when Labour elected to join the multi-party cabinet, it severed its link with Labour and its leader Mick Beddoes became Leader of the Opposition. The NAP, NFP, PANU and VTLP all failed to win seats (Waden Narsey, 'Let's pull together for once', *Fiji Times*, 19 May 2006).

271 *Fiji Sun*, 20 May 2006.

272 *Fiji Times*, 10 June 2006.

273 Ratu Joni Madraiwiwi, 'Making the right choices', 2006.

If the offer to respect the Constitution represented a genuine attempt by Qarase to reset Fiji's politics and move away from the bitterness of the past six years, then he needed the support of both Chaudhry and Bainimarama to ensure success. Neither showed any sign that they would oblige. Chaudhry's initial acceptance quickly became mired in party politics. The unionist Felix Anthony had entered parliament through an exchange deal that promised the sitting member, Vijay Singh, a Senate seat. But when Chaudhry handed his list of Senate nominees to the new Leader of the Opposition, Singh's name was absent. Chaudhry claimed no deal had been made, but the party's management board held a very different interpretation. It requested the list be returned, claiming that Chaudhry had no right to submit it, as he had not been endorsed as party leader.[274]

Fortunately for Chaudhry, his cane-farmer base dominated Labour's National Council and he used it to frustrate the management board's challenge to his authority and impose impossible conditions on Labour's participation in the multi-party cabinet. Cabinet loyalty came second to party loyalty. Chaudhry feared losing control of Labour both to internal dissidents and to the SDL. But his strategy for maintaining control was undeniably shortsighted. Gone were the days when IndoFijians comprised half the population. As a dwindling minority, albeit still a large one electorally, Labour could never hope to win future elections in its own right. Increasingly it would need to demonstrate its capacity to attract Fijians 'if it is not to remain on the sidelines', as Vice President Madraiwiwi advised in an address in June. By frustrating multi-party governance, Chaudhry risked both Labour's future and the kind of compromises that could deliver real win-win gains for Fiji's economy and its peoples. Such moments come infrequently, Madraiwiwi noted.[275]

But Chaudhry had little time for such advice as tension with his senior colleagues escalated. By August the National Council began proceedings against five members of the management board.[276] Few were surprised when two senior Labour ministers – Krishna Datt and Poseci Bune – contradicted Chaudhry's advice, affirmed cabinet solidarity and accepted the SDL's budget proposals, a key element of which – an increase in VAT

274 *fijivillage*, 29 June 2006.
275 Madraiwiwi, 'Making the right choices', 2006.
276 These were ministers Bune and Datt, and backbenchers Anthony, Agni Deo Singh and former senator Atu Bain (*Fiji Sun*, 23 August 2006). They were formally expelled from the party in early 2007 (*Fiji Sun*, 10 January 2007).

from 12.5 to 15 per cent – Labour opposed. Of course the real problem facing Fiji had little to do with VAT. Its long-suffering economy had never fully recovered from the shock of 2000 and now suffered from low levels of investment due, in no small measure, to Fiji's continued dependence on an overstaffed civil service whose cost-of-living adjustments continually forced government to divert resources away from projects. It had made little progress on corporatising government agencies or divesting its shareholding in interests such as Fiji TV.[277] The SDL's nationalist agenda also exacerbated problems facing the sugar industry. Sugar production had fallen 36 per cent over nine years as some 6,000 sugar leases expired and the halcyon years of EU subsidies ended.[278]

The other once bright spot in the economy – the garment industry – had also faltered, employment halving in 10 years. Its single greatest loss came in 2005 when the end of US quotas wiped out 6,000 jobs.[279] Gold production was also down with the Vatukoula goldmine set to close. Little wonder that 35 per cent of the population lived below the poverty line and at least 10 per cent were squatters. The government seemed to have little to offer. GDP growth had averaged only 1.5 per cent since 2000, hardly sufficient to keep up with population growth; hence average per capita GDP growth realised negative 1 per cent over the same period. The government pinned its hopes on tourism becoming a $1 billion industry in 2007 and growth picking up to 3.1 per cent in 2006.[280] The disjuncture between its election promises and the poverty of its economic strategies could not have been starker.

Possibly the state of the economy influenced Chaudhry's decision not to join the cabinet. Instead he chose to become Leader of the Opposition, a move that seemed to dash the high hopes held for the multi-party cabinet. Both he and Qarase may have believed that the arrangement, which had Labour both in and out of government, would soon collapse in any case. Under such circumstances Qarase could at least say that he had genuinely attempted multi-party government as the Constitution stipulated. And Chaudhry could turn to his supporters and say that he had refused to sup with the devil.

---

277 *fijivillage*, 24 October 2006; *fijilive*, 24 September 2006.
278 *fijivillage*, 27 October 2006.
279 *Fiji Times*, 11 October & 21 September 2006.
280 *Fiji Times*, 12, 13 & 25 September 2006.

Unexpectedly for both, then, the multi-party cabinet did not collapse. Despite no ground rules for multi-party cabinet, it muddled on with growing popular support. Brij Lal believes that had Chaudhry participated (in November 2006, as Qarase faced stronger fightback from the military, he was offered posts as deputy prime minister and minister for finance), Bainimarama – the second person on whom multi-party governance depended for success – might have acted differently as the year neared its end. At first Bainimarama did pledge support for multi-party governance. 'Given the right and congenial environment,' he wrote in the military newsletter *Mataivula News*, 'the concept will definitely succeed.' He led a delegation to the Home Affairs Ministry in July and Vosanibola took one to the QEB, urging more cabinet ministers to visit.[281]

Unfortunately, Qarase probably also counted on Chaudhry to maintain his opposition so that he would bear the brunt of popular disapproval. In short, Qarase had embarked on a dangerous game. Outsmarting the military and dividing Labour were becoming mutually exclusive strategies. Qarase could never have his cake and eat it too, particularly once his newfound enthusiasm for multi-ethnic unity demonstrated serious limitations when – against the advice of the Vice President – he blithely returned to his election agenda and reintroduced his controversial bills.[282] Often, as some political commentators noted, it is not the substance of proposed legislation that is at fault but the manner of its introduction. The Qoliqoli Bill was a case in point. Undoubtedly a legal framework would ultimately benefit hoteliers but, without sensible debate and consultation, the Bill quickly became a declaration of nationalist intent. On its introduction to parliament, the Minister for Lands berated hoteliers who questioned its wisdom, telling them to get out of the country if they did not like it. Such political bullying did not auger well for multi-party governance.[283]

The Indigenous Lands Claim Tribunal was similarly flawed. Modelled on New Zealand's Waitangi Tribunal, it sought to settle historic disputes. But such disputes were not always between Fijian entities and the government; they were often between Fijians themselves. As *fijivillage*'s Yellow Bucket column asked, how far back should a tribunal look?

---

281   *Fiji Times*, 28 July 2006.
282   Madraiwiwi had asked in June that 'Six years after the events of May 2000 … is there any purpose served by the [RTU] Bill in the light of the divisions it has caused'? ('Making the right choices', 2006).
283   *fijivillage*, 13 August 2006.

'Does it include marauding chiefs like Ma'afu',[284] the Tongan chief on whose empire the Tovata confederation was built? And who should pay for the golden eggs that the goose would lay to right the wrongs of the past?

Predictably Bainimarama declared Qarase's bills racist: 'only a handful of people will benefit from these [proposals]'.[285] Qarase also reinstated former CAMV ministers and released a new defence white paper, which again proposed reducing the size of the military and curtailing the power of future commanders. He even offered Baledrokadroka – suspended by Bainimarama for failing to support him and facing a possible court martial – a post as Commissioner of Prisons. Most pointedly he began a police investigation into Bainimarama's anti-government activities. The investigation into his alleged involvement in the bloody suppression of the 2000 mutiny rambled on without resolution. Qarase wanted rid of Bainimarama. His government considered surcharging him for his misuse of public funds in the Truth and Justice campaign, but were only beginning to appreciate how out of control their military commander was.[286]

No matter how remarkable his performance, Qarase should have known that Bainimarama would react badly. In late September, Bainimarama told a group of passing-out cadets at a Fijian school in Serua that the government's nationalist bills would drive Fijians back to grass skirts and cannibalism. Soon hoteliers would be leaving the country just as cane farmers had left their farms.[287] Qarase could only repeat his mantra: 'This is a challenge to the legal authority and mandate of a government elected by the people to govern this country'. No political role existed for the military.[288] During the next month Bainimarama stepped up his activism, warning business associates of the government, such as Ballu Khan, a joint owner with the NLTB of Pacific Connex, the company that supplied software services to the Board, to be careful. Khan – a Fiji-

---

284   *fijivillage*, 13 August 2006.

285   C Wilson, 'Lies, lies, lies', *Fiji Sun*, 10 November 2006.

286   Lal & Hunter, 'Smuggled papers', 2012.

287   Following a chance meeting between Bainimarama and a board member for Turtle Island on a flight from Sydney in September 2005, some tourist operators set out to woo the Commander. The owner of Turtle Island, Richard Evanson, who apparently felt cheated by Qarase over the Qoliqoli Bill and went on to back Ganilau's NAP in the 2006 elections, invited Bainimarama and his family to spend Christmas at the resort where he was able to meet a special guest, US Republican senator John McCain (Rory Callinan, 'Fueling Fiji's coup', *Time Magazine*, 20 December 2006).

288   *Fiji Sun*, 23 September 2006.

born New Zealand citizen – angered the military by employing former CRWU prisoners as security guards.[289] Bainimarama also cast his eye over his senior officers once more for signs of disloyalty.[290]

In mid-October 2006, on the eve of his departure to visit troops in West Asia, Bainimarama suddenly delivered an ultimatum: the government had three weeks in which to drop its ethno-nationalist legislation or resign. Rather than maintain stoic normality, Qarase panicked and blundered from disaster to disaster. Naturally enough he declared that his government would not be resigning. And the Police Commissioner refused to release military ammunition that had arrived at the Suva Wharf. It would be 'irresponsible to do so in the current climate', Hughes argued. A couple of days later, on 31 October, soldiers raided the wharf 'commando style' in the early morning and removed 7.5 tonnes of ammunition.[291] Six hours later Qarase went to the President and demanded that the Commander be stood down and replaced with Col Meli Saubulinayau while police investigated his latest threat to take over government. But the President's subsequent directive met a wall of defiance from senior officers. Acting Commander Captain Esala Teleni told over 1,000 territorials and regulars at a two-week camp in Nabua that the army was Fiji's last bastion of law and order, not the Fiji Police.[292] And he released nine demands that, if Qarase complied with them, would prevent a military takeover. Secretly Qarase pleaded with Australia for military assistance only to be turned down and his pleas made public. The military will 'not accept any foreign intervention', Teleni warned. 'Having another armed element is not good for the country,' he added, pointing a finger at the police, 'particularly if the rules of engagement are not clear.'[293]

In desperation, Qarase dropped the amnesty clause from the RTU Bill on 3 November and turned to the GCC for support, claiming that the longstanding impasse between the government and the military was an indigenous problem that should be addressed by the paramount body for Fijian matters. Now back in Fiji, Bainimarama would have none of it. He told the chiefs on 10 November that 'there has never been any public declaration of those who are in government that the 2000 crisis was

---

289 *Fiji Sun*, 26 October 2006.
290 *Fiji Times*, 29 October 2006. In late October, Bainimarama's longstanding head legal advisor, Col Etueni Caucau, went on leave.
291 *Fiji Times*, 30 October & 7 November 2006.
292 *Fiji Times*, 4 November 2006.
293 *Sydney Morning Herald*, 11 November 2006.

wrong … [Qarase] has never educated our people in the villages about the wrongs of 2000 which has resulted in a coup mentality'. Instead he stirred 'the emotions of the common people' and released coup perpetrators under the guise of legal excuses. He had 'given up' on the government: 'Mr Prime Minister, we've had enough of your lies.'

For his part Qarase tried to place his government within historical context. He told the chiefs, 'So long as … undercurrents of unhappiness and discontent … continue, we can never be assured about long term stability in Fiji'. The electoral results of 1987 and 1999 were 'a harsh reminder that Fijian control of government' could no longer be guaranteed in a democracy. 'Fijians feel that they can no longer look to the government of the day for the protective role the British had established,' he concluded: 'This concern was exacerbated by what they perceive to be the anti-Fijian policies of the People's Coalition Government.'[294]

Bainimarama clearly viewed Qarase's performance as irrelevant; so too the GCC's meeting. He dismissed it as 'a waste of taxpayers' money'. Given that many chiefs were tainted by their support for the 2000 coup, they should not be there.[295] With the GCC rejected, Qarase was running out of options and the vacuum of action deafened. 'While the lawful authorities are still in office they should act,' one unidentified legal source told the press in late November: 'If the Commander is to act first, it will be too late for those in lawful authority to do anything.'[296] The police announced seven separate investigations, including the illegal removal of weapons, plotting the overthrow of government, illegally pressing the President to abort a commission of inquiry into Bainimarama's actions, disobeying a lawful order, and financial abuse of office. Investigations into the deaths of CRWU soldiers in 2000 continued but now a new investigation began into 10 politicians, civil servants and former military officers who were inciting Bainimarama to commit treason. On 24 November, police searched the President's office for papers incriminating Bainimarama. The Commander was not amused. 'They want to look for a minute of conversation I had with the President and that conversation was never recorded,' he thundered: 'Qarase is selling our sovereignty to an Australian … [Hughes] should leave the country now for that action.'[297]

---

294 *Sydney Morning Herald*, 11 November 2006; *Fiji Sun*, 11 November 2006; *fijilive*, 11 November 2006.
295 *fijilive*, 11 November 2006.
296 Verenaisi Raicola, 'Who will prevail in the end?', *Fiji Times*, 30 November 2006.
297 *fijilive*, 25 November 2006.

Hughes became increasingly frustrated as he learned the limits to what he could achieve 'as an expat in a country with flawed politics'.[298] He had requested the director of public prosecutions lay sedition charges against Bainimarama but the DPP seemed in no hurry to act. The office that had dismissed its Australian deputy DPP the previous year now refused to appoint the man slated to succeed him. But even without the speedy resolution of police cases, Hughes faced more fundamental issues with regard to Bainimarama. 'The arrest scenario is one that is problematic because he normally accompanies himself with up to 25 fully armed military guards,' Hughes told the press: 'We are an unarmed police force; we are not able to effect a usual arrest.'[299] At the end of November, after three ambassadors from Britain, the United States and Australia visited the QEB to plead with senior officers to pull back, the military raised the stakes higher. It would conduct exercises to train its troops to repel foreign intervention. Acting Commander Esala Teleni declared the ambassadors 'out of line'.[300]

The theatre was far from over. Bainimarama found time in his busy schedule to attend his granddaughter's first communion in New Zealand. There he also found time to express to Auckland media his frustration with the Fiji police investigation into his alleged sedition. Back in Suva, Hughes spied an opportunity and asked NZ police to arrest Bainimarama for 'perverting the course of justice in a foreign jurisdiction'. Such an action might at least avoid an armed confrontation in Fiji at a time when everyone was on edge. New Zealand had already withdrawn all but essential staff from its embassy after Bainimarama told its defence attaché that, if arrested in New Zealand, his troops would storm the High Commission.[301] Hughes held similar fears for his family and sent them to

---

298 *Wikileaks*, 21 December 2010; comment by NZ Deputy Foreign Secretary Alan Williams, 30 November 2006.

299 *fijilive*, 28 November 2006.

300 Raicola, 'Who will prevail in the end?', 2006. Reports from the military suggested they had encouraged senior officers to mutiny, but US Ambassador Larry Dinger later said that they only tried to discourage a coup (*fijilive*, 5 April 2008). The meeting came, however, after Australia had sent three naval vessels to assist in the possible evacuation of Australian citizens. A Blackhawk helicopter crashed during manoeuvres, killing two crew on 29 November. The Fiji military easily escalated the Australian presence outside Fiji waters into a potential invasion threat.

301 www.coupfourandahalf.com, 25 June 2013; report based on High Commissioner Michael Green's posthumous *Persona Non Grata, Breaking the Bond – New Zealand and Fiji 2004–2007* (Auckland: Dunmore Publishing, 2013). NZ police were quietly posted to Suva to assist with evacuation if needed.

Australia.[302] When New Zealand's Prime Minister Helen Clark arranged for Qarase to fly down to New Zealand early on 29 November to meet with Bainimarama for a frank discussion of their differences, Hughes joined Qarase unannounced on the flight from Nausori, Suva's airport.

His plans came to nought. New Zealand preferred a political solution. 'The challenge remains for Qarase to find an adroit way to satisfy the military without exceeding what his domestic political base will tolerate,' the deputy secretary of New Zealand's Ministry of Foreign Affairs and Trade (MFAT) – Alan Williams – believed.[303] Bainimarama and Qarase had not met in nine months. New Zealand had already warned Bainimarama that, should he launch a coup, he and his wife would be banned from entering New Zealand and from visiting their grandchildren.[304] MFAT held no high hopes for success but, to ease the atmosphere, it advised Bainimarama that neither New Zealand nor Australia intended to send troops to Fiji. After two hours and 25 minutes it believed progress had been made. Surreally Qarase gave in to all Bainimarama's demands although with caveats. Bills would be withdrawn *if found illegal*, charges against the Commander would be withdrawn *if the police so recommended*, the military's views on the Police Commissioner would be considered *when his contract was reviewed*, the future of the Tactical Response Unit would be reviewed, and so on. He needed to show 'flexibility while insisting on due process and constitutionality'. Privately Bainimarama agreed to delay the onset of his coup until 4 December in order to give Qarase time to show 'signs of earnest movement'. While Bainimarama headed home via a connecting flight in Auckland, New Zealand quickly returned Qarase directly to Nadi in order to give him a two-hour advantage to 'shape the public perception of the meeting and signal that he is prepared to reach out to the military, the media and civil society in ways that will give Bainimarama reason to conclude that further steps towards a coup are not warranted'.[305]

---

302 Russell Hunter & Victor Lal, 'Fiji police chief tried to get Bainimarama arrested in NZ', *New Zealand Herald*, 18 February 2012.
303 www.coupfourandahalf.com, 20 December 2010, Wikileaks report. New Zealand's Fiji-born Governor General Anand Satyanand opened the 10 am meeting, which was chaired by Foreign Minister Winston Peters.
304 *fijilive*, 22 December 2010.
305 www.coupfourandahalf.com, 20 December 2010.

New Zealand should have heeded the advice of its High Commissioner, Michael Green, who thought Bainimarama had no interest in genuine negotiations but would pocket 'every concession with no reciprocity',[306] or Dinger, who counselled Wellington that 'Being passive with bullies only encourages them'.[307] Dinger also told Washington that Bainimarama:

> is surrounded by a compliant officer corps that is feeding the commander's sense of righteous grievance against the Qarase Government … he does not care about international reactions, including the possible loss of aid money from Australia, the US and New Zealand.[308]

So it came to pass that Qarase returned home, Chamberlain-like, with a peace agreement, waving the agreed outcomes of their meeting. And Bainimarama returned disowning it, calling Qarase a liar. Stung, Qarase repeated his offer to review the three controversial bills and proposed a government information campaign on the 2000 coup. But he also asserted that Bainimarama was not above the law and should still be subject to investigation for the CRWU deaths and for sedition.[309] It was hardly surprising then that, on 30 November, Bainimarama repeated his nine demands, declaring that the police should end its investigations of the military, that the armed Police Tactical Response Unit be disbanded, that the RTU and Qoliqoli Bills be withdrawn, and that the Police Commissioner and all cabinet ministers involved in the 2000 coup should resign. Hughes knew the writing was on the wall and headed for Australia. From Cairns he described Bainimarama as 'deranged' and 'unstable', and possibly still suffering post-traumatic stress from 2000.[310] Bainimarama told Hughes not to return because he had caused all the problems between the army and police.[311]

On 1 December, with the coup's deadline rapidly approaching, Bainimarama's phoney war began to tell. Rumours circulated that the military had tried to capture Qarase the previous evening. Qarase took no chances. He left the capital and flew to Savusavu and later to Nadi. His cabinet similarly went to different locations, 'effectively on the run from the military', according to one observer.[312] Several state CEOs did

---

306 www.coupfourandahalf.com, 25 June 2013.
307 Hunter & Lal, 'Fiji police chief', 2012.
308 Doring, 'US cables', 2011.
309 *Sydney Morning Herald*, 30 November 2006.
310 *Sydney Morning Herald*, 2 December 2006.
311 *Fiji Times*, 3 December 2006.
312 Simon Kearney, 'Army seizes control of Fiji', *Australian*, 2 December 2006.

likewise. Iliesa Duvuloco, one of the perpetrators of the 2000 coup, thought it wise to leave the country. The *Daily Post* called on Australia to grant its staff asylum.[313] The Ministry of Finance hastily issued a memo reminding the military that all ministries had to comply with standard expenditure limits and that it had already overspent its 2006 budget by $31 million.[314]

In contrast, Bainimarama appeared relaxed. He attended the annual rugby match between the army and police, which the police won. Later on the Friday evening he again dismissed Qarase's concessions. Qarase insisted that his government was 'still in control' and that the military's deadline had been extended until midday the following Monday.[315] Back in Australia, Hughes warned of dangers ahead for Bainimarama. The Commander 'doesn't have the support of the government, of the President, of the police, of the churches, of the chiefs, of the people of Fiji,' he told the BBC. Should Bainimarama push ahead, he could 'foresee a popular uprising'.[316] Earlier, *fijivillage* had reached a similar conclusion. Coups were only successful if they enjoyed Fijian support, as Rabuka's had in 1987 and Bainimarama's in 2000. Its Yellow Bucket column argued that the military was now in no position to execute a successful coup.[317]

Both were terribly wrong. On Monday 4 December 2006, Bainimarama's slow-motion coup began with checkpoints erected around Suva and the Police Tactical Response Unit's armoury seized. Eight years would pass before Fiji returned to democratic government.

313 Malcolm Brown, 'Fiji military chief already in power', *Age*, 4 December 2006.
314 *fijilive*, 8 December 2006.
315 *Sydney Morning Herald*, 2 December 2006.
316 *BBC*, 5 December 2006.
317 Yellow Bucket, 'Coup, what coup?' *fijivillage*, 8 November 2006.

4

Plus ça change ...?

Frank Bainimarama's coup on 5 December 2006 shared many features with Sitiveni Rabuka's first coup back in May 1987. On both occasions, the military sought to dismiss the democratically elected government of the day, a goal easily achieved. But, on each occasion, sustaining that achievement under the umbrella of constitutionality proved impossible. Rabuka's solution was a second coup five months later, which led to the formation of a republic and eventually to the creation of a new constitution in 1990. Bainimarama resisted a constitutional response until legal realities caught up with him in 2009. He finally introduced a new constitution in 2013.[1]

What made Bainimarama's coup so different, however, and which partially explains its seven-year delay in constitutional resolution, was its anti-establishment character. Whereas Rabuka in 1987 simply wished to restore the status quo ante and return to power the Fijian elites that Timoci Bavadra's Labour Party had democratically threatened, Bainimarama's coup in 2006 necessitated a wholesale transformation of those elites and their power; indeed, he blamed 'those indigenous Fijians in powerful positions who are power hungry and look after the interests of an elite group' as the cause of Fiji's problems.[2] How extensive that transformation would be was

---

1   The Director of the Fiji Human Rights Commission (FHRC), Dr Shaista Shameem, alluded to this in her report to the UN High Commissioner for Human Rights in mid-2007. She claimed that a coup refers to the removal of the head of state and constitution, not simply the dismissal of a government. Hence there had only been one coup in Fiji's history, that in September 1987, after which Fiji became a republic (*fijilive*, 30 August 2007).
2   *fijivillage*, 23 December 2006.

not immediately apparent. Bainimarama continued to refer to his coup as an overdue clean-up campaign. His early moves leant weight to the assertion. He sacked many state CEOs, began reorganising the police, Fiji National Provident Fund (FNPF) and Native Land Trust Board (NLTB), challenged the leaders of the Great Council of Chiefs (GCC) (many of whom had supported both the 1987 and 2000 coups), and established a new Fiji Independent Commission Against Corruption (FICAC).

A few commentators, such as expatriate journalist Victor Lal, suggested that 'What took place on December 5 cannot even be described as a coup' because Laisenia Qarase and his ministers 'simply abandoned their portfolios and ran away, creating a public necessity for the Commodore to step in and take executive authority in Fiji'.[3] Others supported Bainimarama's necessity defence: 'Given Fiji's turbulent past,' journalist Graham Davis wrote, 'it's arguably a revolution that can happen only at the point of a gun, however much that might offend democratic sensibilities.'[4] Some chose to accept Bainimarama's good governance description of the coup. University of Fiji's Satendra Nandan described it as 'a coup to end all coups',[5] an assertion that gained the support of several civil society groups, but not the Citizens' Constitutional Forum (CCF). Its director, Rev. Akuila Yabaki, declared 'We don't need a coup to end the coup cycle or to end racism, because we cannot break the supreme law of a country to protect the rule of law'.[6] But others, including the Ecumenical Centre for Research, Education and Advocacy (ECREA), as well as some IndoFijian religious organisations and the Catholic Church were more equivocal. Back in 2001 the Roko Tui Bau, Ratu Joni Madraiwiwi, had placed high hopes on civil society to uphold democracy and human rights within Fiji.[7] Clearly that had not come to fruition; many institutions hostile to previous coups were now prepared to grant

---

3   *Fiji Sun*, 8 January 2007. Rabuka made a similar claim, arguing that Qarase could never be compared with Bavadra or Mahendra Chaudhry who 'had to endure the hardships of incarceration as well as their ousting from office' (*Fiji Times*, 15 August 2008).

4   G Davis, 'It's hail to the chiefs no longer', *Australian*, 6 January 2007.

5   'Fiji coup could be its last', *Pacific Islands Report*, PIDP, 21 March 2007. Professor Nandan told the anti-corruption symposium: 'I know the Commander will not take us to heaven, but he may just and justly get us out of the hell-hole we've been digging for the past 20 years. He has not invoked indignity or mawkish religiosity nor mobs marching and bullying defenceless civilians or peasants – and that gives us hope. He has appealed to only one symbol of unity: our beloved country. And race is no longer bandied as the fact of life'.

6   www.coupfourandahalf.com, 14 May 2010.

7   J Madraiwiwi, 'Fiji 2001: Our country at the crossroads', 2001 Parkinson Memorial Lecture, University of the South Pacific, *Wansolwara*, 15 August 2001.

legitimacy to military action. Fiji Human Rights Commission (FHRC) director, Shaista Shameem, even argued in a controversial report released in early January 2007 that the Republic of Fiji Military Forces (RFMF) had a constitutional responsibility to pursue good governance, especially given 'the rampant abuse of power, privilege, illegalities and wastage of wealth of the Qarase government, as well as its proposed discriminatory legislation which, if enacted, would have constituted a crime against humanity under international law'.[8]

Strangely for a coup designed to end Fiji's reputation as 'Coup-Coup Land', it possessed all the by now familiar characteristics of previous coups. For a start Bainimarama – like Rabuka before him – could not control for all eventualities. For some time he had been able to manage President Josefa Iloilo – in his late 80s and displaying signs of dementia – through military personnel and friends in the presidential palace. Iloilo's wife had also minimised government access to the President, and the Commander's alternate office in Strategic Command at Berkley Crescent, adjacent to the Presidential Palace – originally conceived as a way to keep tabs on military commanders – had conveniently given Bainimarama unchecked access to the President.[9] But the Vice President was a different matter. The Bauan high chief and articulate lawyer Madraiwiwi was nobody's puppet. On the eve of the coup he persuaded Iloilo to release a statement declaring that he neither condoned nor supported the actions of the military 'which were clearly outside the Constitution'.[10] Hence, when Bainimarama did finally launch his coup, he did so without the planned endorsement of the President. As he put it on the day: 'I, under the legal doctrine of necessity,

---

8   S Shameem, 'The assumption of executive authority on December 5 2006 by Commodore JV Bainimarama, Commander of the RFMF: Legal, constitutional and human rights issues', Fiji Human Rights Commission, Suva, 3 January 2007, p. 31. This report, like Bainimarama's coup announcement, relied on the repealed provisions in the 1990 Constitution that bestowed a watchdog function upon the military to justify its claims. The report prompted calls for Shameem's resignation, opposition from fellow commissioners like Shamima Ali, the cancellation of NZ funding for the FHRC, and its suspension from the Geneva-based International Coordinating Committee of the National Institute for the Promotion and Protection of Human Rights. Most critics believed the report supported dictatorship rather than constitutional democracy (e.g. Jonathan Edelstein, 'Coups as a human right', Fiji Sun, 7 January 2007; and Graham Leung, 'Lawyers must cry freedom to the challenge in Fiji', Fiji Times, 9 June 2009). Historian Brij Lal declared the notion of a constitutional coup an oxymoron (fijilive, 11 December 2007).
9   Baledrokadroka, 'Sacred king and warrior chief', 2012, pp. 242–44.
10   Baledrokadroka, 'Sacred king and warrior chief', 2012, pp. 266–67.

will step into the shoes of the President given that he has been blocked from exercising his constitutional powers.'[11] He then dismissed Qarase and appointed the 77-year-old military medical doctor, Jona Senilagakali, interim prime minister.

The accidental Prime Minister immediately failed to impress as the harbinger of a new Fiji. In his first statement, he declared that he had 'been called by divine authority to do something for the people of Fiji'. What that might be remained uncertain. In defending the coup, Senilagakali also inadvertently undermined Bainimarama's constitutional claims. 'It's an illegal takeover,' he acknowledged, although its purpose was 'to clean up the mess of a much bigger illegal activity of the previous government,' adding that Fiji needed a different sort of democracy from 'the type ... both Australia and New Zealand enjoy'.[12] This logic, albeit for different reasons, had been employed to justify every coup in Fiji. In the past, nationalists deemed democracy incompatible with indigenous rights, thereby denying Fijians the right to accountability, transparency and equity, the foundations for any form of sustainable development.[13] Now Bainimarama deemed it at odds with Fiji's development status,[14] an assertion that gained the military some unexpected bedfellows.

Aisake Casimira of the Pacific Conference of Churches argued that it was unwise for Fiji to pursue democracy at the same time as a free market economy. He declared that democracy could only be sustained with a strong welfare system. Yet, if history offered any lessons, it is that means are as important as ends. Political democratisation cannot be postponed, as Casimira suggested, in order to achieve economic democratisation. One is not possible without the other, as European countries learned prior to 1945. Economic democratisation also requires accountability, transparency and equity. By 2006, no coup had brought Fiji any closer to realising either political or economic democratisation. Nor had they assisted Fiji to transform its neocolonial economy, make the creativity and skills of all its peoples a driver of economic growth, and extend the boundaries within which they engage. Nationalistic assertions –

---

11   Voreqe Bainimarama, press statement, 5 December 2006.
12   *BBC*, 7 December 2006.
13   Robertson & Sutherland, *Government by the Gun*, 2001, p. 127.
14   Bainimarama declared: 'One must remember that the factors that bring about peace and harmony in any country are not confined to the word democracy. As an example last year I visited China ... [and] witnessed a country that is ... prosperous and peaceful despite the fact that it is regarded by many as not democratic' (*Australian*, 11 December 2006).

whether on the grounds of race or development – were simply weapons of denial; they denied common human interests and needs, they denied opportunities for social partnerships, and they denied prospects for stronger intersectoral linkages and sustainable domestic growth. They did not provide a unique Fiji 'road map to democracy'.[15]

If Bainimarama's coup failed to turn external sources of growth into more balanced internally oriented growth, then it too might go the way of all previous coups. Of course if Fiji's new leader introduced policies that reduced social and economic inequalities, rewarded skills not privilege, stimulated domestic investment and increased real wages, he might transform Fiji society, decrease political instability, reduce emigration and enable the foundations for greater prosperity.[16] All Fiji's postcolonial governments and coup regimes neglected these opportunities in the past, invariably for reasons of race and class, with predictable consequences: *plus ça change, plus c'est la même chose*. Would Bainimarama's contemporary endeavour prove any different? Did the manner of its birth predetermine its outcome?

Undermining human rights

Military force is never an acceptable means to effect change. It simply reinforces coups as the weapon of choice for the disgruntled, as Rabuka conceded.[17] Additionally, military force undermines the very institutions it purports to protect, as human rights activists noted earlier in 2006.

> It is unconstitutional for any institution to threaten to remove a government under any doctrine (legal or otherwise) based on a belief that the government is acting unconstitutionally. It is the function of the courts to determine unconstitutional action.[18]

---

15   A Casimira, 'Democracy in many guises', *Fiji Sun*, 18 February 2007.

16   R Robertson, 'Fiji futuring', paper presented to the Asia-Pacific Development Review Conference *Fiji Forward 2000*, 15–16 June 2006, Raffles Tradewinds, Suva, Fiji, in *Pacific Economic Bulletin*, 21: 2, 2006.

17   *fijilive*, 14 December 2006.

18   *Fiji Times*, 24 March 2006, p. 3; Angie Heffernan of the Pacific Centre for Public Integrity and Virisila Buadromo of the FWRM.

Indeed, the military's own lack of respect for the rule of law, not only in overthrowing an elected government but also in its abuse of human rights and lack of financial transparency, undermined its reach for the moral high ground. In this respect, little distinguished Bainimarama's military from Rabuka's.

The first week of the coup began with Bainimarama declaring that his military would 'respect the international conventions on human rights and humanitarian law'.[19] But, by week's end, a clear pattern of human rights abuses had been established. Former politician Kenneth Zink was first arrested for cursing at Bainimarama's appearance on television while he was at the United Club. Soldiers forced him to run around a sports field at the Queen Elizabeth Barracks (QEB). On a second occasion in early January 2007, he was detained and assaulted in Nadi. Jale Baba, director of Soqosoqo Duavata ni Lewenivanua (SDL), Ted Young (a former Qarase minister) and Mere Samisoni (former MP and owner of the Bread Kitchen chain of bakeries) received similar treatment, sometimes being forced to do press-ups. Journalists were also questioned. *Daily Post* editor, Robert Wolfgramm, faced deportation. Ex–Counter Revolutionary Warfare Unit (CRWU) soldiers at Pacific Connex were arrested and detained.[20]

But worse befell Laisa Digitaki's Young People's Concerned Network. She and colleagues provocatively constructed a shrine to democracy at her Lami office, with banners reading 'Yes to Democracy No to Guns'. A public relations businesswoman and partner of Fijian Holdings Ltd (FHL) managing director, Sitiveni Weleilakeba, she refused to acknowledge that the military's state of emergency had legal validity,[21] a challenge that would increasingly frustrate the regime in coming months. Armed men broke in and tore down the banners four days after the coup. Undeterred, Digitaki participated in a protest against the military government nearly two weeks later and was arrested but bailed. Then, on Christmas Eve, the soldiers came for her, taking her to Nabua where she was eventually united with a small group of dissidents rounded up by the military for special treatment: youth activists Pita Waqavonovono and Jackie Koroi, as well as Virisila Buadromo[22] (Fiji Women's Rights Movement (FWRM)

---

19 *fijilive*, 5 December 2006.
20 *Fiji Times*, 9 December 2006.
21 *Daily Post*, 10 December 2006.
22 The US secretary of state presented Buadromo the International Women of Courage Award on 11 March 2008.

executive director) and her partner, lawyer Arshad Daud. Together and separately they were interrogated (Digitaki alleged that Land Force Commander Pita Driti participated, at one point threatening her with a pistol), before being taken out, assaulted and forced to run 10 kilometres back to their homes.[23]

'The military needs to demonstrate humility not arrogance, altruism not selfishness, in all that it does,' a *Fiji Times* correspondent wrote. But there was little chance of that as Bainimarama soon made clear: 'These individuals should shut their mouths or else the military will shut it for them.' Little wonder that CCF's Jone Dakuvula feared who would be next.[24] 'Look,' the new acting Police Commissioner reportedly argued, 'the reality of things is, whatever legal rights you have, this is not a good time to be claiming them.'[25] Indeed, by 15 February 2007, some 1,193 people had been arrested by the military for a range of offences,[26] some meeting a far worse fate: Tailevu villager and land surveyor Nimilote Verebasaga tortured and beaten to death in early January, and 19-year-old Sakiusa Rabaka dead from injuries received in Nadi in late February. In both instances the military went to great lengths to protect the offenders from charges, even trying to send Rabaka's killers out of the country to serve as peacekeepers in Iraq. 'This is not good governance when the commander can't reflect it within his own army,' Fiji Women's Crisis Centre (FWCC) director Shamima Ali noted pointedly.[27] For their comments, activists like Shamima Ali, Buadromo and Digitaki were regularly prevented from

---

23   'Laisa Digitaki's statement & sequence of events re pro-democracy group of five rounding up and bashing by the RFMF on December 24th–25th, 2006', fijimediawars.blogspot.com.au/2014/09/laisa-digitakis-story.html; *Fiji Times*, 26 December 2007. Driti was reportedly unhappy at being named in Digitaki's statement; his unhappiness pushed Digitaki and Heffernan into hiding in January (*fijilive*, 25 January 2007). *Wikileaks* later reported the US Embassy claiming that Chief of Staff Tevita Mara and Col Sitiveni Qiliho Tukaituraga were also present (www.coupfourandahalf.com, 15 February 2012).

24   *Fiji Times*, 26 December 2006; *Fiji Sun*, 26 December 2006. Bainimarama later alleged that NGOs only spoke out against the coup because they wanted to impress their foreign donors (*Fiji Sun*, 28 January 2007).

25   Richard Naidu, interview, *Fiji Sun*, 16 January 2007.

26   *Fiji Sun*, 25 February 2007.

27   *Fiji Sun*, 30 October 2007. Only one soldier was tried for Nimolote's death, receiving a three-year sentence in April 2009. The men responsible for Sakiusa's death – eight soldiers and one police officer – were finally tried and sentenced to jail for four years in March 2009. They were released under community service orders when the Constitution was abrogated a few weeks later. The police also share the military's penchant for brutality. In mid-2007, Tevita Malasebe, a suspected thief, died in police custody at Valelevu. Two police were later convicted of murder. In September 2008, an escaped prisoner died of injuries received during his recapture by a new Police Strike Back team. FWCC deputy coordinator, Edwina Kotoisuva, claimed the team 'brings out the machoism in the police officers' (*Fiji Sun*, 20 September 2008).

leaving the country to attend conferences or meetings. 'Fiji's Constitution is torn into pieces on a daily basis' by the military's 'abuse of the basic human rights of citizens,' Shamima Ali told the press.[28] Perhaps aware that such abuses cost the military dearly in terms of public support, the new Attorney-General, Aiyaz Sayed-Khaiyum, argued in late February that the military should have the police charge people believed to be inciting instability, not take them to military HQ and interrogate them.[29] And, shortly after, Bainimarama announced that, henceforth, the military would be responsive to public views on human rights and ensure that excesses ceased. But, privately, EU diplomats alleged, he told them that if anyone insulted the army 'of course we must have them taken to the barracks and have them beaten up'.[30]

Asserting constitutionality

Maintaining the pretence of constitutionality proved far more difficult, however, than dealing with human rights activists. Bainimarama had cited the doctrine of necessity as a way to head off such problems but, without doubt, the President's refusal to play ball unsettled him. Taking revenge by dismissing Madraiwiwi and immediately forcing him from his residence,[31] unlike government ministers who were at least given one month's notice, solved nothing. Having the otherwise compliant head of state on side had always been a crucial part of Bainimarama's plan for establishing the veneer of legality. To get back on track, he had now to persuade the GCC to reinstate Iloilo at its forthcoming meeting. But the chair of the Council, Ratu Ovini Bokini, was in no mood to comply. He still recognised the Qarase government and Iloilo as president. As far as he was concerned, Bainimarama's action had no legal effect. He told reporters he had no intention of seeking Bainimarama out: 'He has to make a request to me if he wants to meet me.'[32]

28　*fijilive*, 24 January 2007.
29　*Fiji Times*, 25 January 2007.
30　Doring, 'US cables', 2011. Bainimarama later argued that human rights conventions interfered with sovereignty (*Fiji Times*, 23 February 2008).
31　*Fiji Times*, 7 December 2006.
32　*fijilive*, 8 December 2006.

But Bainimarama could be equally imperious. Australia's Foreign Minister Alexander Downer had just upped the ante by calling on Fiji's citizens to launch a campaign of civil disobedience against the coup.[33] On the same day that the Commonwealth suspended Fiji's membership of its councils, Australia and New Zealand announced their intention to have the United Nations cut Fiji out from its peacekeeping duties, a role the RFMF depended on to maintain its size. In addition, the European Union warned that much of its projected aid to Fiji, particularly for its failing sugar industry, might now be in jeopardy. Back in Suva there was also bad news. With the finance CEO in hiding, the state IT Centre ceased to function, making it impossible to pay the 1,000 territorials called to the QEB. Amidst signs that the tourism industry was about to hit a new low, Emperor Gold Mining announced the closure of its once productive Vatukoula mine in western Viti Levu.

In response Bainimarama sought to shore up popular support. He announced that members of a future interim government would have to apply for their posts following advertisement. He also announced that the prison on Nukulau Island, which housed 21 former coup makers, including George Speight, would be closed and the once popular island restored to Suva's daytrippers. In addition, he scrapped Qarase's planned 2.5 per cent increase in VAT (to 15 per cent) and awarded all public servants a 2 per cent pay rise.[34] Plans were also laid to reverse Fiji's loss of skilled emigrants by enabling dual citizenship.

Targeting dissidents also formed part of the fight back; so, too, the sacking of numerous public officials and raids on SDL headquarters for evidence of corruption. The military needed to project an image of both total control and steadfastness as its clean-up campaign began. It helped that several ECREA members defended the coup from a social justice perspective, declaring it Fiji's first coup for multiracialism and against corruption and economic mismanagement.[35] It helped also that two assumed co-conspirators quickly lent support, albeit qualified. Mahendra Chaudhry intimated that he would help Fiji return to democratic rule if everything was 'constitutionally legal'; Ratu Epeli Ganilau asserted that he

33   *fijilive*, 9 December 2006.
34   *Sydney Morning Herald*, 16 December 2006.
35   Paulo Baleinakorodawa, Father Kevin Barr & Semiti Qalowasa, 'Time of uncertainty, opportunity', *Fiji Times*, 19 December 2006.

supported 'the cleaning up, but not the means'.[36] Even Qarase appeared to give up the struggle, conceding that his government was unlikely to return. He forgave the Commander for his action 'as life must go on'.[37]

But Fiji's chiefs were not so forgiving. They pledged support for the Qarase government, maintained that Iloilo and Madraiwiwi were still in office, and refused to depart from the rule of law, a novel stance given the Council's post-1987 record. But, when the 64-member GCC met on 20 December, Madraiwiwi was the only senior official in attendance. Qarase had not been allowed to return to Suva for the meeting and his Minister for Fijian Affairs probably thought it wise to be absent. Nor did Bainimarama attend. Bokini had refused to invite him as acting president and it seemed unlikely that the Council could guarantee the military the immunity from prosecution it sought for its takeover. Bainimarama even declined to receive a delegation from the Council. 'The GCC has become the last hiding place for those evading the military,' he declared, referring to the many non-members invited, including from the Assembly of Christian Churches in Fiji. The GCC had lost all credibility and its meeting was of no importance, his military spokesperson added.[38] A split within the confederacies did not assist the chiefs' cause. Burebasaga and Kubuna agreed to Iloilo appointing an interim government, but Tovata – whose Lau delegates included Ratu Tevita Uluilakeba Mara, head of the Third Fiji Infantry Regiment – could not reach agreement.

Nonetheless, the Council's stand highlighted a major problem for the military. As Richard Naidu pointed out, the GCC basically told Bainimarama that he was in breach of the Constitution. He could not claim to be the President. Iloilo remained in that role. To reappoint Iloilo as Bainimarama demanded would imply that Bainimarama was indeed the current President. The only way forward now for Bainimarama, Naidu suggested, was 'to get rid of the Constitution'. Madraiwiwi thought similarly. The military were delusional and taking Fiji through 'an Alice in Wonderland journey' when they continue to assert that their actions are within the Constitution, he argued later that year. They would be better off abrogating the Constitution.[39] So too Peter Ridgway, the former assistant director of public prosecutions: a new constitution was the only

---

36   *Daily Post*, 9 December 2006.
37   *fijivillage*, 15 December 2006; Callinan, 'Fueling Fiji's coup', 2006.
38   *Fiji Sun*, 19 December 2006; *fijilive*, 20 December 2006; *Fiji Times*, 22 December 2006.
39   J Madraiwiwi, 'Mythic constitutionalism: Whither Fiji's course in June 2007?' paper to 'The Fiji coup – six months on' workshop, ANU, Canberra, 5 June 2007; *Fiji Times*, 11 June 2007.

way to gain legitimacy and move forward.[40] Not everyone saw things this way. Former Alliance politician and 1987 coup supporter Filipe Bole argued that 'we have gone beyond the point of exploring the legality of the military takeover ... The military has already established control of the country'. Echoing Qarase, he declared that Fiji 'should move on and establish an administration to regain confidence'.[41]

Bainimarama had similar thoughts, but remained flexible, later telling the Melanesian Spearhead Group (MSG) leaders: 'To abrogate the Constitution is no big deal if we have to find a way forward for Fiji'.[42] The GCC, however, maintained its stance of constitutionality. Its solution called on Qarase to tender his resignation and Iloilo to appoint an interim government ahead of fresh elections within 15 months. Bainimarama demurred: 'We will return executive authority but we will not do it in a rush.'[43] He plotted his next move. In early January 2007, after very publicly sending Chief Justice Daniel Fatiaki and Chief Magistrate Naomi Lomaiviti on leave pending a corruption investigation, he reinstated Iloilo as president and announced Senilagakali's resignation as interim prime minister. In a national address on 4 January, Iloilo declared: 'I would have done exactly what the commander of the Republic of Fiji Military Forces ... did since it was necessary to do so at that time. These actions were valid in law.' 'Cultural reasons' had prevented him from acting earlier; now he intended to appoint an interim government.[44]

Although the direct opposite of his statement a month earlier, Iloilo's declaration of support demonstrated Bainimarama's renewed power over the presidential office and, by implication, the GCC.[45] While the chiefs licked their wounds, Iloilo bestowed immunity on the military and announced the formation of a new interim government. Despite promising transparency, many members of the government had not been among the 400 applications received. Nor was there any indication

---

40   *Fiji Times*, 12 January 2007. 'Fiji has to wake up from the dream that the Constitution has not been abrogated,' he later argued. If the Constitution still existed, then all promulgations were null and void (*fijilive*, 18 July 2008).

41   *Fiji Times*, 22 December 2006.

42   *Fiji Times*, 2 June 2008.

43   *Fiji Sun*, 23 December 2006.

44   *fijilive*, 4 January 2006.

45   Graham Davis reported that Ratu Apenisa Cakobau (scion of the Cakobau family that formed 'the hand inside George Speight's glove') told him that 'We still have the support of the ordinary people and he will have to deal with that ... In the old days I would have eaten him' ('It's hail to the chiefs no longer', 2007).

that the lessons of 2000 had been learned, that the new ministers would pledge to forego participation in future elections. And, despite previously dismissing many state board members for holding more than one position, Bainimarama emerged as both prime minister and military commander. No salary statements were disclosed.[46] Four SDL ministers had applied for posts. None were successful. Instead Fiji Labour Party (FLP) (Chaudhry and Lekh Ram Vayeshnoi) and National Alliance Party (NAP) (Ganilau and Bernadette Rounds) members occupied finance, sports, tourism, and Fijian affairs posts respectively. Aiyaz Sayed-Khaiyum became Attorney-General; Poseci Bune, Public Service Minister; and Ratu Epeli Nailatikau, Minister for Foreign Affairs. Altogether there were 16 ministers but, according to economist Wadan Narsey, by failing to include SDL representatives, Bainimarama broke both the letter and spirit of the Constitution regarding multi-party governance and provided 'a recipe for further instability'.[47]

Regression and progression

At least the formation of a new interim government permitted the semblance of normality and an opportunity to pursue the coup's purported agenda of good governance. The new administration was considerably smaller than Qarase's bloated cabinet and its formation was quickly followed by the termination of 23 state CEOs, many only recently appointed, and their replacement by 16 permanent secretaries. This return to pre-reform public service leadership roles reflected Bune's cost cutting measures and also included reducing the retirement age of public servants to 55 years. He argued that retirees could use their pensions to set up new businesses; but no one examined the impact such a policy might have on superannuation schemes, let alone the growing proportion of the population now cut asunder that might otherwise have formed an important market for businesses. Nor, apparently, the loss of skills from the most experienced group in the workforce. The move immediately affected over 900 teachers and 300 nurses, and sparked a series of union

---

46   *Fiji Sun*, 16 January 2007, analysis by Brij Lal. Qarase saw the lineup as proof that the FHRC, the military, FLP and NAP had all participated in the overthrow of his government (*Fiji Times*, 10 January 2007). Others saw it as confirmation of allegations by Andrew Hughes that Bainimarama was simply 'a frontman for power seeking people in Fiji who failed in the last election' (*Fiji Times*, 6 December 2006).

47   *Fiji Times*, 15 February 2007.

strikes in July and August when accompanied by wage cuts.[48] Such back-to-the-past planning demonstrated the paucity of innovative thinking. Initiating policies that might make a crucial development difference had eluded all postcolonial governments; Bainimarama's interim government seemed poised to follow suit.

It did not help that Fiji was soon in the grip of a recession, in part the consequence of past SDL priorities, in part a product of declining access to preferential markets, but in part due also to a collapse of Fiji's only vibrant sector, tourism, caused entirely by the December coup. Overall Fiji's GDP growth in 2007 declined 6.5 per cent from 2006 to − 2.5 per cent, although at least 2 per cent of that decline had been anticipated prior to the coup.[49] Not surprisingly, this mostly military-induced recession reduced the capacity of the interim government to be proactive and grow its $3 billion budget. Losses in sugar earnings were expected eventually to reach 15 per cent and similarly in tourism.[50] Public service wage cuts of 5 per cent reduced Fiji's capacity to make its citizens more economically responsive, with some commentators arguing that it did not help that the new Minister for Finance also seemed stuck in the 1970s and 1980s, unable to see beyond the public sector to drive growth, and using changes in tariffs 'to take revenge on perceived enemies'.[51]

Huge investments in public infrastructure, education and training, health and housing were required for Fiji to break out of its doldrums. Thirty-five per cent of Fiji's population lived in poverty, 12 per cent in squatter settlements. Among them were at least 5,000 affected by the expiry of land leases since 2000. Many were from Vanua Levu or western Viti Levu,

---

48   *Fiji Times*, 22 & 25 January 2007. Strikes by some unions were averted by reducing wage cuts by 1 per cent (*Fiji Times*, 11 July 2007). Union and court challenges prevented the immediate implementation of the new retirement age.

49   *Fiji Times*, 2 March 2007.

50   *fijilive*, 13 February 2007; *fijivillage*, 31 March 2007. Tourism took four years to recover from the 2000 coup, and the 2006 coup was expected to have a similar impact, although an immediate discount on fares and bookings provided some recovery. The sugar industry's prospects seemed bleaker, given the end of preferential trading in 2009, particularly if interim EU support failed to materialise. Since 1997 over 5,250 land leases had expired; 43 per cent were not renewed, sugar cane production had fallen from 4 million tonnes to 3 million by 2006, sugar production from 454,000 tonnes to 310,000, and the number of growers from 22,304 to 15,730 (Bala Dass, 'Ailing sugar industry', *Fiji Times*, 3 August 2015). Employment in the garment industry had halved over the same period. Government debt had increased from 41 per cent of GDP to over 52 per cent during the Qarase government's time in office, although 90 per cent of this was domestically sourced. Growth did eventuate and, by 2018, Fiji's government budget exceeded $5 billion.

51   *fijivillage*, 5 March 2007.

and they moved into the outskirts of Suva where already over 16 per cent of the population were squatters.[52] But none of these much-needed investments were possible without substantial economic growth and capital outlays. And none would be forthcoming with expenditures down and the Reserve Bank of Fiji (RBF) maintaining tight fiscal and monetary policies. In fact the bank did not expect recovery until 2009. Meanwhile, to reach and sustain 5 per cent GDP growth required combined government and private investment to rise from its current level of 14 per cent of GDP to at least 25 per cent. Government alone needed to lift its capital investment to 30 per cent of its annual budget.[53] Given that the post-coup environment made greater foreign direct investment unlikely, any government attempt to compensate with external borrowing could prove ruinously expensive.[54] Not unexpectedly the interim government's revised 2007 budget was little more than a coping mechanism, with few initiatives to promote growth or provide a platform for future investment and growth. 'The economy is barely surviving,'[55] Public Services Minister Bune acknowledged in mid-2007.

Fiji had for too long failed to refashion and grow its agricultural and garments sectors. Bainimarama admitted also that it had failed to diversify its economy and become overly reliant on imported goods and services. Soon it would be buffeted by the headwinds of a global recession, which allowed Bainimarama to claim Fiji's current economic problems were beyond his control.[56] Overspending by the military, by 54 per cent in 2007, did not assist. The *Fiji Times* accused it of double standards: 'despite calling for accountability and transparency in others, the army sees no need to follow the same rules'.[57] Such criticism, its spokesperson retorted, simply demonstrated the media's lack of 'understanding of the important function of the military in national development'.[58]

---

52   *fijilive*, 5 April 2007. Of those in poverty, 43 per cent were IndoFijians and 38 per cent Fijians (*Fiji Times*, 21 September 2006).

53   J Kotobalavu, 'Statistics for Fiji's future', *Fiji Times*, 27 October 2008.

54   *Fiji Times*, 21 September 2006; see also M Reddy, 'Growth policy lacking', *Fiji Times*, 3 March 2007; *Fiji Sun*, 5 March 2007; and *Fiji Times*, 6 & 7 March 2007. Spending on health and education fell by approximately $17 million.

55   *fijilive*, 19 July 2009.

56   *fijilive*, 6 March 2009.

57   *Fiji Times*, 28 November 2008.

58   *Fiji Times*, 27 November 2008. Nonetheless, at the start of 2008 Bainimarama announced 'Good Governance in the RFMF' the military theme of the year (*Fiji Times*, 23 February 2008).

While Bainimarama's coup shared many features with Rabuka's earlier coups, it differed in one crucial aspect. Fiji's military leaders now shunned ethno-nationalism and promised the country a radically different future. Initially they focused on 'cleaning up' governance, but this strategy soon ran out of steam. Proving corruption would take time, possibly years. Efforts to fast track evidence failed dismally. The use of the international conman, Australian Peter Foster, to tape conversations with key SDL officials admitting corrupt practices in the 2006 election backfired when he escaped the country. By then he had tainted almost everyone he dealt with and the military distanced itself from the affair.[59] Even the establishment of FICAC proved problematic. Its constitutionality was immediately challenged. Its newly appointed Malaysian chairman resigned under pressure from international law bodies and its first chief investigator, Inspector Nazir Ali, proved highly controversial. A former head of the Agricultural Scam investigation who had been stood down by Andrew Hughes in 2006, Nazir Ali turned his unwanted attention onto the police, raiding its headquarters in Nasinu and alleging fraudulent practices.[60] FICAC also conflicted with the director of public prosecutions (DPP), until the High Court ruled that it had no right to prosecute cases.[61] Its raid on the Fiji Revenue and Customs Authority (FIRCA) in order to build a case against the suspended Chief Justice prompted the authority's CEO to resign.[62]

---

59   Foster had a long association with Fiji and had helped finance Tupeni Baba's New Labour Party in 2001. Banned from Fiji in 2002, he had returned by 2006 when he was arrested for allegedly manufacturing false internet sites in order to smear a rival tourist resort. Facing fraud charges, he was rearrested by the Police Tactical Response Unit after being on the run for two weeks while attempting to flee to Tonga. After the coup he allegedly did a deal with the military but, in early January, he fled to Vanuatu where he was arrested and deported to Australia to face money-laundering charges (*Fiji Times*, 26 October & 20 December 2006; *fijilive*, 1, 2, 3 & 10 January 2007; *Age*, 6 February 2007). Foster later claimed the Australian Government under John Howard facilitated the rigging of elections in 2006 (interview with Monica Attard, *Sunday Profile*, ABC Radio, 22 May 2009).

60   FICAC seemed out of control. It confiscated items donated by a visiting film crew to an old people's home in Labasa. With the appointment of a new FICAC Deputy Commissioner from the military, and following the appointment of Captain Esala Teleni as Police Commissioner, Nazir Ali was soon transferred back to the police as Assistant Police Commissioner (Crime) (*Fiji Times*, 25 June & 15 July 2007). But after he complained to Bainimarama that Teleni and his deputy were plotting a coup, Nazir Ali was transferred to Levuka as station officer (*Fiji Times*, 4 February 2008).

61   *Fiji Times*, 21 August 2007. Allegedly this did not prevent FICAC from threatening DPP officers with arrest for refusing to prosecute a case about which they had not been consulted. Within days, Nazir Ali was removed from the case and suspended (*Fiji Times*, 8 & 27 November 2007). FICAC gained similar powers to the DPP in 2016.

62   *Fiji Times*, 28 November 2007.

FICAC's lack of success did not appear to trouble the interim government. It simply moved on to the next stage of its Way Forward Reform Agenda, the establishment of a National Council for Building a Better Fiji (NCBBF), first mooted in February as a means to rid Fiji of its 'politics of race'.[63] Race had not always been central to Bainimarama's clean-up campaign, but there were hints that it would form the most significance difference between his coup and those that went before. His quest to ensure justice for those who had led the putative 2000 coup, which had almost cost him his life and crippled the RFMF, had constrained the Qarase government's ethno-nationalist objectives after 2001, but not sufficiently to prevent a showdown. That long lead-time provided ample opportunity for Bainimarama to garner support from an entirely different corner, as Madraiwiwi acknowledged:

> This consisted of the Fiji Labour Party and a large majority of the Indo-Fijian community, scarred by the events of May 2000 and a by sense of alienation from the SDL Government because of some of its policies. A majority of the minority communities also felt likewise i.e. marginalised and deprived of opportunities to benefit from Government assistance. It also included the Roman Catholic Church hierarchy, a significant section of civil society, elements in the judiciary and the professional classes as well as a portion of the private sector.[64]

Such support remained largely unspoken while Bainimarama focused on Qarase, possibly because it held no obvious value for achieving his objective. Immediately prior to the coup he briefly declared, 'We will be one race'.[65] Even after the coup, he made only occasional reference to his new support base. When challenging the chiefs, for example, he pointedly argued that 'Indians are not the cause of the problem'.[66] Instead he sought more diffusely to oppose discrimination, especially that encompassed within the Qoliqoli Bill or in Qarase's affirmative action legislation. In February 2007, Bainimarama's government decreed the removal of discriminatory provisions in the *Social Justice Act* and intimated that it would also review all educational policies; over 15,000 students had been denied educational assistance simply because they attended IndoFijian schools. Racism, Bainimarama declared, remained the principal cause of Fiji's brain drain.[67]

---

63   *Fiji Times*, 21 February 2007.
64   Madraiwiwi, 'Mythic constitutionalism', 2007.
65   *fijilive*, 3 December 2006.
66   *fijivillage*, 23 December 2006.
67   *fijilive*, 14 & 16 February 2007; *Fiji Times*, 21 February 2007.

Charged with developing policies on good governance, economic growth, financial reform, land utilisation and social change to take Fiji forward over the next 15 years, the NCBBF got off to a poor start.[68] Few public submissions were received. The Methodists declared it illegal and the SDL declined to participate. Many provinces refused to permit NCBBF members to speak in their villages. As Madraiwiwi noted, it was 'Impossible for a government that derived its power from the barrel of a gun to enforce cordial community relations'. Ending racial discrimination might be a laudable ideal, but Bainimarama's military leadership provided no shining example for Fiji to emulate.[69]

Nonetheless, the NCBBF persevered under the leadership of Fiji expatriate John Samy, formerly an economist at the Asian Development Bank (ADB). Its principal task was to develop a People's Charter that would establish binding rules for future governance. Samy argued that the Charter represented Bainimarama's exit strategy; others were less charitable. Former Police Commissioner Isikia Savua called it a military prescription for future governments, similar to the demands Rabuka presented to Ratu Sir Kamisese Mara at the end of 1987.[70] Indeed, Angie Heffernan of the Pacific Centre for Public Integrity (PCPI) saw it expanding the military's constitutional role[71] while The Australian National University's Brij Lal declared it a futile exercise that would never garner support or be binding on future governments.[72] Of course the question still remained, could it ever be considered legal?[73] Shamima Ali believed that the NCBBF never considered this question, although how the interim government would seek to legitimise it was, in her opinion, the key issue.[74] And, as the NCBBF extended the reach of its deliberations to include the abolition

---

68   Both Bainimarama and Catholic Archbishop Petero Mataca chaired the NCBBF. There were 45 members invited to attend its first formal meeting in January 2008, mostly representing NGOs and political parties. Only 34 came, including eight cabinet ministers.

69   *Fiji Times*, 2 April 2008.

70   *fijilive*, 31 March 2008.

71   *Fiji Times*, 8 August 2008.

72   *Fiji Times*, 11 January 2008; 3 March 2008. Qarase claimed his government's Strategic Development Plan for 2007–2011 also made it redundant (*Fiji Times*, 7 April 2008). Mick Beddoes of the United People's Party (UPP) called it a 'People's Coalition Charter', highlighting Labour's association with the coup and with Samy, who had apparently been invited back to Fiji in March 2007 by Chaudhry (*Fiji Times*, 3 March 2008; *fijilive*, 28 January 2008). Qarase derided it as a 'Charter to end all coups' (*Fiji Times*, 19 April 2008).

73   Jioji Kotobalavu, Qarase's former CEO, while supporting electoral changes, noted that such changes would not be in accordance with constitutional procedure. Legal challenges might delay a future election (*Fiji Times*, 7 April 2008).

74   *Fiji Times*, 7 August 2008.

of communal seats, the introduction of proportional representation, an end to affirmative action policies based on race, the creation of a new 'Fijian' national name for all Fiji's citizens, the integration of provincial development, and the development of a unified approach to land use, the likelihood of legal challenges grew stronger.

With the release of the 'People's Charter for Change, Peace and Progress' in August 2008, Qarase somewhat predictably argued that Fijians would be marginalised by attempts to mainstream them into national development plans.[75] And, yet, mainstreaming made perfect sense for a country in which Fijians – as long recognised – now formed the overwhelming majority of the population. The 2007 census placed Fijians at 57 per cent of the population and IndoFijians at 38 per cent,[76] a change that reflected both greater IndoFijian emigration rates and lower IndoFijian fertility rates. This change had electoral implications as Narsey later noted:

> [B]y 2027, Indo-Fijians will comprise only 30% of all voters (assumed to be 18 years and over). The ethnic conflicts over political leadership or domination will be well and truly history by then.
>
> And with the incidence of poverty roughly the same for Fijians and Indo-Fijians (a third) if poverty alleviation resources are allocated to the poor only on the basis of need, the Indo-Fijian share will reduce from the current 36% down to a mere 26% by 2027. 'Affirmative action policies' will be a total non-issue.
>
> So also should be ethnic shares of public sector jobs sought by school leavers, another hot political potato in the past.[77]

If this was the future that the People's Charter sought to prepare Fiji for, it would have a hard task convincing those who had profited from ethnic allocations in the past. That included the FLP which recognised that the ending of communal seats and the introduction of voting based on proportional representation spelled the end of its chances of ever forming government in its own right as a predominantly IndoFijian party. Hence it expressed its dismay at the Charter's proposals.[78] The SDL did more than express disappointment. It attempted unsuccessfully to gain an

---

75   *Fiji Times*, 8 August 2008.
76   *Fiji Times*, 1 November 2007. By 2030 Fijians are estimated to comprise 68 per cent of the population, IndoFijians 26 per cent.
77   www.coupfourandahalf.com, 21 March 2010.
78   *Fiji Times*, 11 September 2008.

injunction to prevent further action on the Charter. The NCBBF had already distributed endorsement forms with copies of the Charter during its public feedback meetings. In early December 2008, it claimed to have consulted 80 per cent of Fiji's adult population. Of the 70 per cent who responded, 92 per cent endorsed the Charter.[79] The interim government considered this sufficient evidence of popular support. It knew only too well the risks inherent in a referendum. On 19 December 2008, President Iloilo endorsed the Charter and its implementation.

In part, the response of foreign governments to the December coup prompted the more explicit change in focus that the Charter represented. Australia and New Zealand had both opposed the coup and imposed travel bans on key political and military figures. While Pacific island leaders, especially those from fellow Melanesian states, generally supported non-intervention in Fiji's internal politics, their peak body, the Pacific Islands Forum (PIF), quickly assembled an Eminent Persons Group (EPG) to negotiate an early return to democratic rule. Both it and the European Union called for elections by early 2009. Bainimarama took their call as an opportunity to raise the stakes. In late February, he announced that an election would be predicated on rapid economic recovery, the stability of government finances and, not surprisingly, an assurance of good governance. The earliest he could envisage elections would be in 2010 given the need to hold an overdue census, create new electoral boundaries, re-establish an elections office and, importantly, amend the Constitution. This was the first time constitutional change had been mooted but, given Bainimarama's overriding concerns about the conduct of Fiji politics post-2000, it was unsurprising. As he noted, only a common roll could once and for all get rid of the 'politics of race'.[80]

In March 2007, when PIF foreign ministers met in Port Vila, Nailatikau informed them that to bring the election forward by one year, the NCBBF would have to establish new constitutional principles through its People's Charter.[81] Nonetheless, Bainimarama remained vague on dates, at one stage declaring that the more 'people kept on with their opposition

---

79   *Fiji Times*, 16 December 2008. According to Wikileaks, in late December 2008 Samy told the US ambassador that public approval for the charter had been strongly influenced by army intimidation (*fijileaks.com*, 22 March 2015).

80   *Fiji Times*, 21 February 2007.

81   *fijilive*, 17 & 21 March 2007. Bainimarama later claimed that the military would ensure that no future government ignored it; the military would be the Charter's guardian (*fijilive*, 28 November 2007).

towards the government, [the more] it will prolong the duration to the election'.[82] One year later he declared that there would be no elections in 2009 if people did not adopt the Charter.[83] In August 2008, he postponed the prospect of an election to late 2009 in order to effect changes in Fiji's electoral laws, a stance that he reiterated at the start of 2009 when he told his troops it could take five to 10 years before elections were held.[84] Once the President endorsed the Charter, however, Bainimarama held a political forum to gain consensus on electoral reform. Although unsuccessful, it – along with the earlier appointment of a new supervisor of elections and a decision to develop an electronic voter-registration system – provided evidence of some political movement for an international community grown tired of constant delays. At the start of 2009, the PIF told Fiji that it had 'drawn a line in the sand'; Fiji would be suspended unless it declared a 2009 election by 1 May.[85]

But there were limits to this strategy, as some analysts recognised. Former Australian intelligence analyst Daniel Flitton believed it threatened perpetuating instability, while Jon Fraenkel declared that 'Fiji's military leaders will not be coaxed into democracy by new sanctions or political attacks from Australia and New Zealand'.[86] Divisions within the PIF also threatened to derail its united front. Samoa, whose Prime Minister Tuilaepa Sailele Malielegaoi told Fiji's people to 'wake up' and reclaim government, believed Bainimarama had no intention of relinquishing power. While Vanuatu and smaller Pacific states lobbied for Fiji, Tuilaepa openly supported the position taken by Australia and New Zealand.[87] Bainimarama refused to attend the Forum meeting, citing the devastating floods that had left nearly 2,000 people homeless as his reason. Qarase declared it 'a lame excuse'. Consequently it was left to Aiyaz Sayed-Khaiyum to express his government's frustration. 'Holding elections

---

82   *Fiji Times*, 20 October 2007. He also said that he would not stand in the next election and would probably not form a political party. Tired of being asked when the next election would be held, he gave 13 March 2009 as the date to Radio Fiji Gold listeners (*Fiji Times*, 18 August 2007).
83   *Fiji Times*, 11 January 2008. Bainimarama later argued that elections would only be held once all corrupt practices had been investigated. And, in September, he told radio listeners that if it took 20 years to garner support for the Charter, then elections would wait 20 years (*Fiji Times*, 25 June & 15 September 2008).
84   *Fiji Times*, 28 January 2009.
85   *Sydney Morning Herald*, 28 January 2009. The Commonwealth secretariat followed suit, declaring it would extend Fiji's suspension from its councils to the Commonwealth as a whole if it did not make significant progress (*Fiji Times*, 5 & 6 March 2009).
86   *Age*, 15 April & 23 January 2009. Bainimarama later confirmed Fraenkel's comment: Fiji 'cannot be hurried into this endeavour by outsiders giving ultimatums' (*fijilive*, 13 March 2009).
87   *Fiji Times*, 23 January & 2 March 2009.

for the sake of elections is not going to achieve any proper outcome,' he told Forum delegates at their meeting in Papua New Guinea, 'nor will it achieve any long term democratic stability in Fiji.'[88]

Clearly the dominant issue for the interim government remained unresolved: how could it legally introduce the changes anticipated by the Charter and confirm immunity for the military without first holding elections under the existing Constitution? Such an election provided no guarantees. If the SDL won, as many predicted, Bainimarama's revolution would be transformed into a rout. These issues preoccupied Bainimarama and his government. 'No one will move Fiji to elections,' a defiant Bainimarama told Auckland radio listeners after Commonwealth threats of suspension if Fiji did not demonstrate in 2009 considerable progress on returning to democratic governance. They might as well suspend Fiji now. But at least he could take comfort in the knowledge that the Commonwealth and United Nations were together engaged with Fiji's key stakeholders, unlike the PIF. 'The government has a plan,' he declared at a press conference,[89] but how that might ensure that the past did not repeat itself remained uncertain.

At the second meeting of Leaders of Political Parties (LOPP) on 13 March 2009, to which the media were denied access, Bainimarama pushed the 18 parties represented in the direction he wanted and emerged with an agenda for the upcoming Commonwealth- and UN-sponsored President's Political Dialogue Forum (PPDF). It emphasised constitutional reform and the People's Charter. He urged participants to end the 'blame game', and make the paradigm shifts needed for Fiji to face its challenges.[90] But claiming consensus was easier than demonstrating it and, within days of the leaders' meeting, factions developed among the parties. Naturally Bainimarama gave the SDL special attention. After all, its challenge to the constitutionality of the interim government lay before the Supreme Court. In May 2008, he had recommended that the SDL not be permitted to

---

88   *Fiji Times*, 22 January 2009; *fijilive*, 27 January 2009. New Zealand's new Prime Minister John Key told Aiyaz Sayed-Khaiyum that he should be on trial. The Attorney-General accused him of personalising issues (*Fiji Times*, 29 January 2009).

89   *Fiji Times*, 5 & 6 March 2009. The plan focused on rebuilding the economy, not holding elections.

90   *Fiji Times*, 13 March 2009. Robin Nair claimed that the future role of the military was dropped from the agenda (*Fiji Times*, 17 March 2009). The Soqosoqo ni Vakavulewa ni Taukei (SVT) and several smaller parties proposed a bloc at the next LOPP to oppose rushing into early elections (*Fiji Times*, 7 April 2009).

contest future elections.[91] Driti also suggested in late March 2009 that it, the National Federation Party (NFP) and several civil society organisations should not participate in political dialogue, citing the need to prevent Fiji falling into an 'abyss of lawlessness and disorder' and to encourage constructive debate.[92] Accordingly Bainimarama's office sent letters to all political parties prior to the 9 April meeting in Suva making mandatory commitments to electoral reform to abolish communalism, support for government economic strategies, non-involvement with partisan media outlets, and working honestly to expedite the political process if parties wished to participate in political dialogue. Four parties, including the SDL, refused to agree to the terms and pulled out of the process.[93]

Bainimarama's determination to transform Fiji's politics demonstrated a previously overlooked side to the man. Oppositional blog sites regularly referred to the coup as an Indian coup (because of Labour's support) and later as a Muslim coup (largely because of Aiyaz Sayed-Khaiyum's leading role). Hughes initially fed this perception when he described Bainimarama as 'a front man for power-seeking people in Fiji'.[94] Among themselves, diplomats described him as erratic, violent, thin-skinned and insecure. But Bainimarama's more extensive agenda soon altered these perceptions. Since his appointment as Commander of the RFMF in 1999, he had become more resolute. Having seized power, another transformation began. As one journalist later noted, 'Bainimarama [now] sees himself as Fiji's Atatürk. He will never allow his democratic opponents to return to power, and he will relinquish power only on his terms'.[95] Claims that the Commander was merely a front man disappeared.

Bainimarama's determination to challenge Fiji's chiefs in December 2006 marked the start of this transformation, although anger and petulance often seemed more in play. In April 2007, prior to Iloilo's departure to Australia for a medical examination, Bainimarama asked the GCC to appoint as vice president his Foreign Minister, Ratu Epeli Nailatikau. When it refused on the grounds that Nailatikau was part of an illegal regime, Bainimarama suspended future meetings of the Council and simultaneously ceased all

91   *Fiji Times*, 28 May 2008.
92   *Fiji Times*, 27 & 29 March 2009.
93   *Fiji Times*, 9 April 2009. The SDL, NFP, Nationalist Vanua Tako Lavo Party (NVTLP) and UPP pulled out and signalled they would hold a press conference instead.
94   *Fiji Times*, 6 December 2006.
95   Doring, 'US cables', 2011. Atatürk was the military leader who, after the First World War, transformed the Ottoman Empire into a modern secular Turkish state.

membership by proclamation. There were shades here of Rabuka's early 'angry young man' stance against the chiefs. Indeed, tongue-in-cheek, Rabuka fired off an article to the press envisaging a chiefless Fijian society where all Fijian 'command structures' were militarised. Qarase warned of a violent Fijian reaction.[96] Neither response occurred. Instead the GCC threatened legal action, prompting its eventual restoration in August, but with new rules that reduced its membership.[97] Nonetheless, Bainimarama kept up the pressure, extending his anger also to the equally recalcitrant Methodist church. Chiefs, politicians and the *talatalas* (church ministers) kept Fijians suppressed and took advantage of them, he declared.[98]

At the start of 2008, the rules were again clarified. No chief could be part of the GCC if he or she belonged to a political party, held dual citizenship or residency rights or had been a politician, a prisoner or bankrupt in the past seven to 10 years. Additionally, chiefs must have been officially installed by their *vanua*. Bainimarama now became chair of the GCC in order to reflect government views in council deliberations. The new rules created a storm of controversy. Ratu Naiqama Lalabalavu, whose past would clearly exclude him, claimed chiefs had of necessity to be involved in politics. 'We are born to lead,' he asserted.[99] No longer, claimed CCF director, Rev. Yabaki. Many Fijian institutions had 'passed their sell-by date'.[100] Others criticised Bainimarama's presence; he was not a chief and, as head of government, he would politicise the very body the reforms were meant to depoliticise. The rule on installation also generated controversy. Possibly 80 per cent of all chiefs had never been formally installed; indeed many did not need to be.[101] Predictably, the rule changes threw the chiefs into confusion, as probably intended, and Bainimarama did not call an immediate meeting of his new-look GCC. Instead, in mid-December

---

96   *Fiji Times*, 15 April 2007; *Fiji Sun*, 19 April 2007.

97   *Fiji Sun*, 13 & 19 April 2007. The restored GCC possessed 52 members. The President, Vice President and Prime Minister were no longer members. All commoners (like Rabuka) were excluded (*Fiji Times*, 28 August 2007). In addition, the Ministry of Fijian Affairs was 'downgraded' to a Department of Indigenous Affairs, Provincial Development and Multi-ethnic Affairs after a cabinet reshuffle in November.

98   *Fiji Times*, 31 October 2007.

99   *fijilive*, 13 February 2008; *Fiji Times*, 19 February 2008.

100   *Fiji Times*, 26 February 2008. Even the now-reformed Conservative Alliance – Matanitu Vanua (CAMV) appeared to agree. It demanded the NLTB change the redistribution of rental monies to advantage landowning units and not chiefs (*fijilive*, 8 January 2009).

101   *fijilive*, 1 April 2008. Later, the Minister for Indigenous Affairs became the designated GCC chair.

2008, he brought together district chiefs in a Bose ni Turaga, the first since 2000, to demonstrate engagement and to gain its support for the People's Charter.[102] It was another snub to the GCC.

Bainimarama also targeted the deposed Prime Minister, this time issuing 14 new declarations against him, including aiding and abetting foreign powers to intervene in Fiji affairs. These declarations justified stripping him of any benefits as a former prime minister, including security, transport, medical treatment and pension. After eight months in exile, Qarase had returned to Suva for an SDL meeting in early September 2007. Bainimarama declared him 'a radical racist' and a security risk; he did not 'deserve anything from government because he has brought disaster to the country'.[103] More substantial charges of corruption were laid in March 2008, however, alleging that Qarase had failed to declare his interest in family companies that had bought shares in FHL in the early 1990s. Charges were later laid against the CEO of FHL.[104]

This was the first major new evidence of corruption for a government that had come to power promising to weed out the corrupt practices of the past. Two months later, a wider set of more contemporary allegations surrounding the NLTB enveloped its board members and Qarase. After 2001 the NLTB had diverted trust funds belonging to extinct *mataqali* into its commercial arm, Vanua Development Corporation Ltd. Bainimarama revealed that some $12 million had been lost through VDCL schemes that flowed to Pacific Connex.[105] But these charges were important for

---

102 *fijilive*, 12 December 2008. Of 285 invitees, only 47 per cent accepted. A retreat to the Officers Mess in Nabua occupied the second of three days.

103 *fijilive*, 5 & 6 September 2007; 25 November 2007.

104 See Chapter 2 for further details. FHL had received a loan from the Fijian Affairs Board (FAB) in 1987 to boost provincial ownership. The 1992 FHL annual report, however, showed that 27 private companies now owned 70 per cent of FHL, including companies associated with Qarase and Weleilakeba, financed by the Fiji Development Bank (FDB). Qarase was the managing director of the FDB, a FHL board member, and a financial advisor to the FAB. Weleilakeba was the FHL's CEO. Private companies received 10 per cent dividends, the provinces 5 per cent. In 2012, the High Court found Qarase guilty on nine charges and sentenced the 71-year-old to one year in jail (*Guardian*, 3 August 2012).

105 *Fiji Times*, 12 May 2008. In July 2014, NLTB former general manager Kalivati Bakani and board member Keni Dakuidreketi were sentenced to four and six years respectively after pleading guilty to using extinct *mataqali* funds and government grants to finance a private company (*Fiji Times*, 5 July 2014). The team investigating Fijian institutions was suddenly disbanded without explanation in March 2008. The focus on Pacific Connex took a new turn when the military beefed up security around Bainimarama in October and a few weeks later announced that it had foiled a plot by Pacific Connex personnel and others to assassinate the Commander (*fijilive*, 4 November 2007).

another reason also. As time wore on, the interim government increasingly showed signs that it was not as divorced from the sins of its predecessors as it pretended.[106]

Human rights abuses certainly continued to reveal a military unwilling to exercise restraint. Sixteen people were arrested at the start of November 2007, charged with plotting to assassinate Bainimarama, Chaudhry and Aiyaz Sayed-Khaiyum among others, and incite a military mutiny. The arrests, which bore all the hallmarks of a military sting, drew in a veritable list of known government opponents: Pacific Connex executives including Ballu Khan, Takiveikata, five former CRWU employees of Pacific Connex, as well as Baledrokadroka and Metuisela Mua.[107] Khan was severely beaten during his arrest and nearly died. Only the intervention of the NZ High Commission secured him hospital treatment. The High Court eventually threw out the conspiracy charges against Khan because he had been detained unlawfully and denied access to a lawyer.[108] He returned to New Zealand. For many observers the fear remained that the operation formed a pretext to discredit and detain people known to be opposed to the actions of the government,[109] in much the same way Rabuka had used the discovery of weapons in 1988 to introduce a far-reaching Internal Security Decree.

But other examples of dubious practices quickly multiplied. Commander Francis Kean, Bainimarama's brother-in-law, assaulted and killed his son-in-law's uncle at Bainimarama's daughter's wedding in late December 2006.

---

106 US Ambassador Steven McGaan informed Washington on 22 December 2008 that the Attorney-General had been in default on several property loans for the past two years and that his bank refused to foreclose for fear that its expatriate managers would be deported (*fijileaks.com*, 22 March 2015). Lt Col Ratu Mara alleged in 2011 that Khaiyum's difficulties were resolved when the Tappoo company bought one of his properties at an inflated price in return for duty free concessions in the budget (www.coupfourandahalf.com, 23 May 2011), although the US ambassador claimed instead that he had sold the properties to law firms. The government dismissed Mara's allegations as blog-fuelled justifications for his escape (*fijivillage*, 26 May 2011).

107 *fijilive*, 4 November 2007. Undercover military personnel (locally described as *agent vinod*) had worked on the so-called perpetrators for at least three months. DPP officers initially refused to prosecute the case when Nassir Ali presented it to them because they knew nothing about it. They were threatened with arrest (*Fiji Times*, 8 November 2007). The conspiracy, backed by the *vanua*, the Methodist Church and the international community (Takiveikata allegedly told the undercover agent that Australia would chip in $1 billion to kick start Fiji's economy if Bainimarama was assassinated) and financed by Khan, involved blowing up the Nadi airport and the Monasavu dam with munitions from New Zealand (*fijilive*, 3 February 2010). The defence argued that the military floated the assassination plan to draw out opposition elements that might have been planning such an assignment.

108 *fijilive*,13 November 2008. Baledrokadroka served 40 days in jail until his charges were dismissed. Eight men were eventually found guilty in March 2010.

109 *Fiji Times*, 5 November 2007.

Although given an 18-month sentence for manslaughter in October 2007, he remained a salaried officer throughout, even while serving his sentence. Released after six months, he served the rest of his sentence extramurally with the navy. Several observers drew parallels with the case of former Vice President Ratu Jope Seniloli and questioned whether nepotism had really been put to bed.[110] The growing militarisation of civil service positions similarly failed to demonstrate a government determined to place Fiji's governance on a sound footing; so too the lack of transparency over ministerial salaries. It did not help that ministers excused themselves from the 5 per cent cut imposed on all public servants in 2007, ostensibly due to higher workloads,[111] or that Bainimarama received nearly $185,000 for leave owed since 1978. Other military officers were treated similarly.[112]

The military were not so forward at the start of 2009 when the worst flooding in 50 years hit the Western Division and wiped out vital infrastructure such as the Sigatoka and Nadi bridges. It took nearly a week to begin addressing the disarray at evacuation centres and to distribute food.[113] Worse criticism – some international – followed Esala Teleni, seconded from the military as Police Commissioner in July 2007, when he berated IndoFijian police officers at Navosa for apparently telling the *Fiji Sun* that he was forcing them to convert to his brother's New Methodist Church, which was conducting a moral crusade throughout the force. He called them backstabbers and liars. During 2009 he stepped up his Police National Crusade, claiming that its focus on building character was responsible for a 20 per cent decline in crime during the first half of the year. He believed Fiji would be crime free by 2012, telling Radio Legend FM listeners that he made decisions based on what the Holy Spirit told him to do. His comments won him little praise. The Jesus police were no better than the Taliban, *Fiji Times* editor, Netani Rika, claimed.[114] 'That's what madmen who appoint themselves to office do,' Samoa's Prime

---

110　*Fiji Times*, 2 & 3 November 2007. Kean was reappointed naval commander at the start of 2009, sparking comparisons with Ratu Naiqama Lalabalavu, who the SDL released early from jail and allowed to resume his former position as Lands Minister, an act Bainimarama criticised at the time (*Fiji Times*, 17 January 2009). In 2014, Kean became Corrections Commissioner.

111　*fijilive*, 3 April 2008.

112　*Fiji Times*, 20 July 2008. The government refused to release the auditor general's report on the leave payout, claiming it was only following constitutional procedure by insisting it go to parliament first.

113　*Fiji Times*, 15 & 16 January 2009.

114　www.coupfourandahalf.com, 18, 27 & 28 August 2009. In mid-2010, Teleni was moved sideways and became ambassador to China. His replacement declared the police in a state of disarray (*Fiji Times*, 20 December 2010); a health audit found 60 per cent of the force unfit (*Fiji Times*, 24 February 2011).

Minister quipped: 'They appoint other madmen to positions of power'.[115] But they also, allegedly, acted more conventionally to punish officials who did not toe the government's line.

In March 2009, Charles Sweeney accused the government of illegally removing him from his role as Commerce Commission chair in order to shut down an inquiry into whether mobile telecommunications company Vodafone was trying to restrict deregulation of the industry and future competition in order to preserve its market dominance.[116] The new permanent secretary for foreign affairs, Ratu Isoa Gavidi, found himself suddenly dismissed and the High Commissioner to Papua New Guinea recalled when both contradicted the government's position on Bainimarama's attendance at the PIF in Papua New Guinea in January 2009. Robin Nair lost his role as one of the interlocutors engaged to assist in facilitating political dialogue for apparently criticising Fiji's regional policy and diplomacy.[117] Parallels with previous government behaviour were all too obvious. And bizarrely, Joketani Cokanasiga, a former minister in Qarase's interim government who had defended the agricultural scam as politically necessary to secure Qarase's electoral victory in 2001, became Minister for Agriculture in a revamped cabinet in late August 2007.[118]

But the most egregious case concerned that of Finance Minister Chaudhry. Rumours had circulated on social media for some time that Chaudhry had amassed A$1.6 million in Australian accounts, money that had had never been reflected in his tax returns. These were funds raised in India after 2000 to assist in his possible resettlement to Australia, although in the years that followed he had always argued that any funds raised in India had been used to assist refugee farmers dislocated by the violence of 2000 and housed at the Lautoka Girmit Centre and at Valelawa.[119] Two tax inspectors were dismissed for raising the matter with Bainimarama and the Police Commissioner. But, once full details were published in the local press, an act purportedly endorsed by the Military Council,[120]

---

115 *Fiji Times*, 19 February 2009; *fijilive*, 18 February 2009.

116 *Fiji Times*, 3 & 5 March 2009.

117 *Fiji Times*, 24 & 29 January 2009. This did Nair no immediate harm; he later became ambassador to the United Arab Emirates and, from 2016 to 2017, permanent secretary for foreign affairs, until dismissed by Bainimarama in 2017 (*Fiji Sun*, 11 July 2017).

118 *Fiji Sun*, 20 January 2006.

119 *Fiji Times*, 23 August 2008.

120 *Fiji Times*, 23 February 2008. Credit for the revelations belong to Victor Lal (victorlal.blogspot. com) who first published elements of the story in the *Fiji Sun* during August 2007. Chaudhry threatened the *Fiji Times* with a $1 billion lawsuit, but later withdrew it (*Fiji Times*, 24 October 2008).

the government had to take action. It appointed a three-member team to investigate the tax allegations, which very quickly cleared Chaudhry of wrongdoing. But the government also deported the *Fiji Sun* publisher, Russell Hunter, ostensibly for publishing the stories about Chaudhry's alleged tax evasion. An amendment to the *Immigration Act* the very same day prevented the Immigration Minister's decisions from being challenged by court orders.[121] The *Fiji Times* also found itself exposed. The Attorney-General complained to its publisher, Evan Hannah, on 14 March about the newspaper's coverage of a ban on the entry of Australian lawyer John Cameron to represent human rights activists.[122] Two months later the government pounced, bundling Hannah out of the country despite a High Court order from Justice Filimoni Jikoto preventing his deportation.[123] Bainimarama described media reports as 'careless and irresponsible … inciteful and destabilising, posing a threat to national security and stability'. He threatened to shut down the media if coverage of his government did not improve.[124] A new FHRC report by the former unionist and expatriate James Anthony backed the government's assertion, calling for foreigners to be banned from employment by Fiji's media, the creation of a new media tribunal to oversee its activities, and the introduction of sedition laws.[125]

These distractions could not, however, save Chaudhry. When a tax he imposed on Fiji's water companies threatened to close the high-profile exporter Fiji Water in the following July, he found himself once more in the firing line from the Military Council. Police, allegedly acting on direct orders from Bainimarama, who was then in Beijing, questioned a *Fiji Times* journalist over an article critical of Chaudhry.[126] But such intervention could not save the very diminished politician and, in mid-

---

121   *Fiji Times*, 26 & 27 February 2008.

122   *Fiji Times*, 20 March 2008. At the same time Graham Leung, who had been writing an article for the newspaper, claimed his computer had been hacked. A copy of that article found its way to the Attorney-General who warned Hannah not to publish.

123   Justice John Byrne subsequently stayed the order (International Bar Association, *Dire Straits: A Report on the Rule of Law in Fiji*. An International Bar Association Human Rights Institute Report. London, March 2009, p. 58).

124   *Fiji Times*, 1, 2 & 5 May 2008; *Australian*, 29 February & 9 May 2008. Aiyaz Sayed-Khaiyum argued that the newspaper should not have printed material from Cameron then before the courts. Munro Leys lawyers Richard Naidu and Jon Apted obtained a writ of *habeas corpus* from Justice Jikoto, which both Air Pacific and Air Terminal Services honoured, but Immigration placed Hannah on a plane to Korea instead.

125   *Fiji Times*, 4 March 2008. See also J Anthony, 'Freedom & independence of the media in Fiji: A report'. Suva: Fiji Human Rights Commission, 2008.

126   *Fiji Times*, 11 August 2008.

August, he and two Labour colleagues resigned from the cabinet, citing the need to prepare for elections now that the Charter had been completed.[127] Little wonder that Samy warned that it was imperative the government demonstrate 'the highest standards of transparency and good governance'. Bainimarama conceded that his government did not operate as effectively as it might.[128] Naturally his opponents were in rare agreement with him. He had failed to bring about effective change and appeared unable to keep to his 2009 election promise.[129]

Confronting recalcitrant foreign governments and judges

Foreign governments also came in for special treatment, despite Fiji's need to restore relations in order to ensure the continuance of aid and market access. The European Parliament sent a delegation to Fiji in December 2008 to pressure the interim government on its election commitments. Already, much-needed funds to raise standards in the sugar industry had been withheld pending firm developments on returning democracy and, although growing links with China provided some relief, they could not fully compensate.[130] Fiji's apparent vulnerability, however, did little to dampen its anger at what it perceived to be hostile statements from foreign governments. Driti allegedly harangued the US deputy assistant secretary about the conduct of the international community when the latter visited the country in April 2007.[131] When Australia's army chief, Lt Col Peter Leahy, suggested Australia develop stronger peacekeeping capabilities in order to intervene in unstable countries like Fiji, Bainimarama said he

---

127 *Fiji Times*, 17 August 2008. Land Force Commander Col Mosese Tikoitoga later claimed Chaudhry had been dismissed for non-performance (*fijilive*, 28 March 2012). Tom Ricketts and Vayeshnoi also stepped down. Bune, no longer an FLP member, left the cabinet after a reshuffle in January 2008. In July 2010, Chaudhry was finally charged with money laundering, tax evasion and providing false information to the tax authorities (*fijilive*, 23 July 2010). But the case lingered in the courts. By 2012, time-barred tax declaration offences and money laundering charges were dropped, leaving him – at the insistence of the RBF – to face three counts of breaches of the *Exchange Control Act* (www.coupfourandahalf.com, 25 July 2012). In May 2014, the High Court found him guilty and fined him $2 million (*Fiji Times*, 3 May 2014).

128 *Fiji Times*, 23 August & 5 September 2008.

129 *fijilive*, 25 August 2008; both Beddoes and the CCF called for a government of national unity.

130 *fijilive*, 3 December 2008; $334 million of EU funds were suspended in 2008; the 2009 budget only compensated the industry with $5 million. In September, Fiji gained a $230 million soft loan from China for upgrading rural and squatter homes. During 2006 and 2007 Chinese aid to Fiji increased from US$23 million to US$160 million (*Sydney Morning Herald*, 21 April 2009).

131 *Fiji Times*, 29 April 2007.

would 'be waiting for them'.[132] After New Zealand's High Commissioner Michael Green criticised the interim government, Bainimarama expelled him for being 'in our face'. A rugby match between Fiji 15s and the Junior All Blacks proved the last straw. To nominate 'the enemy of the day, a Kiwi, to be the chief guest', Bainimarama thundered, was 'a disservice to the people of our country'. For all the bluster, Fiji did try to negotiate; Green could stay if New Zealand lifted its travel bans. The move backfired; New Zealand refused and extended the ban to senior officials and their families. Its Prime Minister, Helen Clark, accused the military of being 'so self-centred and narcissistic that it can't understand why the rest of the world rejects its spin. It's under pressure and lashing out unpredictably'.[133]

The bans clearly had an impact. Fiji pulled out of the regional PIF meeting in Niue in August 2008 because New Zealand would only give the Fiji delegation transit visas. They were not permitted to stop over in Auckland. Although direct flights to Papua New Guinea weakened the effectiveness of Australia's travel bans, they still rankled, especially after the United States denied Bainimarama a visa in November to attend an International Monetary Fund (IMF) meeting. Certainly they made more difficult Fiji's ability to engage high-level personnel, but they also impacted on 'innocents', as the Attorney-General called them.[134] Two students studying in New Zealand and whose fathers were senior public servants were denied re-entry to complete their studies. Members of sports teams faced similar difficulties. An angry Bainimarama accused Australia and New Zealand of being bullies and informed Wellington that he would deport the acting High Commissioner Caroline McDonald in retaliation, which he did on Christmas Eve. He also placed several journalists on an arrivals blacklist.[135] Not unsurprisingly, Australia and New Zealand hit back. New Zealand expelled the Fiji High Commissioner. Both left Fiji off the list of Pacific countries eligible for participation in their Pacific guest workers scheme. Fiji accused AusAID of providing financial inducements to critics of its civil society. It accused both countries of trying to prevent it accessing World Bank and ADB aid facilitation.

---

132 *fijilive*, 20 June 2007.
133 *fijivillage*, 15 June 2007; *Fiji Times*, 18 June & 3 July 2007.
134 *Fiji Times*, 23 December 2008.
135 *fijilive*, 16 & 20 December 2008. Smart sanctions had a downside. They pushed Fiji to form new alliances, often with China and India. At the start of 2009 the military announced it had reassigned its medical contract from New Zealand's Wakefield Hospital to Batra Hospital in India (*Fiji Times*, 30 March 2009).

Australia's High Commissioner, James Batley, received anonymous death threats, forcing the High Commission to issue a voluntary recall of its diplomatic families.[136]

Foreign opposition, manifested in the main as travel bans, at least provided the government an opportunity to play the nationalist card. When economic consequences might be damaging, as in the case of EU responses, Fiji chose engagement tactics instead. But, in many respects, opposition from its own judiciary and lawyers proved less easy to handle, in part because the interim government's fragile façade of legitimacy depended solely on retaining their support. Assisting it, however, were judicial divisions that derived from former Chief Justice Sir Timoci Tuivaga's advice to the military on its usurpation of power in 2000. Ironically his successor, Daniel Fatiaki, who Bainimarama suspended in early January 2007, had supported Tuivaga's actions. Fatiaki's crime lay in being estranged from justices Nazhat Shameem (sister of the FHRC director), John Byrne and Anthony Gates who had opposed Tuivaga's role in 2000 and were now apparently reunited in their distaste of the former Qarase government and its policies. The coup provided them the opportunity to turn the tables. Accordingly, Gates – as the next most senior judge – replaced Fatiaki as acting chief justice in circumstances that were viewed as suspicious by many in the legal fraternity,[137] including the Fiji Law Society whose Vice President, Tupou Draunidalo, the military regularly detained and prevented from leaving the country. Appeal Court President Justice Gordon Ward lost his home in a suspicious fire, Justice Gerard Winter had his car vandalised, and the military shadowed Justice Roger Coventry after he ruled against it in a case.[138] Lawyer Graham Leung, who was instrumental in securing the withdrawal of the Malaysian FICAC Commissioner, told the June LAWASIA conference in Hong Kong that 'tyranny, arbitrariness and spite' had perverted the rule of law in Fiji and that the judiciary now lacked even the appearance of independence. Gates had assumed responsibility for hearing Qarase's constitutional challenge to the coup while many other senior judges appeared complicit either before or after the event.[139] After six Appeal Court justices resigned en bloc in

---

136 *Fiji Times*, 10 June 2008; *Australian*, 9 May 2008; *Fiji Times*, 16 May 2008; *fijilive*, 22 May 2008. New Zealand travel bans did not apply to international sporting events hosted in New Zealand.
137 International Bar Association, *Dire Straits*, 2009, p. 40. Jitoko also gave support to Tuivaga.
138 International Bar Association, *Dire Straits*, 2009, p. 44.
139 G Leung, 'Lawyers must cry freedom', 2007. The High Court awarded Draunidalo costs after the Attorney-General dropped a case against her for expressing a lack of confidence in the judiciary (*Fiji Times*, 20 November 2007).

September 2007 over Gates' handling of court administration, FWRM's Buadromo accused the interim government of handpicking judges who may decide on its legality.[140] Coventry terminated his contract, declaring 'acquiescence the friend of illegality'.[141]

But not all of Fiji's judges agreed. In October, the High Court finally ruled on Qarase's substantive case against the military coup and Iloilo's subsequent proclamations. Justices Gates, Byrne and Davendra Pathik declared the President's actions lawful and valid, and dismissed the case. Responses were short and resigned. Leung described it a grievous blow 'to the fabric of the Constitution', while Madraiwiwi argued that 'what has been imposed on people will not endure because the majority of the population disagree with it'. Beddoes believed: 'Ultimately it will all come to an end and the truth will come out, and in time all those involved in this large scale deception and fraud against the law abiding citizens of Fiji will be exposed.'[142]

But that moment had yet to come. In December, the embattled Fatiaki gave up his struggle against the government and resigned as chief justice, despite no evidence of misconduct being found to warrant his suspension. Gates formally replaced him.[143] For the moment the façade of legitimacy held, allowing Bainimarama to tell his international critics 'there is no crisis in Fiji. You have a government in place that's been held to be legally and validly appointed'.[144] The High Court ruling made that claim difficult to refute.

The SDL, however, persisted with legal challenges. It registered a treason complaint against the government in September 2008, only to have the police refuse to investigate it and Commissioner Teleni accuse the

---

140 *Fiji Times*, 11 February 2008. Shameem, Jocelynne Scutt, John Byrne, Daniel Gounder, Pathik and Isikeli Mataitoga replaced them. PCPI's Heffernan demanded the interim government appointee, Justice Jocelynne Scutt, resign after she praised the FHRC (*fijilive*, 11 February 2008). Coventry resigned from the High Court citing differences with Gates (*Australian*, 29 February 2008) but most Supreme Court judges stayed on. Not being appointed by the interim government, they could constitutionally still hear cases against it (*Fiji Times*, 3 May 2008). Australian Greg Bullard resigned after only one month as a magistrate, claiming a lack of judicial independence (www.coupfourandahalf.com, 23 November 2012).

141 International Bar Association, *Dire Straits*, 2009, p. 50.

142 *fijilive*, 22 October 2008; *Fiji Times*, 13 October & 20 December 2008. The IBA considered that, since two of the judges had been appointed since the coup, they breached the law of recusal by hearing the case (International Bar Association, *Dire Straits*, 2009, p. 21).

143 *Fiji Times*, 6 December 2008. The state gave Fatiaki $275,000 in settlement and he ended civil proceedings against it.

144 *Australian*, 29 January 2009.

party of instigating instability. The Attorney-General called the SDL 'unpatriotic'.[145] Attempts by the International Bar Association (IBA) to enter Fiji twice in 2008 were similarly unsuccessful, although this did not prevent the IBA reporting that the judiciary's independence had been compromised, an allegation that the Attorney-General dismissed as without evidence.[146] In November, however, when the SDL gained an injunction from Justice Jikoto stopping the NCBBF proceeding and the government making changes to the electoral system, Justice Byrne promptly stayed the injunction on the grounds that there was insufficient evidence that work on the Charter would lead to electoral changes.[147] When the *Fiji Times* published a letter calling the judicial system corrupt for its handling of Qarase's constitutional challenge, the High Court fined the paper $100,000 in January 2009 and sentenced its editor, Netani Rika, to three months' jail, suspended for two years. Although the paper's publisher, Rex Gardner, who had replaced the deported Hannah the previous July, pleaded guilty, he was not convicted. Nonetheless, the government considered his plea grounds for declaring him a prohibited immigrant and ordered him to leave the country immediately.[148] Outspoken human rights activists and their lawyers were similarly dealt with by threats of contempt proceedings.[149]

Although the government seemed to survive every challenge to its authority, in reality it began to confront a perfect storm. International pressure on electoral commitments, media challenges, outspoken human rights activists, a fractured judiciary trumping each other's decisions, and political objections to consensus on constitutional reform all began to converge in early 2009. The façade of legitimacy now wore thin. Into that storm rode three Sydney barristers, all members of Fiji's Court of Appeal, called to judge the validity of the High Court's October ruling on the 2006 coup: Randall Powell, Ian Lloyd and Francis Douglas, the latter only recently appointed. On Thursday 9 April at 3 pm, they delivered a stunning Easter verdict to the nation, ruling that the government was illegal and that the President should immediately appoint a new caretaker prime minister to take the country to fresh elections. That 'independent'

---

145 *Fiji Times*, 7 & 9 September 2008; *fijilive*, 7 September 2008. Beddoes lodged his own complaint the next day.
146 *Fiji Times*, 5 March 2009.
147 International Bar Association, *Dire Straits*, 2009, p. 54.
148 International Bar Association, *Dire Straits*, 2009, p. 62; *Fiji Times*, 27 January 2009.
149 Tupou Draunidalo had experienced this in 2007; so, too, John Cameron and Virisila Buadromo (International Bar Association, *Dire Straits*, 2009, pp. 58–64).

prime minister should be neither Bainimarama nor Qarase.[150] Qarase was certainly not dismayed. He declared justice served. Immediately Solicitor General Christopher Pryde approached the judges for a stay of their ruling, arguing that the result would be a political vacuum while the government sought an appeal. But Powell, Lloyd and Douglas replied that a stay of execution would make no difference. 'The reality is that the country has a Constitution that everyone has to obey,' they argued: 'That's the judgement of the Court and this Government should obey'.[151]

Briefly it seemed it might. That evening Bainimarama appeared on television to announce his resignation as prime minister. His forces would ensure no disruption to law and order prior to an expected decision from the President on the way forward. The judges had already flown to Nadi to await a flight back to Sydney and were home by the time Iloilo addressed the nation late Good Friday morning.[152] The Court had told him to appoint a third party as caretaker prime minister, but the Constitution made no provision for this, he argued. Hence Fiji, in legal terms, had not had a government since 3 pm the day before, but 'you cannot have a country without a government'. Considerable progress had been made since 2006, he continued, citing the People's Charter and the three meetings of political parties that had established the PPDF process. Consequently, after consulting with the Commander, he had decided to abrogate the Constitution in order to facilitate holding truly democratic parliamentary elections by September 2014. He would appoint an interim government to oversee this transition to a 'new legal order' over the next five years. Existing laws would remain in force but all judicial appointments were forthwith revoked.[153] The next morning Iloilo swore in Bainimarama as prime minister and issued a 30-day state of emergency. All remaining nine members of his former government returned, resurrected by decree.[154]

---

150 *Fiji Times*, 9 April 2009.
151 *fijilive*, 9 April 2009.
152 *Sydney Morning Herald*, 11 April 2009.
153 *Fiji Times*, 10 April 2009.
154 *Fiji Times*, 11 April 2009. Aiyaz Sayed-Khaiyum returned as Attorney-General and Minister for Justice, Electoral Reform, Public Enterprises and Anti-corruption; Nailatikau as Minister for Indigenous Affairs, Provincial Development and Multi-ethnic Affairs; Ganilau as Minister for Defence, National Security and Immigration; Cokanasiga as Minister for Primary Industries; Dr Jiko Luveni as Minister for Women, Social Welfare and Poverty; Bole as Minister for Education, National Heritage, Culture and Arts, and Youth and Sports; Captain Timoci Natuva as Minister for Works, Transport and Public Utilities; and Dr Neil Sharma as Minister for Health. Bainimarama, in addition to serving as Commander and Prime Minister, reassumed the portfolios for public service, people's charter, information, finance and national planning, foreign affairs, international cooperation and civil aviation.

The new order begins

This was the reset button that Bainimarama and his colleagues had been preparing for as their façade of legitimacy became more and more difficult to sustain by the start of 2009.[155] For the majority of Fiji's citizens, the change ushered in an unfamiliar world of media censorship and junta dominance but, for older citizens, it brought forth memories of the dark days that followed Rabuka's own reset on 25 September 1987, although with one substantial difference. Whereas Rabuka quickly accommodated those he opposed after his second coup, this time there could be no accommodation and hence no foreseeable end to the drama.[156] Coup 4.5, as some on social media referred to it, had two agendas: to complete the weakening of once powerful institutions such as the GCC and Methodist Church, and to hasten Fiji's transformation without distraction from political parties and courts. But, even with the military as the only institution standing intact, the path forward proved difficult. Old issues did not drop away and past behaviours continued to distract. Most importantly the reset did not come with a new operating system to download. That had yet to be assembled.

Nonetheless, Bainimarama fronted the nation two days after the abrogation with confidence: 'We must rid ourselves of our past prejudices, our past negative influences; we must be focused on building a better Fiji.' And he outlined the tasks ahead: the introduction of modern governance systems, a liberalised economy, better roads and water supply, the eradication of systemic corruption, the integration of land as a benefit for indigenous Fijians with national economic growth, and the removal of politics from government decision-making. 'We cannot be beholden to petty politics, communal politics, provincial politics and religious politics,' he argued. The Appeal Court had tried to force Fiji to an early election under the old system, but the majority of people wanted electoral change first,

---

155   Bainimarama told Al Jazeera's *101East* program in July 2009 that they were always going to get rid of the Constitution at some stage. But it was just a coincidence that the Constitution was abrogated less than 24 hours after the court's judgement (www.coupfourandahalf.com, 15 August 2009).

156   Aiyaz Sayed-Khaiyum also claimed that, unlike Rabuka, they were not locking up judges and treating people in an undignified manner. There was no violence, and law and order prevailed (*Australian*, 15 April 2009). But, like Rabuka, Bainimarama was rewarded by the President for his services, becoming a Companion of the Order of Fiji in late March. Driti and Col Mohammed Aziz were made Officers of the Order of Fiji (*fijilive*, 24 March 2009).

he claimed.[157] Hence the abrogation of the Constitution to make way for reforms and the introduction of Public Emergency Regulations (PER) to prevent opposition from stalling reforms. Freedom of speech had caused problems in the past; now government alone would make decisions.[158] Later, at a pre-budget consultation, he declared, 'We need to change people if they don't think the way we want them to think'. Until an elected government returned, 'we need to keep people in line'.[159]

And it did. Over the course of 2009 and subsequent years a long series of decrees and government pronouncements began to reshape governance and the basis on which Fiji's citizens interacted with each other. Courts were forbidden to entertain any challenge to the abrogation of the Constitution or to any decree issued after 5 December 2006.[160] Some lawyers and judges in Suva and Lautoka – on the recommendation of the Fiji Law Society (FLS) President, Dorsami Naidu, turned up to the courts on the first working day after the Constitution had been abrogated. Police prevented them entering and detained Naidu. Almost immediately the FLS lost its power to issue practising certificates to lawyers or to investigate complaints. A new chief registrar, Major Ana Rokomokoti, fulfilled that role. She and six government officers raided the FLS office to obtain complaint files against FLS members. Police also seized files relating to military personnel held at the DPP's offices. The DPP, Josaia Naigulevu, and his assistant were dismissed. Shortly after, a new Office of Accountability and Transparency came into being to administer code of conduct and freedom of information decrees and, by the end of the year, an independent Legal Services Commissioner oversaw the performance of lawyers.[161] There were other significant changes also. The legal age became 18 years, a change that placed women and men on the same footing for

---

157 *fijilive*, 12 April 2009. Bainimarama argued on NZ's Radio National that the appeal judges wrote the bulk of their 52-page judgement before coming to Fiji (*Sydney Morning Herald*, 16 April 2009).

158 *Australian*, 15 April 2009. Neither police nor soldiers could be held accountable for actions undertaken under the PER, but individuals could be detained without charge for up to seven days. Meetings of more than three people required prior approval. The regulations stayed in place until 7 January 2012.

159 *fijilive*, 17 September 2009.

160 *fijilive*, 23 April 2009. This applied also to the FHRC.

161 *fijilive*, 27 November 2009; www.coupfourandahalf.com, 23 September 2009; *fijilive*, 27 November 2009; *Daily Post*, 15 April 2009; Amnesty International, *Fiji: Paradise Lost – A Tale of Ongoing Human Rights Violations*. London, 2009, p. 27. During 2008 the FLS began examining complaints against the Attorney-General and threatened to debar him. Graham Leung refused to register under the arrangement, but most lawyers did. The new DPP, John Rabuku, allegedly sacked the assistant DPP, Andie Driu, for declaring that she was loyal only to the law and nothing or no one else (www.coupfourandahalf.com, 24 June 2009).

the first time and removed parental approval for those under 21 seeking to marry.[162] Civil servants, with few exceptions, had now no choice but to retire at 55 years. Dual citizenship, again with full future voting rights, also became possible for the first time.[163]

The abrogation of the Constitution and the dismissal of all judges effectively closed down the justice system until new judges and magistrates could be appointed. For six weeks no chief justice existed until Gates resumed the position. Meanwhile, the public lost all legal protection against human rights violations. The police and military continued to detain and intimidate human rights activists and known critics. Driti made clear what they might now expect:

> There are only a few people who I could term as adversaries – but I would discourage them from doing anything ... otherwise they will be in for something really hard in terms of how we will treat them this year.[164]

Lawyer Imrana Jalal had been threatened with rape immediately after the 2006 coup by a mystery phone caller she suspected was military. She believed that the same military lawyer who had orchestrated the call was using FICAC to persecute her and her husband, Ratu Sakiusa Tuisolia, an economist and former deputy CEO of Rabuka's prime ministerial office in the mid-1990s. Tuisolia had been dismissed as CEO of Airports Fiji Ltd after the 2006 coup, the Nadi airport business he transformed from a loss-making venture in 2003 into a profitable operation. Facing unemployment, Tuisolia established a restaurant business in Suva – the Hook and Chook – with his wife as a partner. Immediately FICAC pounced. The couple had briefly operated their restaurant prior to receiving a licence. Normally only a $20 council fine, the infringement suddenly became a major issue for the corruption body. When in late 2009 a magistrate pointed out the inappropriate use of resources being devoted to a case she believed outside FICAC's jurisdiction, she – like other magistrates who opposed FICAC submissions – had her contract terminated. In 2010, the High Court finally exposed the futility of its pursuit of Tuisolia but, of course, FICAC did not really seek judicial

---

162 *Fiji Times*, 20 May 2009; *fijilive*, 17 July 2009. This applied, for example, to marriage, access to alcohol and future voting. Previously, men could marry at 18 and women at 16.
163 crosbiew.blogspot.com, 19 July 2009.
164 stuff.co.nz, 6 January 2010.

resolution; rather it sought to wear perceived opponents down.[165] At the start of 2010 a new decree provided a different weapon to use against critics of the regime – the removal of pension rights. Rabuka became one of the first affected.[166]

Sometimes intimidation brought physically damaging consequences, as Iliesa Duvuloco and five nationalists discovered when they were arrested on 17 April for distributing pamphlets and severely beaten. George Speight's brother, Samisoni Tikoinasau, met a similar fate for distributing anti-government DVDs in early 2011.[167] Other former politicians, like Mere Samisoni, were harassed. At the end of 2011 she and four former politicians were detained for four days and charged with inciting political violence.[168] Trade unionists were also an easy target, although many union leaders had quietly supported the coup. But with Chaudhry's departure from government, a falling-out began which escalated in mid-2011 when news leaked of government proposals for an Essential National Industries Decree designed to depoliticise and curtail union activities in banking, telecommunications, utilities, broadcasting and aviation industries. At the urging of the Fiji Trades Union Congress (FTUC), unable to directly challenge the decree, the Australian Transport Workers Union briefly threatened industrial action, while the Australian Council of Trade Unions (ACTU) urged Australian businesses to stop importing Fiji-made garments. Both actions endangered two crucial industries. Exports in the garment sector were already down 25 per cent since 2009. A similar call for the United States to end preferential access for Fiji goods also threatened Pacific Fisheries Company's (PAFCO) tuna and Fiji Water's exports. Consequently the government moved quickly. Police broke up a FTUC meeting in August 2011 and banned further union meetings, even social events. It regularly arrested and detained union leaders like Felix Anthony and Daniel Urai, who did not always help their cause by appearing with anti-government coalitions in Australia that called for the government's dismissal. Towards the end of 2011, the government

---

165   www.coupfourandahalf.com, 7 January 2010; *fijilive*, 29 January 2010; *Fiji Times*, 2 November 2010. The High Court issued a permanent stay on most of the charges in mid-2010. Tuisolia was later acquitted of additional charges laid against him as CEO of Airports Fiji Ltd. They both moved to Manila to work for the ADB.

166   *fijilive*, 22 January 2010. The ban on pensions for former parliamentarians was lifted in May 2010, but this did not apply to Qarase who had received no pension after his removal in December 2006. Only in late 2014 did Qarase settle for back payment of $584,000 (*Fiji Sun*, 28 December 2014).

167   Amnesty International, *Fiji*, 2009, p. 23; *Fiji Times*, 25 March 2011.

168   *fijilive*, 4 January 2012.

reinforced its anger by turning back a five-member ACTU delegation. In September 2012, it asked an International Labour Organization (ILO) delegation to leave Fiji.[169]

The government had long viewed the human rights community as a thorn in its side because of its incessant public commentary. For example, in May 2011, FWCC director Shamima Ali claimed that it was all very well to issue decrees prohibiting violence against women, but she wanted to see the law actually implemented. Two months later, in a similar vein, the FWRM executive director, Buadromo, urged police to implement a gender sensitisation program before beginning campaigns against sexual offending. The government welcomed neither input. The Commissioner of Police, Brigadier General Ioane Naivalurua, told Buadromo to come into the ring and not talk from the outside: 'If she has nothing to offer, then she should shut up'. When she did not, they dragged her from an internal FWRM planning meeting and closed it down. But Buadromo was not easily cowed.[170]

For high-profile dissidents such as Methodist officials, harassment did not usually arrive with direct violence. In February 2010, 15 ministers were detained after disregarding an order to prevent known Taukeist church ministers, like Manasa Lasaro and Tomasi Kanailagi, attending its planned annual conference, the Bose Ko Viti, in August. General Secretary Rev. Tuikilakila Waqairatu warned Bainimarama of bloodshed should the conference not go ahead at Lomanikoro in Rewa, the home of Ro Teimumu Kepa, Marama Roko Tui Dreketi and head of the Burebasaga confederacy and a former SDL Education Minister. That action resulted in seven additional ministers and Kepa being detained and charged with contravening the *Public Order Act*, breaching PER and inciting public disorder. For some Fijians, Kepa's arrest demonstrated the risks inherent in using Church affairs to advance political agendas.[171] Bainimarama told the Church to refrain from politics and practice being peacemakers

---

169 *fijilive*, 21 July & 13 December 2011; www.coupfourandahalf.com, 8 December 2011; crosbiew.blogspot.com, 20 September 2012. Both were photographed at a Fiji Democracy and Freedom Movement rally in Sydney in July (www.coupfourandahalf.com, 18 July 2011).

170 *Pacific Scoop*, 13 May 2011; www.coupfourandahalf.com, 2 July 2011; *fijilive*, 24 August 2011.

171 www.coupfourandahalf.com, 22 & 23 July 2009. Her children posted a video of the event on YouTube. Crosbie Walsh memorably wrote: 'The prostrate bodies of slaves should no longer be used as rollers to launch [the Catholic] Ro Teimumu's or anyone else's waqa drua' (crosbiew.blogspot.com, 23 July 2009). Apparently the Vunivalu of Rewa, Ro Epeli Mataitini, agreed. He allegedly assisted 16 police officers to slip into Lomanikoro, a village accessible only by river, at night and arrest her (www.coupfourandahalf.com, 26 July 2009). Charges against Kepa were dropped in September 2010.

and nation-builders instead. When they continued to resist conditions placed on future meetings, he banned the Church from holding its annual conference, in all likelihood – he said – for the next five years.[172] Shortly after Bainimarama dealt a similarly decisive blow to another rebellious Fijian institution, the GCC; with the abrogation of the Constitution, he declared, it no longer existed.[173] He also announced Iloilo's retirement as president. In a further snub to the defunct GCC, he replaced Iloilo with the candidate the GCC had refused to endorse as his deputy, Ratu Epeli Nailatikau.[174]

There were, of course, other political issues left hanging by the Constitution's sudden abrogation, but the government was in no mood to be rushed. It announced a new National Dialogue Forum to replace the aborted PPDF in February 2010, stating that this time political parties or communally based organisations could not be represented. Additionally, participants would have to accept the charter, keep focused on the future, and have no criminal record or be facing criminal charges.[175] To make his intentions clear, Bainimarama announced that he would step down in 2014.[176] Consultations for a new constitution would not begin for another three years, however, but once developed the Constitution would mandate racial equality, incorporate the provisions of the People's Charter, and provide for a common name for all citizens to build social cohesion.[177] To that end a new office for a Strategic Framework for Change began implementing the Charter, amending the criteria for scholarships and directing that all race-based names of schools be changed. In September 2009, the Fiji School of Nursing announced that, henceforth, entry would be determined only by grades and geographical criteria, not race. A decree in 2010 officially changed the term used to describe indigenous

---

172 *fijilive*, 31 July 2009; Amnesty International, *Fiji*, 2009, p. 23. Circumstances repeated themselves in 2011 after the Church reappointed its current leadership for a further three years in defiance of government wishes for ministers facing charges to stand down (*Fiji Times*, 24 August 2011). The Church had to await the lifting of PER to hold its first annual general meeting in 2012.
173 *fijilive*, 2 August 2009. The declaration was belatedly formalised in March 2012 with the iTaukei Affairs Revocation Regulation Decree 2012.
174 www.coupfourandahalf.com, 28 July 2009; *fijilive*, 30 October 2009. Immediately after the abrogation, Bainimarama made Nailatikau Vice President. Memberships of troublesome provincial councils were sometimes purged, especially those – such as Rewa – that consistently opposed the coup or the charter (www.coupfourandahalf.com, 20 November 2011).
175 *Fiji Times*, 15 November 2009. The forum never met.
176 *Fiji Times*, 11 February 2010.
177 *fijilive*, 12 June & 2 August 2009.

Fijians to iTaukei.[178] Henceforth all Fiji's citizens were Fijians. But, on the constitution itself, there was little movement. The National People's Charter Advisory Council urged Bainimarama in May 2011 to fast-track constitutional development and to that end recommended the establishment of a Constitution Commission. At the Attorney-General's conference in December, Aiyaz Sayed-Khaiyum outlined the overriding principle behind future elections: one person, one vote, one value. Voter registration for national and municipal elections would be centralised. Electronic voting might be considered, but there would be no more ethnic voting.[179]

When Bainimarama introduced the Strategic Framework for Change on television in July 2009, he specifically focused on non-political issues, in particular land and government reform. The National People's Charter Advisory Committee would establish a monitoring centre to grade the progress of reform in all ministries and departments. A year later, Bainimarama announced that the military would align its corporate plan with the People's Charter and hold regular meetings with the Strategic Framework for Change Committee.[180] It is difficult to determine exactly how transformative these decisions were. With land, however, there were more than just progress reports. The *Agricultural Landlord and Tenant Act* (*ALTA*) disappeared under a new land-reform program, replaced by the *Native Land Trust Act* with leases up to 99 years possible.[181] Bainimarama promised to make the distribution of lease monies to landowners more equitable, and to make more land available for productive use, especially idle land. A land use bank would see to that.[182] He repeated his stand

---

178 *fijivillage*, 21 November 2009; *fijilive*, 8 September 2009. The Ministry for Indigenous Affairs now became the Ministry for iTaukei. The name change, first introduced in 2009, became mandatory in July 2010. Because the *i* is an article, the former description 'Fijians' or 'indigenous Fijians' is rendered as the Taukei from this point on in the text wherever the English 'the' is also used, or simply as Taukei where an article is not appropriate.

179 crosbiew.blogspot.com, 1 June, 12 July & 7 December 2011.

180 *fijilive*, 22 April 2010; crosbiew.blogspot.com, 22 December 2010.

181 *Fiji Times*, 14 January 2010.

182 Monies now went directly to *mataqali* and bypassed chiefs. In 2016, the government preserved $12.5 million of lease monies due to over 30,000 Taukei minors in a trust account. It claimed also that the rate of land leases renewals had risen from 50 per cent in 2006 to 65 per cent in 2010. The NLTB (now rebadged the iTaukei Land Trust Board or TLTB) wanted renewal rates to rise to 90 per cent (*Fiji Times*, 22 February 2011). Lease monies available for distribution also increased, from $24 million in 2000 to $64 million in 2014. In 2016, however, Biman Prasad cast doubt on these figures, claiming that between 2007 and 2014 only 59 per cent of leases were renewed compared with 57 per cent between 1997 and 2006 ('Another view of the sugar industry', *Fiji Times*, 30 July 2016).

when foreshadowing land reforms in December 2009. He would protect Taukei land ownership and tenant security, but he would also ensure the fair distribution of rental income. When the Commissioner Western addressed the Ba Provincial Council a year later with firmer details, the chiefs – principal beneficiaries of existing laws – were clearly unimpressed. The goose still laid golden eggs but no longer for them. Bainimarama wanted rural Taukei integrated into the modern economy, not serving the demands of the chiefly system.[183] The chiefs lost access to 30 per cent of lease monies. Except for the 15 per cent that went to the NLTB, later reduced to 10 per cent, all lease monies were now distributed to *mataqali* members equally.[184] A Land Use Decree in 2010 enabled unused native and crown land to be put into a land bank that the government could use to attract new investors. Sixty per cent of *mataqali* members had to agree, but the bait lay in their potential to earn 100 per cent of lease monies.[185]

Communications also formed part of his strategy, in particular its management. In December 2009, he formed a Central Agency for Roads, which merged the 13 different organisations previously responsible for overseeing Fiji's 9,000 kilometres of roads.[186] For Bainimarama, after three years of politicking, such changes in direction assumed new importance. The economy had to be kickstarted; constitutional change came a poor second in terms of priorities. He had told the media as much in the month before the Constitution's abrogation. Few understood his intent at the time.[187]

---

183 *fiji.gov.fj*, 1 July 2009; *Fiji Sun*, 2 December 2009; *Fiji Times*, 5 November 2010. Deductions from the TLTB fell from 15 per cent to 10 per cent over the course of 2013, adding further to the sums available for distribution to the *vanua*. The chiefs were unimpressed. 'We are the people's leaders,' claimed Nadroga paramount chief, Ratu Sakiusa Makutu, 'and we are not just here to sit idle and do nothing.' Bainimarama told the Naitasiri Provincial Council that the Taukei are educated and do not need chiefs or the GCC to make decisions for them. That the GCC had not met for five years had made no difference to the performance of provincial councils although the ending of payments to chiefs at least reduced conflicts over chiefly titles (*fijilive*, 22 & 25 March 2012).

184 These changes made a considerable difference to *mataqali* members. Sefanaia Sakai cites the example of the Yaya *mataqali* in Makare village that earned $1,600,000 from the Nepani government quarry. Previously its 77 individual members earned only $9,350 each from the lease, with the bulk of benefits accruing to their chief ($480,000) and the NLTB ($400,000). By 2014, with the TLTB proportion at 10 per cent and the special allocation to chiefs gone, individual *mataqali* members earned twice as much as before (Sefanaia Sakai, 'Insecurity of Taukei land as an issue in the 2014 general election: real threat or political gimmick?', in Vijay Naidu & Sandra Tarte (eds), '*No Ordinary Election': The Fiji General Election of 2014*. Special issue. *The Journal of Pacific Studies*, 35:2, 2015, p. 55).

185 Sefani Sakai, 'Native land policy in the 2014 elections', in Steven Ratuva & Stephanie Lawson, *The People Have Spoken*. Canberra: ANU Press, 2016, pp. 147–49.

186 *fijilive*, 2 December 2009.

187 *Fiji Times*, 6 March 2009. He told a press conference that 'All my government and officials need worry about now is our economy,' not electoral deadlines.

There were obvious reasons for Bainimarama's focus. His coup had robbed Fiji of any prospect of growth. The economy contracted sharply in 2007 and again in 2010, in part because of rising food and fuel costs. The global recession also impacted on tourism, although Australian markets were shielded and Fiji became more attractive as a tourist destination for cash-strapped New Zealanders. Cane farmers continued to experience declining returns (down 36 per cent since 2006), their predicament worsened by the loss of EU aid for sugar reforms. Over 3,000 growers abandoned the industry between 2006 and 2009, precipitating a 45 per cent collapse in sugar production by 2011.[188] In September 2009, the government scrapped the farmer-funded Sugar Cane Growers Council in a bid to reduce the influence of rival cane-grower bodies at a time when increased road charges bit into farmer pockets.[189] The Sugar Marketing Board also disappeared as part of a savings drive. Remittances were now the only bright spot in the economy, helping to keep the country afloat.[190]

Tight foreign exchange controls (which remained in place until late 2011) and a currency devaluation of 20 per cent swiftly followed the launch of the 'new legal order' in April, pushing inflation to over 9 per cent and shrinking economic growth to negative 1.4 per cent in 2009; hence the perceived importance for civil servants to retire early. Compulsory retirement forced nearly 2,500 civil servants out by mid-2009. By planning to reduce civil service numbers from 26,000 to 20,000, the government hoped to lower salary costs by 20 per cent. Ending the provision of housing for many public servants also cut costs. In addition, it planned to turn government departments, such as those dealing with water and government supplies, into statutory bodies in order to raise productivity.[191] Here too were shades of Rabuka's 'New Fijian' privatisation programs after 1987. Necessity drove uncomfortable

---

188 Dass, 'Ailing sugar industry', 2015.
189 *Fiji Times*, 9 September 2009. The NFP had earlier dominated the Sugar Cane Growers Council. But Chaudhry had sacked its chairman and councillors, put his own people in charge and disallowed fresh elections until 2010. The council was replaced in 2015 by a nine-member council comprising three government and six cane-producer nominees, still paid for by a levy on growers. The government proposed adding appointed reps from eight sugar districts in 2016. The Fiji Sugar Corporation (FSC) also struggled to repay a $85 million loan from the Indian Exim Bank and required injections of $164 million from the state. Works associated with the Qarase-era (2005) loan to upgrade the four FSC mills were three years behind schedule by 2010 and allegedly suffered from poor Indian workmanship and substandard equipment.
190 Between 2007 and 2010 remittances probably earned Fiji some $400 million per annum, surpassing both sugar and tourism as the sector with the greatest impact on the Fiji economy (B Prasad, 'Growth must result in more for us', *Fiji Times*,12 September 2015).
191 *fijilive*, 15 July & 31 December 2009; *Sydney Morning Herald*, 10 January 2012. Critics argued that early retirement compromised the quality of education (*fijilive*, 2 September 2009).

similarities. A 3 per cent increase in bus fares pushed ECREA to collect 20,000 signatures demanding reduced fares for school children. Stung, Bainimarama granted free bus travel for school children[192] and included in the budget for 2010 a new food voucher program for the elderly and disabled, adding bus concessions for them also in 2011. Additionally, squatter assistance and relocation programs, housing-rehabilitation loans, improved family assistance, free text books and caps on school fees projected government resolve to assist the poor. A new low-cost housing project for nearly 2,000 families began with Chinese support at Tacirua East in Suva.[193] It would never be enough. By early 2010 new estimates placed 45 per cent of the population in poverty and the government applied for an IMF loan of $1 billion to pay for all its proposed civil service, public enterprise, FNPF, land and agricultural reforms.[194] By the close of the year, government debt and liabilities comprised 92 per cent of GDP, far above the 60 per cent level recommended by economists. To compensate, the government increased VAT from 12.5 to 15 per cent, but lifted its imposition on basic food items. The end result could only be less growth and more pain.[195]

The state of the economy demonstrated the dangers facing the new legal order. With emergency regulations extended every month and imposing indefinite censorship, with critics once more arrested, detained, prevented from leaving the country or forbidden to speak at conferences, it was hard to see how the government truly believed that it enabled a 'stable socio-political platform conducive for nation-building initiatives'.[196] No news

---

192   crosbiew.blogspot.com, 9 September 2009; *fijilive*, 26 November & 16 October 2009.

193   *fijilive*, 13 September 2010.

194   *fijilive*, 20 April 2010; crosbiew.blogspot.com, 14 April 2010. The loan was never taken and the government obtained the required finances at greater cost from alternative sources. FNPF lost $327 million on its investment in the Natadola and Momi tourism developments, forcing it to reassess the viability of its fund, in particular the subsidy given pensioners by current members. In 2012, it cut the conversion rate for its pensions from 15 per cent to 8.7 per cent (G Rashbrooke, 'Reform of the Fiji National Provident Fund', www.actuaries.org/HongKong2012/Papers/MBR12_Rashbrooke.pdf).

195   Kevin Barr argued in a letter that the *Fiji Times* refused to publish that devaluation and delays in raising basic wages and VAT increases would have negative impacts, particularly for those living below the poverty line (www.coupfourandahalf.com, 1 February 2012). In August 2012, he resigned as chair of the Wages Council in frustration at the government's consistent failure to implement wages orders since 2008 (*Fiji Times*, 18 August 2012).

196   *fijilive*, 21 July 2009; Bainimarama's address to the Asia Pacific Institute for Broadcasting Development Conference in Nadi. Chaudhry attacked Bainimarama's thinking, arguing that it isn't possible to just shelve resolution of the political crisis for three years to focus on economic development. Only a stable inclusive democratic political environment would restore investor confidence (www.coupfourandahalf.com, 15 July 2009). The IMF agreed. A visiting team in 2011 warned that medium growth prospects would remain weak without improvements in the political situation (*Sydney Morning Herald*, 14 January 2012).

is not always good news, and silence is not necessarily golden; certainly not for investors pondering the potential Fiji offered. If anything PER weakened confidence and provided the diverse opposition a platform on which they could agree. At the forefront of this contest lay the media and foreign governments. Neither survived their exchanges well.

Decreeing compliance and respect

PER immediately hit the media hardest. ABC and New Zealand journalists were deported. Radio Australia's FM relay stations in Fiji were closed. PACNEWS relocated to Brisbane. The newly promoted information permanent secretary, Lt Col Neumi Leweni, warned media to comply with directives and not focus on the negative. PER gave him authority to revoke the licences of any media outlet that failed to comply.[197] To assist implementing indefinite censorship, censors from the Ministry of Information and police were stationed in news offices to filter stories. The newspapers protested. The *Daily Post* published a pointedly nonsensical article about the amazing feat of a man getting onto a bus; the *Fiji Times* printed blank pages. Fiji TV cancelled its regular evening news. They were told to desist. Articles about popular protests in countries like Thailand were also denied. Radio talkback shows had to submit topics of discussion to the Ministry for Information one week in advance.[198] In late 2009, economist and University of the South Pacific (USP) dean of Business, Biman Prasad, cautioned the government while launching a special journal issue on the media:

> Because of censorship, people are turning to blogs to get their news. These blogs are not governed by any rules or standards. People are being misled and are being incited. Government will have more legitimacy if it allows the media to operate freely and independently.[199]

---

197 *fijilive*, 13 May 2009.

198 *Daily Post*, 15 April 2009; www.coupfourandahalf.com, 29 July 2009 & 17 February 2000.

199 www.coupfourandahalf.com, 14 October 2009. Crosbie Walsh argued that anti-government blogs recorded 5,000 visits per day, over 1,000 from within Fiji (crosbiew.blogspot.com, 12 December 2010). The military also relied upon the blogs for information. Solely on the basis of information on various websites, Driti and Lt Col Jone Kalouniwai (head of Military Intelligence) told Bainimarama in September 2010 that he should sack Aiyaz Sayed-Khaiyum because of his alleged dealings. Bainimarama told them to come back when they had evidence (*Fijileaks*, 21 November 2013).

The government did not respond. Amnesty International believed media censorship existed solely to hide the government's actions and breaches of human rights, and to suppress critical comment.[200] Already prior to September 2009, 20 journalists had been intimidated by detention and the *fijilive* website temporarily taken down after it posted pictures of a bomb scare in Suva.[201]

Fiji news websites had proliferated after the late 1990s. Their presence made a significant difference to reporting during the 2000 coup compared with 1987, when Rabuka could more easily control the dissemination of news nationally and internationally by simply closing down media outlets or imposing strict controls on their operation. All international communications went through Fiji International Telecommunications Ltd (FINTEL) and could be monitored or stopped. But automated telecommunications and the internet rendered these measures obsolete, as the interim government discovered immediately after December 2006 when a plethora of new blog sites emerged, many drawing on rumour and gossip and being, in the main, hostile to what they saw as an illegal military junta running roughshod over the wishes of Fiji's people.[202] Hence the government began targeting individuals thought to be contributing to hostile blogs.

When, in late May 2009, the pro-regime *Real Fiji News* website accused lawyers of being behind *Raw Fiji News*, police again detained Richard Naidu and Jon Apted, along with Qarase's lawyer, Tevita Fa, seizing their computers and copying their hard drives for forensic examination.[203]

---

200 Amnesty International, *Fiji*, 2009, pp. 16, 19 & 21.

201 www.coupfourandahalf.com, 28 May 2009. It would be taken down again in August 2010 and its editor, Richard Naidu (the journalist, not the lawyer), detained when it leaked news of the end of Police Commissioner Teleni's tenure ahead of a government announcement (www.coupfourandahalf. com, 30 July 2010). Foreign media were also targeted; the ABC's Sean Dorney, Fairfax's Michael Field and NZ TV One's Barbara Deaver were banned from Fiji (www.coupfourandahalf.com, 13 April 2009).

202 Raw Fiji News (www.matavuvale.com/forum/topics/raw-fiji-news-your-live), Soli Vakasama (solivakasama.wordpress.com), Stuck in Fiji Mud (stuckinfijimud.blogspot.com.au/), Fiji Today (fijitoday. wordpress.com/), Tears for Fiji (tearsforfiji.blogspot.com.au/), fijicoup2006 (www.fijicoupin2006.com/), Luvei ni Viti (solivakasamablog.wordpress.com/2009/04/21/luvei-viti-children-of-fiji/), Discombulated bubu (discombobulatedbubu.blogspot.com/), Intelligentsiya (intelligentsiya.blogspot.com.au/) and coupfourpointfive (www.coupfourandahalf.com/) were but a few of the critical websites. Others like the Graham Davis's grubsheet (grubsheet.blogspot.com.au/) and Crosbie Walsh's site *Fiji: The Way It Was, Is and Can Be* (crosbiew.blogspot.com), were more nuanced. Additional sites belonged to media outlets, academic programs and journals, and individuals. It may have been a jungle, misleading for the unwary, but it was certainly an improvement on the media poverty Rabuka induced and that Bainimarama was powerless to emulate.

203 *Australian*, 21 May 2009.

Smart phones had yet to make an impact in Fiji, but Fiji's citizens took to the internet with gusto.[204] If sites could not be taken down (and some sites were blocked), then restricting access could be tackled more conventionally. In late May 2009, the government announced that internet cafes (along with amusement centres and billiard rooms) could only operate from 6 am to 5 pm. Restrictions applied to other businesses also.[205] But, still, the websites persisted, even attempting to organise by blog a surprise anti-government demonstration in late 2010 by riding on the coat tails of an approved women's and children's human rights gathering in Suva's central Sukuna Park. A twitchy government banned both. But, as Crosbie Walsh, now a blogger himself, pointed out, this was no longer simply a law and order matter but a propaganda war. Crude and clumsy government responses to challenges did little to win the hearts and minds of the people it claimed to be working for.[206]

There were other, similarly unsubtle, ways that the pesky media could be dealt with. Ministries were ordered to cancel advertising contracts with the *Fiji Times* in September and not publish notices in the paper. In November 2009, a National Spectrum Decree cancelled ownership of all radio and television frequencies. Existing frequencies used by stations were deemed temporary, subject to reallocation by the Attorney-General as he saw fit without compensation and without recourse to the courts. The decree potentially advantaged the state-owned Fiji Broadcasting Corporation (FBC), whose CEO was the Attorney-General's brother, Riyaz Sayed-Khaiyum. When talks were later held on a new media decree, the Australian News Ltd–owned *Fiji Times* and the Yasana Holdings–owned Fiji TV were excluded for not recognising the contemporary legal system and the status of government.[207] Worse was to come. A new

---

204   About 34 per cent of Fiji's population were internet users by 2014, and nearly 30 per cent or 260,000 were Facebook users (Jope Tarai, Romitesh Kant, Glen Finau, Jason Titifanue, 'Political social media campaigning in Fiji's 2014 elections', in Naidu & Tarte, '*No Ordinary Election*', 2015, p. 92). Broadband usage increased fourfold and mobile phone usage increased 7 per cent per annum between 2007 and 2014 (*Fiji Sun*, 26 November 2016).

205   www.coupfourandahalf.com, 26 May 2009. Only essential businesses (pharmacies, bakeries and service stations) could open until 9 pm, for the cost of a $20 weekly permit. Service stations and bakeries could also remain open after 9 pm.

206   crosbiew.blogspot.com, 12 December 2010.

207   crosbiew.blogspot.com, 8 September 2009; *Australian*, 21 November 2009; *Fiji Times*, 17 December 2009. Yasana Holdings owned Fiji TV on behalf of Taukei provincial councils. It also owned PNG's EMTV.

Singapore-inspired Media Industry Development Decree came out in early April 2010 for discussion and mandated that all media organisations had to be 90 per cent locally owned. The implications for the News Corporation *Fiji Times* and for the 51 per cent Australian-owned *Daily Post* were obvious.[208]

The government had long claimed that, once the media decree came into force, PER would go. Now critics understood why: a Media Industry Development Authority (MIDA) would enforce self-censorship as well as oversee media and cross-media ownership rules, a Media Tribunal would deal with complaints, and all stories over 50 words had to carry the author's name. Penalties for non-compliance could go as high as $100,000 for individuals and $500,000 for organisations.[209] Immediately critics pounced. The CCF claimed the new rules violated the principles of the People's Charter, while Auckland journalism professor David Robie claimed it would open 'the door to vindictive abuse in a climate of dictatorship and the singling out of media organisations that do not toe the media line'. The blog site *coupfourpointfive* believed it spelled the end of investigative journalism of the kind that brought down Chaudhry.[210] Not everyone agreed. The Pacific Islands News Association (PINA) thought it too early to adopt a position, while former *Daily Post* editor Thakur Ranjit Singh lamented the failure of mainstream media to tell the real story behind the coup and thought Bainimarama only wanted journalists to take greater responsibility for shaping a new modern Fiji.[211] Indeed, whether they wanted to or not, the media had to comply. The decree came into force at the end of June 2010 and, by the close of the following September, the *Fiji Times* had been sold to Mahendra Patel, a long-serving member of its board and owner of the Motibhai group of companies, who in 2011 would be sentenced to one year's jail for abuse

---

208 The cross-media rules also created uncertainty. Hari Punja owned shares in both Communications Fiji and Fiji TV while William Parkinson's Communications Fiji also operated stations in Papua New Guinea (*Australian*, 5 July 2010).

209 *fijilive*, 8 April 2010. Professor Subramani became chair of MIDA with Matai Akauola (PINA manager), Christopher Pryde (Solicitor General), Aselika Uluilakeba (children's representative), Peni Moore (women's representative) and Jimaima Schultz (consumers' representative).

210 www.coupfourandahalf.com, 9 & 10 April 2010.

211 www.coupfourandahalf.com, 10 April 2010; *Pacific Scoop*, 15 April 2010. PINA's response saw a rival Pasifika Media Association attack it for being under Bainimarama's spell (*fijilive*, 22 August 2010). CCF director Akuila Yabaki claimed that Bainimarama was obsessed with the potential for elements of previous coups to overthrow him and feared a return to 2000 circumstances and popular uprisings; hence PER and new media laws (*Sydney Morning Herald*, 14 January 2014).

of office while chair of PostFiji.[212] It remained to be seen, however, whether the Media Industry Development Decree would produce the compliant and respectful media the government craved.

Diplomatic cold war

Certainly, compliance and respect were not forthcoming from many foreign governments and international organisations. The Australian Foreign Minister, Stephen Smith, set the tone after the abrogation of the Constitution by immediately declaring the regime 'a military dictatorship'[213] and, with New Zealand, lobbied the United Nations to cease using Fiji peacekeepers.[214] Because Fiji had failed to nominate an election date by 1 May, the condition laid down by the PIF at its Port Moresby meeting in January, it faced automatic suspension from the regional body. Aiyaz Sayed-Khaiyum seemed certain it would not happen. 'I admire his optimism,' NZ Foreign Minister Murray McCully quipped. Fiji was suspended, the first such suspension in the regional body's 38-year history. Bainimarama immediately asked for a summit with Australia and New Zealand. They refused. Bainimarama had used the same strategy prior to expelling the NZ High Commissioner in 2007, hoping – according to *Wikileaks* – to show Australia and New Zealand as the problem and drive a wedge between the two countries and PIF members. The British High Commissioner told McCully 'that the time had come to push Fiji down the list of priority until conditions deteriorated sufficiently to allow

---

212 *Australian*, 9 October 2010; *Fiji Times*, 13 April 2011. The change in ownership brought in a new publisher, Dallas Swinstead (previously with the *Herald Weekly* and *Age* in Melbourne and *Fiji Times* editor in the late 1970s), and a new editor, Fred Wesley. Existing editor Netani Rika resigned temporarily to allow the paper to begin on a fresh note. Patel appealed his sentence, lost an appeal in 2014 and failed to return from Sydney for sentencing (*Fiji Sun*, 25 November 2014; *Australian*, 25 November 2014).

213 *Fiji Times*, 14 April 2009.

214 *Fiji Times*, 17 April 2009. This was more than a symbolic matter. Fiji had some 578 soldiers, police and military observers on UN missions in Sinai, Israel–Syria, Iraq and Sudan in 2009. In late April, Australian Prime Minister Kevin Rudd implied that lobbying had been successful but, at the start of May, 12 Fiji police left for Darfur (*fijilive*, 1 May 2009). In September, UN Secretary General Ban Ki Moon told NZ Prime Minister John Key that reductions in Fijian numbers would only apply to future operations (*Fiji Times*, 26 October 2009). However, fresh Fijian peacekeepers were still being sent to Iraq in October (*Australian*, 4 November 2009) and, by 2011, 1,252 were engaged in Iraq (275), Sinai (994) and Sudan (six), one third of the RFMF's regular troops (*fijilive*, 25 February 2011).

for improved engagement'.[215] If only it was so simple. Within a short time, Bainimarama met a 25-member Chinese delegation at the Shangri-La Fijian Resort in Sigatoka to discuss Chinese investment and, in early 2010, the Chinese ambassador described Fiji as a paradise for investors under the leadership of the Bainimarama government.[216]

The mutually convenient love affair had been long in the making. China sought to use Fiji's apparent isolation as a way to demonstrate its usefulness to the Pacific. Premier Wen Jiabao's early plans to raise China's stakes in Fiji had become mired in the turmoil of 2006 but, in early 2009, then Vice President Xi Jinping visited Fiji, much to the chagrin of Australia, which attempted unsuccessfully to prevent him transiting through Australia. Xi's visit consolidated the growing links between the two countries: direct air services, relaxed visa regulations and direct shipping links. Fiji now looked north, not south or west. It appointed Isikeli Mataitoga its first ambassador to Russia. It began steps to join the Non-Alignment Movement and formed new relationships with 17 countries, including Cuba. In 2011, it opened embassies in Indonesia, South Africa and Brazil.[217]

Fiji's foreign policy assertiveness strengthened its hand against Australian and New Zealand pressure. Bainimarama told Mark Davis on an episode of SBS's *Dateline* entitled 'Perfectly Frank' that he could not simply give in and have an election to please Australia and New Zealand: 'We're trying to change the mindset of the people from racial issues that developed in the last ten years to what we want to take Fiji to – equal suffrage.' Change is not an easy thing to do; it takes time, he argued. Only ending the race card 'will stop all coups'.[218] But, like the PIF, the Commonwealth Ministerial Action Group refused to listen. It urged Fiji to reactivate the PPDF process and inform it by September of its intention to hold an election before

---

215 www.coupfourandahalf.com, 29 December 2010. Suspension also meant that Fiji was barred from participating in the Pacific Island Countries Trade Agreement (PICTA) and PACER regional trade discussions, something Fiji, as the second largest economy in the Pacific after Papua New Guinea, saw as both counterproductive and illegal. The Forum promised only to brief Fiji officials after trade talks (*fijilive*, 7 & 8 August 2009).

216 crosbiew.blogspot.com, 13 April 2010. Chinese investment comprised 37 per cent of foreign direct investment by 2014, compared with only 2.9 per cent in 2009 (*Fiji Times*, 30 October 2014).

217 www.coupfourandahalf.com, 28 April 2011; crosbiew.blogspot.com, 17 August 2009; *Fiji Sun*, 26 May 2010; *fijilive*, 25 September 2011.

218 *fijilive*, 27 July 2009; www.sbs.com.au/news/dateline/story/perfectly-frank.

October 2010.[219] Bainimarama did not and Fiji was fully suspended from the Commonwealth on 2 September 2009. 'Two democratic, non-racist institutions oppose a military regime and so unwittingly continue to extend support for undemocratic, racist policies,' Crosbie Walsh observed, and 'undermine the wobbly efforts of the military regime (sic!) to impose democratic non-racist policies'.[220]

In some respects the Suva-based PIF came out worst from these suspensions, not Fiji. The divisions – apparent since 2006 – now became raw. Bainimarama accused Samoa's Prime Minister Tuilaepa of trying to engineer the removal of the PIF secretariat to Apia[221] and criticised Australia and New Zealand – who funded the PIF – of exercising undue pressure on its Pacific member states. The PIF remained important to Fiji. Its former director of economic governance, Roman Grynberg, claimed the PIF is part of what makes Fiji the centre of the Pacific. Yet Bainimarama's beef was not with the PIF per se but with Australia and New Zealand, although at the time the distinction became blurred.[222] Bainimarama did have, however, a means to lobby among the Pacific states that bypassed the PIF. That way took the form of the Melanesian Spearhead Group (MSG), which comprised the three largest Pacific states (Papua New Guinea, Solomon Islands and Vanuatu). In July, Vanuatu supported Bainimarama's roadmap and promised to lobby for Fiji's right to remain in the PIF and have a place at Pacific trade talks. In October, Papua New Guinea also promised to lobby Australia and New Zealand on Fiji's behalf.[223] It was a small opening and Bainimarama and his new

---

219 *fijilive*,1 August 2009. When Sir Paul Reeves visited Fiji as the Commonwealth envoy a week later, he emphasised that the Commonwealth still intended to assist Fiji return to democracy (www.coupfourandahalf.com, 10 September 2009).

220 crosbiew.blogspot.com, 2 September 2009.

221 Tuilaepa invited Bainimarama to Samoa for a chat but Bainimarama wanted Tuilaepa to come to Fiji instead; 'It might change the way he sees us', adding 'don't come alone. Bring your friend Toke Talagi with you'. At the Cairns PIF meeting in August, the Niuean premier had called on Fiji's people to rise up against Bainimarama (*Pacific Scoop*, 12 September 2009).

222 *Islands Business*, January 2010. This did not stop Fiji pressuring the Forum secretariat by delaying a work visa to its new director of economic governance, Australian Chakriya Bowman, in January 2010.

223 *fijilive*, 11 July & 16 October 2009.

Foreign Minister, Ratu Inoke Kubuabola,[224] took care to cultivate it, hinting that the MSG might open its next meeting – which Fiji would chair – to other Forum island states.[225]

Fiji also sought to assuage EU sensitivities, telling Brussels that the government would decree parts of the 1997 Constitution dealing with the rule of law, human rights and democracy. The European Union responded, promising substantial dialogue and a new bilateral agreement. And Fiji reminded the United States of its current and past support for American initiatives in Iraq and the Sinai and of its role in the Solomon Islands.[226] But it could do little to make Australia or New Zealand adopt a more conciliatory approach. Not surprisingly, in the absence of economic sanctions – which both countries and the European Union claimed not to be contemplating – the focus of the Fiji Government's anger fell once more on the issue of travel bans and, in particular, their impact on Fiji's ability to staff its judiciary.

The Chief Justice, Anthony Gates, claimed that Australian travel bans made it difficult for him to recruit judges from Sri Lanka, which he had toured in August. Most appointees had to endure lectures from Australian High Commission officers in Colombo about the dangers in accepting positions in Fiji. Australia claimed it approved their visas, but apparently failed to tell the Sri Lankans, who withdrew their applications and flew, instead, via Korea to avoid transiting Australia. Gates regarded Australian interference as an attempt to undermine Fiji's judiciary and he took to Bainimarama a tape that one Sri Lankan judge had made of a conversation with Australian officials.

NZ travel bans also concerned Gates. In October, Justice Anjala Wati applied to the New Zealand High Commission for a humanitarian visa. Her baby needed urgent eye surgery. Its response indicated that the request fell within 'the parameters of New Zealand's travel sanctions'. An appeal brought no relief. Only when Gates raised the matter in the media did New Zealand relent and offer a visa, but 'subject to absurd restrictions' such as

---

224 The former High Commissioner to Papua New Guinea and ambassador to Japan appeared a strange choice as Foreign Minister because of his background. A former secretary to the South Pacific Bible Society, he had gained notoriety as a founding member of the Taukei Movement, which supported Rabuka's 1987 coups. He served also as a cabinet minister in Rabuka's governments in the 1990s and became leader of the SVT in 1999. He again served in Qarase's interim government in 2000 and 2001, before losing his seat to CAMV.
225 www.coupfourandahalf.com, 2 November 2009.
226 *fijilive*, 19 November 2009.

'no shopping'.[227] 'If you bully there will be some retaliation,' Bainimarama later told NZTV's *Sunday* program. He accused New Zealand of trying to destroy first its economy and now its judiciary.[228] And retaliate he did by immediately expelling New Zealand's acting Deputy High Commissioner Todd Cleaver and Australia's High Commissioner James Batley, and simultaneously recalling Fiji's envoys in the two countries. In Suva, Brij Lal told the ABC that Bainimarama wanted to be seen as standing up to two bullies in the region and defending Fiji's sovereignty and honour. But the real issue, he said, concerned the integrity and impartiality of the judiciary. The military seized him, interrogated him at the QEB, and deported him.[229] Contrary views were not permitted.

Bainimarama immediately offered talks with Australia and New Zealand, as he had done before. He held meetings with EU representatives to demonstrate the value of dialogue. An IMF team visited the country in early December. The United Nations still received Fiji troops for peacekeeping duties and China maintained its aid program. Australia is 'pissing in the wind', the *Sydney Morning Herald* quoted *Fiji Times* editor, Netani Rika. Australia and New Zealand might have had more success had they done more earlier to demonstrate the difference between democracy 'and the form of government we have had for the last 40 years', he said. Instead their silence now posed as 'complicity in the problems we face'.[230]

Fiji needs incentives to democratise, not punishment, the former Constitutional Review Committee chair and now Commonwealth envoy Paul Reeves remarked. Australia's parliamentary secretary for the Pacific islands, Duncan Kerr, agreed. In August 2009, he met US officials privately to seek American support for re-engagement with Fiji. He believed Australia close to exhausting its diplomatic options on Fiji with little apparent effect. Forcing economic collapse on Fiji would only cost Australia dearly and weaken other Pacific states as well. Australia – Kerr added – had secured Fiji's suspension from the PIF but did not know what to do next. Bainimarama could not simply give up power, as Australia wanted, 'as he would end up at the mercy of his enemies'. Either find a safe

---

227 *Fiji Times*, 4 November 2009; *Pacific Scoop*, 3 November 2009.
228 www.coupfourandahalf.com, 16 November 2009.
229 www.coupfourandahalf.com, 4 & 5 November 2009; *Australian*, 4 November 2009. Two months later the government completed its revenge on the outspoken Brij Lal. It denied his wife, Padma Lal, a former advisor to the PIF secretariat but then working in Fiji for the International Union for Conservation of Nature, entry into Fiji and declared her a prohibited immigrant.
230 *fijilive*, 2 December 2009.

way for him to exit or do business with him.[231] His colleagues, however, insisted on maintaining Australia's hardline stance and Kerr resigned as parliamentary secretary in mid-December. Prime Minister Rudd preferred to look north to Asia and – in the eyes of many Pacific leaders – had little time for them.[232] He did not replace Kerr. Two weeks later, New Zealand Prime Minister John Key took up Kerr's mantle, offering to re-engage. Bainimarama's perseverance appeared to have paid off, but the cold war was far from over. He claimed only to be encouraged by New Zealand's change in stance.[233]

Nonetheless, Bainimarama immediately tested the waters, announcing in January 2010 his intention to appoint Lt Col Neumi Leweni, formerly military attaché to China and permanent secretary for information but subject to Australasian travel bans, Fiji's new High Commissioner to New Zealand. Two weeks later, New Zealand and Australia's foreign ministers met to discuss Fiji and agreed to reopen their missions but not appoint heads of mission. Fiji had first to learn how to agree to disagree, 'to conduct a good civilised diplomatic conversation'.[234] Foreign Minister Kubuabola met briefly with McCully and Smith and received their determination. Leweni would not be going. Worse followed.

Fiji had hoped to regain the initiative when it chaired the next MSG meeting at Natadola in late July 2010. Bainimarama called it MSG Plus, having invited 10 other Pacific states to attend in a clear challenge to the Forum. But his ambitions were trumped by Australia, which had rapidly increased aid to Vanuatu. Somewhat undiplomatically, Australia announced that the MSG meeting would not take place, leaving a weak-looking Vanuatu Prime Minister, Edward Natapei, to claim that the MSG had been cancelled because Fiji failed to restore democracy. An angry Bainimarama told Auckland Radio Tarana that such constant interfering

231 *Age*, 19 December 2010.

232 *Islands Business*, March 2010. Peter Thomson, a former Fiji diplomat, had advocated a similar position since 2006: Australia was punishing Fiji without achieving anything and destabilising the region. He returned to Fiji in 2010 and became Fiji's very successful permanent representative to the United Nations (*Australian*, 22 July 2010).

233 *fijivillage*, 4 December 2009; *fijilive*, 23 December 2009; www.coupfourandahalf.com, 24 December 2009.

234 www.coupfourandahalf.com, 5 February 2010. Steven Ratuva had counselled Fiji not to act triumphantly but to pursue 'quiet diplomacy' in its cold war with Australia and New Zealand. Win-win, not attack and counterattack strategies were more likely to succeed (*Pacific Scoop*, 5 February 2010). Bainimarama tried to seize the moral high ground after the event by claiming Australasian High Commissioners could not be reappointed until travel sanctions ended (www.coupfourandahalf.com, 25 February 2010).

might make Fiji unprepared for elections in 2014. To drive home his point, he expelled Australia's acting High Commissioner, Sarah Roberts, for 'unfriendly acts' and for interfering in Fiji's internal affairs.[235] And he went ahead with his Natadola meeting, renaming it 'Engaging with the Pacific'. In all, 11 of the 14 PIF nations came, including the largest states – Papua New Guinea, Solomon Islands and Vanuatu. Was this a new south-west Pacific bloc in the making, one that excluded Polynesia and particularly Samoa? Bainimarama kept everyone guessing. He had denied Forum representatives the right to observe progress towards democratic change in Fiji, and he now temporarily suspended Fiji from MSG meetings. He told his guests that it was time to move beyond 'the traditional sphere of influence dictated to by our colonial past by certain metropolitan powers'.[236] And, as if to demonstrate that intent, he travelled next to the Shanghai Trade Fair where he declared that Fiji should ditch its ties with Australia and turn to China for support. Fiji had already relaxed immigration rules for Chinese students and tourists; now it announced that Rabuka's former Finance Minister, Jim Ah Koy, would head Fiji's mission in Beijing. China promised a government delegation for Fiji's 40th anniversary of independence on 10 October 2010, the auspicious triple 10. And it agreed to fund a MSG secretariat in Port Vila.[237]

Bainimarama was on a roll. He wanted both Australia and New Zealand out of the PIF. When Key offered to bring Fiji back into the regional Pacific Agreement on Closer Economic Relations (PACER) trade talks, Fiji demurred. PACER was no longer a promising instrument for development. It had been corrupted by regional politics. If Fiji came back, it would be on its own terms.[238] With Australia and New Zealand's strategy for dealing with Fiji in tatters and with no new approach forthcoming, Steven Ratuva believed fragmentation now threatened the Pacific's regional bodies.[239] Indeed, when PIF leaders met in Vila in August 2010, many were absent and sent senior officials instead; even Australia's new Prime Minister, Julia Gillard, failed to attend. The MSG, however, patched up its differences and, at the long-delayed meeting in Honiara, Vanuatu handed over leadership to Fiji after a reconciliation ceremony.[240] It was time for

---

235 *Sydney Morning Herald*, 13 July 2010; *Australian*, 14 July 2010.
236 *fijilive*, 23 July 2010. Bainimarama mooted the idea of a Regional Police Academy.
237 *Age*, 12 August 2010; *fijilive*, 22 August 2010.
238 www.coupfourandahalf.com, 10 August 2010.
239 *Fiji Times*, 9 August 2010.
240 *fijilive*, 15 December 2010. It helped that a vote of no confidence in the Vanuatu parliament had seen Natapei replaced as prime minister by Sato Kilman in early December.

Australia and New Zealand to step back and allow Pacific countries to take the lead, former New Zealand diplomat, Gerald McGhie, argued.[241] Kerr stepped out of the shadows to urge Australia to focus on practical steps to help Fiji address poverty, land reform and the plight of the sugar industry. It should get Fiji back into trade talks, and not focus on the democracy agenda to the detriment of all else.[242] Fiji responded positively. Solo Mara, now permanent secretary for foreign affairs, claimed Fiji was willing to re-engage with Australia and New Zealand. But the two countries had first to treat Fiji with respect and recognise its government.[243]

Relations with the United States had, of necessity, to be handled more delicately. Fiji had enacted a comprehensive anti-human trafficking law in its Crimes Decree, which replaced the old Penal Code, and begun a series of training programs on trafficking for law-enforcement officers. These measures assisted to reduce its risk level for human trafficking sufficiently to remove US Congress mandated sanctions on approvals for loans needed from the World Bank, the IMF or the ADB.[244] These were important safeguards for Fiji, but the United States itself sent mixed signals. It clearly wanted to resist the build-up of Chinese interests in the Pacific and its demonstration of intent to stay with Fiji took shape in the form of a large new embassy complex in Suva's Tamavua Heights. The Chinese had also constructed an embassy complex on the waterfront at Nasese. In late September 2010, the United States signalled its intention to re-engage with Fiji but, almost immediately, Secretary of State Hillary Clinton announced that she intended to work with Asia and Australia to persuade Fiji to introduce democratic government. Bainimarama responded quietly. The United States should work directly with Fiji instead.[245]

For the RFMF, this hardening stance was particularly worrying. The intended withdrawal of US troops from both Iraq and Afghanistan promised greater opportunities for Fiji soldiers on UN and civil contracts, but only if the United States did not oppose their presence.[246] US travel bans also impacted on senior Fiji officials, including the Chief Justice,

241 crosbiew.blogspot.com, 9 October 2010.
242 *Radio Australia*, 9 November 2010.
243 *fijilive*, 29 November 2010.
244 *Islands Business*, July 2010.
245 *fijilive*, 30 September 2010; www.coupfourandahalf.com, 8 November 2010; *fijilive*, 9 November 2010.
246 J. Baledrokadroka, 'Showtime as the US call's Bainimarama's bluff', www.coupfourandahalf.com, 8 November 2010.

the Attorney-General and the Solicitor General who had travel visas to the United States denied in 2010. Not until the next year did Fiji get the United States to rethink the issue of visas for UN and multilateral fora. Even the United Nations could be problematic. It blocked Driti from leading an Iraqi peacekeeping mission. Fiji recalled Berenado Vunibobo as its permanent representative at the United Nations in April 2010 and replaced him with Peter Thomson, hoping for more active promotion of Fiji's interests in New York.[247] The wider international context could never be taken for granted, no matter Fiji's mostly pyrrhic victories against Australia and New Zealand. But Bainimarama could hardly complain. After all, he alone had chosen to ride the tiger. And he appeared to be riding well.

In March 2011, the long-awaited MSG summit took place in Suva, funded by the Chinese. It gave Bainimarama everything he wanted, recognition of the Charter and the roadmap. The meeting included representation from Indonesia and Luxembourg, the latter lobbying for a seat on the Security Council 'in Australia's backyard', according to Graham Davis. 'Bainimarama is getting the last laugh,' he added.[248] Foreign Minister Rudd, already lobbying in Africa for Australia's own tilt at a seat, remained unmoved; he would not legitimise 'what has been a very ugly military coup'. He maintained the same line at the Commonwealth Ministerial Action Group in London during May, relenting only on Fiji's engagement with the United Nations as peacekeepers.[249] So too PIF in September 2011, when it met in Auckland and refused to alter sanctions against Fiji but agreed to reconsider Fiji's participation in PACER talks. But, again, New Zealand had second thoughts. Foreign Minister McCully pondered allowing Fiji officials to attend the 2012 Rugby World Cup in Auckland in return for concessions. 'We should hold our nerve,' the *NZ Herald* counselled; it just might give Bainimarama 'one more chance to make us look foolish'.[250]

247 *fijilive*, 14 January & 8 December 2011.
248 grubsheet.blogspot.com, 28 March 2011.
249 *Australian*, 10 May 2011. Kubuabola claimed that there could be no real re-engagement with Australia as long as Rudd remained in office.
250 *NZ Herald*, 4 April 2011.

The Lowy Institute's Fiji poll, released in September, added to that concern. It found that 66 per cent of Fijians supported Bainimarama, 39 per cent strongly; hence the Fiji Government's claim that three-times more Fijians supported Bainimarama than Australians supported Gillard.[251] If Bainimarama's government had not previously fully appreciated the need to properly manage public relations – especially to the outside world, it certainly did now. In October 2011, it hired the Washington-based public relations firm, Qorvis Communications, for this purpose, resulting in a splurge of new government websites, twitter accounts, YouTube profiles and newswire reports all promoting a very upbeat message. Bainimarama's December *Huffington Post* article, 'A win for the 99 per cent', became an early example, its title a direct appeal to the sentiments of Americans angry at the inequalities the global financial crisis had brought into stark relief. Here was a small country prepared to reduce or eliminate taxes for 99 per cent of taxpayers.[252] What greater evidence of its progressivism did people require?

Riding the tiger

For any leader coming to power through the sheer weight of military muscle, longevity depends overwhelmingly on the maintenance of military support. Bainimarama understood this well, always insisting on amnesty for military offences and quickly coming to the defence of soldiers caught breaking the law. 'I cannot afford to discard my men after they finished the job done for you and your family,' he declared after soldiers were videoed beating captured prison escapees in September 2012: 'I will stick by my men.'[253] Bainimarama's opponents understood this also. Whenever possible they spread rumours through their websites that suggested rumblings in the Military Council or hinted at major divisions within the military itself. Often their whispers were malicious, implying, for example, that Bainimarama intended to assume the presidency in order

---

251 *Sydney Morning Herald*, 8 September 2011. Carried out by Tebbutt Research and supervised by a former chair of Newspoll, the survey of 1,032 citizens found that 98 per cent wanted democracy and 47 per cent thought the government could be doing more to restore it. Wadan Narsey questioned the survey's results, given that it was conducted only in urban and peri-urban areas of Viti Levu and not truly random (*intelligentsia.blogspot.com*, 9 September 2011).
252 crosbiew.blogspot.com, 24 December 2011; *Huffington Post*, 13 December 2011. Allegedly Fiji paid Qorvis $86,200 per month for its services (*Fiji Times*, 1 September 2015). The 2017–18 budget made provision for a $1 million payment to Qorvis.
253 *Australian*, 12 March 2013.

to allow Muslims under the leadership of their pet hate – the Attorney-General, Aiyaz Sayed-Khaiyum – to take over government. Sometimes they were opportunistic, seeking to exploit changes in military personnel to suit a preconceived narrative. But, with PER still in force and local media censored, government silence merely deepened the vacuum in which rumours thrived. As Walsh argued, prior to Qorvis's appointment, government inaction not only played into the hands of opponents but also ensured its continued misrepresentation overseas.[254] Events in 2010 and after demonstrated just how dangerous this could be.

By 2010, Fiji Water had become Fiji's most recognisable export. In many ways, the iconic little bottle and its contents represented the value of utilising the success of one industry – tourism – to leverage another. That Fiji's tourism included a number of very exclusive resorts also helped ensure that America's fashionable and environmentally conscious elite wanted to be seen with a product that the company's managers sold as ancient water untouched by humans. They product-placed it wherever appropriately possible, including at the White House, to enhance its exclusive appeal. Thus connectivity and marketing made Fiji Water the fourth-most imported water bottle in the United States by 2004, with the company valued at some US$50 million. By 2009, it was number one. Little wonder former Finance Minister Chaudhry thought he had hit upon a goldmine when he announced a new 20-cent tax on water exports in 2008. After all the company paid next to no tax, sheltered assets in tax havens, employed a 700-strong workforce confined largely to the Yaqara Valley (near Rakiraki) – which sits above the aquifer from which the company draws its water – and contributed comparatively small sums to local charities, at least until government attention spurred it to become more charitably active.[255] But Chaudhry had not counted on the influence of Fiji Water's director of external affairs, David Roth, who was close friends with the Mara family, in particular Ratu Epeli Ganilau. Roth

---

254   crosbiew.blogspot.com, 2 March 2011.
255   Anna Lenzer, 'Fiji Water: Spin the bottle', *Mother Jones*, September–October 2009. The company is allegedly owned by an entity in Luxembourg while its trademarks (including the capitalised word FIJI) are registered in the Cayman Islands. By 2010 Fiji Water was involved in the renovation of a primary school, paid funds into a local village trust and contributed to local clean water, education and health projects for local villages at a cost of around $4 million. In addition, it paid Yaqara Pastoral Company $1.8 million per annum for using its land. But it had paid less than $1 million in corporate taxes since 1995 and the new tax could bring in about $22 million (compared with $0.5 million under the old tax) to the government for a product that annually earned Fiji Water about US$170 million or $330 million in local currency.

instantly closed the plant, took the opportunity to sack 300 workers, and waited. The knives had been out for Chaudhry for some time; this time they fell and Chaudhry went.

Fast-forward to 2010 and a financially strapped government again put new water taxes back on the table. This time Bainimarama drove the reform and was in no mood to be swayed. When Fiji Water objected, he went on the offensive, reiterating the government's case. Despite being Fiji's fourth-largest export, water brought the government little in export revenue. Fiji Water practiced transfer pricing. This time, when Fiji Water threatened to close its business, Bainimarama – in China with a trade mission – declared he would reopen it and call for international tenders.[256] He ordered Roth out of the country for interfering in Fiji's internal affairs and sent Homelink, a security company comprising former soldiers, to guard the site. Epeli Ganilau, then acting prime minister as well as Minister for Immigration, allegedly attempted to get his brother-in-law, President Nailatikau, to block Roth's deportation. He failed and resigned on 16 November in protest. The next day Roth flew out of Fiji and two weeks later Fiji Water caved in.[257]

Fiji Water was never the catalyst for the events that unfolded, but it did present a rare public manifestation of a growing rift between some of Bainimarama's political and military supporters, most notably those connected with the Mara family. The falling-out was not sudden and may well have been the result of resentments or disquiet stretching back over many years. We do not know. The people involved have not said. But Epeli Ganilau's sudden departure from office for 'personal reasons' followed other initially unexplained changes in military roles and appointments. In late October 2010, Bainimarama unexpectedly announced that he had replaced Driti as Land Force Commander with Col Mosese Tikoitoga. Simultaneously he replaced the 3FIR Commander, Lt Col Ratu Tevita Uluilakeba Mara with Major Amani Suliano. No reasons were given, but Driti and Mara were sent on leave. Additionally, Major Ana Rokomokoti, who had lost her role as chief registrar in June 2010, was dismissed as a military officer. Then, in January 2011, Brigadier General Mohammed

---

256 *fijilive*, 30 November 2010. The tax increased from 0.33 cents to 15 cents per litre.
257 www.coupfourandahalf.com, 17 November 2010. Fiji Water executives seemingly believed they were indispensible to Fiji's economy, one claiming 'Without Fiji Water, Fiji is kind of screwed' (Lenzer, 'Fiji Water', 2009). The increase in tax did not harm Fiji Water. By 2015, its exports exceeded $200 million, it had added a third production line, and diversified into mango and pawpaw production (*Fiji Times*, 19 July 2016).

Aziz inexplicably resigned as deputy chair of FHL for 'personal reasons'. Shortly after Bainimarama announced investigations into fraud at FHL had ceased.[258] All four were allegedly close colleagues.

In February 2011, Bainimarama indicated that he would determine the status of Driti and Tevita Mara in April after they had taken their leave. It was not enough for anti-government bloggers who suggested that the Presidential Palace had been raided, that the President was about to be sacked and that a purge of the military forces was underway. Tikoitoga denied the existence of any split in the military[259] but the sudden appearance of Driti and Mara in the Suva Magistrates Court in May on charges of sedition and incitement to mutiny immediately suggested otherwise. A raid in early 2011 on the home of Ben Padarath, a former NAP candidate in 2006 and nephew of Driti, had allegedly uncovered papers detailing a plot against Bainimarama.[260] Mara at least was unbowed. Out on bail, he announced that Lau province no longer supported the People's Charter.[261] Such defiance could not be sustained for long, and Mara plotted an escape, pretending to go fishing off the coast of Kadavu on 9 May. In reality he had a Tongan naval patrol boat

258 *fijilive*, 25 October 2010, 19 January & 11 February 2011; www.coupfourandahalf.com, 25 October 2010. FHL's chair and managing director also resigned. Aziz retained an important military role as chief of staff, the second-ranked position in the military. Social media sites alleged that Aziz conspired with Driti and Tevita Mara to remove Bainimarama and Aiyaz Sayed-Khaiyum, but saved his job by cooperating with Bainimarama (www.coupfourandahalf.com, 10 May 2011). Driti argued that Mara and Aziz had brought him in and that he had approached Bainimarama in September 2010 to request Aiyaz Sayed-Khaiyum's removal but Bainimarama refused to act, telling him to get evidence before raising the matter again (*Fijileaks*, 21 November 2013). Driti allegedly also told a disaffected Major in October that he would remove Bainimarama when the latter visited Sudan in late October and revoke his passport so he could not return. A new administration would be appointed to take the country to elections in 2011. Apologies would be made to the Methodist Church and GCC, and Australian and NZ troops used to contain any potential internal threats. But unfortunately for Mara, the Major informed the head of Military Intelligence who told Bainimarama of the plot. On 24 October 2010, Mara and Driti were summoned to Bainimarama's office and sent on leave, after which – they were told – they would have to resign their posts and leave the military (High Court Judgement, Criminal Case 0005 of 2012, State v Driti, 26 November 2013).
259 crosbiew.blogspot.com, 2 March 2011; *fijilive*, 7 March 2011.
260 The Suva Magistrates Court subsequently dismissed the case against Padarath.
261 crosbiew.blogspot.com, 4 & 5 May 2011. Michael Field argued that the original fallout resulted from sexual improprieties, although Tevita Mara insisted it derived solely from the Military Council's desire to soften the government's image by removing Aiyaz Sayed-Khaiyum (crosbiew.blogspot.com, 16 May 2011). The evidence against Mara came from a conversation with a disaffected fellow officer, Major Manasa Tagicakibau, during a trip to Korea in July 2010, the same officer who testified against Driti (*Tonga Chronicle*, 26 May 2011; *Fijileaks*, 26 November 2013). That officer had conducted his own surveillance operation on Mara in February 2010 and noted the undocumented movement of weapons and ammunition from the QEB to the Grand Pacific Hotel, which housed some of Mara's 3FIR troops. He watched Mara closely over coming months and recorded their conversations.

pick him up and take him to the safety of Nuku'alofa where, as a close relative of King George Tupou V, he gained immediate refugee status and eventually citizenship.[262]

Once in Nuku'alofa, however, the fugitive issued a series of increasingly strident statements. He declared Commodore Bainimarama 'weakened by ill health, morally and intellectually bankrupt', 'no more than Aiyaz Khaiyum's hand puppet', and a megalomaniac 'inspired entirely by the self importance of a lowly and inadequate man'. His depravity was such that he had even beaten three female human rights activists immediately after the 2006 coup; the women in question had actually identified Driti as their torturer. His intellectual weakness meant that he 'hardly understands the speeches prepared for him by Khaiyum'. 'Navy people are stupid,' he stated. His evidence: the devious Aiyaz Sayed-Khaiyum had convinced the weak Bainimarama in mid-2010 to rule indefinitely; his roadmap for 2014 no more than 'a deceitful plan'.[263] All in all, the ideals of 2006 that had so inspired Tevita Mara and the RFMF had slowly morphed into schemes for self-enrichment. But Mara had awoken from his dreams. Like a true chief he would lead Fiji back to democracy and, to start the process, he called for tougher sanctions against the regime.[264]

Tevita Mara did not have it entirely his own way. Bainimarama called him 'immature' and 'shallow'. He was sidelined for 'things that he did' that he was not supposed to do 'and it started from there and he talked against the government and went against the government'. But for a man who now expected to work with expatriate democracy movements 'to end the dictatorship', Mara did not enjoy the respect he might have anticipated.

---

262   Tevita Mara's casual departure had severe costs for those who inadvertently helped him escape. An Estonian fisherman, who had taken him out to the island from which he made his escape, spent nearly 17 months fighting obstruction of justice charges. A close friend was deported. For a time, Tonga's breach of Fiji's territorial waters raised tensions between the two countries and, at one stage, Tonga stationed a naval boat at Minerva Reef in Fiji's EEZ (exclusive economic zone). Fiji did make an extradition request. The *Economist* speculated how that might have been handled by Tonga's Chief Justice Michael Scott, a former Fiji High Court judge, refugee from Fiji and opponent of Fiji's Chief Justice Gates (21 May 2011). Both Australia and New Zealand ignored Fiji's extradition requests.

263   *Fijileaks'* claim that Aiyaz Sayed-Khaiyum had secretly bought the internet domain for the FijiFirst Party in November 2009 contradicts Tevita Mara's assertion that the Attorney-General manipulated Bainimarama and plotted perpetual dictatorship in 2009. *Fijileaks* inadvertently revealed an Attorney-General purposefully taking the necessary steps to provide a political platform for the government as it planned the country's return to democracy (22 March 2015).

264   crosbiew.blogspot.com, 16 May 2011; www.coupfourandahalf.com, 16 & 23 May 2011. He also alleged collusion with businesses in return for backhanders and that both Aiyaz Sayed-Khaiyum and Bainimarama received incomes of over $700,000 per annum for handling multiple portfolios.

Coupfourpointfive presented an interview with Mara interspersed with comments on his role in the events of 2006 and after, accusing him of forming the hit squad that burned down the homes of dissidents and intimidated the judiciary. He did not deny the allegations; he claimed only to be acting under the command of Bainimarama and that ultimately he would answer to the people. When he visited New Zealand to speak to the Fijian diaspora, Nik Naidu from the Coalition for Democracy in Fiji filed a criminal complaint against Mara for the torture of hundreds of Fiji citizens.[265] His grand tour of Pacific states similarly ran into difficulties. Solomon Islands officials refused to meet him. The Mara phenomenon fizzled out and, in Fiji, he became a nonperson.[266] Driti, however, became a prisoner. On 26 November 2013, Justice Paul Madigan found Driti guilty of inciting mutiny and sedition and sentenced him to jail for five years.

The clumsy actions of two of the most senior officers in the RFMF served to demonstrate Bainimarama's mastery of his role as Commander. Deliberations on a new constitution in 2012 and 2013 demonstrated similar mastery of his political role as prime minister. According to his government's roadmap, 2012 was the start of constitutional consultations, and to that end Bainimarama announced on 2 December 2011 that he would lift the onerous PER on 7 January. He used the occasion to list his government's many achievements, pointing out that none would have been possible if politicians, religious organisations and self-interested individuals had been permitted to fan the flames of prejudice and intolerance 'behind the façade of a free press'. Thus PER – he claimed – had provided the necessary stability for reform and change.[267] But to ensure his government's achievements were not lost, a new constitution had to include certain non-negotiable principles: common and equal citizenry, a secular state, the removal of systemic corruption, an independent judiciary, the elimination of discrimination, good and

---

265 www.coupfourandahalf.com, 19 July 2011.

266 The government's Land Use Unit confiscated the Seaqaqa Sugarcane Estate that his father had established and which Mara managed, purchasing it from the FDB and leasing it to the FSC. The land had been left idle and the estate had defaulted on loan repayments for machinery (www.coupfourandahalf.com, 24 August 2012).

267 *Age*, 7 January 2012; *Address to Nation*, no. 13. Suva: Ministry of Information, 2012. The removal of PER, however, did not mark a return to the status quo ante; a new Public Order (Amendment) Decree addressed issues such as terrorism, offenses against public order, racial and religious vilification, hate speech and economic sabotage. Individuals could be held for two days without charge and up to 14 days with the approval of the Commissioner of Police and responsible minister. In February 2012, a State Proceedings (Amendment) Decree gave ministers legal protection (and media organisations that might quote them) (*fijilive*, 10 February 2012).

transparent governance, social justice, one person – one vote – one value, the elimination of ethnic voting, proportional representation, and a voting age of 18 years.[268] Immunity remained the one unmentioned non-negotiable principle, although it featured in the decree establishing a Constitutional Commission and in the military's late submission to the Commission.[269]

In March 2012, came the appointment of 73-year-old Kenyan professor Yash Ghai – a renowned constitutional expert who had recently worked on the Kenyan and Nepalese constitutions – as chair of the Fiji Constitution Commission (FCC).[270] Its commissioners comprised Fijians Taufa Vakatale, Satendra Nandan and Penelope Moore, as well as South African Christina Murray. Directed to hold public consultations and receive submissions during the course of the year, the FCC would submit a draft constitution to the President in December. That draft would then be reviewed by a constituent assembly, comprising representatives from civil society organisations, political parties, churches and government, with the end result presented to the President in late February 2013. Meanwhile government would undertake voter registration. It had already purchased over 380 Canadian electronic voter registration units and put together a military-led registration team that included two electoral consultants from Australia and New Zealand.[271] Elections would now be held over one day instead of the customary week.[272]

After years of false starts and delays, Fiji at last appeared on the cusp of democratic restoration, although not everyone viewed the coming consultations positively. Unionist Felix Anthony queried the government's mandate for a new constitution and, from Tonga, Tevita Mara questioned the neutrality of the commissioners, while Qarase argued that the last

---

268 Fiji Constitutional Process (Constitution Commission) Decree (no. 57 of 2012), fiji.gov.fj, 18 July 2012.

269 *fijilive*, 22 December 2012. The military submitted that the Prescribed Political Events Decree 2010 be extended to cover the period up until the formation of a new government in 2014. The unconditional amnesty, however, did not include the takeover of government on 19 May 2000 and the subsequent military mutiny.

270 The FCC cost $2,514,507 to operate, funded entirely by Australia, New Zealand, the European Union, the United States and Britain.

271 crosbiew.blogspot.com, 24 May 2012. By the end of 2012, some 504,588 voters were registered, 80 per cent of all domestic voters; 40 per cent being in the Central Division, 38 per cent in the West, 17 per cent in the North and 5 per cent in the East (*fijilive*, 5 September 2012; *Fiji Times*, 12 December 2012).

272 *fijilive*, 3 September 2013.

parliament should be reconvened instead.[273] Aiyaz Sayed-Khaiyum dismissed them as critics who wanted to return Fiji to the dark ages of nepotism, elitism and racism.[274] Tikoitoga asserted that, because the new constitution would end the race-based politics that had previously drawn in the military, it heralded an end to the era of coups.[275] Indeed, Commissioner Nandan predicted that the new constitution would become a sacred document that no one would want to destroy.[276]

Nonetheless, Bainimarama feared losing control. Rival politicians who attempted to influence the constitutional process by privately meeting with Ghai unsettled him. So too the public airing of views that the government had successfully suppressed during the past six years. In fact Ghai had quickly established the FCC's independence by criticising continued government media restrictions.[277] By mid-October, his Commission had held 120 meetings around the country and received over 7,000 oral and written submissions, some of them unreconstructed declarations of resistance: Fiji should become a Christian state, only the Taukei should be called Fijian, the GCC should be reinstated, dual citizenship should be ended and all soldiers involved in the 2000 coup stripped of their medals. Chaudhry wanted the 1997 Constitution returned; his son, Rajendra Chaudhry, called for the return of the GCC. Rabuka wanted old Taukei schools like Ratu Kadavulevu School, Queen Victoria School and Adi Cakobau School exempted from zoning because they were 'the last bastion of iTaukei identity in a country that can have its indigenous community very rapidly marginalised'. Krishna Datt called for a civic education program and a truth commission.[278]

273 www.coupfourandahalf.com, 9 March & 31 May 2012.
274 *fijilive*, 22 March 2012.
275 *fijilive*, 21 March 2012.
276 *Fiji Times*, 4 September 2012.
277 *Economist*, 30 March 2013. At the start of October 2012 the High Court fined the *Fiji Times* $3,000 for quoting a foreigner who questioned the independence of Fiji's judiciary. The CCF was fined $20,000 for a similar offence in May 2013 and its director, Akuila Yabaki, sentenced to three-months jail, suspended for one year (CCF, *An Analysis: 2013 Fiji Government Constitution*. Suva: CCF, 2013, p. 56).
278 crosbiew.blogspot.com, 18 & 19 October 2012; *Fiji Times*, 14 & 16 October 2012. An SDL submission encompassed many of these features, although its recommendations for a 71-seat parliament promised to reduce the number of communal seats and introduce a mixed member proportional voting system. Of the 7,170 submissions, 66 per cent were from iTaukei; 24 per cent, IndoFijians; and 10 per cent, Others.

Many of these submissions potentially threatened the government's plans for Fiji if the Commission took them seriously. The all-embracing nature of the Commission's public seminars at the USP also concerned the government. Not surprisingly, tensions between it and the Commission grew, flaring up in October over the issue of appointments. In accordance with the provisions of its establishment decree, the FCC appointed Madraiwiwi in October as a legal consultant, and he sat in on a series of Commission meetings, including a two-day workshop on the 'Military in Transition' that I attended at the request of the Commission.[279] To me the commissioners seemed troubled. They received mixed messages from the government. Allegedly the Attorney-General would countermand agreements reached with Bainimarama. But there was no confusion around the government's response to Madraiwiwi's appointment. It declared a conflict of interest and questioned his impartiality; he had participated in the Bauan submission that called for the creation of a Christian state. Madraiwiwi withdrew and Ghai rightly called the attack unfair.[280]

The government saw red and rushed out a Fiji Constitution Process (Constitution Commission) (Amendment) Decree 2012 at the end of October to reduce its exposure to risk. Because the Commission had already travelled extensively and received a large number of consultations, the government deemed further public consultations following the production of a draft constitution no longer necessary. In addition, it no longer required the FCC to seek and present to the President public reactions to its draft. Further, the Commission had now to publish each month a statement of its accounts and a list of all staff, including consultants.[281] The sudden change angered Ghai. To change the rules halfway through violated the Commission's independence.[282] But Bainimarama insisted Ghai had only to produce a constitution, not solicit the opinion of people opposed to government. Ample scope existed for public discussion once the constituent assembly began, he claimed.[283] Events quickly proved him wrong.

---

279 Held in the Veiuto parliamentary complex, 18–19 October 2012. The workshop canvassed the possibility of government moving towards personalised authoritarianism masquerading as democracy. Several participants believed Fiji had reached a dangerous moment as the government had seen the conservative submissions from the countryside.

280 *fijilive*, 1 & 4 November 2012; *Fiji Times*, 8 November 2012. Commissioner Moore later argued that 'we were getting a strong feeling from government that we were out to get them' (*Fiji Times*, 15 January 2013).

281 fiji.gov.fj.

282 crosbiew.blogspot.com, 31 December 2012.

283 *Fiji Times*, 8 November 2012.

On 21 December 2012, Ghai presented his Commission's draft Constitution to the President. In the days before and after he made very clear that he found Fiji to be a state but not a nation, its society deeply fragmented, 'full of anxiety' and unable to cope with the rapid changes that had taken place over the past 30 years. The challenge, he believed, was to give people a sense of all things at play, and an understanding of how they might reconcile highly valued traditional principles with change and build a nation out of diverse communities suspicious of each other. To assist, the Commission had crafted a constitution that it hoped would shift the identity, politics and institutions of Fiji from their community bases to ones derived from equal citizenship. To achieve this, culture had to be separated from the state and the common interests of communities given preference over their differences. The alternative had always cost Fiji dearly in terms of social harmony, the retention of skilled labour, the productive use of resources, cultural and artistic development, and cooperation. No longer![284]

Herein lay danger for Bainimarama. In striving to create the basis for a vigorous democracy as a way to reduce the risk of future coups, the Commission's Constitution trod on many toes, and rightly so; however, many of those toes belonged to military feet. Its leaders did not take kindly to the loss of their role as guardian of the Constitution and the people's welfare, and their restriction to defence only. No longer would the President be associated with the military, even as Commander-in-Chief. Instead, under this Constitution, parliament possessed total control over the RFMF. Discipline forces could not obey illegal orders and their much-coveted immunity came with a caveat; immunity applied only to soldiers who renounced their crimes and swore an oath of allegiance disowning their previous support of illegal regimes. Immunity would not be possible for future offences.

The Commission's Constitution also brought the GCC back to life, although only as a civil society organisation with no parliamentary role as before. Because the Taukei now comprised the overwhelming majority of the population, they no longer required special protection. Hence there would be no Senate. Instead there would be a single house of parliament made up of 71 members. Sixty members would be elected from four multi-member districts (24 from the Central Division, 22 from the West,

---

284 *Fiji Times*, 13 December 2012; www.coupfourandahalf.com, 27 December 2012.

nine from the North and five from the East). The remaining 11 would come from party lists depending on their party's proportion of votes. The Commission believed that this system would make it easier for small parties to get in, but not so many as to be destabilising. It would avoid racially divisive contests and enable quotas for women (one third of candidates in the first two elections, and half thereafter). In addition, parliament would have a reduced four-year term, cabinets would be limited to a maximum of 14 ministers (up to four of whom could be brought in from outside parliament), and a prime minister could serve for no more than eight years. Uniquely, it mandated an annual national people's assembly consisting of the President, Speaker, Prime Minister and Cabinet, Leader of the Opposition, 10 Members of Parliament and 95 representatives of local government, constitutional commissions and civil society nominees. This assembly would assist parliament to elect a president and change the Constitution, consider challenges confronting the nation, and examine progress towards national goals.[285] While laudably promoting a democracy that gave its citizens greater voice, the Commission's assembly added yet another complication for Bainimarama to digest.

The prospect of having to surrender to a caretaker government six months before the election equally worried an already anxious Bainimarama. The Commission's transitional arrangements also called for an independent interim electoral commission and a transitional advisory council that, among other tasks, would amend or repeal any decrees inconsistent with the new Constitution. By removing the prospect of continuity, such measures potentially doomed Bainimarama's 2006 experiment. Not surprisingly, he struck back.

A day after presenting the draft Constitution to the President, police confronted Ghai as he attempted to collect 600 copies of the Constitution. They seized the copies and burned galley proofs in front of him. The incident became a public relations disaster; newspaper headlines screamed 'Government burns Constitution'. Ghai told Radio Australia that the incident 'shows such contempt for our work and in turn contempt for the people who had come out in their thousands and thousands to give us their views [and] participate in the process'. Clearly dejected, he added, 'I felt not just a betrayal, I felt will Fiji ever have a democratic constitution?'[286] But the government had no intention of letting him off

---

285 FCC, *Explanatory Report on the Draft Constitution*. Suva, December 2012.
286 www.coupfourandahalf.com, 28 December 2012.

the hook. Tikoitoga accused Ghai of wilfully ignoring the government's amended decree and usurping the role of the constituent assembly. His behaviour was 'unbecoming'. Foreign powers funded the FCC; hence it did not feel that it was answerable to Fiji. It took advisors from unions, political parties and NGOs, with the result that its Constitution was not all its own work.[287] A short campaign to undermine the Commission's Constitution had begun.

At the start of January 2013, the President issued a decree allowing the government to amend the FCC Constitution, suggesting that it represented a recipe for over-governance and financial ruin.[288] Tough new rules for political parties were also released. Party names had to be in English (to reduce ethnic appeals), the signatures of 5,000 members from across Fiji were required with applications, and a fee of $5,005 paid. Union officials could no longer serve as party officials nor, of course, public officers (excluding the President and members of the government). Companies and unions could not make donations to political parties, and anyone sentenced for a period of six months or more during the past five years would be unable to hold office in a party.[289] Regional or provincial parties were clearly a thing of the past. So too the future of many of the country's current 16 political parties, not to mention the plans for a new party made at the start of January by some 400 trade unionists and NGOs in Nadi. In fact, by May, only the FLP and NFP had successfully navigated the registration process although, by this time, the FLP had become a shadow of its former self.[290] The SDL did not believe it had time to meet its own constitutional requirements and elected to form a completely new party, the Social Democratic Liberal Party with the same SDL acronym. Ro Teimumu Kepa became its president. When a late amendment to the Political Parties Decree forbade the use of acronyms derived from deregistered parties, the SDL had no alternative but to use

---

287   *Fiji Times*, 5 January 2012; *fijilive*, 9 January 2013.
288   *Fiji Times*, 11 January 2013.
289   *Fiji Times*, 16 January 2013. The Political Parties Registration, Conduct, Funding and Disclosure Decree 2013 determined that the 5,000 signatures (previously only 180) be comprised of 2,000 from the Central Division, 1,750 from the Western Division, 1,000 from the Northern Division and 250 from the Eastern Division.
290   Chaudhry remained the focus of division within the party, with many members believing that he wished to see his son installed as a future leader. As a shadow leader, he remained firmly in control. At a FLP conference in Nadi on 25 August 2012, 83 per cent of delegates were NFU officials or members and a further 13 per cent were beholden to Chaudhry, according to one report (www.coupfourandahalf.com, 28 August 2012).

the clumsier SODELPA as its abbreviated name.[291] The United People's Party (UPP) terminated itself and its former leader Mick Beddoes joined SODELPA.[292]

On 21 March 2013, Bainimarama presented a much delayed new draft Constitution to the nation, announcing also a change to the consultation process: 'My fellow Fijians, you will be the new Constituent Assembly.' No doubt dropping the requirement for review by a constituent assembly enabled some of the three months lost in rewriting the Constitution to be made up, particularly as the public were now given only 15 days to respond to the draft. But most likely Bainimarama wished to avoid empowering yet another body – this time a populist one – to determine the future of the nation and the role of the military. The *Economist* argued that this decision cost him the opportunity to preside over a new durable and legitimate political order.[293] It is just as likely, however, that Bainimarama believed his action regained him that opportunity. The very next day he announced that he would run for election.

Bainimarama presented Fiji with a slimmed-down draft Constitution, half the size of its ill-fated predecessor, outlining an equally slimmed-down four-year single house of parliament, comprising just 45 members proportionally drawn from an open list system comprising Fiji's four divisions.[294] Candidates would have to be Fiji citizens only, resident in Fiji for at least two years prior to an election, and not been subject to 12 months imprisonment or longer during the previous five years. Significantly there would be no caretaker government, no National People's Assembly, no GCC, no re-examination of its decrees, the President would be chosen by the parliament for a three-year term, and the military would regain its 1990 role to secure the welfare of Fiji's people. The Prime Minister would be all-powerful, being the Commander-in-Chief of the RFMF (to reduce the possibility of future coups)[295] and responsible for advising the President on appointing the military commander, the Chief Justice

291 Pio Tabaiwalu, 'The genesis of the Social Democratic Liberal Party: A struggle against the odds', in Ratuva & Lawson, *The People Have Spoken*, 2016, p. 194.
292 *fijilive*, 28 January 2013. The United Voters Party (formerly the General Voters Party) changed its name to the UPP in 2004.
293 *Economist*, 30 March 2013.
294 The numbers were 18 members from the Central Division, 16 from the Western Division, seven from the Northern Division and four from the Eastern Division.
295 Comment by Aiyaz Sayed-Khaiyum, crosbiew.blogspot.com, 18 April 2013.

and the President of the Appeal Court, the latter two in conjunction with the Attorney-General, who would also advise the Judicial Services Commission on the appointment of all judges.

Nailatikau stressed that this less bureaucratic constitution incorporated the salient features of the FCC Constitution and gave prominence to an elected parliament, rather than 'an unelected assembly of NGOs'. He also commended it for introducing for the first time an extensive range of socio-economic rights and for including recognition of customary land ownership.[296] The President did not acknowledge, however, that the Constitution now contained no provision for the rights of women or for cultural and linguistic rights, and that customary land ownership brought no specific protections.

The short time allowed for public responses clearly indicated where government priorities lay. Although the Attorney-General and his team subsequently held 19 public meetings on the draft Constitution, none of the 1,093 written submissions was ever released for public scrutiny.[297] Instead on 22 August 2013 the President approved an amended Constitution. It became law with still further changes on 6 September, much to the dismay of 14 FWRM and youth protestors who objected to the assent process and were arrested for assembling without a permit.[298] Days later the CCF released a damning assessment of Fiji's fourth Constitution, claiming that it failed to satisfy many of the government's non-negotiable principles by concentrating power in the executive, undermining the independence of the judiciary and incentivising future coups by making constitutional change more difficult.[299]

Specifically, the CCF criticised the powers given parliament to limit the extensive rights and freedoms outlined in the Constitution's Bill of Rights, which it claimed transformed them into aspirations. Courts were no longer bound to interpret the Bill of Rights with reference to international law and could only deal with cases brought by individuals whose rights had been directly contravened. Parliament had now gained five additional

---

296 *Fiji Times*, 13 April 2013. It did however recognise indigenous rights for an equitable share of royalties resulting from the exploitation of land or seabed.
297 crosbiew.blogspot.com, 26 August 2013.
298 *Fiji Times*, 7 September 2013.
299 Changing the Constitution required a 75 per cent majority in parliament and in a referendum. The following section draws on the CCF's *An Analysis*, 2013. See also Wadan Narsey's 'The costs of compromise: A dead-end parliamentary farce', *narseyonfiji.wordpress.com*, 21 February 2016.

members since the earlier draft, in itself not an issue, but a new provision required that parties and individuals win at least 5 per cent of the total vote in order to gain a seat in what was now a single national constituency, even if they obtained more individual votes than successful candidates. The provision consolidated the power of large parties. Strangely, given the rationale for its birth, no constitutional check existed to prevent the return of communal politics. The government clearly believed a single constituency sufficient to promote trans-ethnic voting and doom once powerful ethnically based parties. But nothing compensated for the failure to present measures to raise the proportion of women in parliament.

Despite originating from a disregard for due process, this was no poorly conceived and rushed Constitution.[300] It specifically maintained the powers government had grown accustomed to after 2006. Although the President regained the ceremonial role of Commander-in-Chief and could now serve up to two three-year terms, the Prime Minister retained enormous powers, appointing all independent offices through the Constitutional Offices Commission and determining – among others – the salaries of the Chief Justice and the President of the Court of Appeal. The Attorney-General also continued to enjoy wide powers over the judiciary and independent bodies. The CCF believed the Public Service Commission, the Judicial Services Commission, even the Electoral Commission, would all become highly politicised. Not surprisingly, the new Constitution diminished the influence of the Opposition in parliament. Its leader no longer participated in appointments. Nor did the Opposition automatically chair the Public Accounts Committee. Unaccustomed to oversight, government had no intention to insist on it now. Hence parliament would also no longer scrutinise the rules and regulations of constitutional offices and commissions. Existing decrees would remain, unchallengeable in court even if they contradicted the Constitution. And, predictably, no caretaker administration would control the transition to this brave new world.

---

300   Chantelle Khan, director of the Social Empowerment Education Programme, argues that 'by intercepting, circumventing and overriding due process', the government has consistently undermined the 'practices of democracy at all levels' ('Reflections on the September 2014 elections: A CSO perspective', in Naidu & Tarte, *'No Ordinary Election'*, 2015, p. 67).

Most political parties preparing for participation in the 2014 elections resigned themselves to the new Constitution, only demonstrating their displeasure by boycotting the government's official constitutional presentation. An ad-hoc grouping of SODELPA, FLP and NFP – the United Front for a Democratic Fiji – claimed to reject the Constitution and presented a submission to the President's office. Kepa argued that the Constitution had been designed to prevent the perpetrators of the 2006 coup from ever having to account for their unlawful actions, and did not reflect the will of the people.[301] But Fiji's political parties had no appetite for a boycott; perhaps they hoped that history might repeat itself. After all, Labour and the NFP had both participated in the 1992 election under a Constitution they despised and had succeeded in influencing its change. Indeed, Rabuka declared the new Constitution 'a better starting point' than the 1990 one and urged people to accept it and move forward. He had already announced his departure from politics and once more apologised for his role in the 1987 coups.[302] Even former Constitutional Commissioner Nandan stressed its positives; there could no longer be a Leader of the Opposition from a party with only one other member and elected with only a few thousand votes.[303] Surprisingly, international responses were also muted.

The EU's director of External Action Services said simply that the new Constitution provided sufficient grounds for the European Union to restart political dialogue with Fiji.[304] Australia's position throughout Fiji's process of constitution-making had been complicated by its own political turmoil. Rudd had become Foreign Minister when Gillard assumed the prime ministership in June 2010. He stood down from that role prior to his first challenge to her leadership in February 2012. Fiji anticipated that Australia might change its approach with Bob Carr as the new Foreign Minister. Hence, Bainimarama used the occasion to criticise Australian policy, claiming it had been governed by pride not policy. Rudd 'personalised issues' and failed to follow New Zealand and

---

301 *Australian*, 7 September 2013; www.coupfourandahalf.com, 24 October 2013.
302 *fijilive*, 26 August 2013, 30 January 2013. Rabuka had issued another more comprehensive apology for 'the wrong' committed in 1987 in a paid advertisement with the *Fiji Times* (1 January 2012).
303 crosbiew.blogspot.com, 31 August 2013. He alluded to the status of Mick Beddoes as Leader of the Opposition after the 2006 election, representing the UPP with only two MPs.
304 *fijilive*, 27 October 2013.

the United States in renewing ties with Fiji.[305] For 'short-term political gain', he had 'arrogantly' dumped his country's asylum seeker problem on Melanesia.[306] Julie Bishop, the opposition spokesperson on foreign affairs, echoed Bainimarama's concerns and dared Carr to lead a new direction on Fiji and open dialogue.

Carr refused, however, despite acknowledging Fiji's progress towards democratic elections. In May, Australia pressured Japan to deny Bainimarama a seat at the Pacific Alliance Leaders Meeting Forum.[307] It also pressured the World Bank to reject a $88 million loan for hydropower construction, with the result that the China Development Bank stepped in with a $70 million soft loan for a project now to be built by the Chinese company, Sinohydro.[308] With China's presence in the Pacific visibly increasing and with the American FBI training Fiji police in Suva, the pressure was on Carr to make a formal change to Australia's stance on Fiji. Australia had already quietly doubled its aid to Fiji in 2012 and, at the end of July, Carr finally announced the implementation of full diplomatic relations. Travel sanctions would ease and be dealt with on a case-by-case basis. Hence, when the Attorney-General travelled to Brussels to chair the African, Caribbean and Pacific Group of States (ACP) Ministerial Trade Committee and its talks with the European Union, Australia permitted him to transit through its airports.[309]

In 2013, Fiji chaired both the G77 plus China grouping at the United Nations and the International Sugar Council.[310] By this time Pacific ACP leaders had severed their link with the PIF in order to allow Fiji's

305 *Fiji Times*, 28 February 2012.
306 *Guardian*, 29 July 2013.
307 *Australian*, 8 March & 18 May 2012; *ABC News*, 9 March 2012.
308 *Australian*, 29 May 2013. Chinese foreign direct investments in Fiji increased from $194 million in 2011 to $389 million in 2014 (*Fiji Times*, 25 October 2014); aid stood at US$333 million between 2006 and 2013, compared with US$252 million from Australia (*Economist*, 25 March 2015).
309 *Fiji Times*, 27 June 2012; *Age*, 31 July 2012; crosbiew.blogspot.com, 24 October 2012. Australian aid rose from $33.7 million to $65.6 million.
310 Peter Thomson actively engaged with the United Nations as Fiji's permanent representative and helped Fiji develop diplomatic relations with 63 new nations after 2009. At the same time Fiji secured a new Asia-Pacific Island Developing Group within the UN Asia Group for lobbying purposes (Makereta Komai, 'Fiji's foreign policy and the new Pacific diplomacy', in G Fry & S Tarte (eds), *The New Pacific Diplomacy*. Canberra: ANU Press, 2015, pp. 114–17). In 2014, Thomson became president of the executive committee for the UN Development Program, the UN Population Fund and the UN Office of Project Services.

full participation.[311] Australia's strategy lay in tatters. Jon Fraenkel, now at Victoria University of Wellington, claimed that Bainimarama had cleverly used anti-Australian rhetoric to gain credibility in the region. Of course the siege mentality it induced also played an important role in Fiji, especially 'among the new elite that cluster around the interim government'.[312] 'To them, we are a land of coups, failed institutions and a military dictator,' Kubuabola reflected: 'There exists a condescending and patronising tone to almost every statement and media report that comes out of Australia and New Zealand.'[313] New Zealand similarly lifted some travel bans. Bainimarama called it 'insincere, unneeded and too late'.[314]

At the Australian Strategic Policy Institute, Richard Herr and Anthony Bergin agreed with the changed stance of Australia and New Zealand. 'Using the Pacific Island Forum against Fiji,' they wrote, 'was tantamount to cutting off our nose to spite our public face in the Pacific Islands.' Bainimarama had sidelined the PIF in a way that excluded Australia and New Zealand.[315] In late August 2012, he held another 'Engaging with the Pacific' meeting in Nadi, deliberately prior to a PIF meeting in the Cook Islands to maximise attendance and embarrass the PIF. Shortly after, in September, China's second-most senior leader, Wu Bangguo, visited Fiji and denounced 'strong countries' for bullying Fiji and excluding it from the PIF. Fiji was now a port for China's satellite communication vessels and Wu handed over a $200 million concessional loan for road construction.[316]

Having been wrong-footed for so long by Fiji and under pressure to adopt a different policy, Australia's response to Fiji's constitutional shenanigans suddenly became uncharacteristically muted. Unlike New Zealand, it declined to slap Fiji for trashing the Ghai Constitution. Carr

311 Relations with Papua New Guinea soured at the end of 2013 when Fiji objected to High Commissioner Peter Eafeare continuing as dean of the diplomatic corps in Fiji. PNG's Prime Minister, Peter O'Neill, withdrew the offer for a Fijian to chair the proposed Pacific ACP secretariat (*Islands Business*, January 2014). In 2016, the relationship degenerated further when Fiji proposed continuing to ban imports of canned beef, biscuits and rice from Papua New Guinea under the MSG Trade agreement on biosecurity grounds. Papua New Guinea threatened to invoke a trade dispute and ban Fiji poultry imports (*Fiji Times*, 1 & 8 September 2016).
312 *Australian*, 18 February 2014.
313 *Australian*, 27 January 2012.
314 crosbiew.blogspot.com, 17 September 2013.
315 R Herr & A Bergin, 'Fiji vital to an effective regional system', *Australian*, 3 August 2012.
316 *Age*, 26 September 2012.

said he understood why the Constitution had to be amended; recreating 'an unelected GCC would seem to give rise to the suggestion that ethnic divisions in the country were going to be exaggerated'.[317] The *Australian's* Rowan Callick wondered whether Carr could really come to terms with what Bainimarama wants. 'After 6 years of steadily chiseling away at Fiji's Parliament, the courts, the media, the chiefs, the Methodist church, the army has this year suddenly accelerated the process of embedding itself in sole command for the long term,' he wrote: 'It is difficult, however, to understand … how absolute power does not lead, in this single case alone in world history, to absolute corruption.'[318] However, the Opposition's Julie Bishop told the Australia–Fiji Business Forum in Brisbane in July 2013 that 'It is now time to rebuild the bridges'.[319] Unsurprisingly, the Constitution barely received a mention. Australia needed a strong presence in Fiji, the *Australian's* foreign editor Greg Sheridan argued, to pursue its interests in the South Pacific.[320]

In September 2013, Bishop's Liberal–National Coalition won office in Australia and quickly moved to cement what Carr had timidly begun. In mid-February 2014, she met Bainimarama in Suva, offering full restoration of defence ties and Fiji's participation in its New Colombo Plan and seasonal worker program. PIF's Ministerial Contact Group also offered Fiji restored membership following its elections. But Bainimarama had no intention of restoring the status quo ante. He had fashioned a more independent and stronger international presence. In September 2013, he told the UN General Assembly that his quest for a constitution 'worthy of the Fijian people' had lost his country many friends:

> They abandoned us and sought to punish us with sanctions; we sought their assistance but they turned their backs on us. They chose to support a form of democracy, governance and justice in Fiji that they would never have accepted for themselves.[321]

---

317 *Australian*, 12 & 16 January 2013.
318 R Callick, 'Poll tests diplomatic will of Canberra', *Australian*, 2 April 2013.
319 crosbiew.blogspot.com, 31 July 2013.
320 *Australian*, 17 February 2014. ANU academic Scott MacWilliam claimed that the real reason Australia changed tack was because it needed the MSG to help with the resettlement of refugees (crosbiew.blogspot.com, 16 February 2014).
321 crosbiew.blogspot.com, 26 September 2013.

Savouring the moment, he held the first Pacific Islands Development Forum (PIDF) in Nadi in late April and announced that this new coalition of Pacific island governments, civil society organisations and business would be headquartered in Suva. The PIF no longer served the interests of Pacific islanders. Australia and New Zealand should not be both members and donors, Kubuabola added. They would not be members of the new PIDF.[322]

Tasting victory

With his international critics in their place, Bainimarama confidently moved his country towards elections on his terms. In January 2014, with Aiyaz Sayed-Khaiyum as the Elections Minister, he established a new Electoral Commission under Fiji Law Society President, Chen Bunn Young.[323] The acting permanent secretary for justice, Mohammed Saneem became the Supervisor of Elections, with an Australian as his deputy. Over the months leading up to the 17 September elections, new rules and procedures were rolled out. Voters were issued with identity cards that contained biometric data and photos. To prevent vote stacking, each polling station could accommodate only 500 voters. No political party flags or signs would be permitted within 300 metres of polling stations and, during the novel single election day, which was declared a public holiday, no political advertising would be allowed.[324] In addition, all electioneering would stop two days before polling in order to give the electorate space to reflect unencumbered by politicking.[325]

The 2014 budget similarly prepared the way for Bainimarama's elections, providing salary increases for public servants and huge concessions in education: subsidised bus fares, free textbooks and free schooling. At last Bainimarama had an expanding economy to assist him, boosted by infrastructure projects and growing business confidence after years of

---

322 *Fiji Times*, 27 April 2014; *Australian*, 29 April 2014. The PIDF also represented Fiji's frustration with the MSG and its determination to launch a regional body it could control. At the last moment, the PNG Prime Minister cancelled his attendance at the Forum (*Islands Business*, January 2014).

323 Its members were elections specialist Father David Arms, civil-society activist Alisi Daurewa, playwright Larry Thomas, businessman James Sloane, accountant Jenny Seeto and sociologist Professor Vijay Naidu.

324 crosbiew.blogspot.com, 1 June 2014. Pre-polling would enable up to 60,000 isolated voters to participate. In addition, Fiji nationals living overseas could also register and pre-vote.

325 This did not prevent the use of government billboards ostensibly promoting non-political matters such as development projects and road safety.

decline.[326] Bainimarama had announced his intention to run for election with a new political party back in August 2013. In November, he indicated that he would quit the military in order to lead the party, stepping down on 5 March 2014. Tikoitoga succeeded him as Commander of the RFMF. Bainimarama's new party did not materialise, however, until the end of that month when he began a two-day bus tour of Viti Levu to collect the signatures needed to register the party to be known as FijiFirst (FFP). The process of collecting signatures around the country took over one month, at the end of which it could boast over 40,000 signatures. FijiFirst also proved an apt slogan for Bainimarama. His was a party for Fiji, not a select few, a charge he had plenty of opportunity to repeat.[327]

SODELPA played directly into his hands. The 68-year-old Ro Teimumu Kepa, Marama Bale na Roko Tui Dreketi, the traditional head of the Burebasaga confederacy, represented everything Bainimarama opposed: tradition, privilege, the status quo ante. When she gave her inaugural address to SODELPA in March 2014, Kepa declared it her mission to defeat the dictatorship that had stolen the last elected government. She would stop the beatings, threats and incarcerations, of which she had personal experience. She would rededicate Fiji to God[328] and resume the multi-party cabinet model the SDL began. She would ask the Supreme Court to provide its opinion on the status of the 1997 Constitution, clearly placing the new Constitution in jeopardy. She would re-establish the ethnic divisions for scholarships and review the changes made to the distribution of lease monies that had so disadvantaged the chiefly elite. She would review the whole question of land leases and bring back the GCC.[329] In short, she would 'Reclaim Fiji'.

326   GDP growth wavered around 2 and 3 per cent between 2010 and 2012. In 2013, it grew by 4.7 per cent, in 2014 by 5.3 per cent (tradingeconomics.com/fiji/gdp-growth-annual).

327   *Fiji Times*, 6 May & 31 March 2014.

328   Perhaps deliberately, there was always some confusion as to whether this meant Fiji would be declared a Christian state. Qarase suggested it did, although Kepa emphasised only SODELPA's Christian mission (see Jacqueline Rye, 'Religion, the Christian state and the secular state: Discourses during the 2014 Fiji General Election', in Naidu & Tarte, *'No Ordinary Election'*, 2015, pp. 35–48). In August, the newly elected President of the Methodist Church, Rev. Tevita Nawadra Banivanua, forthrightly declared that his Church would remain apolitical and accept a secular state (*Fiji Times*, 26 August 2014). This did not prevent the secretary for Christian Citizenship and Social Services, Rev. Iliesa Naivalu, from circulating a letter two weeks prior to the elections to 56 Methodist divisions endorsing SODELPA (*Fiji Sun*, 25 September 2014).

329   crosbiew.blogspot.com, 14 March 2014.

Kepa's promise to restore the GCC drew the ire of Aiyaz Sayed-Khaiyum. Qarase, whose recent imprisonment prevented him from standing for election, retorted that 'as an IndoFijian', the Attorney-General had no right to tell iTaukei what to do.[330] But, of course, like every Fijian, he had a right to speak about any institution that might impact on Fiji's governance and all its citizens. Predictably, Bainimarama accused SODELPA of wanting to take Fiji back to the politics of fear: 'It is the same old tired political faces who brought Fiji to its knees in the first place through their petty squabbling and division.'[331] When SODELPA 'sacked' Rabuka because of his role in 1987, Bainimarama's attack appeared vindicated.[332] It was the same when the party used Kepa's personal connections to chiefly houses to open doors for its candidates. SODELPA represented a past Bainimarama claimed he wanted to put behind Fiji. 'We will consign them to history, once and for all bury them, ignore their false promises – and set our eyes on the future we can build together, One Nation, putting Fiji first to make Fiji great,' Bainimarama argued: 'Don't judge me by my promise. Judge me by the achievements I've already delivered.'[333]

SODELPA's focus constrained its ability to take on FijiFirst. The *vanua* should retain its distance from political parties, Madraiwiwi warned, and allow the Taukei to choose freely. It would, however, take at least a generation for the perceptions that Bainimarama wanted to foster to be realised.[334] Nonetheless, as journalist Nemani Delaibatiki noted, SODELPA's discriminatory policies reduced its appeal to non-Taukei voters at a time when it could not match the FFP in organising large public meetings. To minimise the potential for dissent, it held small pocket meetings without the presence of the media.[335] Meanwhile the 60-year-old Bainimarama presented himself as an agent for change, an image with traction across the Pacific because he had stood up to Australia and New Zealand. Tongan politician Akilisi Pohiva believed Bainimarama had the political will to make things happen. Newspaper polls prior to the election appeared to confirm FijiFirst's popularity. At the end of June 2014, the *Fiji Sun*–Razor poll gave it 59 per cent of popular support

---

330   www.coupfourandahalf.com, 13 July 2014.
331   crosbiew.blogspot.com, 14 March 2014.
332   crosbiew.blogspot.com, 2 May 2014. Beddoes declared Rabuka's most recent apology insufficient.
333   crosbiew.blogspot.com, 21 July 2014; see also Nicola Baker & Haruo Nakagawa, '"Known unknowns and unknown unknowns" in the 2014 Fiji election results', in Naidu & Tarte, *'No Ordinary Election'*, 2015, p. 126.
334   *Fiji Sun*, 19 May 2014.
335   *Fiji Sun*, 4 September 2014.

compared with 8 per cent for SODELPA, 5 per cent for the FLP and 8 per cent for the NFP. Bainimarama received an outstanding 73 per cent as preferred prime minister; no other party leader exceeded 7 per cent.[336] As Brij Lal later noted, 'He had all the advantages of incumbency, name recognition, a public profile, media on his side, campaigning on the public purse, and a desire on the part of the voters for stability, which he promised'.[337]

And he retained the loyalty of the military, which remained centre stage in the consciousness of many voters, in part because, during the weeks leading up to the election, 45 Fijian peacekeepers were captured by the rebel Al Nusra group after evacuating Camp Faouar on the Syrian side of Golan Heights, where 500 Fiji troops monitored the border between Israel and Syria as part of a UN Disengagement Observer Force. They were held for two weeks in captivity, before being released on 11 September after Fiji requested Qatar mediate on its behalf.[338] Five days later and one day before the election, in an exercise that echoed Bainimarama's own actions prior to the 2006 election, the military marched through Suva. Journalist Rowan Callick reported that the exercise delivered a clear message to all Fijians: the army was still there and would tolerate no nonsense.[339] On the same day, during the media blackout, Bainimarama held a public thanksgiving ceremony for the safe release of his peacekeepers.[340]

It is tempting to suggest that FijiFirst's confidence heading into the election dictated the late release of its manifesto just 10 days before the election, but it may also have been tactical, enabling it to minimise the impact of criticism from rival parties. In many respects, FijiFirst had mixed results to crow about when it came to the economy. Certainly Bainimarama's government had dismantled the telecom monopoly and no longer bowed to powerful Taukei interests or big business. It had seized back control of Air Pacific from Qantas in 2012 and renamed it Fiji Airways, bought new airliners and returned the company to profitability in 2013–14. Similarly,

---

336 crosbiew.blogspot.com, 5 July 2014.
337 *Australian*, 17 August 2014.
338 Two separate groups of Filipino peacekeepers evaded capture (*Daily Mirror*, 12 September 2014).
339 *Australian*, 17 September 2014. Allegations that Qatar paid US$2.5 million for their release have never been confirmed by the United Nations.
340 David Robie, '"Unfree and unfair?": Media intimidation in Fiji's 2014 elections', in Ratuva & Lawson, *The People Have Spoken*, 2016, p. 90. The Methodist Church refused to attend the interfaith service on the grounds that it might be a political event (Lynda Newland, 'From the land to the sea: Christianity, community and state in Fiji and the 2014 elections', in Ratuva & Lawson, *The People Have Spoken*, 2016, p. 120).

its stewardship of Fiji Pine and Tropik Woods returned profits for the first time in 40 years.[341] It had formed its own Fiji National University (FNU) in 2010, and had belatedly stimulated long-overdue infrastructure development, much of it funded by rising debt, increasingly denominated in Chinese yuan.[342] And private investment now reached 15 per cent of GDP. Historically the level was significant (private investment managed only 3.5 per cent of GDP in 2010), enabling the government to reach its investment target of 28 per cent of GDP. Success now reflected badly on the record of the government after 2006, and infrastructure did not bring immediate opportunities to reduce unemployment or raise minimum wages.[343] Nonetheless, in 2013, the economy's growth rate had finally recovered from coup-induced shrinkages and risen over 4 per cent; the year 2014 promised to be even better.

Low growth carried dangers for FijiFirst; hence its focus on policies for amelioration, which had the added advantage of impacting more directly on the average voter: increased electricity subsidies and free medicines for low-income families, a basic level of free water and an extension of clean water initiatives, the maintenance of zero VAT on basic food items and medicines, lowered age eligibility for social security, increased scholarships and education loans for tertiary education, and the extension of free education to preschool. But there were new initiatives also: an increase in teacher numbers, an emergency package for farmers, a new agricultural research council, fertiliser subsidies, affordable housing programs and squatter development, first home grants, $10 million to assist iTaukei develop their own lands, and major highway developments. Surprisingly,

---

341 *Fiji Sun*, 10 December 2014.

342 Government debt rose 40 per cent (2006–14) to 56 per cent of GDP in 2010 (above the IMF's 40 per cent target, although this had been adjusted to 60 per cent after the GFC), with domestic sources of debt (mostly the FNPF) shrinking from 83 per cent to 73 per cent of all loans. Foreign lenders comprised 12.8 per cent of GDP by mid-2017. Chinese loans represented one quarter of Fiji's foreign debt ($158.5 million) in 2014, up from 2.6 per cent or $7.6 million in 2008 (*Fiji Times*, 30 October 2014, 12 September 2015, 30 May 2016, 7 July 2017). Under the energetic leadership of Dr Ganesh Chand, the first vice chancellor, the FNU brought together six once separate institutions (Fiji Institute of Technology, Fiji School of Nursing, Fiji School of Medicine, Fiji College of Agriculture, Fiji College of Education and Lautoka Teachers College) across 33 campuses and centres serving over 20,000 students.

343 Biman Prasad argues that remittances, low interest rates and credit prompted recovery based on consumption, not growth-based on production. Key performing sectors like retail, construction and transport were not the largest sectors of the economy where employment was greatest ('Growth must result in more for us', *Fiji Times*, 12 September 2015). Minimum wages remained at $2 per hour because of employer pressures on the government. Only in 2014 were they raised to $2.32, still far below the poverty line of $4.20 (crosbiew.blogspot.com, 7 July 2015).

FijiFirst (temporarily) resurrected Ratu Mara's plan to nationalise the purchase of oil (more eggs for the nest), but it called also for the introduction of digital TV, the rollout of e-governance platforms and the greater provision of microfinance to individuals and small businesses.[344]

Predictably the Labour Party saw the manifesto as a blatant vote-buying tactic to offset its poor record in government. Electricity subsidies were needed because the government had overseen a 10-fold increase in electricity costs to the average family, free water to 80 per cent of the population could not be achieved, and free milk to class one students overlooked its responsibility for doubling the price of milk. Chaudhry argued that Bainimarama's 'record in government showed unprecedented increases in poverty levels, unemployment and cost of living'. His promises now were hollow. He could not be trusted.[345]

But Chaudhry faced his opponent from an unfamiliar position. His recent conviction barred him from participation and effectively left the FLP leaderless. Long-simmering tensions over his leadership produced a breakaway faction (the People's Democratic Party or PDP) and provided Fiji's oldest political force, the National Federation Party, an opportunity to regain ground it had lost since 1999. Economics professor Biman Prasad became its new leader at the end of March and attempted to refashion the party and – more actively than other parties – to court the new youth vote.[346] Draunidalo became its new president. A human rights activist, she was intimately connected across the political spectrum.[347]

---

344   FijiFirst, 'Our manifesto', *fijifirst.com*.

345   *flp.org.fj*, 12 September 2014.

346   See Patrick Vakaoti, 'Fiji elections and the youth vote: token or active citizenship?', in Ratuva & Lawson, *The People Have Spoken*, 2016, pp. 157–75. No evidence exists that youth represented a singularly different cohort, although with the reduction in voting age to 18 the potential existed for under 25s (now 19 per cent of voters) to demand more nuanced policies. No one in that age group was elected to parliament, however, and only four from the 30 to 39 cohort. Combined, the two cohorts possibly comprised over 50 per cent of the voting population (Tarai et al, 'Political social media campaigning', Naidu & Tarte, *'No Ordinary Election'*, 2015, pp. 90–92; David Arms, 'Analysing the open list system of proportional representation in Fiji's 2014 General Election: A perspective from the Fiji Electoral Commission', in Naidu & Tarte, *'No Ordinary Election'*, 2015, p. 14).

347   Her late father, Col Savenaca Draunidalo, was a senior military officer under Nailatikau and Rabuka, a politician, public servant and, allegedly, a 2000 coup conspirator. Her late mother, Adi Kuini Vuikaba, was equally well connected within the Fijian chiefly elite and served as leader of the Labour Party following the death of her second husband, Dr Timoci Bavadra, the man who first led the Labour–NFP Coalition to victory in 1987. Vuikaba also led the Fijian Association Party after 1998 until 2000.

Nonetheless, the party's efforts to produce a stronger multicultural face to the electorate were seriously damaged when three of its Taukei candidates were deliberately targeted in late July by unilateral government changes in electoral laws and forced to withdraw.[348] And, like the FLP and SODELPA, it was left lamenting the past eight years lost to good governance and human rights, and promising to deliver a more positive future: average annual GDP growth since 2006 had languished at 0.6 per cent since Bainimarama seized power, national debt had nearly doubled, youth unemployment had growth massively, poverty – by some estimates – had risen from 31 per cent to over 45 per cent, and Bainimarama had regressed towards import substitution strategies and an ill-conceived retirement policy.[349] But, as Narsey later noted, FijiFirst's bread-and-butter pledges (and its delivery of infrastructure into long-neglected rural communities) carried far more weight with an electorate keen to move forward than dwell on constitutionality, law or revenge.[350] And, as a harbinger of life under FijiFirst, Fiji's economy did grow in 2014 by over 5 per cent and tourism boomed.

On 17 September 2014, Fiji finally went to the polls under the watchful eyes of 92 multinational observers.[351] Only 18 per cent of the 247 candidates were women. IndoFijians comprised just 38 per cent of the electorate. With an impressive 85 per cent turnout and a low informal vote (0.75 per cent, despite the complexities around identifying candidates by number), FijiFirst achieved a landslide victory, winning 60 per cent of the vote and 32 of the 50 seats; SODELPA gained only 28 per cent of the vote and 15 seats; and the NFP 6 per cent and three seats. Four parties (including the FLP) and two independents failed to make the 5 per cent threshold and received no seats. Only eight women were elected (another joined parliament several months later following

---

348 They were academic Jone Vakalalabure, former magistrate and lawyer Makereta Waqavonovono and former national rugby player Seru Rabeni (*Fiji Times*, 8 August 2014). The requirement for a two-year residency prior to voter registration had been removed earlier but now returned, affecting candidates who had studied overseas. The rule did not apply to public servants who lived overseas in the performance of their work.

349 Biman Prasad's address to the Fiji Teachers Union (www.coupfourandahalf.com, 30 April 2013).

350 *Fiji Times*, 21 September 2014.

351 The Multinational Observer Group reported the elections free and fair, but recommended that political party identification be included on candidate lists, that the requirements for registering parties be less onerous, that parties should be able to hold meetings without permits, and that the poll numbers assigned to candidates be drawn earlier in order to allow their parties time to publicise them (*fijivillage*, 14 April 2015).

a resignation).[352] Seventy-one per cent of IndoFijians, 50 per cent of Taukei and 80 per cent of other minorities voted for Bainimarama's party; 0.4 per cent of IndoFijians, 46 per cent of Taukei and 1.4 per cent of other minorities voted for SODELPA.[353] With 16 Taukei, 15 IndoFijian and two Other MPs, FijiFirst also became the most representative party in parliament. SODELPA comprised only iTaukei, while the small NFP managed one Taukei and two IndoFijian MPs.

This was, as Vijay Naidu and Sandra Tarte note, an historic election in so many ways: the first held in Fiji under proportional representation, one person – one vote – one value, a single national constituency, and a single electoral roll. All these features were designed to remove past gerrymanders and reduce the impact of ethnic appeals on electoral outcomes. There were other firsts also. All successful political parties were headed by a woman either as president or leader. Eighteen-year-olds could now vote, with the result that youths (18–25 years) comprised nearly 20 per cent of the electorate.[354] In fact, 47 per cent of voters were under 35 years, 75 per cent of whom voted in 2014 for the first time. Hence the significance of social media in this election, utilised with varying effectiveness by all the

---

352   The 5 per cent threshold equated to 27,000 votes. Four seats were effectively transferred to FijiFirst (three) and SODELPA (one). Many FijiFirst members sneaked into parliament with low personal votes, the lowest being 600 votes (Wadan Narsey, 'Critical issues for 2017', *Fiji Times*, 31 December 2016). Women clearly earned no advantage from the new voting system. Although they gained 16 per cent of seats compared with 11 per cent in 2006, the number of women elected remained the same.

353   *Fiji Times*, 21 September 2014; *Australian*, 20 September 2014; Steven Ratuva, 'Shifting democracy: electoral changes in Fiji', in Ratuva & Lawson, *The People Have Spoken*, 2016, pp. 28–34. Dr Jiko Luveni also became Fiji's first female Speaker of parliament. See also Asenati Liki & Claire Slatter, 'Control, alt, delete: How Fiji's new PR electoral system and media coverage affected election results for women candidates in the 2014 election', in Naidu & Tarte, *No Ordinary Election*, 2015; and Gordon Nanau, 'Representative democracy, the Constitution & electoral engineering in Fiji: 2014 & beyond', in Naidu & Tarte, *No Ordinary Election*, 2015, pp. 71–88, 17–34. Had the People's Democratic Party not split from the FLP, the FLP might have been able to achieve two seats. But with only 3 per cent of the vote each, they were excluded by the 5 per cent threshold rule, as were the two independents. The rule, not an uncommon feature with proportional representation (Germany and New Zealand have a similar threshold), is designed to favour political parties and reduce the potential for parliamentary instability (Nanau, 'Representative democracy', 2015, pp. 23–24). Chaudhry, however, believed the FLP's loss was due solely to his inability to contest the election (*Fiji Sun*, 10 July 2017). Because of its narrow electoral appeal, SODELPA required 80 per cent of the Taukei vote to win, an impossible task given many Taukei did not register or vote, and others viewed FijiFirst as a way to address the past dominance of eastern chiefs (Baker & Nakagawa, 'Known unknowns and unknown unknowns', 2015, pp. 116, 123).

354   'Introduction', Naidu & Tarte, *No Ordinary Election*, 2015, p. 5. Unlike previous voting systems based predominantly on closed lists, the open list provided more power to voters than parties in determining who would be elected.

parties.[355] It was also the first time an election had been held in a single day, and without the long queues that had once been a feature of polling. Over 2,000 polling stations and 14,000 polling officials saw to that.

The *Economist* noted that 'The result, by in effect legitimising the coup, has shocked the country's intellectual elite',[356] although Narsey more accurately reflected that the Bainimarama government could never have survived so long had it not enjoyed the support of that intellectual elite:

> Lawyers, former High Court judges, business men and women, accountants and auditors, public relations experts, university administrators and academics, opportunists from abroad, and at some critical times, some of our own colleagues and friends from the union movement.[357]

Yet it is also important to bear in mind that Bainimarama could also never have survived had his government not become responsive to popular needs and pushed ahead with long-neglected infrastructure development. That alone distinguished him and FijiFirst from SODELPA's chiefly sponsored forebears: Qarase's SDL, Rabuka's Soqosoqo ni Vakavulewa ni Taukei (SVT), and the final decade of Mara's Alliance. Indeed, FijiFirst rode into office on Bainimarama's popularity as a leader for change and stability, demonstrating how far he had travelled since 2006 when many diplomats found him unpredictable and angry.[358] He alone won 41 per cent of the popular vote and drew in 70 per cent of FijiFirst's support.[359] By removing the gerrymander of provincialism and communalism, the single electorate

---

355 Tarai et al., 'Political social media campaigning', 2015, pp. 89–114. FijiFirst outdid all other parties and independents in terms of the number of subscribers to its Facebook pages, but responded to and engaged less with its audience than SODELPA. The image that the parties conveyed on social media, however, probably mattered more: Bainimarama came across as a friendly family man, Kepa as a formal chief, while NFP candidates presented themselves with stilted studio images (Tarai et al., 'Political social media campaigning', 2015, p. 109). Joseph Veramu's report ('Our rising generation', *Fiji Times*, 5 January 2017) claimed that 91 per cent of 15–35-year-olds (35.5 per cent of the population) possessed mobile phones (72 per cent possessed mobiles with the internet), 83 per cent held Facebook accounts, and 38 per cent Twitter accounts.

356 *Economist*, 20 September 2014.

357 crosbiew.blogspot.com, 29 March 2014, Address to the Fiji Public Servants Association AGM.

358 Sometimes the old Bainimarama resurfaced. He sent an abusive text to Father Kevin Barr after Barr tweeted that the Chinese flag should replace the Union Jack in the corner of any new Bainimarama-endorsed Fiji flag. Barr was also threatened with expulsion (*Australian*, 18 January 2013). In June 2013, a FTV sports editor was forced to resign for accusing Bainimarama's daughter – the CEO of the Fiji Sports Council and organiser of a nearby high school event – of playing music too loudly (Robie, 'Unfree and unfair?', 2016, p. 86).

359 Bainimarama won four times more votes than Kepa, enabling his party to win many more seats than might have been the case had distribution been determined by individual candidate votes (Ratuva, 'Shifting democracy', 2016, p. 32).

open list proportional system advantaged his nationally inclusive party and disadvantaged those based on sectional, provincial and communal interests. So too the weakening of traditional politics as Fiji's population grew more urban and Viti Levu based. The 2014 election and the rules under which it was conducted represented an unprecedented rout of the old order.

Conclusion: Playing the politics of respect

Hubris

In the months that followed Rear Admiral (Ret) Voreqe Bainimarama's electoral victory, the rout did not dissipate. Almost immediately the Pacific Islands Forum (PIF) announced Fiji's readmission and Australia's Foreign Minister, Julie Bishop, visited Bainimarama to proclaim the formal removal of sanctions, new investments in job-creation programs, the relaunch of senior officials' meetings and the inclusion of Fiji in its seasonal workers and New Colombo programs.[1] Bishop's quick response did not, however, check Bainimarama's determination to consolidate Fiji's changed foreign policy position. Fiji returned to PIF but refused to participate in its leaders' meetings or back away from its desire to reform PIF's architecture.[2] Fiji also maintained its 'hardline' on the Pacific Agreement on Closer Economic Relations (PACER) Plus trade talks.[3] In Brisbane for an Australia–Fiji Business Forum later in 2015, Bainimarama reminded his audience: 'It is a great shame … Australia and

---

1   *Fiji Times*, 1 November 2014.
2   *Islands Business*, 21 January 2015. Fiji proposed that its former Foreign Minister, Kaliopate Tavola, be PIF's new secretary general. He supported Bainimarama's stance that Australia and New Zealand become donors and development partners of PIF only, and not sit at the leaders' table. Bainimarama deliberately avoided PNG's Prime Minister at the Japanese Pacific Islands Leaders Meeting in early 2015, fearing he would be lobbied to attend the forthcoming Moresby Forum.
3   Fiji rejoined the trade talks but held out for long-term improved market access, the maintenance of policy space, and binding commitments on labour mobility and development cooperation. There were 'not enough pluses in the PACER for Fiji to commit', Bainimarama claimed (*Fiji Times*, 8 & 17 May 2016). In September 2016, Bainimarama refused to sign PACER Plus: it was 'too one-sided, too restrictive, places too many obligations on us that we cannot afford to meet' (*Fiji Times*, 15 October 2016). Australia and NZ officials, however, believed it possible to conclude the agreement in 2017, the eighth year of negotiations (*Fiji Times*, 1 February 2017).

New Zealand – our traditional friends – turned their backs on us when we set out to substitute a flawed democracy in Fiji with a proper one like theirs.' And he added:

> How much sooner we might have been able to return Fiji to parliamentary rule if we hadn't expended so much effort on simply surviving. If you had been more understanding. More engaged. Been able to recognize that defending the status quo in Fiji was indefensible, intellectually and morally.[4]

The lesson, Foreign Minister Inoke Kubuabola claimed shortly after the elections, was simple: Fiji 'can never again permit [itself] to be dependent – politically, strategically or economically – on a narrow group of powerful countries'.[5]

Days later, Bainimarama hosted both India's new Prime Minister Narendra Modi and China's President Xi Jinping in Fiji. They came, Bainimarama declared, because they regard Fiji as important: 'They acknowledge us as a regional leader – a preeminent island nation that is also playing an increased role on the wider global stage.'[6] Fiji's years in the cold had permitted it to develop a powerful sense of difference with the past. It had established new diplomatic missions, joined the Non-Alignment Movement, gained alternative military support from Russia,[7] chaired the G77 + China and the International Sugar Organization, and created a new regional body, the Pacific Islands Development Forum (PIDF), the latter still a bone of contention with Australia and New Zealand.[8] Its UN ambassador, Peter Thomson, became President of the UN General Assembly in September 2016. And Fiji had developed a Green Growth Framework as a blueprint

---

4   *PACNews*, 15 November 2015.

5   *Fiji Sun*, 15 October 2014.

6   *Fiji Sun*, 18 November 2014.

7   Russian support was long in the making. Its Foreign Minister visited Suva in 2012 and Bainimarama pushed for a deal to supply much-needed new weaponry to its Golan Heights peacekeepers when he went to Moscow in 2013. In January 2016, some 25 containers of Russian arms and equipment, worth an estimated $19 million, arrived in Suva, initially creating public confusion as to its purpose. Bainimarama later declared that the Blackrock military base in Nadi would become a new peacekeeping training institute (*Economist*, 23 January 2016).

8   *Fiji Times*, 1 September 2015; *Australian*, 8 September 2015. Bainimarama accused the two neighbours of continuing to lobby Pacific countries not to attend PIDF meetings. Only eight of 14 PIF leaders attended the 2015 PIDF. Its acting secretary general, Amena Yauvoli, soon left to become – briefly – ambassador for climate change and oceans. In April 2016, he emerged as the new director general of the Melanesian Spearhead Group (MSG), a sign perhaps that Fiji wished to reinvigorate an organisation its former leader claimed lacked sufficient support from MSG governments (*Fiji Sun*, 9 April 2016). Samoan François Martel replaced him as PIDF Secretary General in September 2015, hoping to focus the PIDF on sustainable development through blue-green economies.

for development that allowed it to challenge the climate change policies of its large neighbours, gain prominence on the world stage for green leadership, become chair of the 23rd session of the Conference of Parties (COP 23) 2017 to the UN Framework Convention on Climate Change at the latter's secretariat in Bonn,[9] and co-chair the UN Conference on Oceans. 'Make no mistake, our resolve in the last eight years, our strategic direction as a nation and our ability to think outside the box,' Bainimarama asserted, 'has gained Fiji much respect around the world.'[10] This stance was not going to change.[11]

At home, Bainimarama delivered the same message. When parliament met for the first time in mid-October 2014, it was at the old parliament site in the downtown Government Buildings, not at Rabuka's former Veiuto complex. There is 'something deeply symbolic about having brought history full circle to this chamber', Bainimarama declared. His President agreed; it served to 'draw a line under the years of division that have held Fiji back and herald a new era of unity and purpose'.[12] But, as Nailatikau gave his address to the newly assembled parliament, it became apparent that FijiFirst had no intention of reaching out to its opposition, especially over the Constitution and parliamentary procedures. Instead it would focus on programs already begun: increasing

---

9   *Fiji Sun*, 2 June 2015. Fiji became the first nation in the world to ratify the Paris Agreement following the UN Climate Change Conference in December 2015, promising to generate all its electricity needs from renewable sources by 2030 and to cut emissions by 30 per cent (*Guardian*, 16 February 2016). Climate change is a real issue for Fiji. By mid-2015 it had spent $2 million relocating three villages threatened by rising sea waters and had identified another 45 (*Fiji Times*, 24 June 2015) under threat. The World Bank estimated Fiji would spend $478 million by 2020 on coastal protection, much of it on sea walls (*Fiji Times*, 31 July 2016). Fiji also offered to provide a permanent refuge to people from Kiribati and Tuvalu should they be displaced as a result of rising seas (*Fiji Times*, 25 May 2016).

10   *Fiji Sun*, 18 November 2014. Anna Powles and Jose Sousa-Santos are uncertain as to the long-term impact of new players such as China and Russia on the Pacific. Fiji has not supported China's position on South China Sea access, despite receiving nearly $700 million in Chinese aid between 2006 and 2013 (more than Australia's $620 million contribution), but it did abstain during the UN General Assembly vote on Russia's annexation of the Crimea in 2014. Nonetheless, Fiji's courting of new partners has effectively shifted its foreign policy and challenged the South Pacific's traditional security orthodoxy ('Principled engagement: rebuilding defence ties with Fiji', Lowy Institute Analysis paper, Sydney, July 2016).

11   Greg Fry and Sandra Tarte are more circumspect, believing this a journey with no obvious end (G Fry & S Tarte, *The New Pacific Diplomacy*. Canberra: ANU Press, 2015, p. 15). Powles and Sousa-Santos are similarly uncertain as to how the PIF rift will play out, but believe that Australia and New Zealand 'will have to be smarter in their engagement' with Fiji and the Pacific ('Principled engagement'). Meanwhile Bainimarama continues to push boundaries, requesting Fijian visa-free access to Europe's Schengen zone in 2016 (*Fiji Times*, 7 December 2016).

12   *Fiji Sun*, 14 October 2014. Of course Veiuto represented both Rabuka's failed communal politics and the site of the 2000 coup.

water and electricity subsidies to the poor, providing squatters with long-term leases, encouraging the commercial development of Taukei land, extending the Tertiary Education Loan Scheme, providing free education also to preschools, raising the minimum wage and supplying low-income earners with free hospital procedures and medicine.[13] When combined with funding for long-neglected infrastructure, the government believed it had a winning formula that could take it beyond the next election. In 2016, Aiyaz Sayed-Khaiyum described as unprecedented the economic growth in excess of 4 per cent that had occurred over the past three years, and proudly noted that government interventions for those at the bottom of the socio-economic scale meant that, rather than widen disparities between rich and poor, growth had actually reduced poverty levels by more than 3 per cent.[14] 'Compassion for the vulnerable' represented a hallmark of Bainimarama's leadership, he argued.[15]

The strategy caught the opposition parties off guard; they accused the government of remaining in campaign mode. But the real problem, Steven Ratuva noted, lay with their refusal to respect the election process.[16] The National Federation Party (NFP), he argued, needed to expand its appeal. It began the parliamentary session focusing on decrees, media restrictions, deteriorating services, and the unexplained discrepancies highlighted in the tabled Auditor-General's reports from 2010. It demanded a review of the 2013 Constitution and supported the Social Democratic Liberal Party's (SODELPA) petition to reinstate the Great Council of Chiefs (GCC) on the grounds that the public were not consulted on its abolition.[17] It called for a government of national unity and requested dialogue on 'critical issues'. It opposed the government's repeal of the death penalty in the *Royal Fiji Military Forces Act*.[18]

---

13   *Fiji Times*, 8 October 2014. In 2016, Bainimarama claimed that he wished to be known as the first prime minister to make education free to all Fijians (*Fiji Sun*, 13 January 2016).
14   *Fiji Sun*, 21 July 2016.
15   *Fiji Sun*, 10 December 2016.
16   *Fiji Sun*, 10 April 2015.
17   *Fiji Sun*, 30 April 2016.
18   As NFP President, Draunidalo expanded the debate, calling the United Nations a useless institution that sponsored mercenaries and let genocides occur (*Fiji Sun*, 20 February 2015).

With such a huge majority, Bainimarama felt no pressing need to deviate from his revolution. Instead he announced plans for a new flag for Fiji to better reflect his achievement in creating a new Fiji.[19] And he indulged in petty politics. An unforeseen discrepancy in the registration of the NFP auditors saw the small party threatened with exclusion from parliament at the start of 2016,[20] leaving its leader, Biman Prasad, impotently railing against the lack of bipartisanship, the continuance of draconian media decrees, the lack of fundamental rights, dictatorial and inconsistent economic management, and the development of a culture of servility and sycophancy.[21]

The larger SODELPA presented a different challenge. Certainly it raised similar issues as the NFP, with MP Niko Nawaikula provocatively suggesting that the government's refusal to review the Constitution was tantamount to inviting another coup.[22] He and his leader, Ro Teimumu Kepa, were members of the Fiji Native Tribal Congress, which, since 2010, had claimed that Bainimarama – and later his Constitution – breached UN-mandated indigenous rights by abolishing the GCC and the exclusive Fijian name, and by denying iTaukei self-determination.[23] The matter quickly came to a head in late 2014 when small groups of Taukei in Nadroga and Ra, under the influence of a Taukei expatriate

---

19   *Fiji Times*, 10 March, 7 July & 24 December 2015. Public responses to the proposal were muted and the opposition refused to engage in the process. Bainimarama argued that the flag carried both colonial and Bauan features, and Fiji now needed a more modern design. But, after witnessing how Fijians rallied around the flag during Fiji's first Olympic gold win in August 2016, he dropped the new flag from his list of priorities (*Fiji Sun*, 18 August 2016).

20   The NFP's auditors were not registered with the Fiji Institute of Accountants. Nineteen days later on 19 February 2016, the suspension ended when the NFP filed legal action in the High Court. Wadan Narsey argues that the suspension enabled the government to seize control of the Public Accounts Committee and change standing orders (*Fiji Times*, 21 February 2016). Undoubtedly this move assisted the government to reduce scrutiny of the Auditor-General's 2010–14 reports, which revealed that salaries to then ministers had bypassed Finance and been paid through a private accounting form, Aliz Pacific Ltd, owned by a relative of the Attorney-General. The Auditor-General questioned the lack of supporting documentation. The government did not respond to questions from then PAC chair, Biman Prasad (*Fiji Times*, 7 November 2014; 17 September 2015).

21   *Fiji Times*, 30 January 2016. Prasad highlighted the Prime Minister's pettiness: telling opposition leaders to 'jump in a deep pool' and advising gay people to shift to Iceland if they wished to marry, did not – he claimed – produce a worthy legacy. See also Prasad's address at the Centre for Strategic Studies, Victoria University of Wellington, 26 May 2016 (*Fiji Times*, 4 June 2016).

22   www.coupfourandahalf.com, 17 October 2014.

23   *Fiji Times*, 20 April 2015. In 2016, Kepa admitted in parliament that she now supported the use of 'Fijian' as a common name. To date, however, the party has not officially corrected its stance (*Fiji Sun*, 13 February 2016).

who urged them to rise up against the Bainimarama government, declared their provinces sovereign Christian states. As a consequence, by September 2015, 63 persons had been arrested and charged with sedition.

Although SODELPA distanced itself from the Taukeists, it sang from the same hymn sheet. Both Kepa and her deputy, Ratu Naiqama Lalabalavu, used much of their parliamentary time attacking government policies as anti-Taukei. Lalabalavu criticised the government's planned divestment of shares in state enterprises on the grounds that the entry of foreign companies reduced opportunities for Taukei investments and exposed the country to human trafficking, drugs and terrorism.[24] Kepa complained that government moves to prioritise places at state boarding schools for rural students would victimise iTaukei, and she insisted that the Constitution be put to a referendum.[25] As late as May 2016, Kepa referred to the government as a dictatorship and suggested that, when SODELPA becomes the government in 2018, it would take to task those journalists 'who are props of the dictatorship'.[26]

Such attacks enabled Bainimarama to assume the high moral ground. 'SODELPA keeps summoning up the past and preying on the fears of the iTaukei people about the security of their land and their way of life,' he told the Kadavu Provincial Council in February 2015: 'It is divisive. It is offensive. And it simply isn't true ... There is no threat to iTaukei – to our land, culture, institutions or religion.'[27] He told school cadets in Nadi that 'The future for Fiji isn't one of a privileged few keeping only the best for themselves and not sharing with other ordinary common Fijians'.[28] But he was not above baiting SODELPA. Only English could be spoken in parliament and chiefly titles were not to be used. 'When you walk out,' he declared, 'you can pick it up again, your Ratu, your Adi, and you walk out with it.'[29]

24   *Fiji Times*, 13 December 2014. The Fiji Electricity Authority (FEA) became an early target for divestment.
25   *Fiji Times*, 13 April & 24 December 2015.
26   *Fiji Sun*, 4 May 2016.
27   *Fiji Sun*, 20 February 2015.
28   *Fiji Sun*, 23 April 2015.
29   *Fiji Times*, 11 February 2015.

As Ratuva commented, SODELPA was a dream opposition for FijiFirst. By constantly focusing on Taukei issues and the 2006 coup, it placed itself exactly where the assertively inclusive FijiFirst wanted it.[30] Discontent within SODELPA did the Opposition no favours either. Discontent derived in part from its stunning defeat in the 2014 elections. Kepa blamed her party's defeat on Bainimarama's fear-mongering. Prior to voting, Bainimarama implied that Suva would burn again if FijiFirst lost power and Kepa claimed that fear drove voters into his arms.[31] But, having focused so much on Taukei matters during the election campaign, it soon became clear that some of her MPs held different views on what mattered to iTaukei. In fact, some issues around which the party appeared to present a united front were potentially destabilising. For example, while Kepa and Nawaikula regarded the disestablishment of the GCC as a pivotal symbol of Bainimarama's trashing of indigenous rights, MPs like Mosese Bulitavu believed that indigenous rights should not be used as a reason for the re-establishment of the GCC. Far from being a traditional indigenous institution, he argued, the GCC had been a colonial-era ploy by Bau to assert dominance over Fiji and eradicate the influence of once powerful *tikina* such as Verata. Indeed, the whole chiefly system, he asserted, was politicised by the descendants of the dominant chiefs of 1874 to augment their authority.[32]

These were not new arguments, and equating Taukei rights with indigenous rights had long been bedevilled by the problem of how to define the group. Who are Taukei? Who are not? Prior to 1990, most Fiji-born descendants of Pacific islanders were considered Taukei for voting purposes. Rabuka's 1990 Constitution stripped that status from them. Attempts were then made to excise Taukei of those with mixed heritage. Hence Ratu Sir Kamisese Mara's fears that the same fate awaited Lauans in Viti Levu.[33] Group rights, as opposed to human rights, always carry this risk.

---

30   *Fiji Sun*, 10 April 2015. SOLDELPA's weakness is potentially FijiFirst's weakness also. Should SODELPA abandon its communal and chiefly focus and transform itself into a national party like FijiFirst, it may become a credible alternative government in the future.

31   *Fiji Sun*, 28 September 2014. Mick Beddoes claimed SODELPA lost because 'the election process was compromised' (*Fiji Sun*, 25 October 2015).

32   *Fiji Sun*, 10 October 2015.

33   *fijilive*, 16 October 2000. Qarase's government attempted to impose Taukei colonial patrilineal criteria on Rotumans also.

Unsurprisingly, then, confusion over indigeneity abounds. Bainimarama has described iTaukei, Banabans and Rotumans as indigenous peoples of Fiji, although Banabans (from Kiribati) only settled in Fiji (on Rabi Island) after 1945. When Rotuman Jioji Konrote became the new Fiji President in October 2015, Brij Lal welcomed him as Fiji's first 'non-indigenous' president.[34] Clearly indigeneity and Taukei identity are not one and the same. iTaukei and Rotumans may meet one UN criterion by having 'historical continuity with pre-invasion and pre-colonial societies', even if in different parts of Fiji. They do not, however, satisfy other criteria, for example, that they 'form at present non-dominant sectors of society'.[35] Add to that the complexities of colonial institutions and customs that are accorded traditional status by some indigenous peoples but not others, and a recipe for division and hatred soon emerges. Hence Bainimarama's desire to call everyone Fijian, to reject ethno-nationalism, and move on with what he sees as more important issues facing modern Fiji. 'We drew a line under the past,' he declared: 'We reset the national compass.'[36]

Not so SODELPA, but its problems were not solely confined to its backward-looking agenda. Many within the party blamed Kepa and Laisenia Qarase for its failure to win the 2014 election. They were unhappy with the party's management. Kepa did not inform them of Mick Beddoes' appointment as principal administration officer in the Opposition office or of her support for Biman Prasad as chair of the Parliamentary Public Accounts Committee and Richard Naidu as a member of the Constitutional Services Commission. When shadow portfolios were apportioned, Kepa chose education, not the iTaukei affairs and sugar portfolios that Bainimarama held in addition to being prime minister. Thus she lost the opportunity to directly confront Bainimarama on the floor of the parliament; that role went to her deputy instead.[37]

---

34   www.coupfourandahalf.com, 19 October 2015.

35   *The UN Declaration on the Rights of Indigenous Peoples: A Manual for National Human Rights Institutions.* Sydney & Geneva: Asia Pacific Forum of National Human Rights Institutions and the Office of the UN High Commissioner for Human Rights, 2013, p. 6.

36   *Fiji Times*, 4 March 2015. Bainimarama told the UN Human Rights Council in Geneva that the UN Declaration on the Rights of Indigenous Peoples did not readily apply in Fiji. The Taukei had not been dispossessed of their land; their land, culture, traditions and languages were protected in the Constitution and were not under threat (*Fiji Sun*, 4 March 2015).

37   *Fiji Sun*, 20 October 2014. Some MPs in her party wanted Aseri Radrodro, an accountant and auditor, as the Public Accounts Committee chair instead. Additionally, some SODELPA MPs opposed granting NFP members front bench seats in parliament, given that the NFP had rejected being in coalition with SODELPA prior to the elections (*Fiji Sun*, 15 May 2016). Such dissatisfaction weakened Opposition solidarity.

By boycotting the special sitting of parliament for an address by Indian Prime Minister Narendra Modi, she failed to rise above party politics. She also led SODELPA out of the chamber during the budget address. She undertook an unendorsed and reportedly disorganised tour of Vanua Levu. And she returned from the United States without attending a UN indigenous conference, claiming that she had been treated with disrespect.[38]

A report on the state of SODELPA in mid-2015, requested by five MPs led by Bulitavu and Aseri Radrodro, criticised party governance, financial management and leadership. It recommended Kepa's expulsion. A disciplinary committee meeting subsequently cleared her of wrong doing[39] but, with the party divided, no clear way forward seemed possible, especially after its deputy leader, Lalabalavu, seen by some as a possible successor, was banned from parliament for two years in May 2015 for making a derogatory comment about the Speaker of the House. He had also attempted to bring Sitiveni Rabuka into the party prior to the elections.[40] Later he tried to install him as a vice president, but Kepa refused and Rabuka reportedly resigned from the party. With the subsequent resignations of general secretary Pio Tabaiwalu, Beddoes and Pita Waqavonovono from their posts, SODELPA appeared to reach a new low. Even if Lalabalavu had assumed the leadership, it is unlikely he would have received the support of dissidents, who wanted to keep chiefs out of the frontline.[41]

To foster unity, SODELPA pardoned Kepa instead. But, during 2016, discontent rumbled on, focusing on her unadvertised appointment of Adi Laufitu Malani as her personal assistant and her dogged pursuit of the GCC lost cause.[42] Kepa seemed unwilling or unable to escape her chiefly straitjacket. Perhaps for that reason she announced in June 2016 her intention not to recontest party leadership. In the tussle that quickly followed, Rabuka finally made his way back into political leadership,

---

38   *Fiji Sun*, 24 May 2016. No one met her at Los Angeles from where she intended to transit to New York.

39   *Fiji Sun*, 13 December 2015.

40   *Fiji Sun*, 3 & 11 September, 22 October 2015. In June 2016, the NFP's Tupou Draunidalo was similarly excluded for the remainder of the parliament for making a derogatory comment (*Fiji Times*, 4 June 2016); the same fate awaited Opposition Whip Ratu Isoa Tikoca – for making anti-Muslim remarks (*Fiji Sun*, 30 September 2016).

41   *Fiji Sun*, 12 July 2016.

42   *Fiji Sun*, 3 February, 12 & 26 April 2016; see Neelesh Gounder, 'The Opposition in an effective democracy', *Fiji Times*, 28 May 2016.

hoping to repeat his 1992 performance as leader of the Soqosoqo ni Vakavulewa ni Taukei (SVT), and promising to make SODELPA relevant to more Fijians by abandoning ethno-nationalism.[43]

Nonetheless, some party members were unhappy with yet another return to the past. They believed that Rabuka was too close to the military machine they conveniently blamed for all Fiji's political woes. Indeed, no Opposition leader except Rabuka attended Constitution Day ceremonies in September 2016. The national interest, he declared, should always come before party interests, a line that distanced him further from some of his new colleagues. Party resignations soon followed and – in the absence of clear party policies on cooperation – the task of creating an effective Opposition coalition and widening its support base ahead of elections in 2018 remained a work in progress.[44] When the government proposed an increase in parliamentary allowances, SODELPA could not even maintain unified opposition.[45]

Bainimarama did not have it all his own way, however. The militarisation of the police force remained an ongoing issue after the resignation of Commissioner Ben Groenewald, a South African appointed only in May 2014 to secure organisational and operational changes ahead of elections and to end its reputation as 'a brutal force'. He cited continued military interference in policing, a reference to three police officers who had beaten and sexually assaulted an escaped prisoner in 2012. Groenewald had reopened the case after the military recruited the officers, claiming the police had abandoned them. Brigadier General Sitiveni Qiliho now replaced Groenewald as Police Commissioner in November 2015 but, before long, found himself embroiled in controversy when he re-employed

---

43   Kepa remained the parliamentary Opposition leader, indicating that she would not contest the next election. Both Kepa and Lalabalavu officially announced their withdrawal in January 2017. Reportedly Lalabalavu approached Rabuka in April 2016 to succeed Kepa as party leader (*Fiji Sun*, 8 May 2016; 14 January 2017).

44   *Fiji Sun*, 2 & 25 June, 8 & 28 September 2016. Former youth wing member Pita Waqavonovono and Beddoes were reported to be establishing their own political party and planning a grand coalition ahead of the 2018 election (*fijivillage*, 19 November 2016). Opposition to Rabuka centred on his coup leadership in 1987 and the similarity of his credentials and outlook with Bainimarama's. Beddoes called removing a leader (Kepa) who had polled the SODELPA's largest votes (35 per cent of its votes) 'an act of lunacy' (*Fiji Sun*, 26 June 2016). NFP President Draunidalo took the opportunity to claim her party the only one fit to contest the next elections; its members and leaders had never planned or taken part in coups. She argued that the NFP had to differentiate itself and would not engage with people involved in coups. Her leader, however, did not endorse this strategy (*Fiji Times*, 27 June 2016; *Fiji Sun*, 27 June 2016).

45   Lalabalavu and Rabuka presented contradictory advice on the parliamentary allowance vote to their parliamentary members (*Fiji Sun*, 6 October 2016).

police officers who Groenewald had stood down over the 2014 sexual assault and death of a robbery suspect in Nadi and the sexual assault of another prisoner. Qiliho claimed they were needed in the fight against Fiji's rising crime rate. The Chief of Intelligence and Investigations, Harry Brown, resigned in protest.[46]

Another resignation surprised in late 2015. Brigadier General Mosese Tikoitoga had only been Commander of the Republic of Fiji Military Forces (RFMF) for one year, but allegedly proved too independent, promoting officers of his choice into senior roles and denying Bainimarama's personal bodyguards access to the Queen Elizabeth Barracks officers' mess. Not long after, Rear Admiral Viliame Naupoto became the new RFMF Commander and Tikoitoga was 'exiled' as ambassador to Ethiopia.[47] Fresh human rights issues also arose; a Lautoka internet café owner alleged that he had been tortured by police in late November 2015 after he sent copies to the Police Commissioner and the Attorney-General of plans to destabilise the government. His house was later firebombed in an attack reminiscent of military special ops after 2009. Bizarrely, historian Brij Lal and his economist wife, Padma Lal, remained barred from returning to Fiji.[48]

Disturbing as these matters were, they did not unsettle the government or force it to reach out to the Opposition parties. Instead, strong economic growth bolstered government confidence. Four per cent GDP growth in 2015 permitted an optimistic budget at the end of the year, with VAT reduced to 9 per cent, and record spending on land development, roads, water and electricity. To much fanfare, the government announced a new $103 million infrastructure loan from the World Bank and Asian Development Bank (ADB), the first for Fiji in 23 years. Bainimarama claimed only to be reversing the neglect of former governments and predicted that unemployment would fall and that tourism, already

---

46   *Fiji Sun*, 9 February 2016; *Fiji Times*, 3 April 2016. The police, like the military, had also to confront its own violent past. In July 2016, images of Colo villagers beaten and tortured during drug raids in 2009 circulated on social media (*Fiji Times*, 13 July 2016). Eight former police officers and one soldier were found guilty in late 2016 of the sexual assault and rape of robbery suspects near Sigatoka in 2014, one of whom who later died of his injuries. They were sentenced variously from seven to nine years (*Fiji Sun*, 12 November 2016; *Fiji Times*, 22 November 2016). Burglaries increased 31 per cent between 2014 and 2015. In 2016, carjackings and home invasions also increased.

47   *Fiji Times*, 12 & 20 November 2015; *Fiji Sun*, 10 November 2015; *Economist*, 23 January 2016. At the same time, Mohammad Aziz returned from long service leave as Deputy Commander.

48   *Fiji Sun*, 17 December 2015; *Fiji Times*, 16 December & 4 July 2015.

comprising 30 per cent of GDP, would soon be a $2 billion industry.[49] Fiji Airways opened new services to Singapore and San Francisco. Barry Whiteside, governor of the Reserve Bank of Fiji, predicted growth in mineral water, garments, timber, mining and manufacturing in the years ahead and noted that remittances had become the largest foreign exchange earner for Fiji after tourism. He also predicted that attention to micro and small-to-medium enterprises would 'make growth more inclusive for rural dwellers'.[50]

But there were dangers. Despite the International Monetary Fund praising Fiji for becoming a more equal society, ECREA's Father Kevin Barr doubted government claims that poverty had fallen to 28.1 per cent: Fiji's cost of living had risen over 40 per cent since 2009, domestic violence and crime had increased, so too the number of squatters.[51] VAT may have fallen, but not necessarily in a way that assisted the poor, given that exemptions for basic food and medicines were removed. In addition, continued economic growth remained too dependent on debt, and increased debt (46 per cent of GDP and projected to rise to 50.4 per cent by mid-2017) potentially threatened both Fiji's B+ credit rating[52] and the viability of its major internal lender, the Fiji National Provident Fund (FNPF).

---

49   *Fiji Times*, 18 April & 25 May 2016; *Fiji Sun*, 17 November 2015; *Financial Review*, 18 November 2015. The World Bank opened a new liaison office in Suva in May 2016.

50   *Fiji Times*, 19 July 2016. Remittances reached $492 million in 2015, 28 per cent higher than in 2014 ($354 million), reinforcing the government's claim that its focus on the education and welfare of its people would pay dividends in the long run. In 2016, remittances rose a further 6 per cent to $530 million and to $605 million in 2017 (*Fiji Times*, 1 September 2016, 7 July 2017). Whiteside anticipated that an expansion in Australia's seasonal worker program for agriculture, tourism and aged care, together with British army recruitment, would strengthen labour mobility further. He also congratulated the garment industry for developing niche products such as designer and sportswear that enabled it finally to realise the value of high end products. It now earned $100 million annually, and employed 7,000 workers, 90 per cent being women. Dependence on Australasian markets for sales, however, and a falling Australian dollar hampered growth. The rising US dollar increased the cost of raw materials (*Fiji Times*, 9 December 2016; 28 February 2017). Whiteside believed a similar niche awaited micro and small enterprises with virgin coconut oil and seaweed production.

51   *PACNews*, 21 April 2016; crosbiew.blogspot.com, 29 April 2009.

52   *Fiji Times*, 28 April & 23 June 2016. Welfare and debt promised a bleak future, according to Biman Prasad (*Fiji Times*, 3 December 2014); however, due to economic growth, the debt to GDP ratio had fallen from 56 per cent at the end of 2010, where it had been stuck since 2000, and is forecast to fall to 43 per cent of a much larger economy by mid-2017 (*Fiji Times*, 30 May 2016; Joseph Veramu, 'Budget and Prospects', *Fiji Times*, 7 July 2017). Over 70 per cent of Fiji's debt is held internally.

Once more, the consequences of agricultural neglect loomed large, especially in the long-suffering sugar industry where the government proposed legal sanctions to compel greater production.[53] Pine and mahogany industries were also affected by longstanding neglect, their potential for value-adding largely unrealised. Land-tenure laws and policies similarly constrained investment in agriculture.[54] Neglect imposed a drag on growth, but was not responsible for the sharp fall in projected GDP growth for 2016, from 3.7 per cent to 2.4.[55] On this occasion, the cause lay in the unexpected. Cyclone Winston – a category 5 hurricane, the strongest ever recorded in the southern hemisphere – struck Fiji on 20 February and left a $2 billion trail of disaster as it tracked between the two main islands with wind speeds up to 233 kilometres per hour: 44 lives

---

53   *Fiji Times*, 9 May 2016. Only 52.5 per cent of cane-farming land remained cultivated in 2016, sugar production had fallen 30 per cent since 2006 (from 310,000 to 220,000 tonnes), and the number of growers had also fallen 30 per cent (from 18,636 to 12,872). With costs of production close to $50 for a tonne of cane, returns from the $75 price for a tonne of cane put the average grower on an income of $4,500, well below the minimum wage. Further problems loomed for the industry; EU sugar quotas end in October 2017 and British importer Tate & Lyle ceased purchasing Fair Trade sugar from Fiji in August 2015. Some 5,000 members of the Lautoka Cane Producers Association had relied upon Fair Trade income since 2012 to subsidise sugar production (*Fiji Times*, 4 December 2016). Prasad urged the government to boost production by guaranteeing growers $90 a tonne (*Fiji Times*, 30 July 2016). Instead, its 2016 Sugar Cane Industry Bill proposed the complete nationalisation of the financially stricken Fiji Sugar Corporation and the introduction of draconian penalties to enforce harvesting and planting (*Fiji Times*, 14 May & 23 November 2016). Diversification plans for two mills were put on hold (*Fiji Times*, 31 May 2016), despite the lack of cane for crushing making all the four mills unviable (Biman Prasad, 'Sugar sector anaysis: Caught up in cobwebs', *Fiji Times*, 4 March 2017; the cyclone-damaged Penang mill in Rakiraki closed in early 2017). So, too, plans to pay farmers for the quality of cane they delivered to the mills, rather than its weight (*Fiji Times*, 30 December 2016). Fiji still dreamed, however, of replacing agricultural imports with local produce, especially for the tourist sector, but also made slow progress (*Financial Review*, 18 October 2015). Indeed, agriculture's contribution to GDP continued to decline, from 12 per cent in 2006 to 8 per cent in 2016 (*Fiji Sun*, 1 December 2016).

54   *Fiji Times*, 19 July 2016. Address by Reserve Bank of Fiji governor Whiteside to the 2016 ADB Pacific Update Conference held at University of the South Pacific. Mahogany stagnated, with little investment in replanting (*Fiji Times*, 14 November 2016). Bainimarama commited to redevelop the pine industry, with new resources to extend the industry in 2017 to maritime islands like Kadavu (*Fiji Sun*, 22 January 2017).

55   This was temporarily restored to 3 per cent at the time of the 2016–17 budget. Projections of 3.6 per cent GDP growth for 2017 and 3.2 per cent in 2018 and 2019 allowed Sayed-Khaiyum to forecast an unprecedented nine consecutive years of growth from 2010 (*Fiji Sun*, 21 July 2016).

and 40,000 homes lost, 419 schools damaged, 160 schools destroyed, and an estimated $200 million loss in crops. The devastation impacted nearly 40 per cent of Fiji's population and drove up inflation.[56]

Bainimarama's government rose quickly to the challenge and introduced novel initiatives. It launched a successful adopt-a-school program as a target for foreign aid,[57] as well as an adopt-a-village fund. 'Help for Homes' provided $88 million in immediate financial assistance for home owners earning less than $50,000. Depending on the nature of damage, a home owner received a card loaded with up to $7,000, redeemable at any hardware outlet.[58] The FNPF also allowed members to withdraw up to $5,000 and, by May 2016, it had disbursed nearly $300 million. In addition, government paid social welfare benefits as a lump sum for three months to assist some 44,000 families recover.[59] In its budget in

---

56   *Fiji Times*, 5 March 2016, 27 March 2017; *Fiji Sun*, 21 January 2017. Sugar production fell over 26 per cent to 164,330 tonnes in 2016 (*Fiji Times*, 31 December 2016); however, major tourism areas were less affected, enabling a faster recovery for the Fiji economy (*Fiji Times*, 30 May 2016; *Fiji Sun*, 4 December 2016). Fiji Electricity Authority infrastructure damage alone stood at $30 million. The Fiji Development Bank, which allocated 20 per cent of its loans to agriculture, reported losses of $4 million and immediately provided assistance to farmers and businesses affected (*Fiji Times*, 24 January 2017). Inflation peaked at 6.8 per cent in January 2017 (*Fiji Times*, 28 February & 26 March 2017), with half attributed to kava price increases. By May 2017, inflation had fallen to 2.5 per cent (*Fiji Times*, 5 July 2017).

57   India, for example, pledged to adopt 20 schools and gave the government $2.7 million. In 2016, India also donated $10.6 million in cash, relief materials, equipment and seeds. Indonesia contributed to the reconstruction of Queen Victoria School, and other governments, including Japan, which contributed $3.2 million for four schools, also committed resources to the school-rebuild effort. The Fiji Government committed $207.9 million in the 2016–17 budget (*Fiji Times*, 26 January & 2 February 2017; *Fiji Sun*, 21 January 2017).

58   The program was extended in late 2016 with an additional $20 million. Of course its success depended on retail hardware outlets being able to deliver the materials required. Evidence soon emerged that many were unable to deliver as promised, especially concrete blocks, roofing iron and timber (*Fiji Sun*, 5 August 2016; *Fiji Times*, 6 September 2016). Additionally, many areas were excluded from the first round of assistance and had to endure a long wait until the second round began at the end of 2016. A lack of documentation also frustrated tendering for school rebuilding, with deadlines for completion pushed back until October 2017. Until then students had to make do with tents (*Fiji Sun*, 23 December 2016).

59   *Fiji Times*, 9 & 22 March, 28 & 30 April 2016. Parliament rushed through a *False Information Act* in April 2016 to prevent abuse of cyclone assistance. By the end of May, some 22,100 homes had been assisted through the Help for Homes initiative. But the constant impact of withdrawals for education, housing, medical bills, unemployment and funeral costs from the $5 billion FNPF meant that 75 per cent of its 403,316 members now had less than $10,000 remaining in their pension accounts. Only 14 per cent had balances above $50,000 (*Fiji Times*, 1 & 2 August, 13 October 2016). Its chair, Ajith Kodagoda, believed inadequate financial literacy misled 200,000 members into withdrawing funds after Winston and neglecting the consequences for their retirement (*Fiji Sun*, 1 March 2017).

June it reinforced its welfare credentials further, expanding poverty and pension schemes for the disadvantaged, and continuing medical, electricity and water subsidies to the poor.[60]

Inevitably, politics entered reconstruction efforts. Bainimarama refused a SODELPA request to rebuild damaged churches. A secular state had of necessity to restore buildings and public infrastructure that benefited all Fijians; hence it would remain focused on homes, schools and health centres, and prioritise the provision of water and electricity services.[61] Rabuka accused Bainimarama of deliberately fostering a culture of dependency that denied people the capacity to be resilient.[62] Prasad called for an investigation into the two large hardware firms most responsible for long delays in providing materials under the Help for Homes initiative. They had accepted government money but apparently found it more profitable to export scarce materials than deliver them to cyclone victims. The government, Prasad claimed, failed to confirm their stocks prior to handing over money.[63] But, if anything, Cyclone Winston demonstrated – at least in the short term – both the government's competence and its resolve to maintain its goals.[64] Certainly the World Bank celebrated its efforts, declaring it a model for the Pacific. The government's individual lump sum of $600 to 10 per cent of the population pumped nearly $20 million into the economy in the three months following Winston, when pump-priming was most needed to keep the economy going.[65] Additionally, Fiji's Rugby Sevens gold win at the Rio Olympic Games in August 2016 gave Fiji's people and its government an important psychological boost, and a rare moment to come together to celebrate an historic achievement after such a difficult year.

---

60 Recovery after Winston (assisted by remittances and foreign aid) permitted the government to push on with expanding medical training and services, to plan the establishment of a new pilot training academy in association with Boeing and Airbus, to develop Nadi's Black Rock military facility as a peacekeeping centre, to obtain special vehicles for disaster relief, to shift the target of infrastructure development from large projects to rural roads, bridges and wharves, and to increase its focus on education.

61 *Fiji Times*, 21 & 30 April 2016.

62 *Fiji Times*, 29 August 2016.

63 *Fiji Times*, 5 & 13 December 2016. The two companies were dropped from the second phase of the initiative and the Attorney-General threatened them with penalty and interest charges.

64 Sayed-Khaiyum, as Minister for Economy, drew attention to the work of the Construction and Implementation Unit within the ministry for progressing the rebuild and 'building back better within budget' (*Fiji Sun*, 21 January 2017).

65 *Fiji Sun*, 22 February 2017.

Nonetheless, dangers still lay ahead. At the end of 2016 the Reserve Bank revised GDP growth for the year down to 2 per cent, acknowledging both the greater damage Winston had inflicted on Fiji's cane belt, forests and aquaculture than originally supposed and the slow pace in rehabilitation efforts forced by crippling shortages in building materials and persistent wet weather.[66] Major flooding from a tropical depression at the end of 2016 inflicted further hardship on many of the same areas that Winston had hit. So, too, did an unexpectedly prolonged decline in tourism arrivals after Winston.[67] The Reserve Bank's GDP downgrade potentially threatened hopes for 3.8 per cent growth in 2017 and the government's boast of nine consecutive years of strong growth. A new $840 million ADB and European Investment Bank loan in December 2016 for water supply and waste management in greater Suva promised to maintain the government's infrastructure drive, and the Attorney-General quickly reminded Fiji that Bainimarama's commitment to modernise Fiji for all Fijians, 'not just a select few', remained a core feature of his leadership.[68]

Nonetheless, 2016 demonstrated FijiFirst's inability to anticipate external shocks to the economy. Growth could never be taken for granted and decline now might even embolden Fiji's opposition parties ahead of elections in 2018.[69] Any political or economic stumble could puncture FijiFirst's aura of invincibility. Hence the Attorney-General's concern at the end of 2016 to remind Fijians what FijiFirst had achieved.

---

66   *Fiji Times*, 17 November 2016.

67   *Fiji Times*, 13 December 2016. The tropical depression (TD04F) hit Ra hard; 66 per cent of Ra's river crossings were damaged by TD04F and Winston. The cost of repairs could only be sustained over several years. Cyclone Winston also had a long-term impact on tourism and, although tourist numbers rose during the year (principally from New Zealand and China), earnings in the September quarter were 10 per cent lower than in 2015. From November 2015 to November 2016 visitor arrivals rose 5 per cent, although Australian arrivals (50 per cent of the tourism market) fell 1.2 per cent. However, data for the year up until May 2017 suggested tourist numbers had increased 7.7 per cent (*Fiji Times*, 4 July 2017). Fiji Airways retained its plan for a new service to Adelaide in mid-2017, and with new resorts opening in 2017, Fiji still hoped to achieve one million tourist arrivals by 2020 (*Fiji Times*, 31 December 2016, 31 January 2017).

68   *Fiji Sun*, 10 December 2016.

69   Indeed, sociologist Tui Rakuita suggested that FijiFirst would struggle to retain the support it gained in 2014 because of substantial rebuild delays after Winston ('Analysing the polls', *Fiji Times*, 25 February 2017). The Tebutt-Times poll at the start of February gave FijiFirst only 37 per cent of the vote, compared with 13 per cent for SODELPA and one per cent for the NFP. Forty per cent of those polled remained undecided (*Fiji Times*, 26 February 2017).

It may seem a simple thing, but by establishing our shared identity as 'Fijians', the Constitution sent a clear message that every Fijian is equal under the law and equally entitled to the benefits of our nation's progress. That mantra has driven the progress we have made over the past decade to reverse the years of discrimination that plagued Fijian society and stagnated our national development.[70]

But for opposition parties, the past did not always appear so simple. Hence, Amnesty International's report on torture in Fiji in mid-December 2016 provided an ideal opportunity for them to come together against FijiFirst. The report noted Bainimarama's concession that beatings are 'deeply engrained in parts of the Fijian psyche', but argued that: 'When the military is involved in policing matters, human rights violations are more likely to occur and they are less likely to be held accountable for their actions.'[71] Immediately Draunidalo launched an attack on the decrees and immunity provisions inserted in the Constitution as a cause of Fiji's dangerous culture of impunity. Silence reigned from her opposition colleagues, however, leaving an unchallenged Sayed-Khaiyum to declare the report selective and biased. Chief Justice Gates also reinforced Bainimarama's claim that beatings were common long before 1987 and the coups. The report, he maintained, neither offered solutions nor acknowledged government responses.[72]

Responsibility for the opposition's paralysis lay in part with Rabuka's resurrection. No sign existed by the end of 2016 that he could revitalise SODELPA or heal the differences within and between the parties to lead a united struggle against FijiFirst or at least enhance cooperation. SODELPA's continued claim for preferential Taukei treatment risked the broader multicultural appeal it required to challenge FijiFirst, while Rabuka's leadership created tensions, especially within the NFP, which

---

70   *Fiji Sun*, 8 December 2016. Bainimarama's attendance at the launch of a dubious Instacharge app in late 2016 could have become such a stumble. Foreign media claimed he endorsed the app, which its promoters claimed enabled mobile phones to recharge within 30 seconds (*Guardian*, 3 December 2016), but local media only reported that he sought to spruik Fiji's fast growing information and communications technology sector, now comprising 6 per cent of GDP (*Fiji Times*, 4 December 2016).

71   Amnesty International, *Beating Justice: How Fiji's Security Forces Get Away with Torture*. London: 2016, pp. 4–5. Fiji ratified the UN Convention against Torture (CAT) in March 2016 and hosted a regional workshop on CAT at Natadola in October. It sought a seat on the UN Human Rights Council.

72   *Fiji Times*, 13 December 2016; *Fiji Sun*, 11 December 2016. The British government and the UNDP were working with Fiji to establish new procedures for interviewing prisoners.

could ultimately disadvantage both parties.[73] If anything, Rabuka's past haunted him: If we cannot work together, he argued, then any electoral victory against the government will be hollow, like Mahendra Chaudhry's in 1999 when opposition parties 'ganged up against the SVT, they won, and then they saw who the winner was … They did not like it'. 'If we combine to defeat someone, then what?' he pondered.[74] Fiji's electoral landscape was reset in 2014, but political parties born from the struggles of a past era could not be remade.

Perspectives

Bainimarama's election victory in 2014 is now part of Fiji's history. But histories are of necessity confined by their parameters; the shorter the timeframe for analysis, the narrower their context. To some extent this effect is understandable, but it can distort perceptions. This study focuses only on Fiji's postcolonial years and, in particular, on a coup-riven period of nearly 30 years. That might seem a long time but, against Fiji's three millennia of human settlement, it is very short. We know very little about that greater epoch to enable valuable comparisons for contemporary studies. Only from the late 18th and 19th centuries, when the world began to envelop the Pacific islands, are Fiji's histories better understood, and their complexities suggest that it would be foolish to read into contemporary history the detail of what preceded. This, however, is precisely how many people do read their past, with the result that their reimagined 19th century has become the tempting tradition against which all change is judged; temptation being greatest when contemporary advantage is sought.

---

73   *Fiji Sun*, 23 & 24 December 2016. When Rabuka called for a united struggle against FijiFirst, he made clear that other opposition parties should recognise SODELPA's superior status. Their supporters should unite behind SODELPA (*Fiji Times*, 30 November 2016). That clearly did not accord with Draunidalo's preferences, and at the start of 2017 she quit as President of the NFP. SODELPA replaced Prasad as shadow Minister for Economy with its own Radrodro in July 2017 (*Fiji Times*, 10 July 2017). Rumours suggested she might join Waqavonovono's proposed Hope party. Meanwhile Rabuka began coalition talks with the Fiji Labour Party and its breakaway United Fiji Freedom Party. At the start of 2017, it is unclear whether the NFP will join in a coalition against FijiFirst or if sufficient common interests could sustain a coalition divided over so many issues (*Fiji Sun*, 28 January 2017). The formation of a new Unity Fiji Party in May 2017, along with the campaign ambitions of the People's Democratic Party, seemed to suggest that FijiFirst would find itself pitted against a very divided opposition in 2018 (*Fiji Sun*, 30 May 2017).
74   *Fiji Times*, 28 September 2016.

But the past is never so bound. Because we stand with one foot in the past and with the other reaching for the future, when we do look back or stare ahead, the perpetually changing present constantly challenges what we glimpse. Like ancient navigators on high seas, we seek a star to guide us. For many people in Fiji, the Constitutions have become their stars, with each new deviation scrutinised to ascertain distance from the original reference. But this way of viewing change can be misleading if it carries the assumption that the first reference point, a constitution embedded in the politics of communalism, represents a national lodestone with deep roots in an ancient past of Taukei order.

How, then, might we view Fiji, a country that is both clearly and simplistically the product of very different migratory histories: early settlement by Lapita Polynesians followed much later by waves of Melanesians from the Solomons and Vanuatu? To that mix we should add the influx of Tongans during the past three centuries, the distortions of early globalisation visited upon Fiji by trade, guns and disease, the rising power of Bau in the mid-19th century and the growing consolidation of political alliances. Bau's ambitions were in part thwarted by British colonialism although, thereafter, the Tongan-dominated Lau and small Bauan powerhouse found new ways to extend their influence as colonial allies. Consequently, a fundamentally different Taukei order under the rule of eastern chiefs and colonial officials quickly took shape in the late 19th century, characterised by the subjugation of Colo and the introduction of still more migrants, this time indentured labour from northern and southern India engaged to establish an economy on which colonial government could depend for income. This new order established the modern features of Taukei tradition: standardised language, Christianity, *mataqali* land ownership, consolidated village settlements and provincial identities, as well as stable chiefly governance, at the apex of which stood the newly created (Great) Council of Chiefs. Similar processes of change impacted on the fragmented Indian population; small-scale cane farming, urbanisation, education, political–industrial organisation, the withering of caste, and the immigration of a business class from Gujarat and Punjab began to produce a new IndoFijian community. The wider world had come to Fiji and transformed it beyond recognition.

Then, after nearly 100 years, a global wave of decolonisation caught up with Fiji, pushing colonial officials to conspire with leaders from both communities, which remained largely disparate, to establish an independent state. Their vision: to perpetuate chiefly influence by positioning the Taukei against the country's most recent immigrants, whose labour had assisted to develop an economy that was the envy of Pacific island countries and – ironically – enabled the chiefly elite to retain its largely rural Taukei support base. The 1970 Constitution gave General Electors (Europeans, Chinese and people of mixed descent) the balance of power in the lower house of parliament but, in the upper house, the Taukei dominated, courtesy of GCC nominees. Communal democracy, however, possessed a crucial flaw; it worked only for as long as communal unity survived. For countries like Fiji embarking on a new adventure of independence and development in an increasingly globalised world, such unity could never be guaranteed, particularly since – given its very recent roots – no homogeneous communities existed outside of their political constructs.[75]

Britain had form when it came to paying lip service to democracy in its former colonies, particularly those it had ruled over by fostering division. In Fiji's case, Britain's failure to transcend its own narrow colonial strategies cost the country dearly after 1970. True, Mara preached multiracialism and Fiji prospered in the brief flush of independence. But, by 1977, new economic realities set in and the communal dream soured with Sakeasi Butadroka's resistance to chiefly domination, rural neglect and the continued presence of IndoFijians. Fiji faltered. By 1982, Mara's multiracialism had become a protectionist façade. Enter Timoci Bavadra and his new Labour Party with an issues-based agenda in 1987 and the whole edifice crumbled as Rabuka and his military – itself a product of globalisation – swept them aside in the country's first military coup.

Rabuka sought to preserve the very interests Bavadra wanted to reform but, in doing so, he inadvertently transformed them in ways that ultimately weakened them further. Absolute Taukei paramountcy had always been the dream of Taukeists (although they disagreed on its form) but its

---

75   Brij Lal, 'Where has all the music gone? Reflections on the 40th anniversary of Fiji's independence', *Contemporary Pacific*, 23: 2, 2011, p. 416. Fiji has always been something of a Pacific melting pot, as its long history demonstrates. To disregard diversity by constructing the notion of a Taukei race or, for that matter, an IndoFijian race was always bound to turn out badly. Race is a social invention designed to cause division, as philosopher Kwame Anthony Appiah reminds us in his 2016 BBC Reith Lectures, *Mistaken Identities* (www.bbc.co.uk/programmes/b00729d9/episodes/guide). Madraiwiwi similarly argued that the notion that the Taukei could only protect their rights by maintaining racial unity 'is an arid concept conveniently used by politicians to advance their own interests and agendas'. He also argued that 'With the erosion of traditional structures and authority, pre-existing differences have begun to re-emerge' ('Ethnic tensions and the law', 2004). See also Ratuva ('Politics of ethno-national identity', 2008) for a discussion of the syncretic nature of communalism.

achievement removed the one element that fostered communal unity – the threat of IndoFijian political dominance. Hence Taukei differences quickly multiplied, energised by the provincial basis for Taukei politics enshrined in Rabuka's 1990 Constitution and by continued rural neglect. With party loyalty near impossible, dysfunction soon followed. Stung also by declining economic growth and rising poverty, Rabuka sought allies from his erstwhile IndoFijian rivals with a constitutional reset in 1997.[76] Unfortunately, it did no more than put icing on what remained fundamentally a communal cake. It could never escape the confrontational straitjacket communalism inflicted on Fiji's politics, as Taukei nationalists and rogue soldiers demonstrated again during George Speight's 2000 civilian coup when they seized parliament and launched raids across the country to keep out the IndoFijian-led People's Coalition government that Rabuka's unpopularity had inadvertently brought into power the previous year through a new voting system designed to promote cross-communal cooperation. Thus Fiji arrived at its second lost decade.

Of course it could be said that nothing in politics is certain. But, in 2000, this was not how many people in Fiji read their politics. Instead, stargazers asserted that Fiji had merely corrected its course, history had repeated itself, confirming a veritable coup cycle in 'Coup-Coup Land'. Once again the military stepped in, swept aside both the Coalition government and Speight's rebels, and handed power to a new alliance of Taukei politicians, business leaders and chiefs. Fiji's subsequent history might have been very different had its recently appointed military commander imposed on Fiji the wishes of the populist Speight and his clique of chiefly allies and military supporters. But he did not. Instead he allowed the re-establishment of what many Taukei viewed as the natural status quo. And yet, there was something very different about the ambitious Bainimarama that was not immediately apparent. He was no princeling or chief handed a leadership role in the military because of his status, as had been the case with some of his predecessors. He hailed from a province sceptical of the eastern chiefly elite. He struggled with army officers who disrespected his naval background or believed that they were more deserving of military leadership. He endured an assassination attempt during an unprecedented rebel mutiny in 2000. That background set him apart from the elite that

---

76   *Fiji Times*, 6 September 2016. Rabuka later claimed that his 1997 Constitution returned constitutional power to the people. But while processes of consultation have varied considerably, no constitution in Fiji has ever been put to the popular vote.

he restored to power, a separation that became ever more apparent each time it sought to accommodate the former rebels. In the end, alienation and ambition transformed separation into divorce.

Despite superficial appearances, Fiji's fourth coup in late 2006 differed from its predecessors. Bainimarama sought to avoid Rabuka's mistakes after 1987 by maintaining the levers of power and the Constitution. Even when left no choice but to abrogate the Constitution nearly three years later, he refused to rush into a new constitution. Instead he began to transform elements of Fiji: Taukei deference to tradition, the provision of golden eggs to sustain the old elite, the power enjoyed by the media and judiciary, rural neglect and infrastructural inertia. And he brazenly navigated international hostility to his illegal regime. Then, having accepted an independent process for developing a new constitution, he rejected its outcome, fearing it threatened his hold on power and would restore much of what he had undone. Instead he reset electoral rules, abolishing communalism in order to remove the base of the old elite and to provide Fiji's people a non-communal foundation for voting. This, Steven Ratuva and Stephanie Lawson argue, brought Fiji's political system – for the first time in its history – closer to the standard model of liberal democracy.[77]

Government still remained the familiar goose but, this time, its golden eggs were distributed more equally than before through lease monies that now bypassed chiefly hands; through welfare and educational programs that were no longer racially determined; and through massive public road, water and electrification projects. True – like Mara, Rabuka and Qarase – Bainimarama had cronies, and the military continued to benefit excessively from his ascendency. But Bainimarama's outstanding controversial achievement remains undoubtedly his rebooting of Fiji's operating system in 2013. Gone were the single-member electorates favouring rural areas and Fiji's aristocrats. Instead, to paraphrase Scott MacWilliam, he marginalised the 'indigenous buccaneers' who used the 'screen of identity' to justify their access to state assets and power.[78] Rabuka had once pondered just such an outcome:

77   Steven Ratuva & Stephanie Lawson, 'The people have spoken', in Ratuva & Lawson, *The People Have Spoken: The 2014 Elections in Fiji*. Canberra: ANU Press, 2016, p. 2.
78   Scott MacWilliam, '"Not with a bang but a whimper": SODELPA and the 2014 elections', in Ratuva & Lawson, *The People Have Spoken*, 2016, p. 217.

hopefully we can introduce certain policies and systems in which we can work at getting our chiefs into an effective ruling group, not to the extent that they rule the politics of the nation, but they rule their own little *vanua*s and the divisions of the *vanua* effectively, capable of understanding the modern democratic systems that we now live in.[79]

But he could never bring himself to realise it. Restoring multiracialism in 1997 remained his sole achievement.

In essence, Bainimarama had become Bavadra Mark II, returned as a military avenger, and that difference goes some way to explain the cost of Fiji's misadventure. From late 2006 until September 2014, Bainimarama and his government rode roughshod over human rights, legal and constitutional systems, business rights and media freedoms, acts Bavadra would never have contemplated or endorsed.[80] His was a military dictatorship that transformed itself into what MacWilliam calls a 'militarised democracy', albeit an unreconstructed military subject to none of the equal opportunity reforms imposed on Fiji.[81] How that democracy performs and survives remains yet to be seen.[82] It helps that the dividing line is, at least officially, no longer communal, as Ratuva and Lawson note,[83] and as the Attorney-General emphasises:

> When politicians are elected through an electoral system that divides society on the basis of ethnicity, it encourages an ethnic way of thinking and incentivises ethnic favouritism. Racism has been at the base of Fiji society since Colonial times, and it has always been used as a means to preserve the power and influence of the elites. When Fijians are homogenised into groups on the basis of ethnicity, we are unable to address intragroup injustices, such as gender, economic participation and socioeconomic rights. Government's work is therefore focused on those Fijians on the margins of society. We are using the promotion of socioeconomic rights to overcome the racist paradigm that has been used by the elites to withhold resources and opportunities for the rest of society.[84]

---

79   *Islands Business*, July 1991.
80   Some readers may object to the comparison, but Bainimarama and Bavadra shared much in common: both objected to the focus on race, they wanted all citizens to be called Fijians, they wanted to democratise Fijian institutions, and they wanted greater equalisation in the distribution of wealth.
81   MacWilliam, '"Not with a bang but a whimper"', 2016, pp. 225–26.
82   Politics academic Sandra Tarte believes that, while 'coup leaders may be the enemy of democracy … they can also reinvent themselves as its strongest ally' ('What Rabuka's return means for Fijian politics', *eastasiaforum.org*, 5 August 2016).
83   Steven Ratuva & Stephanie Lawson, 'Concluding note: the election to end all coups', in Ratuva & Lawson, *The People Have Spoken*, 2016, pp. 278–79.
84   *Fiji Sun*, 8 December 2016. Comments made during a meeting on contemporary forms of racism and intolerance with the UN Special Rapporteur, Matuma Ruteere, in Suva.

But Sayed-Khaiyum's promotion of what he sees as Bainimarama's most impressive achievement overlooks the greatest challenge to his legacy, namely the legitimacy of the new parliamentary system, and in particular – to quote Ratuva and Lawson again – that it becomes 'integral to a democratic political culture and is accepted by all'. They argue that extra parliamentary processes have been painful and destructive, leaving Fiji desperately in need of greater democratic space. Means are as important as ends and can also have a lasting impact if a sense of victimhood generates a cycle of vengeance and counter vengeance.[85]

Jon Fraenkel makes a similar point. Fiji may not be 'a consolidated semi-authoritarian state', but it remains politically highly fragile: 'Much of its present orientation depends on the prime minister and his attorney general'. Without them, 'Fiji would probably change direction', Fraenkel argues, assuming of course that the military permits change.[86] Rabuka directly acknowledged that dilemma in late 2016, as we noted earlier: 'If we combine to defeat someone, then what?'[87] Hence the importance of FijiFirst reaching out to Opposition parties rather than playing the politics of respect, bringing them along on the journey and, above all, providing them a stake in a constitutional reset.

At the close of 2016, Fiji's longest reigning public intellectual, Wadan Narsey, outlined what that journey might involve in 2017, a series of much-needed constitutional changes: an end to the 5 per cent threshold which (he argues) disenfranchises candidates and mocks the notion of one person – one vote – one value, the reintroduction of constituencies to restore MP accountability to electorates, the addition of a closed-list system to ensure proportionality and raise the number of women in parliament, the use of party symbols on ballot boxes, the removal of government control over the Election Office, Electoral Commission and the Media Industry Development Authority, and the removal of legislation and decrees that discourage the media from performing its watchdog role. For the sake of future generations, Narsey argues, mere tinkering will not suffice.[88] No process as formal as he suggests, however,

---

85   Ratuva & Lawson, 'Concluding note', 2016, pp. 275–77. As Vice President, Madraiwiwi had similarly argued that 'Diversity is a strength rather than a weakness' but, to gain from it, Fiji needed 'a practical vision of how to affirm and strengthen diversity in the context of uniting the nation' ('Challenges and opportunities in Fiji today', *fijilive*, 20 April 2006). Only engagement would succeed.

86   Jon Fraenkel, 'In the Pacific, two cheers for democracy', *Inside Story*, 13 December 2016.

87   *Fiji Times*, 28 September 2016.

88   Wadan Narsey, 'Critical issues for 2017', 2016.

has emerged since 2014. Instead, Opposition leaders have been harassed for attending a constitutional forum[89] and Prasad has been left bemoaning the lack of a middle ground and questioning whether democracy is really working in Fiji. Military dictatorship, he believes, has simply transformed itself into parliamentary dictatorship.[90]

How different might Fiji be today had Rabuka accepted Bavadra's legitimacy in 1987? Lawyer Richard Naidu once remarked 'that Fiji would have been a better place, with a better vision, if the doctor [Bavadra] had been allowed to see out his shift'.[91] Of course we will never know how the confines of communalism would have played out under Bavadra. But we do know what Rabuka's actions ultimately cost Fiji in terms of political and economic misadventure, and more. Economically, according to Narsey, the coups have cost Fiji some $10 billion between 1987 and 2010. This equates to about two years' GDP, or two years' income for every household and company, an effective decline in GDP of 30 per cent. This, he argues, 'is not just a failure on the part of our political and military leaders, but a failure of the populace at large'.[92] Indeed, Narsey notes, the coups have left Fiji 'morally gutted, from the top down' and, because people turned a blind eye to corruption, treason and injustice, a silence now enshrouds the country.[93] Back in 2005, the former deputy director of public prosecutions, Peter Ridgway, wrote:

> The silent majority in Fiji is too big. Too many people are comfortable making a quid and not wanting to rock the boat. Too many people see themselves as powerless to change things but they are not. Public opinion is a most powerful motivator for all government to behave ethically. I don't think Fiji understands the importance of participation in their own democracy. My message to Fiji is: it is your democracy, use it.[94]

---

89   On 5 September 2016, Chaudhry, Prasad and Rabuka attended a Pacific Dialogue forum on the 2013 Constitution. Five days later, they and organiser Jone Dakuvula, unionist Attar Singh, and SODELPA's Tupeni Baba were arrested and detained for two days by police for attending a forum held without a police permit. Eventually the director of public prosecutions refused to proceed with the case, arguing that the arrests had been highly selective (*Fiji Sun*, 18 October 2016). Police also shut down a three-day Sugar Forum at the Pearl Fiji Resort in Pacific Harbour in early September because its organisers had similarly gained no permit.

90   *Fiji Times*, 16 & 30 January 2016, 4 June 2016.

91   Griffen, *With Heart and Nerve and Sinew*, 1997, p. 356.

92   Wadan Narsey, 'Costly coups: No catching up', *Fiji Times*, 11 December 2007.

93   Wadan Narsey, 'The moral gutting of Fiji and coming economic collapse: To raise our voices as one', *narseyonfiji.wordpress.com*, 13 July 2009.

94   Peter Ridgway, 'Use your democracy', *Sunday Sun*, 26 July 2005.

The late Ratu Joni Madraiwiwi similarly argued that 'Ultimately the best guarantor of the rule of law is not the State and the branches which comprise it but the recognition by people of its value and their willingness to fight for and uphold it'.[95] Lawyer Graham Leung also had his own take on Fiji's contemporary misadventure:

> The real problem in Fiji is feudal cliques refusing to relinquish power, an army that refuses to recognise its limitations in a democracy, and failed politicians of all persuasions and opportunistic businessmen who support them, see nothing wrong in undermining electoral verdicts.[96]

That may still be Fiji's future, unless Bainimarama's government works hard to combine economic and social reforms with greater democratic space for popular voices. The 2012 FCC draft Constitution proposed such a space and its rejection has given Fiji's democracy the potential for more authoritarian practices. 'At the end of the day, democracy and pluralism are fragile human experiments,' the London-based historian Sunil Khilnani warns, 'and they are also very easy to destroy.'[97] Reforming the 2013 Constitution, without returning to its mythical communal lodestone, now remains Fiji's greatest challenge and it is one that the Bainimarama government should proactively address, rather than push its divided opposition parties into constitutional confrontation. Similarly, alienating business leaders and cane farmers by failing to consult about important reform initiatives can needlessly transform allies into enemies ahead of elections when democratic support from many fronts will be required.[98] And, when that day comes, as inevitably it will, Fiji's future prosperity and stability will be better assured if all parties and all Fiji's people accept the cosmopolitan basis of Bainimarama's 2013 reset and not resort to identity politics.

---

95   Madraiwiwi, 'Ethnic tensions and the law', 2004. He added: 'Until that point is reached, the journey to it must be seen and appreciated for what it is. In a society such as ours where divisions exist both inter-ethnically and within communities, the process of nation-building of which the rule of law is an integral part, requires a deft balancing of priorities in a fair and inclusive manner. This allows everyone to be part of the challenge that we need to face together'.

96   *Australian*, 7 May 2009.

97   *BBC*, 15 March 2016; the director of London's India Institute reflecting on India's moment for change and the need for leaders to take a long view.

98   The *Fair Reporting of Credit Act* and the Sugar Cane Industry Bill are examples where the government has allegedly failed to consult adequately prior to legislating reforms, thus creating the impression that it remains in its pre-election decree mode (Neelesh Gounder, 'Elective dictatorship', *Fiji Times*, 7 May 2016; Richard Naidu, 'True democracy and the cost of credit', *Fiji Times*, 30 April 2016).

Speaking of an earlier opportunity 'to develop a new paradigm and ways of doing things', Madraiwiwi believed such moments rare in Fiji's collective experience. '*Kunekune na yaloka ni dilio* is a Fijian expression that captures the essence,' he argued. It refers to a bird so adept at hiding her eggs that they are mostly never found. 'Having found the egg on this occasion,' he asked, 'what are we going to do with it? The choice is ours to make.'[99]

But the bird also deserves attention. There is always the danger that, without reform, a time will come when Fiji's leaders find not only their much-coveted eggs missing or broken but Rabuka's bird well and truly cooked.

---

99   Ratu Joni Madraiwiwi, 'Making the right choices', 2006.

Bibliography

Books, reports & theses

Akram-Lodhi, H (ed.), *Confronting Fiji Futures*. Canberra: Asia Pacific Press, 2000.

Amnesty International, *Beating Justice: How Fiji's Security Forces Get Away with Torture*. London: Amnesty International Publications, 2016.

——, *Fiji: Paradise Lost – A Tale of Ongoing Human Rights Violations*. London, 2009.

Anthony, J, 'Freedom & independence of the media in Fiji: A report'. Suva: Fiji Human Rights Commission, 2008.

Baledrokadroka, J, 'Sacred king and warrior chief: The role of the military in Fiji politics', PhD Thesis, The Australian National University. Canberra, 2012.

Ball, N, *Security and Economy in the Third World*. Princeton University Press, 1988.

Baran, P, *The Political Economy of Growth*. New York: Monthly Review Press, 1957.

Beattie, A, *False Economy: A Surprising Economic History of the World*. London: Viking, 2009.

Britton, S, *Tourism & Underdevelopment in Fiji*. Canberra, The Australian National University, 1983.

Brookfield, HC, Ellis, F & Ward RG, *Land, Cane & Coconuts: Papers on the Rural Economy of Fiji*. Canberra: The Australian National University, 1985.

Bullock, A, *Hitler: A Study in Tyranny*. London: Penguin, 1962.

Burns, AAC, *Fiji*. London: Her Majesty's Stationery Office, 1963.

Carstairs, R & Prasad, R, *Impact of Foreign Direct Investment on the Fiji Economy*. Suva: Centre for Applied Studies in Development, University of the South Pacific, 1981.

Citizens' Constitutional Forum, *An Analysis: 2013 Fiji Government Constitution*. Suva: Citizens' Constitutional Forum, 2013.

Cliff, AD & Haggett, P, *The Spread of Measles in Fiji & the Pacific*. Canberra: The Australian National University, 1985.

Cole, R & Hughes, H, *The Fiji Economy May 1987: Problems & Prospects*. Canberra: National Centre for Development Studies, The Australian National University, 1988.

Collier, P, *Wars, Guns & Votes: Democracy in Dangerous Places*. London: The Bodley Head, 2009.

Dean, E & Ritova, S, *Rabuka: No Other Way*. Sydney: Doubleday, 1988.

Derrick, RA, *A History of Fiji*. Suva: Government Press, 1950.

Durutalo, A, 'Of roots & offshoots: Fijian political thinking, dissent & the formation of political parties, 1960–1999'. PhD Thesis, The Australian National University. Canberra, 2005.

Durutalo, S, 'Internal colonialism & unequal regional development: The case of western Viti Levu, Fiji'. MA Thesis, University of the South Pacific. Suva, 1985.

Field, M, Baba, T & Nabobo-Baba, U, *Speight of Violence: Inside Fiji's 2000 Coup*. Auckland: Reed Publishing, 2005.

Fiji Bureau of Statistics, *2007 and 2009 Population Census of Fiji*. Suva: Fiji Island Bureau of Statistics, June 2012.

Fiji Constitution Commission, *Explanatory Report on the Draft Constitution*. Suva, December 2012.

Fiji Independent News Service, *Fiji Situation Report*. Sydney, 13 November 1990.

Fijian Initiative Group, *Nine Points Plan*. Suva, 1988.

Fraenkel, J & Firth, S (eds), *From Election to Coup in Fiji: The 2006 Campaign and its Aftermath*. Canberra & Suva: ANU E Press & Institute of Pacific Studies, University of the South Pacific, 2007.

Fraenkel, J, Firth, S & Lal, BV (eds), *The 2006 Military Takeover in Fiji: A Coup to End All Coups*, Canberra: ANU E Press, 2009.

France, P, *The Charter of the Land: Custom & Colonization in Fiji*. Melbourne: Oxford University Press, 1969.

Fry, G & Tarte, S (eds), *The New Pacific Diplomacy*. Canberra: ANU Press, 2015.

Furnivall, JS, *Netherlands India: A Study of Plural Economy*. Cambridge University Press, 1939.

Gillion, KL, *Fiji's Indian Migrants – A History to the End of Indenture in 1920*. Melbourne: Oxford University Press, 1963.

Green, M, *Persona Non Grata, Breaking the Bond – New Zealand and Fiji 2004–2007*. Auckland: Dunmore Publishing, 2013.

Griffen, A (ed.), *Election Watch II: A Citizen's Review of the Fiji General Election 2001*. Suva: CCF, 2002.

——, *With Heart and Nerve and Sinew: Postcoup Writing from Fiji*. Suva: Christmas Club, 1997.

Grynberg, R, Munro, D & White, M, *Crisis: The Collapse of the National Bank of Fiji*. Suva: USP Book Centre, 2002.

Halapua, W, *Tradition, Lotu & Militarism in Fiji*. Lautoka: Fiji Institute of Applied Studies, 2003.

Harrison, L, *Culture Matters: How Values Shape Human Progress*. New York: Basic Books, 2000.

Howard, MC, *Fiji: Race and Politics in an Island State*. Vancouver: University of British Columbia Press, 1991.

Huntington, S, *Political Order in Changing Societies*. New Haven: Yale University Press, 1968.

International Bar Association, *Dire Straits: A Report on the Rule of Law in Fiji*. Human Rights Institute Report. London, March 2009.

Kelly, JD & Kaplan, M, *Represented Communities: Fiji & World Colonization*. University of Chicago Press, 2001.

Kermode, R, 'Report of the Commission of Inquiry into the Deed of Settlement dated 17.09.92 between Anthony Frederick Stephens and the Attorney General of Fiji', Parliamentary Paper 45. Suva: Government Printer, 1993.

Knapman, B, *Fiji's Economic History 1874–1939: Studies of Capitalist Colonial Development*. Pacific Research Monograph 15. Canberra: National Centre for Development Studies, The Australian National University, 1987.

Kuper, L & Smith, MG (eds), *Pluralism in Africa*. Berkeley: University of California Press, 1969.

Lal, BV, *Fiji and the Coup Syndrome*. Special issue: *The Round Table. Commonwealth Journal of International Affairs*, 101: 6, December 2012.

———, *Islands of Turmoil: Elections and Politics in Fiji*. Canberra: ANU E Press, 2006.

———, *A Vision for Change: AD Patel and the Politics of Fiji*. Canberra: National Centre for Development Studies, The Australian National University, 1997.

———, *Broken Waves: A History of the Fiji Islands in the Twentieth Century*. Honolulu, University of Hawaii Press, 1992.

———, 'Girmitiyas: The Origins of the Fiji Indians'. Canberra: *Journal of Pacific History*, 1983.

Lal, BV & Chand, G (eds), *1987 and All That: Fiji Twenty Years Later*. Lautoka: FIAS, 2008.

Lawson, S, *The Failure of Democratic Politics in Fiji*. Oxford: Clarendon Press, 1991.

Leckie, J, *To Labour with the State: The Fiji Public Service Association*. Dunedin: University of Otago Press, 1997.

Leys, C, *Underdevelopment in Kenya: The Political Economy of Neo-Colonialism*. London: Heinemann, 1975.

Malcomson, SL, *Tuturani: A Political Journey in the Pacific Islands*. New York: Poseidon Press, 1990.

Mamak, A, *Colour, Culture & Conflict: A Study of Pluralism in Fiji*. Sydney: Pergamon Press, 1978.

Mara, K, *The Pacific Way: A Memoir*. Honolulu: University of Hawai'i Press, 1997.

Mausio, A, 'Boomerangs & the Fijian dilemma: Australian aid for rural development 1971–1987'. PhD Thesis, The Australian National University. Canberra, 2006.

McNaught, TJ, *The Fijian Colonial Experience: A Study of the Neo-Traditional Order under British Colonial Rule prior to World War II*. Canberra: The Australian National University, 1982.

Naidu, V, *Violence of Indenture in Fiji*. Lautoka: Fiji Institute of Applied Studies, 2004.

Naidu, V & Tarte, S (eds), *'No Ordinary Election': The Fiji General Election of 2014*. Special issue. Journal of Pacific Studies, 35: 2, 2015.

Narayan, J, *The Political Economy of Fiji*. Suva: South Pacific Review Press, 1984.

Nayacakalou, RR, *Tradition & Change in the Fijian Village*. Suva: University of the South Pacific, 1978.

——, *Leadership in Fiji*. Melbourne: Oxford University Press, 1975.

Nicole, R, *Disturbing History: Resistance in Early Colonial Fiji*. Honolulu: University of Hawai'i Press, 2011.

Overton, J, 'Fiji Since the Coups'. *Pacific Viewpoint*, 30: 2, October 1989.

——, *Land and Differentiation in Fiji*. Pacific Research Monograph 19. Canberra: National Centre for Development Studies, The Australian National University, 1989.

Powles, A & Sousa-Santos, J, 'Principled engagement: rebuilding defence ties with Fiji', Lowy Institute Analysis paper, Sydney, July 2016.

Prasad, S (ed), *Coup & Crisis: Fiji – A Year Later*. Melbourne: Arena Publications, 1988.

Ratha, D & Xu, Z (eds), *Migration and Remittances Factbook 2008*. Washington: World Bank, 2008.

Ratuva, S & Lawson, S, *The People Have Spoken: The 2014 Elections in Fiji*. Canberra: ANU Press, 2016.

Ravuvu, A, *The Façade of Democracy: Fijian Struggles for Political Control, 1830–1987*. Suva: Reader Publishing House, 1991.

Reeves, P, Vakatora, T & Lal, BV, *The Fiji Islands: Towards a United Future*. Report of the Fiji Constitutional Review Commission, Parliamentary Paper 34. Suva: Parliament of Fiji, 1996.

RFMF Board of Inquiry Report into the Involvement of the First Meridian Squadron in the Illegal Takeover of Parliament on 19 May 2000 and the Subsequent Holding of Hostages until 13 July 2000, 24 October 2000, www.truthforfiji.com/uploads/8/4/2/3/8423704/1st_meridian_report_rfmf_opt2.pdf (unauthorised).

Rist, G, *The History of Development: From Western Origins to Global Faith*. London & New York: Zed Books, 1997.

Robertson, R (ed.), *Livelihoods and Identity in Fiji*. Suva: University of the South Pacific, 2006.

——, *Multiculturalism & Reconciliation in an Indulgent Republic. Fiji after the Coups: 1987–1998*. Suva: Fiji Institute of Applied Studies, 1998.

Robertson, R & Sutherland, W, *Government by the Gun: The Unfinished Business of Fiji's 2000 Coup*. Sydney & London: Pluto Press & Zed Books, 2001.

Robertson, R & Tamanisau, A, *Fiji: Shattered Coups*. Sydney: Pluto Press, 1988.

Robinson, P, 'The Crown Colony Government & the regulation of relations between settlers & Fijians, 1880–1910'. Master of Letters Thesis, Oxford University, 1984.

Rostow, WW, *The Stages of Economic Growth: A Non-Communist Manifesto*. Cambridge University Press, 1960.

Routledge, D, *Matanitu: The Struggle for Power in Early Fiji*. Suva: University of the South Pacific, 1985.

Scarr, D, Fiji, *Politics of Illusion: The Military Coups in Fiji*. Sydney: NSW University Press, 1988.

SDL, *Government Paper to the National Economic Summit*. Suva, 2006.

——, *Strategic Development Plan 2007–2011*. Suva: National Economic Summit, 2006.

Sen, A, *Development as Freedom*. Oxford University Press, 1999.

Singh, A, *Silent Warriors*. Suva: FIAS, 1991.

Shameem, S, 'The assumption of executive authority on December 5 2006 by Commodore JV Bainimarama, Commander of the RFMF: Legal, constitutional and human rights issues', Fiji Human Rights Commission, Suva, 3 January 2007.

Sharpham, J, *Rabuka of Fiji*. Rockhampton: Central Queensland University Press, 2000.

Spate, OHK, *The Fijian People: Economic Problems & Prospects*. Suva: Legislative Council of Fiji, 1959.

Stubbs, R, *Rethinking Asia's Economic Miracle*. London: Palgrave Macmillan, 2005.

Sutherland, W, *Beyond the Politics of Race. An Alternative History of Fiji to 1992*. Canberra: The Australian National University, 1992.

Swainson, N, *The Development of Corporate Capitalism in Kenya, 1918–1977*. London: Heinemann, 1980.

Thomson, P, *Kava in the Blood: A Personal & Political Memoir from the Heart of Fiji*. Auckland: Tandem Press, 1999.

UN Declaration on the Rights of Indigenous Peoples: A Manual for National Human Rights Institutions. Sydney & Geneva: Asia Pacific Forum of National Human Rights Institutions and the Office of the UN High Commissioner for Human Rights, 2013.

Walsh, C, *Fiji: An Encyclopaedic Atlas*. Suva: University of the South Pacific, 2006.

Wangome, J, 'The African "neocolonialism" that is self-inflicted'. MA Thesis, Marine Corps University Command and Staff College. Quantico, Virginia, 1985, www.globalsecurity.org/military/library/report/1985/WJ.htm.

Warren, B, *Imperialism: Pioneer of Capitalism*. London: Verso, 1980.

Ziemann, W & Lanzendorfer, M, 'The state in peripheral societies', *The Socialist Register 1977*. London: Merlin Press, 1977.

Articles & media presentations

Acemoglu, D, Ticchi, D & Vindigni, A, 'A theory of military dictatorships', *American Economic Journal: Macroeconomics*, 2: 1, January 2010. doi.org/10.1257/mac.2.1.1.

Appiah, KA, *Mistaken Identities*, 2016 BBC Reith Lectures, www.bbc.co.uk/programmes/b00729d9/episodes/guide.

——, 'There is no such thing as Western civilisation', *Guardian*, 9 November 2016.

Arms, D, 'Analysing the open list system of proportional representation in Fiji's 2014 General Election: A perspective from the Fiji Electoral Commission', in Vijay Naidu & Sandra Tarte (eds), 'No Ordinary Election': *The Fiji General Election of 2014*. Special issue. *The Journal of Pacific Studies*, 35: 2, 2015.

Baker, N & Nakagawa, H, '"Known unknowns and unknown unknowns" in the 2014 Fiji election results', in Vijay Naidu & Sandra Tarte (eds), 'No Ordinary Election': *The Fiji General Election of 2014*. Special issue. *The Journal of Pacific Studies*, 35: 2, 2015.

Baledrokadroka, B, 'Showtime as the US call's Bainimarama's bluff', www.coupfourandahalf.com, 8 November 2010.

Baleinakorodawa, P, Barr, K & Qalowasa, S, 'Time of uncertainty, opportunity', *Fiji Times*, 19 December 2006.

Ball, N, 'The military in politics: who benefits & how?', *World Development*, 9: 6, 1981. doi.org/10.1016/0305-750X(81)90006-1.

Barbour, P & McGregor, A, 'The Fiji agricultural sector', *Pacific Economic Bulletin*, 13: 2, November 1998.

Bettelheim, C, 'Theoretical comments', in A Emmanuel, *Unequal Exchange: A Study of the Imperialism of Trade*. New York: Monthly Review Press, 1977.

Bogidrau, W, 'Inside a palace coup', *Fiji Times*, 25 June 2005.

——, 'Checkmate: Why the army and state went head-to-head', *The Review*, 1 July 2003.

Brown, M, 'Fiji military chief already in power', *Age*, 4 December 2006.

Callick, R, 'Poll tests diplomatic will of Canberra', *Australian*, 2 April 2013.

——, 'No ready way out of Speight's big hole', *Australian Financial Review*, 24 July 2000.

——, 'Fiji grasps for a bonanza', *Australian Financial Review*, 30 November 1988.

Callinan, R, 'Fueling Fiji's coup', *Time Magazine*, 20 December 2006.

Casimira, A, 'Democracy in many guises', *Fiji Sun*, 18 February 2007.

Cawthorne, P, 'Fiji's garment export industry: An economic and political analysis of its long term viability', Faculty of Economics & Business Working Paper, University of Sydney, 2000.

Chand, S, 'Coups, cyclones & recovery: The Fiji experience', *Pacific Economic Bulletin*, 15: 2, November 2000.

Chandra, R, 'Manufacturing in Fiji: Mixed results', *Pacific Economic Bulletin*, 11: 1, May 1996.

——, 'The political crisis and the manufacturing sector in Fiji', *Pacific Viewpoint*, 30: 2, October 1989.

Chippendale, M, 'Qarase sees a future of affirmative action', *Sydney Morning Herald*, 19 February 2001.

Chung, M, 'Ethnic politics and small business: The case of the Fiji poultry industry', *Pacific Viewpoint*, 30: 2, October 1989.

Cole, RV, 'The Fiji economy: From go to woe', *Pacific Viewpoint*, 30: 2, October 1989.

Collier, P & Hoeffler, A, 'Grand extortion: Coup risk & the military as a protection racket', Second Workshop on Political Institutions, Development And a Domestic Civil Peace (PIDDCP), 19–20 Jun 2006, ora.ox.ac.uk/objects/uuid:ff727e54-408e-4288-a202-cf46a61d7187.

——, 'Coup traps: Why does Africa have so many coups d'état?', August 2005, ora.ox.ac.uk/objects/uuid:49097086-8505-4eb2-8174-314ce1aa3ebb.

'Cyclone George', *Four Corners*, Australian Broadcasting Corporation, 15 November 2000, www.abc.net.au/4corners/stories/4Cprograms _151295.htm.

Dagney, MF, 'RFMF in Fiji's defence policy', in *Background Paper on the RFMF and Fiji's Defence Policy*, CCF papers submitted to the Defence Review Committee, October 2003.

Dakuvula, J, 'The unresolved issues at stake over the commander controversy', *Asia-Pacific Network*, 30 January 2004.

——, 'More land gossip from the grassroots', *Citizens' Constitutional Forum*, ccf.org.fj, 2 May 2001.

Dass, B, 'Ailing sugar industry', *Fiji Times*, 3 August 2015.

Davis, G, 'The camera doesn't lie', 15 June 2011, www.grubsheet.com.au/ the-camera-doesnt-lie/.

——, 'It's hail to the chiefs no longer', *Australian*, 6 January 2007.

——, 'Fiji – democracy by the gun', *Sunday*, 7 May 2006, Nine Network, www.vanuatu.usp.ac.fj/sol_adobe_documents/world/paclaw/davis_ debate_fiji.htm.

Davis, M, 'The origins of the Third World', in S Chari & S Corbridge (eds), *The Development Reader*. Oxon & New York: Routledge, 2008.

Davis, M, 'Perfectly Frank', *Dateline, SBS*, 26 July 2009, www.sbs.com. au/news/dateline/story/perfectly-frank.

Digitaki, L, 'Laisa Digitaki's statement & sequence of events re pro-democracy group of five rounding up and bashing by the RFMF on December 24th–25th, 2006', fijimediawars.blogspot.com. au/2014/09/laisa-digitakis-story.html.

Digitaki, T, 'Dangerous tinkering', *Review*, April 2000.

Dobell, G, The Canberra column: 'The Pacific Way wanes', *The Interpreter*, Lowy Institute, Sydney, 8 August 2008, www.lowyinstitute.org/the-interpreter/pacific-way-wanes.

Doornbos, M, 'The African state in academic debate: Retrospect and prospect', *The Journal of Modern African Studies*, 28: 2, 1990. doi.org/10.1017/S0022278X00054410.

Dore, C, 'Just another day in paradise', *Australian*, 27–28 May 2000.

Doring, P, 'US cables reveal the brutality of Fijian regime', *Age*, 27 August 2011.

Dropsy, A, 'The church & the coup: The Fijian Methodist coup of 1989', *Review 20*, September 1993.

Durutalo, S, 'The liberation of the Pacific Island intellectual', *Review*, 4, September 1983, SSED, University of the South Pacific.

Edelstein, J, 'Coups as a human right', *Fiji Sun*, 7 January 2007.

Field, M, 'Farewell to Coup-Coup Land', *Fiji Times*, 8 August 2000.

Fiji Constitutional Process (Constitution Commission) Decree (no. 57 of 2012), fiji.gov.fj, 18 July 2012.

'Fiji coup could be its last', *Pacific Islands Report*, PIDP, 21 March 2007.

FijiFirst, 'Our manifesto', *fijifirst.com*.

Firth, S & Fraenkel, J, 'The Fiji military and ethno-nationalism: Analysing the paradox', in J Fraenkel, S Firth & BV Lal (eds), *The 2006 Military Takeover in Fiji: A Coup to End All Coups*. Canberra: ANU E Press, 2009.

Foley, R, 'Rabuka says interim government a "sideshow"', *Canberra Times*, 11 August 1988.

Forsyth, D, 'Fiji at the crossroads', *Pacific Economic Bulletin*, 11: 1, May 1996.

Fraenkel, J, 'In the Pacific, two cheers for democracy', *Inside Story*, 13 December 2016.

——, 'Fiji's December 2006 coup: Who, what, where and why?', *The 2006 Military Takeover in Fiji: A Coup to End All Coups*. Canberra: ANU E Press, 2009.

Frank, AG, 'The development of underdevelopment', in S Chew & R Denemark (eds), *The Underdevelopment of Development: Essays in Honour of Andre Gunder Frank*. Thousand Oaks: Sage Publications 1996.

Gebhart, S, 'The role of the military in a democracy: Civil–military relations in Fiji', in *Background Paper on the RFMF and Fiji's Defence Policy*, CCF papers submitted to the Defence Review Committee, October 2003.

Godfrey, M, 'Kenya: African capitalism or simple dependency?', in M Bienefeld & M Godfrey (eds), *The Struggle for Development: National Strategies in an International Context*. New York: John Wiley & Sons, 1982.

Gounder, N, 'The Opposition in an effective democracy', *Fiji Times*, 28 May 2016.

——, 'Elective dictatorship', *Fiji Times*, 7 May 2006.

Grynberg, R, 'The WTO incompatibility of the Lomé Convention trade provisions', Working Paper 98/3. Canberra: Asia Pacific Press, 1998.

Heartfield, J, 'You are not a white woman: Apolosi Nawai, the Fiji Produce Agency and the trial of Stella Spencer in Fiji, 1915', *Journal of Pacific History*, 38: 1, 2003. doi.org/10.1080/00223340306076.

Herr, R & Bergin, A, 'Fiji vital to an effective regional system', *Australian*, 3 August 2012.

Hunter, R & Lal, V, 'Fiji police chief tried to get Bainimarama arrested in NZ', *New Zealand Herald*, 18 February 2012.

Kaplinsky, R, 'Capitalist accumulation in the periphery – the Kenyan case re-examined', *Review of African Political Economy*, 16, 1980. doi.org/10.1080/03056248008703416.

Kearney, S, 'Army seizes control of Fiji', *Australian*, 2 December 2006.

Keith-Reid, R, 'Fiji's simmering election pot', *Islands Business*, April 2006.

Khan, C, 'Reflections on the September 2014 elections: A CSO perspective', in Vijay Naidu & Sandra Tarte (eds), '*No Ordinary Election*': *The Fiji General Election of 2014*. Special issue. *The Journal of Pacific Studies*, 35: 2, 2015.

Knapman, B, 'Afterword: The economic consequences of the coups', in R Robertson & A Tamanisau, *Fiji: Shattered Coups*. Sydney: Pluto Press, 1988.

Komai, M. 'Fiji's foreign policy and the new Pacific diplomacy', in G Fry & S Tarte (eds), *The New Pacific Diplomacy*. Canberra: ANU Press, 2015.

Kotobalavu, J, 'Statistics for Fiji's future', *Fiji Times*, 27 October 2008.

Kotoisuva, E, 'When reconciliation is unjust', *Fiji Times*, 11 January 2006.

Lal, BV, 'Where has all the music gone? Reflections on the 40th anniversary of Fiji's independence', *Contemporary Pacific*, 23: 2, 2011. doi.org/10.1353/cp.2011.0040.

——, 'Anxiety, uncertainty and fear in our land: Fiji's road to military coup', in J Fraenkel, S Firth & BV Lal (eds), *The 2006 Military Takeover in Fiji: A Coup to End All Coups*. Canberra: ANU E Press, 2009.

Lal, P, Lim-Applegate, H & Reddy, M, 'Fijian landowners and IndoFijian tenants have their cake and eat it too', *Pacific Economic Bulletin*, 16: 1, November 2001.

Lal, P & Reddy, M, 'Old wine in a new bottle: Proposed sugar industry restructuring and land conflict in Fiji', *Pacific Economic Bulletin*, 18: 1, May 2003.

Lal, V, 'Bainimarama's behind-the-scenes backers were in the judiciary', *coupfourandahalf.com*, 24 May 2012.

Lal, V & Hunter, R, 'Details of the death of CRWU soldier Selesitino Kalounivale revealed', *coupfourandahalf.com*, 19 March 2012.

——, 'Smuggled papers show Bainimarama's lust for power', *New Zealand Herald*, 25 February 2012.

Lawson, S & Lawson, EH, 'Chiefly leadership in Fiji: Past, present, and future'. State, Society & Governance in Melanesia Discussion Paper 2015/5. Canberra: The Australian National University.

Lenzer, A, 'Fiji Water: Spin the bottle', *Mother Jones*, September–October 2009.

Leung, G, 'Lawyers must cry freedom to the challenge in Fiji', *Fiji Times*, 9 June 2009.

Leys, C, 'Capital accumulation, class formation, and dependency – the significance of the Kenyan case', *The Socialist Register 1978*. London: Merlin Press, 1978.

Liki, A & Slatter, C, 'Control, alt, delete: How Fiji's new PR electoral system and media coverage affected election results for women C=candidates in the 2014 election', in Vijay Naidu & Sandra Tarte (eds), *'No Ordinary Election': The Fiji General Election of 2014*. Special issue. *The Journal of Pacific Studies*, 35: 2, 2015.

Luvenitoga, J, 'The vision', *Sunday Post*, 14 March 2004.

Maclellan, N, 'Fiji, the war in Iraq and the privatization of Pacific Island security', *Australian Policy Forum*, Nautilus Institute, 6 April 2006.

MacWilliam, S, '"Not with a bang but a whimper": SODELPA and the 2014 elections', in Steven Ratuva and Stephanie Lawson, *The People Have Spoken: The 2014 Elections in Fiji*. Canberra: ANU Press, 2016.

Madraiwiwi, J, 'Mythic constitutionalism: Whither Fiji's course in June 2007?', *Fiji Times*, 11 June 2007.

——, 'Making the right choices', keynote address to the 34th Annual Congress of the Fiji Institute of Accountants, Sofitel Resort Spa, 23 June 2006.

——, 'Challenges and opportunities in Fiji today', *fijilive*, 20 April 2006.

——, 'Building the peace', *Fiji Times*, 17 March 2005.

——, 'Ethnic tensions and the law', *Fiji Times*, 25 September 2004.

——, 'Fiji 2001: Our country at the crossroads', 2001 Parkinson Memorial Lecture, University of the South Pacific, *Wansolwara*, 15 August 2001.

Mar, T, 'A village based eco-tourism venture: A case study of Tai village', in R Robertson (ed) *Livelihoods and Identity in Fiji*. Suva: University of the South Pacific, 2006.

Mara, K, interview, *Closeup*, Fiji TV, unofficial transcript on pcgovt.org.fj, accessed 29 April 2001.

Mara, T, 'Fiji's dictator Frank Bainimarama's truth revealed', *Truth for Fiji*, www.truthforfiji.com/uploads/8/4/2/3/8423704/fijis_dictator_frank_bainimarama_revealed.pdf.

Mataca, P, 'Churches must preach unity', *Fiji Times,* 9 February 2005.

Mottram, M, 'Speight meets his match', *Age*, 5 June 2000.

Naidu, R, 'True democracy and the cost of credit', *Fiji Times*, 30 April 2016.

Nanau, G, 'Representative democracy, the Constitution & electoral engineering in Fiji: 2014 & beyond', in Vijay Naidu & Sandra Tarte (eds), *'No Ordinary Election': The Fiji General Election of 2014*. Special issue. *The Journal of Pacific Studies*, 35: 2, 2015.

Narayan, PK, 'A tourism demand model for Fiji. 1970–2000', *Pacific Economic Bulletin*, 17: 2, November 2002.

Narsey, W, 'Critical issues for 2017', *Fiji Times,* 31 December 2016.

——, 'The costs of compromise: A dead-end parliamentary farce', *narseyonfiji.wordpress.com*, 21 February 2016.

——, 'Fiji's cancerous conspiracies of silence', www.coupfourandahalf.com/2011/11/fijis-cancerous-conspiracies-of-silence.html, 5 November 2011 (see also narseyonfiji.wordpress.com/2012/03/18/fijis-cancerous-conspiracies-of-silence-5-november-2011-on-blogs/).

——, 'Fiji's far reaching population revolution', 21 March 2010, www.usp.ac.fj/fileadmin/files/schools/ssed/economics/Wadan_Narsey/Media_articles/2010_C____Fiji_s_population_revolution.pdf.

——, 'The moral gutting of Fiji and coming economic collapse: To raise our voices as one', *narseyonfiji.wordpress.com*, 13 July 2009.

——, 'Just wages & coup impacts', *Fiji Times*, 15 April 2009.

——, 'The struggle for just wages in Fiji: Lessons from the 2009 wages councils and the continuing coups', the Rev. Paula Niukula Lecture, University of the South Pacific, 15 April 2009.

——, 'Incidence of poverty & the poverty gap in Fiji: Unpalatable facts for ethnocentric parties', *Pacific Economic Bulletin*, 23: 2, November 2008.

——, 'Costly coups: No catching up', *Fiji Times*, 11 December 2007.

——, 'Truth behind our poverty', *Fiji Times*, 10 June 2007.

——, 'Let's pull together for once', *Fiji Times*, 19 May 2006.

——, 'Great concept, bad reality', *Fiji Times*, 31 May 2005.

——, 'What's the plight of women garment workers', *Fiji Sun*, 10 November 1985.

——, 'Monopoly, capital, white racism and superprofits in Fiji', *Journal of Pacific Studies*, 5, 1979.

Nesian, 'The forces coalesce', *Croz Walsh's Blog – Fiji the Way it Was and Can Be*, crosbiew.blogspot.com.au (hereafter *CW*), 31 January 2010.

Newland, L, 'From the land to the sea: Christianity, community and state in Fiji and the 2014 elections', in Steven Ratuva & Stephanie Lawson, *The People Have Spoken: The 2014 Elections in Fiji*. Canberra: ANU Press, 2016.

Norton, R, 'The changing role of the Great Council of Chiefs', in J Fraenkel, S Firth & BV Lal (eds), *The 2006 Military Takeover in Fiji: A Coup to End All Coups*. Canberra: ANU E Press, 2009.

O'Callaghan, M-L, 'Rabuka legacy: Rule by the gun', *Australian*, 26 May 2000.

O'Callaghan, M-L & Dore, C, 'Shadowy figures thicken the plot', *Australian*, 24 May 2000.

OPS FMF, Unsigned Military Document, 30 March 1988.

Overton, J & Ward, RG, 'The coups in retrospect: The new political geography of Fiji', *Pacific Viewpoint*, 30: 2, October 1989.

Parkinson, T, 'The rebels had military chief in their sights', *Age*, 3 November 2000.

Phillips, A, 'The concept of development', *Review of African Political Economy*, 8, 1977. doi.org/10.1080/03056247708703308.

Prakash, S, 'Return to theatrics', in S Prasad, *Coup & Crisis: Fiji –A Year Later*. Melbourne: Arena Publications, 1988.

Prasad, B, 'Sugar sector anaysis: Caught up in cobwebs', *Fiji Times*, 4 March 2017.

——, 'Another view of the sugar industry', *Fiji Times*, 30 July 2016.

——, 'Growth must result in more for us', *Fiji Times*, 12 September 2015.

——, 'Why Fiji is not the "Mauritius" of the Pacific? Lessons for small island nations in the Pacific', Discussion Paper 23. Canberra: Development Policy Centre, The Australian National University, September 2012.

Prasad, BC & Asafu-Adjay, J, 'Macroeconomic policy & poverty in Fiji', *Pacific Economic Bulletin*, 13: 1, May 1998.

Prasad, BC & Kumar, S, 'Fiji's economic woes: A nation in search of development progress', *Pacific Economic Bulletin*, 17: 1, May 2002.

Prasad, S, 'Civic challenges to Fiji's democracy and the CCF's agenda for the next decade', in Arlene Griffen (ed.), *With Heart and Nerve and Sinew: Postcoup Writing from Fiji*. Suva: Christmas Club, 1997.

Premdas, R, 'The foundations of political conflict in Fiji', Suva, mimeo, 1986.

Qalo, S, 'Champion of rights or lawbreaker?', *Fiji Times*, 16 March 2006.

Rabuka, S, 'Divine intervention', *Fiji Times*, 26 October 2008.

Raicola, V, 'Who will prevail in the end?', *Fiji Times*, 30 November 2006.

——, 'Doctrine of necessity', *Fiji Times*, 29 March 2006.

Rakuita, T, 'Analysing the polls', *Fiji Times*, 25 February 2017.

Rashbrooke, G, 'Reform of the Fiji National Provident Fund', www.actuaries.org/HongKong2012/Papers/MBR12_Rashbrooke.pdf.

Ratuva, S, 'Shifting democracy: Electoral changes in Fiji', in *The People Have Spoken: The 2014 Elections in Fiji*. Canberra: ANU Press, 2016.

——, 'Politics of ethno-national identity in a post-colonial communal democracy: The case of Fiji', *Identity & Belongingness in Fiji*, 18 June 2008, ecreanfriends.wordpress.com/2008/06/18/politics-of-ethno-national-identity-in-a-post-colonial-communal-democracy-the-case-of-Fiji.

——, 'Officers, gentlemen and coups', *Fiji Times*, 25 January 2006.

——, 'Addressing inequality? Economic affirmative action and communal capitalism in post-coup Fiji', in H Akram-Lodhi (ed.), *Confronting Fiji Futures*. Canberra: Asia Pacific Press, 2000.

Ratuva, S & Lawson, S, 'Concluding note: The election to end all coups', in Steven Ratuva and Stephanie Lawson, *The People Have Spoken: The 2014 Elections in Fiji*. Canberra: ANU Press, 2016.

——, 'The people have spoken', in Steven Ratuva & Stephanie Lawson, *The People Have Spoken: The 2014 Elections in Fiji*. Canberra: ANU Press, 2016.

Reddy, M, 'Growth policy lacking', *Fiji Times*, 3 March 2007.

'Reflecting on the Fiji experience and USP', *University of the South Pacific Bulletin*, 23: 4, 2 March 1990.

Ridgway, P, 'Use your democracy', *Sunday Sun*, 26 July 2005.

Robertson, R, 'Cooking the goose: Fiji's coup culture contextualised', *The Round Table*, 101: 6. December 2012. doi.org/10.1080/003585 33.2012.749095.

——, 'Coups & development: The more things change, the more they stay the same', in BV Lal & G Chand (eds), *1987 and All That: Fiji Twenty Years Later*. Lautoka: FIAS, 2008.

——, 'Elections & nation-building: The long road since 1970', in J Fraenkel & S Firth (eds), *From Election to Coup in Fiji: The 2006 Campaign and its Aftermath*. Canberra: ANU E Press, 2007.

——, 'Fiji: Opportunities & challenges', in CCF, *Reviewing Fiji's Electoral System*. Suva: Citizens' Constitutional Forum, 2006.

——, 'The parliamentary system', in C Walsh, *Fiji: An Encyclopaedic Atlas*. Suva: University of the South Pacific, 2006.

——, 'Fiji futuring', paper to the Asia-Pacific Development Review Conference: *Fiji Forward 2000*, 15–16 June 2006, Raffles Tradewinds, Suva, Fiji, in *Pacific Economic Bulletin*, 21: 2. 2006.

——, 'A house built on sand', *Time* (Sydney), 24 July 2000.

——, '"The greenery of well-engineered factory complexes": Fiji's garment-led export industrialization strategy', *Bulletin of Concerned Asian Scholars*, 25: 2, 1993.

Robie, D, '"Unfree and unfair?": Media intimidation in Fiji's 2014 elections', in Steven Ratuva & Stephanie Lawson, *The People Have Spoken: The 2014 Elections in Fiji*. Canberra: ANU Press, 2016.

——, 'Coup Coup Land: The press and the putsch in Fiji', paper presented to the Journalism Education Association Conference, Queensland, 5–8 December 2000.

——, 'Taukei Plotters Split Forces', *Dominion*, 7 January 1988.

Rye, J, 'Religion, the Christian state and the secular state: Discourses during the 2014 Fiji General Election', in Vijay Naidu & Sandra Tarte (eds), *'No Ordinary Election': The Fiji General Election of 2014*. Special issue. *The Journal of Pacific Studies*, 35: 2, 2015.

Sakai, S, 'Native land policy in the 2014 elections', in Steven Ratuva & Stephanie Lawson, *The People Have Spoken: The 2014 Elections in Fiji*. Canberra: ANU Press, 2016.

——, 'Insecurity of Taukei land as an issue in the 2014 general election: Real threat or political gimmick?', in Vijay Naidu & Sandra Tarte (eds), *'No Ordinary Election': The Fiji General Election of 2014*. Special issue, *The Journal of Pacific Studies*, 35: 2, 2015.

Sampford, C, 'Dare to call it treason', *Overhere.com*, May 2001.

Sayed-Khaiyum, A, 'Political support and the law', *Fiji Times*, 13 January 2005.

Schumpeter, 'Khaki capitalism', *Economist*, 3 December 2011.

Singh, S, 'The thin line', *Review*, December 2000.

Singh, TR, 'Shame on our banana republic', *Fiji Sun*, 18 April 2006.

Slatter, C, 'Women factory workers in Fiji: The "half a loaf syndrome"', *Journal of Pacific Studies*, 13, 1987.

Su, B, Jin, L, Underhill, P, Martinson, J, Saha, N, McGarvey, ST, Shriver, MD, Chu, J, Oefner, P, Chakraborty, R & Deka, R, 'Polynesian origins: Insights from the Y chromosome', *Proceedings of the National Academy of Science*, 97: 15, July 2000. doi.org/10.1073/pnas.97.15.8225.

Tabaiwalu, P, 'The genesis of the Social Democratic Liberal Party: A struggle against the odds', in Steven Ratuva & Stephanie Lawson, *The People Have Spoken: The 2014 Elections in Fiji*. Canberra: ANU Press, 2016.

Tagicakibau, E, 'The politics of forgiving', *Fiji Times*, 23 October 2004.

Tarai, J, Kant, R, Finau, G & Jason Titifanue, J, 'Political social media campaigning in Fiji's 2014 Elections', in Vijay Naidu & Sandra Tarte (eds), *'No Ordinary Election': The Fiji General Election of 2014*. Special issue. *The Journal of Pacific Studies*, 35: 2, 2015.

Tarte, S, 'What Rabuka's return means for Fijian politics', *eastasiaforum. org*, 5 August 2016.

——, 'Fiji: 1989 in review', *Contemporary Pacific*, Fall 1990.

Vakaoti, P, 'Fiji elections and the youth vote: Token or active citizenship?', in Steven Ratuva & Stephanie Lawson, *The People Have Spoken: The 2014 Elections in Fiji*. Canberra: ANU Press, 2016.

Veramu, J, 'Budget and prospects', *Fiji Times*, 7 July 2017.

Veramu, J, 'Our rising generation', *Fiji Times*, 5 January 2017.

Walsh, C, 'Fiji's prehistory: Lapita', in C Walsh, *Fiji: An Encyclopaedic Atlas*. Suva: University of the South Pacific, 2006.

——, 'Fiji's prehistory: Ring-ditch fortifications, in C Walsh, *Fiji: An Encyclopaedic Atlas*. Suva: University of the South Pacific, 2006.

Williams, G, 'Class relations in a neo-colony: The case of Nigeria', in P Gutkind & P Waterman (eds), *African Social Studies, A Radical Reader*. London: Heinemann, 1977.

Wilson, C, 'Lies, lies, lies', *Fiji Sun*, 10 November 2006.

Wolpe, H, 'The theory of internal colonisation: The South African case', in I Oxaal, T Barnett & D Booth (eds), *Beyond the Sociology of Development*. London: Routledge & Kegan Paul, 1975.

Yellow Bucket, 'Coup, what coup?', *fijivillage*, 8 November 2006.

Newspapers, journals & websites

abc.net.au

Age (theage.com.au)

aljazeera.com

American Economic Journal

Auckland Star

Australian (theaustralian.com.au)

Australian Financial Review (afr.com)

bbc.co.uk

Canberra Times (canberratimes.com.au)

Citizens Constitutional Forum (ccf.org.fj)

Contemporary Pacific

Croz Walsh's Blog – Fiji: The way it was, is and can be (crosbiew.blogspot.com.au)

Daily Post (Fiji)

Dateline (sbs.com.au/news/dateline)

Dominion Post (stuff.co.nz/dominion-post)

EastAsiaForum (eastasiaforum.org)

Economist (economist.com)

Far Eastern Economic Review (Hong Kong)

Fiji Coupfourpointfive (coupfourandahalf.com)

Fiji Daily Post

FijiFirst (fijifirst.com)

FijiLeaks (fijileaks.com)

fijilive.com

Fiji Sun Online (fijisun.com.fj)

Fiji Times (fijitimes.com)

fijivillage.com

Grubsheet Feejee (grubsheet.com.au)

Guardian (theguardian.com/au)

Inside Story (insidestory.org.au)

Islands Business (islandsbusiness.com)

Journal of Pacific History

Journal of Pacific Studies

Lowy Institute (lowyinstitute.org)

Monthly Review Press

Mother Jones (motherjones.com)

NarseyOnFiji: Fighting censorship (narseyonfiji.wordpress.com)

New Zealand Listener

nzherald.co.nz

overhere.com

Pacific Economic Bulletin

Pacific Islands Monthly

Pacific Islands Report

Pacific Scoop (pacific.scoop.co.nz)

Pacific Viewpoint

PACNews (pina.com.fj)

pcgovt.org.fj

Proceedings of the National Academy of Sciences (USA)

Radio Fiji (fbc.com.fj)

rawfijinews.wordpress.com

Review, news and business magazine of Fiji (Suva)

Review of African Political Economy

Sangharsh (Suva)

Scoop (scoop.co.nz)

Sydney Morning Herald (smh.com.au)

The Fijian Government (fiji.gov.fj)

The Round Table (Commonwealth Journal of International Affairs)

The University of the South Pacific Bulletin

Time magazine

Truth for Fiji (truthforfiji.com)

Wansolwara

Weekender (Suva)

World Development

Index

www.ingramcontent.com/pod-product-compliance
Lightning Source LLC
Chambersburg PA
CBHW050806270326
41926CB00026B/4577